Ethics of Spying

A Reader for the Intelligence Professional

Edited by
Jan Goldman

The Scarecrow Press, Inc.
Lanham, Maryland • Toronto • Oxford
2006

SCARECROW PRESS, INC.

Published in the United States of America
by Scarecrow Press, Inc.
A wholly owned subsidary of
The Rowman & Littlefield Publishing Group, Inc.
4501 Forbes Boulevard, Suite 200, Lanham, Maryland 20706
www.scarecrowpress.com

PO Box 317
Oxford
OX2 9RU, UK

British Library Cataloguing in Publication Information Available

Library of Congress Cataloging-in-Publication Data

Ethics of spying : a reader for the intelligence professional / edited by
Jan Goldman.
p. cm.
Includes bibliographical references.
ISBN 0-8108-5640-9 (pbk. : alk. paper)
1. Espionage—Moral and ethical aspects.   2. Espionage, American—Moral
and ethical aspects.   3. Intelligence service—Moral and ethical aspects.
4. Intelligence service—United States—Moral and ethical aspects.   5. Military
interrogation—United States—Moral and ethical aspects.   6. Spies—
Professional ethics.   7. Political ethics—United States.   I. Goldman, Jan.
JF1525.I6E895   2006
172′.4—dc22   2005031311

All statements of fact, opinion, or analysis expressed in these articles are those of
the authors. They do not necessarily reflect official positions or views of the
Department of Defense or any other U.S. government entity, past or present.
Nothing in this book's content should be construed as asserting or implying the
U.S. government's endorsement of an article's factual statements and
interpretations.

To Reta,
For helping me figure out right from wrong,
and everything in between.

Contents

Foreword   ix

Preface   xi

Acknowledgments   xv

Part 1: Ethics and the Intelligence Community

1   Ethics and Intelligence   1
    J. E. Drexel Godfrey

2   Intelligence Ethics   18
    R. V. Jones

3   Ethics and Morality in U.S. Secret Intelligence   39
    Arthur S. Hulnick and David W. Mattausch

4   The Need for Improvement: Integrity, Ethics, and the CIA   52
    Kent Pekel

5   Bungee Jumping off the Moral Highground: Ethics of
    Espionage in the Modern Age   66
    Tony Pfaff

Part 2: Ethics and Intelligence Collection and Analysis

6   Moral Damage and the Justification of Intelligence Collection
    from Human Sources   104
    John P. Langan, S. J.

7   Intelligence Collection and Analysis: Dilemmas and Decisions   114
    John B. Chomeau and Anne C. Rudolph

8   An Ethical Defense of Torture in Interrogation   126
    Fritz Allhoff

9   Interrogation Ethics in the Context of Intelligence Collection 141
    Michael Skerker

10 Guarding against Politicization: A Message to Analysts   171
    Robert M. Gates

11 Memorandum: One Person Can Make a Difference   185
    *Veteran Intelligence Professionals for Sanity (VIPS) and
    Andrew Wilkie*

12 The Ethics of War, Spying, and Compulsory Training   190
    J. E. Roscoe, Rev.

Part 3: Ethics and Covert Action

13 Legitimacy of Covert Action: Sorting out the Moral
    Responsibilities   193
    Lincoln P. Bloomfield Jr.

14 Covert Intervention as a Moral Problem   206
    Charles R. Beitz

15 "Repugnant Philosophy": Ethics, Espionage, and Covert
    Action   221
    David L. Perry

16 Managing Covert Political Action: Guideposts from Just War
    Theory   248
    James A. Barry

17 Ethics of Covert Operations   266
    Loch K. Johnson

18 Military and Civilian Perspectives on the Ethics of Intelligence:
    Report on a Workshop at the Department of Philosophy   300
    Jean Maria Arrigo

Part 4: Related Professions

19 Sociology: Ethics of Covert Methods   314
    Roger Homan

20 Comment on "The Ethics of Covert Methods"   329
    Martin Bulmer

21 Science: Anthropologists as Spies   336
    David Price

22 Business: Ethical Issues in Competitive Intelligence Practice   343
     Linda K. Trevino and Gary R. Weaver

23 Business: The Challenge of Completely Ethical Competitive
     Intelligence and the "CHIP" Model   362
     Darren Charters

Appendix A: Principles, Creeds, Codes, and Values   379

Appendix B: Case Studies   394

Contributors   409

Foreword

Clandestine intelligence gathering, covert action, torture, and targeted killing—all are dramatic yet familiar themes to seasoned observers of world history and international conflict. Over the centuries, rules governing such activities have evolved and restraints have been developed to regulate these darker aspects of human conflict.

For Americans, reconciling secret activity and democracy has been a long struggle. The last major public point of reference was the Church Committee hearings of the 1970s. The result of this investigation into past practices was a new set of procedures, standards, and limits.

But the norms that seemed settled since the 1970s are now under stress. The new pressures of the post-September 11, 2001, security environment have compelled a rethinking of the duties and restraints that have guided American foreign policy since the end of the Cold War.

Where does one go for guidance on the tough moral choices that confront us today? How do we calculate the trade-offs that are demanded by the imperfect world in which we live? How do we evaluate the institutional arrangements of today's intelligence community and the actions of those professionals who must act within its system?

Surprisingly, there is no central address for reflection on the ethical dimensions of the intelligence profession. Until now, there has been no textbook cataloguing the key themes and showcasing the best ideas.

With this book, Professor Jan Goldman has created a central reference point for ethics in the intelligence profession. Intelligence professionals will recognize it as vital for their personal and professional development. A wider audience of concerned citizens will benefit too. Readers will find a compilation of the best work of the past generation—all in one easily accessible and highly readable volume.

Many of the articles in this book address the systemic problem inherent in a profession where "truth" is the goal, yet deception, secrecy, and morally troubling compromises are often necessary. How does a society design institutions and agencies to accommodate such discrepancies between ends and means? Other articles focus on the dilemmas of the individual. How does one navigate between seemingly contradictory codes of ethics?

The answers offered may appear ambiguous. Yet the direction is clear. Institutional design is not merely aesthetic. It is decisive in producing morally favorable results. Proper oversight, reporting, and accountability procedures go a long way to tipping the balance toward creating intelligence agencies that yield morally desirable outcomes. Similarly, hiring and promoting people of integrity in the profession—men and women with a strong moral compass—will encourage morally favorable outcomes at the level of personal decision-making.

Perhaps the most powerful force for ethics in the intelligence profession is open and honest reflection. Free debate is the beginning of the education process. Forthright discussion is what distinguishes the American approach from many others. Self-criticism makes us strong. Analysis of tough cases becomes our ally as we think about the values and standards that will guide us in the future.

This book appears at a propitious moment. The way forward is not entirely clear. We are in a moment of moral self-discovery that will define for our generation the values and standards we will live by. It will be up to men and women of good will, long experience, and moral sensibility to lead the way. The ideas in these pages offer them an excellent place to start.

—Joel H. Rosenthal
President, Carnegie Council on Ethics and International Affairs (NY)

Preface

You know, I don't think the films of James Bond and romantic views of
spies have done anything to alter the public revulsion to what espionage
really is, any more than you know, people, despite law-and-order,
tough-on-crime views are likely to really like the public hangman. That
stench is there. And it's deeply compromising to the people in institutions that practice it. But does it lead to a later betrayal? No, I don't
think so, I don't think so. I don't think that a KGB officer, a CIA officer, an SIS officer, out pandering to betrayals on the part of the people
that he's recruiting and handling—I don't think that the corruption and
perversion of ethics, and the way you believe that happens to him,
expresses itself in any natural way in a willingness for himself to go out
and do it. I don't think so. I think what it does is, it makes a person
calloused. I mean, I take it for granted that doing these things has to have
an effect on you, just as a professional soldier who has overseen the
deaths of thousands of people, you know, for this great cause, as his professional duty, it has an effect on him. It doesn't turn him into a sadistic
killer, or at least for most it doesn't (laughs) but it has a deeply forming
and shaping effect on character. And I'll just have to leave for others to
try and figure that out.

> —Aldrich Ames, convicted for spying against the United States
> (Episode 21: Spies, CNN interview transcript at National
> Security Archives, http://www2.gwu.edu/~nsarchiv/coldwar/
> interviews/episode-21/aldrich7.html accessed 12/11/04)

The role of ethics in intelligence work has always been either misunderstood
or poorly appreciated, by both policymakers and the public, leading to the
stale joke that "ethics" and "intelligence" form an oxymoron. In other
words, "doing what's right" (i.e., doing your job, which may require you to
act immorally) should not interfere with doing "the right thing" (i.e., acting
with moral principles). Of course, most work done by intelligence profes-

sionals does not involve a moral dilemma, such as providing accurate analysis or collecting information. Sometimes, however, conflicting requirements and tasks impose significant ethical and moral dilemmas upon people doing their job. Consequently, public servants must make a decision or take an action that could be considered inappropriate or unethical for a similar circumstance in their private lives.

The typical notion the American public holds of intelligence work is mostly generated by a long and rich history originating in Hollywood and from a lack of understanding, limited by secrecy and myth. The public is inundated with the perception that intelligence professionals will say or do anything to accomplish their jobs and that to be employed as an intelligence professional is to abandon any sense of moral judgment. Bookstores and theaters are filled with stories of people who are sanctioned by the government and thus they have a "license" to lie, cheat, steal, or kill. This license is bestowed on the individual, in the name of society, to act as we dare not. They are not responsible for their actions, and morality be damned.

Professionals in many fields have standards of ethical conduct with established codes of ethics, to include psychologists (by the American Psychological Association), lawyers (by the American Bar Association), doctors (by the American Medical Association), organists (by the American Guild of Organists), music teachers (by the Music Teachers Association), real estate appraisers (by the Society of Real Estate Appraisers), funeral directors (by the Funeral Ethics Association), travel agents (by the American Society of Travel Agents), and speleologists (i.e., people who study caves, by the National Speleological Society). The list goes on and on.[1] All these professions have a concern with the issues and ethical conflicts that those who work in that field may encounter. These concerns may include problems of honesty, confidentiality, privacy, impartiality, accountability, and conflicts of interest. In the intelligence business, these concerns are as real as in any other profession.

The recent events at Abu Ghraib prison in Iraq and the allegations of the politicalization of intelligence that led the United States into that conflict have cast a spotlight on how the intelligence community collects and analyzes information. Lacking legal directives or guidance, intelligence professionals are left to decide for themselves how far they, and the country they represent, can go before losing the moral high ground. And if it is legal, is it ethical? According to media reports, in the months since the Abu Ghraib prison scandal, government officials have insisted that America does not and will not use torture; but at the same time, the government has tried to preserve maximum leeway in the interrogation of terrorism suspects by not drawing a legal and clear line between where rough treatment ends and torture begins.[2]

It is time to discuss the role of ethics in intelligence work. Contrary to the war fighter, with a rich history in "just war theory," the intelligence professional has no theoretical and ethical foundation to work with in his decision-making process. Most ethics and intelligence education, which is really training, normally consists of management and leadership techniques, learning the legal ramifications for conducting certain actions and decisions, associating the intelligence profession with the military profession, or learning from previous ethical mishaps through case studies. Although all of these are excellent teaching tools, they fail to take into consideration the moral underpinnings of this very volatile and possibly morally damaging profession. None of these pedagogical methods seeks to establish a theory upon which a code of ethics can be built, a framework that can transcend the intelligence community.

This book represents the first collection of articles to seriously study ethics for and about intelligence professionals. The goal of this book is to develop a body of literature that may initiate the building of an ethical code for the intelligence professional not dependent on any particular agency, department, or even country—a standardized code of ethics for the intelligence professional that would enable practitioners to define their responsibilities, provide guidance, inspire, motivate, raise awareness and consciousness, as well as improve the quality and consistency of the work they perform.

This book is for intelligence professionals, whether they are collectors, analysts, or operators working with human intelligence, electronic intelligence, signals intelligence, imagery intelligence, or all-source intelligence; students of international affairs, political science, and philosophy; and citizens to think critically about the work that is being done for their security. Ultimately, this book seeks to lay the groundwork for discussion, education, and research, so that "ethics and intelligence" will be taken more seriously rather than relegated to an old joke.

NOTES

1. An excellent source for different professional codes of ethics is at the Illinois Institute of Technology Code of Ethics website (http://ethics.iit.edu/codes) and general information at the Association for Practical and Professional Ethics (http://www.indiana.edu/~appe).

2. *Los Angeles Times*, January 23, 2005, p. 1.

Acknowledgments

First and foremost, I want to thank all the authors for allowing me to use their articles, and the publishing companies and organizations that allowed me to reprint them. A long time ago I began thinking about this topic when I met Dr. Phyllis O'Callaghan at Georgetown University. It was there that I learned about the intangible elements of international affairs. Also, I want to thank the faculty and students at the Joint Military Intelligence College, specifically Rebecca Bolton, Patricia Manchester, John Prout, Leo McCormick Jr., Walter Coryell Jr., Tim Christenson, Dennis Cox, Elizabeth Yerkes, Mark Marshall, Karen Albert, Kristina Young, Michael Trevett, and Tivo Romero for contributing to the cases studies; Solveig Brownfeld, Nancy Jemiola, and William Spracher for their resourcefulness in helping me pull this manuscript together. Finally, I want to thank my wife, Reta, for her patience and support, and to my children, Dacia, Oliver, and Mallory, for allowing me to work on the computer, even when my time was up.

Grateful acknowledgment is made to the following sources for permission to reprint material copyrighted or controlled by them:

"Ethics and Intelligence" by J. E. Drexel Godfrey, reprinted by permission of *Foreign Affairs*, issue 56(3), April 1978. Copyright © 1978 by the Council on Foreign Relations, Inc.

"The Ethics of Covert Methods" by Roger Homan and "Comment on 'The Ethics of Covert Methods'" by Martin Bulmer, reprinted by permission by *The British Journal of Sociology*, Blackwell Publishing.

"Ethics and Morality in United States Secret Intelligence" by Arthur S. Hulnick and David W. Mattausch, reprinted by permission from *Harvard Journal of Law & Public Policy*, Spring 1989.

"The Legitimacy of Covert Action: Sorting Out the Moral Responsibilities" by Lincoln P. Bloomfield Jr., *International Journal of Intelligence and Counterintelligence.* Copyright 1990. Reproduced by permission of Taylor & Francis, Inc., http://www.taylorandfrancis.com.

Excerpt from *Secret Agencies: U.S. Intelligence in a Hostile World* by Loch K. Johnson, reprinted by permission from Yale University Press. Copyright © 1979.

"Guarding against Politicization" by Robert Gates and "Managing Covert Political Action" by James A. Barry both appeared in *Studies in Intelligence*, fall 1992.

"Moral Damage and the Justification of Intelligence Collection from Human Sources" by John Langan, S. J., appeared in *Studies in Intelligence*, Summer 1981.

"The Need for Improvement: Integrity, Ethics, and the CIA" by Kent Pekel appeared in *Studies in Intelligence*, Spring 1998.

"Terrorism and Torture" by Fritz Allhoff is reprinted by permission from *International Journal of Applied Philosophy*, fall 2003. Copyright © 2003.

"Covert Intervention as a Moral Problem" by Charles R. Beitz, reprinted by permission from *Ethics and International Affairs* by the Carnegie Council on Ethics and International Affairs. Copyright © 1989.

"Anthropologists as Spies" by David Price is reprinted by permission of *The Nation*, copyright © 2000.

"Ethical Issues in Competitive Intelligence Practice: Consensus, Conflicts and Challenges" by Linda Trevino and Gary R. Weaver, copyright © 1997. Reprinted with permission of John Wiley & Sons, Inc.

"The Challenge of Completely Ethical Competitive Intelligence and the 'CHIP' Model" by Darren Charters, copyright © 2001. Reprinted with permission of John Wiley & Sons, Inc.

"Intelligence Collection and Analysis: Dilemmas and Decisions" by John B. Chomeau and Anne C. Rudolph appeared in *Ethics & National Defense: The Timeless Issues* by James Gaston and Janis Bren Hietala (edited), National Defense University Press, Washington, DC.

1

Ethics and Intelligence

J. E. Drexel Godfrey

Editor's note: At the time this essay was written, two Congressional Committees had completed their investigations into alleged CIA abuses of power, finding that the agency had a history of committing excesses abroad.

The three-year public agony of the Central Intelligence Agency may be coming to an end. Richard Helms has been convicted, the President has issued a new set of regulations restricting certain surveillance activities, and the torrent of public exposés by "insiders" seems to be abating. What remains to be seen is whether the traumas suffered since the sweeping congressional investigations began in 1975 have made any significant impact on the heart and guts of the Agency.

There are some suggestions, of course, that nothing much has changed. When Mr. Helms returned from receiving a suspended sentence, he was given a hero's welcome by an indulgent group of ex-colleagues. Simultaneously the announced intention of Admiral Stansfield Turner, the present Director, to reduce Agency operational personnel by several hundred was met by smear campaigns so powerful that the President soon felt obliged to publicly declare his continuing support for the Admiral. These responses from traditional intelligence officers may not be all that significant, however. Angry reactions to reductions in force are not, after all, new in Washington. Any pruning of career public servants can result in mid-level bureaucrats making high-level mischief.

The Helms case was quite another matter. Far from resolving any of the deeper issues of recent Agency conduct, it did not even address them. The case did, however, expose the persistent failure of several administrations to establish appropriate congressional arrangements for the exercise of intelligence operations. All post-war Presidents have permitted Directors of Central Intelligence to appear before congressional committees in the full knowledge that they would be closely questioned about secret operations approved and placed under tight security restrictions by the National Security Council. A long tradition had been built up over the years with the leaders of the Congress itself, that the facts concerning political operations (or clandestine intelligence operations) should be revealed only to selected members of Congress, and denied to formal committees at least in open session.

From time to time efforts were made by individual Presidents, or their staffs, to reach an accommodation with Congress that would reduce the vulnerability of CIA officials, caught between the professional obligation for secrecy and the legislative thirst for candor. No true resolution of this dilemma was achieved until President Ford declared for candor and so instructed Mr. Helms' successor. By then, of course, Mr. Helms had presented the testimony on operations in Chile to a Senate committee, which a federal judge subsequently found to be not only misleading but false.

Not unnaturally many intelligence officials felt their ex-Director had been victimized. In a narrow sense he had. Lacking a presidential mandate to reveal the full nature of the U.S. involvement in the Chilean elections, Mr. Helms opted to give testimony that was less than truthful.

The irony of the case, however, is not that Mr. Helms was forced to choose between two ethical imperatives, one honoring his oath of secrecy, the other telling the truth. Far more significant is the fact that because it focused on such a narrow issue—and one where responsibility for the sorry turn of events could be laid as much at the doors of a succession of Presidents and leaders of Congress as to the Agency Director—the trial and judgment ignored a whole range of ethical problems concerning intelligence practices in a free society.

⁎   ⁎   ⁎

To some the mere juxtaposition of ethics and intelligence may appear to be a contradiction in terms. But at heart, intelligence is rooted in the severest of ethical principles: truth telling. After all, the end purpose of the elaborate apparatus that the intelligence community has become is to provide the policymaker with as close to a truthful depiction of a given situation as is humanly possible. Anything less is not intelligence. It may be useful opinion—in some cases it may even be more accurate than prevailing intelligence—but if it is, the opinion maker is lucky, or in the particular instance possessed of more facts and sharper judgmental skills than the professional intelligence officer. Even the CIA has long recognized the centrality of truth telling. As a contributor to *Foreign Affairs* observed several years ago, the motto of the CIA, chosen by the doughty old Presbyterian, Allen Dulles, is "And the Truth Shall Make You Free."[1]

Even as the motto was being chosen in the mid-1950s, however, the point was being lost and the purpose of the Agency corrupted. Perhaps because of the personality of Mr. Dulles and his operational successes in Switzerland during World War II, emphasis on activities having little or nothing to do with the pursuit of truth grew to preoccupy the CIA. The Church Committee's excellent report on intelligence activities makes it abundantly clear that foreign operations won top priority under Mr. Dulles's leadership; worse, foreign operations expanded from a tiny "psych warfare" section of the clandestine collection division to absorb a major share of the Agency's budget, its personnel, and skills. Operations both foreign and domestic, with a host of concomitant and now familiar malpractices, became the bread and butter of the Agency during the 1950s and 1960s.[2]

To accept the approximation of truth as the purpose of intelligence is one thing. To accept the methods by which truth can be obtained poses ethical dilemmas. The truth, after all, is often a set of facts, or concrete physical entities, or intentions, which the party with whom they are entrusted will guard jealously as a precious, not to say sacred, element of the national preserve. Ferreting out the truth under these circumstances often requires means and techniques not ordinarily employed in human intercourse.

At this point the ethical absolutist is compelled to say, "Exactly. An ethical society should renounce foreign intelligence altogether; given the new Administration's emphasis on human rights, domestic intelligence might best be scuttled, too." In this formulation the argument that other nations will not cease intelligence-gathering activities simply because the United States renounces them carries little weight. Ethical conduct is a force of its own; powerful nations lead by example; renunciation of intelligence gathering would be an act of moral courage with untold beneficial international consequences, etc.

But we are not all ethical absolutists. Value trade-offs are probably the best that most people in an uncertain world will accept. And it is because intelligence offers security that bizarre methods to obtain it are acceptable to most. Foreign policy making without an intelligence input of some kind would be capricious; in the uncharted waters of world crisis situations it would be scandalously foolhardy. It follows that the more ambiguous the international situation, the greater the value of intelligence in the decision-making process. Put another way, of course, this means that where intelligence does not add to international security, but rather, say, to the obsessive comfort of knowing more about Ruritania than even the Ruritanians, or where it merely facilitates the feeding of salacious tidbits about foreign leaders to inquisitive Presidents, questionable methods to collect it are not acceptable.

The security returns of intelligence are probably inestimable, and they are welcomed by both world superpowers and tacitly condoned by almost all active participating nations on the world stage. Satellites monitor the missile developments of the superpowers; microwave telephone messages between foreign embassies and capitals are intercepted for critical information. Without technology of this kind in the hands of both the United States and the Soviet Union, there would of course have been no SALT talks; there would not now be any form of SALT agreement. Nikita Khrushchev implied just this when he half-seriously suggested to President Eisenhower in 1958 that the two countries exchange intelligence chiefs. Both leaders recognized that inspections in each other's countries would probably be out of the question for many years to come; each knew that in order to make any progress on arms limitation he would have to rely on the safety of his own intelligence monitoring system and avert his eyes to monitoring by the other.

In a world where the two great powers can no longer guarantee international stability and where weaponry is no longer the exclusive currency of power, intelligence monitoring must sweep targets other than the principal antagonist—e.g., China or the Middle East. It must also be as concerned with economic and energy considerations as missiles. But the principle governing the choice of targets remains the same. Intelligence must promote international security, or the ethical compromises necessary to accommodate the requisite collection methods cannot and should not be stomached.

Intelligence monitoring substitutes for full faith and credit between nations, and technology provides a pitiful but workable substitute for the joyful conditions of a distant One World. The tensions of the nation-state system are, in other words, held in bounds not only by diplomacy and by mutual common sense but by carefully calibrated monitoring systems.

Assuming, then, that intelligence can help toward security in a dangerous international order, how can the intelligence function be carried out at the least risk to other values in our society? To put this most succinctly, how can a professional intelligence service operate so that officials within it perform their roles in an ethical manner? Most public officials would prefer that this be the case; certainly most private citizens expect nothing less.

The traditional easy answer, of course, is that in international affairs a double standard operates. What is unacceptable human behavior at home or in one's own society can be forgiven in dealings with foreign societies or with the representatives abroad of those societies. War is the ultimate expression of this double standard. But the assassination of foreign leaders in peacetime stretches the standard furthest, beyond, as is now wholly agreed, its breaking point. Under the shelter of the double standard, self-justification usually takes the form of: "Someone's got to do the dirty work"; or "Distasteful as the task was, it served the national purpose." On examination both statements contain implicit assertions by the makers of ethical standards. This, then, is the nub of the matter.

Foreign intelligence is not, by and large, conducted by people lacking the capacity to recognize ethical standards, but standards are lowered to accommodate the perceived national purpose. Once lowered, they can be more easily lowered a second time, or they can be lowered further and further as routine reduces ethical resistance to repugnant activities. This is the area of human dynamics where yesterday's managers of the intelligence community have been the most irresolute. Management rarely blew the whistle on subordinates. When subordinates succeeded in operations of questionable morality, they were as often rewarded with promotions as reprimanded for using dubious methods.

A high management official of one intelligence agency—in this case the FBI—blurted out to the Church Committee an incredibly candid confession of amorality. In response to questions as to whether any supervisory official of the Bureau had voiced reservations about the legitimacy of the infamous Operation Cointelpro (active disruption of citizen groups) he answered:

> We never gave any thought to this line of reasoning, because we were just naturally pragmatists. The one thing we were concerned about was this: Will this course of action work; will we reach the objective that we desire to reach? As far as legality is concerned, morals or ethics, it was never raised by myself or anyone else. I think this suggests really that in government we are amoral.[3]

To disagree with this official's conclusion is easy; to refute the implicit charge that government itself contributes to, if not insists, on amorality, is more difficult. Presumably, the official, like most Americans, entered government service with some sense of ethics and acceptable norms of moral behavior. He came to believe, apparently, that the responsible intelligence officer *should not* concern himself with such matters. They are, he said, irrelevant to the conduct of his government business.

                    *   *   *

Most professions, such as the law and medicine, have for centuries provided themselves with fail-safe systems to ensure that ethical norms are not compromised out of existence, or rusted from misuse. Some of these systems work better than others, some are susceptible to corruption themselves and a few are mere shams, but the fact that they exist and generally are taken seriously by the members of the profession is critically significant. At the very least, it means that there are limits to a professional's freedom and that those limits are defined by ethical codes sanctioned by colleagues.

A profession whose end purpose it is to root out the truth cannot afford to resist asking where its limits should be set. However, the intelligence professional has in the past operated under the simple guideline, "don't get caught." Recently there have been signs that suggest that the intelligence community is busily, if somewhat ponderously, groping toward a limit-setting policy for its professionals.

The business of limit setting will not be easy, particularly for the center-piece of the community, the CIA, and specifically for its large clandestine services element. It will not be easy because of the grim ethos of clandestine collection and operations, developed long before orbiting photographic satellites or sophisticated interception systems were ever conceived. That ethos is rooted in a concept as old as human society: the weak or the vulnerable can be manipulated by the strong or the shrewd. Human intelligence collection is a major preoccupation of the clandestine service. Simply put, this is the process of extracting from others information or national assets they would not willingly part with under normal circumstances.

In some cases the creation of appropriate circumstances is relatively easy. This is where the source is a willing volunteer acting out of his own sense of patriotism. Anti-Soviet émigré Hungarians providing detailed information on Russian military units occupying their country fall into this category. The clandestine officer must provide the means whereby the émigré can return to his country. By and large the clandestine officer can content himself with the knowledge that the Hungarian is as anxious to reenter his homeland illegally as he is anxious to have him make the effort.

But the highest art in tradecraft is to develop a source that you "own lock, stock, and barrel." According to the clandestine ethos, a "controlled" source provides the most reliable intelligence. "Controlled" means, of course, bought or otherwise obligated. Traditionally it has been the aim of the professional in the clandestine service to weave a psychological web around any potentially fruitful contact and to tighten that web whenever possible. Opportunities are limited, but for those in the clandestine service who successfully develop controlled sources, rewards in status and peer respect are high. The modus operandi required, however, is the very antithesis of ethical interpersonal relationships.

Sometimes the information obtained by these methods can be important. It is, however, rarely of critical importance. At best it may provide a measure of confirmation of some already suspected development or fill in a missing piece of a complex mosaic of facts. There have been occasions when controlled sources have been successful in snatching internal documents off high-level desks in their own governments, but even in these instances the "take" has not been earthshaking. Perhaps the faintly disappointing record of achievement by clandestine operatives is explainable in bureaucratic terms. Well-placed officials with immediate access to critical policy-making circles—and for the most part this means they are part of the policy-making process—are generally well rewarded by and well satisfied with their own governments. If they were not, they would not hold powerful positions. The main targets for clandestine collectors are usually second- and third-level officials who may not be fully privy to policy developments.

Finally, there is the human consideration. Most controlled sources are ambivalent about the roles they are obliged to play. On the one hand, there may be gratification that their retainer fees enable them to reduce some crushing personal debts, or to meet other expenses incurred as a result of weaknesses or personal misjudgments. On the other hand, they will almost certainly feel a sense of guilt in betraying trusts they are expected not to betray; they may also feel more than a little self-loathing that they have been too weak to resist being used by those who pay them or blackmail them. How these feelings subconsciously affect what they report and how they report is anybody's guess. It is at least possible that the clandestine officer who "owns" a controlled source may not have the extraordinary asset that his "tradecraft" teaches him he should have.

Quality of information obtained aside, a fundamental ethical issue concerning clandestine human collection remains. That issue is the impact on the clandestine officer of his relationship with his source. The former's bread and butter is the subversion of the latter's integrity. The officer is painstakingly trained in techniques that will convert an acquaintance into a submissive tool, to shred away his resistance and deflate his sense of self-worth. Of course, the source may be thoroughly cynical, even a venal merchant of his country's privacy, and in that case the task of the clandestine officer is less burdensome—although he may come to find the relationship just as repellent as if the source had slowly and resistingly been bent to compliance. Whatever the chemistry between the two individuals, collector and source, or perhaps more pointedly, dominant and dominated, the biggest loser is the one whose ethical scruples are most damaged in the process. Depending on the techniques he may have to use to bring the source under control and maintain that relationship, the biggest loser may be the clandestine officer.

Another prime concern of the clandestine services is the development of methodologies and devices to thwart the defensive measures of other intelligence agencies and other national political systems. While much of this activity is purely technical electronic engineering, a significant investment has also been made in such exotica as "truth drugs," complex psychological warfare strategies, bizarre bugging devices, and the like. Some of these devices and techniques have been used with profit and success by clandestine officers operating overseas; others have proved impractical in the field or have stalled on the drawing board as development costs got out of hand. But the search for new ways to penetrate other societies goes on. Today's drug experimenters (if there are indeed any left) may become tomorrow's experts in long-range behavior-modification processes.

Whatever the state of these arcane arts, they have two things in common. First, their purpose is almost always to facilitate the manipulation of man by man. In this sense they are not dissimilar in effect and impact to the process of controlled source development. Secondly, the practitioners of these arts and the "psych warfare" experts are obliged by the very nature of their trade to presume that they are operating in hostile environments. The end point of their efforts, after all, is to bypass normal authority, or at the least, to use semi-legal means to overcome obstacles placed in their path by the authorities of other nations. The professional premise of the officers engaged in these practices, then, is the constructive use of illegality. While revolutionaries around the world have lived long and comfortably with this paradox, it is quite another matter for sober and presumably accountable U.S. public servants to be exposed to its temptations.

In this connection it is important to note that over the years officers whose careers have primarily been spent in clandestine activities have occupied the preeminent roles in the management of the CIA. At least until recently, when heavy reductions in clandestine staff were ordered by the current Director, Admiral Stansfield Turner, roughly two-thirds of the highest executive positions at any given time were filled by officers whose careers blossomed in the clandestine services. Years of hardening in the ugly business of source control and penetration of foreign capitals have surely taken their toll. Little wonder that the CIA's top leadership did not traditionally spend much time setting "limits" on the Agency's activities. Little wonder that management developed a process of compartmentalizing what it recognized to be questionable activities. The most bizarre operations, such as Chaos (to be discussed below) and human drug experimentation, have been traditionally walled off even from other Agency colleagues whose questions might have been embarrassing. Mr. Helms himself testified before the Church Committee that in many instances the CIA's General Counsel was simply excluded from knowing of the existence of particularly exotic activities and operations.[4] The inference is inescapable that he was shut off out of fear that he would, as he had occasionally done in the past, advise that the operations overstepped legal limits. Similarly, the Church Committee report makes clear that even the recommendations of the Agency's elaborate Inspector General system could be, and sometimes were, rejected by the Agency Director.[5]

Thus, a picture emerges of a highly compartmentalized bureaucracy whose direction has been largely controlled by officials with long experience in the seduction of other human beings and societies. Not immoral or even without ethical standards themselves, they had lost the habit of questioning where they should set limits on their official conduct. And other officers who might have been expected to remind them of these limits were kept in ignorance. This state of affairs is particularly distressing when it involves an organization where high premiums are paid for inventiveness, for "outsmarting the opposition."

In an organizational context where the edge of possibility is bounded only by the stretch of the imagination, special arrangements for limit setting are necessary. Each management level of the clandestine services, from the most immediate and parochial to the highest, should have an officer who plays the role of "naysayer." His task would be to review operational plans for their ethical consequences and occasionally to remind the imaginative subordinate that daring and innovativeness must sometimes bow to prudence. Every organization has informal "naysayers" seeded through its ranks. In traditional bureaucracies they are almost always negative influences, cruel stiflers of initiative and zeal. In intelligence organizations, institutional "naysayers" could have just the opposite effect: they could be critical to a rediscovery of ethically acceptable limits of activity.

*   *   *

That element of the CIA whose job it is "to tell the truth," as opposed to collecting the truth overseas, is the overt Intelligence Directorate. It would appear at first glance to have the easier job. But this is not necessarily so. For one thing, truth is rarely simple fact; it is almost always a combination of fact and judgment and as such almost always subject to second guessing. The intelligence analyst has no monopoly on wisdom and prescience, but he does have one advantage. He is not subject to the policy considerations of the operating departments, such as State and Defense. He is, in this respect, free to call the shots as he sees them, whether or not they substantiate or confirm some fundamental premise of U.S. policy. Ignoring the policy assumptions of the Administration in a search for the most defensible judgment can be an unhappy affair, as those analysts who toiled through the Vietnam years can testify. While support from Agency superiors for the views of the analysts was strong during the Johnson and Nixon Administrations, the analytic product—that is, the truth as the analysts saw it—was not always palatable to higher consumers. The "truth" more often than not implicitly cast doubt on the outcome of the U.S. efforts in Indochina. Reaction to such judgments at White House and National Security Council levels was at worst unfriendly, and at best indifferent.

Nevertheless, the obligation remains for the analytic component of the CIA to produce what it believes to be the least assailable version of a given situation and its consequences for the future course of events. In this lonely and sometimes scorned pursuit, there are ethical pitfalls no less severe than those encountered by the overseas clandestine collectors.

A case in point is the unusual episode surrounding the studies of radical youth produced by the Agency at the demand of both Presidents Johnson and Nixon in the late 1960s and early 1970s. The original order for such a study coincided with one of the peak points in protest against the Vietnam War, protests conducted in Europe and the Far East as well as in the United States. When the order was first relayed to the Agency by Walt Rostow, then National Security Special Assistant to the President, it was accompanied by the hypothesis that the protest actions were so vociferous and so universal that they must be orchestrated by communists. Dubious at best, this became the principal theme of the first study and the several successive versions that were subsequently ordered. The Agency undertook, in other words, to determine whether communist instigation lay behind the worldwide protests.

The first edition of the study concluded that there had been no discernible communist involvement in the student protests, with a purely theoretical aside that, at least as far as U.S. student protests were concerned, there were a variety of justifications for protest that made communist intervention unnecessary. The study was ill received by the White House. In effect, it was rejected out of hand with the pointed question: "Are you sure of your conclusions? Have you turned over every rock?" These injunctions were to be repeated twice more as the Agency, confident of its original judgments, tried to produce the evidence, or demonstrate the absence of evidence, that would similarly persuade two reluctant Presidents and a host of presidential advisers.

The costs to the CIA of "turning over every rock" were shatteringly high. The dearest cost was the decision to expand greatly the patently illegal "Operation Chaos," which had begun modestly with the intention of collecting evidence for the analysts preparing the first version of the student paper. To this end U.S. agents under control of the Clandestine Services' counterintelligence component were infiltrated into student groups within the United States and abroad. Once again the operation was carefully compartmentalized so that few even of the most senior Agency officials were aware of its existence—including those responsible for the production of the study. When the first study was rejected, Chaos was built up into a sizable operation, with access to computer technology and a network of overseas and domestic employees keeping book on many thousands of U.S. and foreign students. Not only was the Agency's legislative charter, which mandates *only* overseas espionage, violated, but so too were privacy rights of thousands of young Americans.

The second cost was a natural concomitant of the first. As more and more "rocks got turned over," the pursuit of evidence became an end in itself. A tendency developed among the collectors to believe that if they hunted long enough and assiduously enough, some communist involvement might be found, and if it were, the President would be satisfied. In short, the collection effort lost perspective. Had it found communist affiliations—say, in the leadership of a particular student organization—it would not have been of much significance given the overwhelming negative findings elsewhere in the great majority of student movements. The notion that an assertion can be converted to a truth if there is one scrap of positive evidence to support it is dangerous nonsense—in this case nonsense entertained by desperate Presidents and abetted by officials who might better have said: "We have turned over enough rocks, Mr. President." Thus, at the end of the unhappy affair called Chaos, one side of the Agency was unwittingly engaged in what was a corruption of the search for truth, to say nothing of extensively illegal activities, while the other side of the Agency was frenetically trying, under heavy fire, to stick to its best judgment.

In retrospect, it can be rationalized that all the actors in this unhappy drama were victims of the curious political climate of Washington as the Vietnam conflict ground to a conclusion. The psychological ingredients were all there: bureaucratic weariness with a clearly failing U.S. policy to which the Agency had already committed much of its manpower energies for a decade was one. Presidential frustration as various ways out of the dilemma were closed off was another. When all is said and done, however, there can only be one satisfactory explanation for the Agency's plunge into massive illegal activities. Top management had the means, the manpower, and the mind-set to do the President's bidding and to do it without arousing suspicion or inviting investigation. Only in the waning days of Chaos (and the War) did complaints from lower echelons of the Agency begin to be registered around Washington. What top management lacked was the habit of limit setting, the reflex that warns of dangerous consequences—not of being found out, but of transgressing minimal ethical standards. Presidents can perhaps be forgiven for obsessiveness, but for the servants of Presidents, particularly those whose business is truth, the first duty is to guard against those personal and institutional frailties that make a mockery of the search for truth.

*   *   *

Is it possible, then, to introduce, or better, to revive a sense of ethics in the intelligence community? Certainly much can be accomplished simply by strong leadership that sets an appropriate tone. Presumably some efforts are being made in this direction now. But rhetoric alone cannot do the job that is required. Some specific prescriptions are offered in the following paragraphs.

The time would appear ripe, from the perspective both of history and the complexities of a world where energy resources, food supply, and technological sophistication carry as much, if not more, weight than weapons superiority, for the intelligence community to get out of political operations. The massive investment in these activities in recent years has paid off only rarely in terms of advancing U.S. interests. At times, as in the Congo, they have done more to confuse and unsettle an already fluid situation than to stabilize it. Some operations have probably cost the United States goodwill for years to come. Cost-benefit factors apart, political operations are often, although not always, illegal activities in which the greatest skill is to thwart the established authorities of foreign countries. To live clandestinely, to manipulate others, to distress the political ecology of another society—these are all activities that induce an amoral view of life. While they may or may not produce critical effects in the countries where they are undertaken, they almost certainly will affect those who engage in them. They are, finally, activities that have little or nothing to do with intelligence.

It can be argued that there are occasions, or there may be occasions, when political action of a clandestine nature may be the only feasible way to produce a desirable circumstance beneficial not only to the instigating country, but to a larger portion of the world's peoples. One can imagine, for example, such operations mounted in South Africa that might have positive consequences throughout the southern part of the continent. U.S. policy interests could be served at the same time as the interests of South Africa's neighbors. Indeed, there have been occasions when massive infusions of U.S. funds and skills have turned the tide in tightly balanced and critical political contests. Support for the noncommunist parties in Italy and France in 1948 comes to mind as does the far less obtrusive (and, one gathers, predominantly European) support in 1975 for democratic elements threatened by hard-line (and Soviet-supported) Communists in Portugal.

The opportunity for U.S. intervention in political events of high international significance would not be lost by the abolition of a political operations capability. Private citizens recruited for the occasion have carried out such tasks for Presidents before and could again. On the other hand, there could be two salutory consequences for the United States in abandoning political operations as an ongoing activity of the CIA. First, Presidents would have to shoulder the burden themselves and create ad hoc arrangements for each instance. This would almost certainly sharpen their discrimination and force them to concentrate on interventions with the highest chance of success and the least chance of exposure. Second, the elaborate network of clandestine operators currently in place could be drastically reduced. No longer would it be necessary to nurture and maintain agents around the world on a contingency basis. The temptation to indulge in operational mischief of low or ambiguous priority for the sake of keeping agents alert would be foreclosed.

Many of the arguments used to question the efficacy and suitability of political operations can be applied to the process of human clandestine intelligence collection: the product is not all that impressive, the moral damage to the collectors is high, intelligence tends to be collected as an end in itself, and there is always the risk of exposure. Nevertheless, intelligence must be collected in selected areas and against specific subject targets. Technology is now the workhorse of the collection business and it should remain so. The present Director has in effect recognized this evolution in collection methods; he has justified his reduction of covert officers on this ground. Photographic and audio satellites and other interception devices are immensely expensive, but they have the advantage of doing only minimal damage to the ethical standards of the operators and processors. As noted above, technological intelligence collection is in at least one highly significant area—that of arms limitation control—tacitly accepted as essential to security by both superpowers.[6]

Of course, even with the phasing down of clandestine human collection, the need will remain for residual capability in certain esoteric collection techniques. Atmospheric conditions in some geographic locations may be so unfavorable that short-range collection devices will be needed to supplement "stand-off" equipment, such as satellites. There will always be the need for personnel skilled in the techniques of situating these devices. Similarly, there must be those who can exploit the defector or the "walk-in" source.

Counterintelligence is another field of clandestine intelligence activity which probably cannot be dispensed with for some years to come. But if counterintelligence is to survive, it should be organized on a purely defensive basis as a protection against foreign penetration of the U.S. intelligence services and their technical capabilities. It should be a small, lean component with a sophisticated understanding not only of the technological capabilities of major foreign intelligence services, but also of those countries' political dynamics. Far from being walled off from other Agency components as in the past, it should be a vital part of Agency life, as much to gain from exposure to varying points of view as to influence those points of view.

A vigorous reexamination of the entire collection function, both in terms of techniques and targets, would be salutary at this point in the intelligence community. Collection that goes beyond what the satellite and the intercept station provide cannot be forsaken altogether. Indeed, it should be improved with renewed emphasis on (a) analytic collection and (b) the old-world expertise of the open dialogue replacing the controlled source. Collectors with the training to mine and exploit technical materials in archives and specialized libraries or statistical centers could be the intelligence pick-and-shovel men of the future.

For those tightly closed societies where access to such material is almost completely denied to the United States, a different methodology will be necessary. Third-country officials with some access privileges in the host country must be assiduously cultivated, but (breaking with past practice) in an open and reciprocal manner. Collectors with substantive knowledge of their data targets should be authorized to disseminate "trading materials" to their foreign counterparts in exchange for hard-to-get data and technical material. This will be a delicate business. Maladroit handling of such negotiations could result in even tighter controls over information by the host country. Needless to say, negotiations could not be conducted *in* the target country without risking the expulsion of third-country nationals. New expertise in content evaluation both of the materials desired by the United States and the data to be used as trading currency will have to be developed.

At the higher levels of intelligence collection—that is, gaining insight into the sensitive complex of issues concerning political, economic, and military developments in a target country—emphasis should be on the old-fashioned method of diplomatic dialogue. Reports that contribute to an understanding of social or economic trends or that sort out shifting national priorities are almost always more significant and useful than the one-shot item that reveals a specific decision or records some finite act. "Think pieces" have traditionally been the preserve of the ambassador or senior Foreign Service official. Their quality has, however, been uneven; they suffer from irregularity. Part of the problem is that few Foreign Service officers stay long enough on a single posting to become in-depth analytical experts. Only a few of the largest embassies have enjoyed the luxury of having one such person on their staffs for a number of years. What is being proposed here is that CIA officers fill the roles of permanent in-country experts. These would be senior officials, chosen for their substantive familiarity with the political and economic cultures of the countries to which they are posted. They would be expected to cultivate openly the widest circle of acquaintances and to report selectively both to headquarters and the ambassador. Clandestine would give way to substantive expertise.

The finely trained and highly skilled clandestine collection officer with years of service in the field is likely to scoff at these suggestions. It has always been the contention of the clandestine collector that overt techniques could indeed uncover immense amounts of data about the capabilities of a foreign nation target, but that the intentions and plans of the same country could only be unlocked by controlled penetrations. There is, of course, some truth to this proposition. Final and critical decisions—e.g., to go to war with a neighbor, to begin the development of nuclear weaponry—are so tightly held and originate from such complex motivations that they do not suddenly spring off printed pages being turned by a lonely researcher. On the other hand, neither have such decisions been revealed with any great degree of success by penetration agents in the past.

Once the CIA has begun to turn itself around by the actions suggested above, it will have taken the most painful steps. But backsliding into old habits and behavior patterns will surely occur unless other, less dramatic moves are made. The influence of the clandestine service in the Agency remains strong and, given the sheer weight of numbers, it will have a significant voice in internal Agency affairs for years to come.

Something of the flavor of how that voice might express itself can be inferred from the hero's welcome given to Richard Helms when he appeared at a reception of recently retired covert officers fresh from his conviction in federal court. The old methods of compartmentalization and tightly controlled operations have become a way of life not easily shaken in the insular bureaucracy of an intelligence service. Radical rearrangements of traditional procedures must be considered.

At the least the Inspector General's function should be strengthened, as the Church Committee has recommended. Specifically, this officer's role should be expanded beyond its traditional one of internal control and response to employee complaints. One ex-Agency official who is a careful student of its recent history has suggested the creation of an ombudsman accessible to employees who felt they were being used in improper activities.[7] This would be a helpful addition to the Inspector General's staff, freeing him for the vital task of constructively intervening in questionable plans and programs throughout the Agency.

Similarly, the Legal Counsel must be given more steel to put under his velvet glove, particularly when his rulings are ignored or overturned by the Director. Traditionally matters of legal propriety have been referred to the Legal Counsel by other senior officers when and if they chose to do so; in effect his role has been passive. It should be a relatively simple internal matter to reverse this pattern. President Ford followed up one Church Committee recommendation by giving the Legal Counsel access to the Executive Oversight Board in the event that one of his rulings was ignored by the Director. This is a significant step in strengthening the legal review function in the Agency.

*   *   *

A more sweeping structural change for the Agency has been suggested from time to time. This would entail a complete divorce of overt and covert intelligence activities. Overt functions (analysis, reporting, estimates, etc.) would be aggregated under one organizational roof and covert functions (collection, operations, counterintelligence, technical development of human control devices, etc.) under another. The objective behind such proposals has usually been to remove from the intelligence end product the taint of the methods used to obtain the raw data, in other words to strengthen the dignity and credibility of the Agency's truth-telling function.

There are merits to these suggestions, but perhaps the optimum time for divorce has passed. Indeed, if political operations were now eliminated and clandestine collection minimized, the temptation to breach ethical standards by the clandestine services would be reduced significantly. Moreover, cutting the clandestine services adrift would result in the concentration in one organization of most of those officers—now at high positions—who have been exposed to the highest ethical risks. Backsliding would be a great temptation, managerial control an administrator's nightmare.

But the measures discussed above will amount to little more than tinkering if not buttressed by a radical new personnel policy that places a premium on ethical values. Beyond native intelligence, recruitment criteria have in the past emphasized such psychological factors as stability, intellectual curiosity, and phlegm. Once selected on the basis of favorable readings on these counts, the candidate had, of course, to survive the polygraph test—a final screening against the possibility of penetration by a foreign agent or a duplicitous adventurer. To this battery a test of ethical values should be added.

Law enforcement agencies in a few communities have provided something of a model in an area almost as contentious. A handful of larger police departments have been including in their selection procedures a "violence test" for rookie candidates.[8] The tests are basically psychological, designed to determine which applicants, in the normal course of their duties, would resort too readily to heavy-handed or bullying tactics. The results are not yet wholly clear—in part, one suspects, because there is little or no reinforcement of the desired value level as the new patrolmen become acculturated by their older colleagues, who possessed badges years before consideration of behavior patterns became a professional concern.

An ethics test could be constructed from an array of situational choice problems inserted into the Agency's selection instruments. Such problems would present difficult ethical decision choices for the test taker in a variety of interpersonal and organizational settings. To prevent the job applicant from tilting his answers toward problem solutions he presumes the testers are seeking, the questions would have to be scattered throughout the various portions of the questionnaires used—psychological, intelligence, etc. All ethics questions could then be selected out of the various test parts and reviewed separately. One hopes that a rough profile of the applicant's personal ethical standards could be obtained by this device, but at best it would probably do no more than single out applicants with unacceptably low or hopelessly confused ethical standards. Follow-up tests for those who enter the Agency and have served for several years would be considerably more difficult to design, but they are not beyond the skills of Agency psychologists.

Surely this is slippery ground. One man's ethical floor may be another's ethical ceiling. Who is to define what the acceptable level of ethical beliefs should be? How would Agency management keep its ethical sights straight in a period of rapidly changing moral values? The issues raised are immensely difficult, but dismissing the concept will not solve the problem of the current low estate of the Agency in the public mind. Tackling the problem head on would, if nothing else, constitute a clear signal of top Agency management's concern to current employees, prospective recruits, and the general public.

*   *   *

Finally, the real purpose of intelligence—truth telling—must be placed at the center of Agency concerns. This is a harsh prescription; it is certainly the most difficult objective of the lot. But it must be the principal purpose of

Agency leadership to establish beyond question the capacity of its experts and its facilities to seek out and find the truth, or the nearest approximation of the truth possible. Public cynicism will have to be dispelled before this is possible; it will take time. There are no easy paths to this objective. Indeed, the present mood of the public toward the Agency militates against its succeeding. The best graduate students do not gravitate to the Agency; its name is suspect in much of academia; business and professional groups are fearful of association.

Where such circumstances exist they must be met with new and probably at first none too credible approaches. Insistence on being primarily in the business of truth telling will not automatically convince the skeptic that it is so. But CIA leadership that condones no other competing role and that demands that ethical questions be asked before internal Agency policies are decided upon will have made a beginning in the long journey back to public accountability. None of these steps, of course, would avert the damage that an unscrupulous President, intent on misusing intelligence talents, could produce. Only loud, angry public resignations by intelligence leaders could in such a case underscore a professional's ethical commitment to truth.

NOTES

1. Chester L. Cooper, "The CIA and Decision-Making," *Foreign Affairs*, January 1972, p. 223.

2. *Final Report of the Select Committee to Study Governmental Operations with respect to Intelligence Activities*, U.S. Senate, 94th Congress, 2nd session, April 14, 1976, seven volumes.

3. Testimony of William Sullivan, *Final Report, op. cit.*, Book II, p. 141.

4. *Final Report, op. cit.*, Book I, p. 282.

5. *Ibid.*, p 286.

6. Harry Rositzke in "America's Secret Operations: A Perspective," *Foreign Affairs*, January 1975, pp. 334–51, has presented a sophisticated view of the remaining need for clandestine human intelligence and counterintelligence collection. And Herbert Scoville, Jr., writing from a consumer's viewpoint (as I do) has laid, I think, the right stress on the predominant need for technological methods today. "Is Espionage Necessary for our Security?" *Foreign Affairs*, April 1976, pp. 482–95.

7. See Harry Rositzke, *CIA's Secret Operations*, New York: Reader's Digest Press, 1977, Chapter 13.

8. The "Machover DAP" test is one frequently used to detect overly aggressive personalities. Sophisticated screening instruments are described in the publication *Police Selection and Career Assessment*, issued by the Law Enforcement Assistance Administration, National Institute of Law Enforcement and Criminal Justice, U.S. Department of Justice, 1976.

2

Intelligence Ethics

R. V. Jones

When resources on a national scale can be applied in secrecy, as they have to be in intelligence, the power of public scrutiny cannot always be brought to bear against their prospective misuse. In the absence of such scrutiny, and particularly because of the opportunities for malpractice that intelligence offers, the only safeguard is a firm sense of ethics among its operators. This chapter therefore discusses some of the ethical problems that are involved.

RESPECT FOR ALLIES

Since intelligence often involves prying into another country's secrets, the question arises of the extent to which this can be justified. In my days in intelligence we observed a rule handed down to us that we should not spy on allies. The tradition was so strong that Churchill himself ordered that there should be no espionage against Russia once the German attack in 1941 had brought the Russians into alliance with us. And even after the alliance had dissolved in the Cold War, we have seen how Lord De L'Isle ruled that we should refrain from any reconnaissance against the *Sverdlovsk* at the Coronation Review of 1953.

Such a ruling, however, evidently had little effect at the later visit of the warship *Ordzhinikidze* which brought Khrushchev and Bulganin to Portsmouth in 1956, for it resulted in the affair in which Commander Crabb lost his life while attempting an underwater reconnaissance; and on the same visit the rooms to be occupied by Khrushchev and Bulganin were "bugged," according to Peter Wright's account in *Spycatcher*.[1] It could, of course, be pleaded that this discourtesy was merely a reciprocation for the similar measures the Russians had long taken against us. But Peter Wright also relates how he and his colleagues "bugged" the French Embassy between 1960 and 1963. It was clever work which resulted in our reading the French high-grade cipher coming in and out of the French Embassy in London. "Every move made by the French during our abortive attempt to enter the Common Market was monitored."[2] It is true that, as far as the Common Market was concerned, the French could no longer be regarded as our allies, and yet for me the episode jars.

The reason is that it brings back a memory of a very different episode in which we and the French were involved with ciphers. This was in 1945 when the British cryptographers at Bletchley were anxious to interrogate their German counterparts after the German surrender. We traced their flight from the wartime headquarters at Treuenbritzen and found that they were now in the relatively small zone of Germany that had been allocated for French control. After their wartime history the French were tending to reestablish their dignity whenever occasion arose, and this was one: they would not allow a mission of British and American cryptographers to enter their zone, and all representations, both military and diplomatic, had failed. I heard about the problem at Bletchley, and put it to my French colleague, Professor Yves Rocard, the Director of Research of the Free French Navy, whose contributions I described in *Most Secret War*.[3]

He said that he would see what could be done, and within a day he returned to my office to tell me that our cryptographers would now be welcome to go in, and to talk to the Germans. The French would not even ask to be present at the interrogations, and their only request was that if we discovered anything that affected the security of France, they would be grateful to know. Such a change had been brought about simply by the complete trust that the events of war had forged between Rocard and myself, and it shows how such a trust may prove much stronger than the wary relationships of diplomacy. With that memory, I for one could not have bugged the French Embassy.

DIPLOMATIC BAGS

A classic way of spying on embassies is, of course, the interception of diplomatic bags and the clandestine opening of the mail they contain. Much skill can be exerted in this process, as Peter Wright describes in *Spycatcher*, to avoid any sign that the contents have been read.[4] He also says that the simple application of Sellotape to the original sealing of the envelope makes it very difficult to open without giving the ultimate recipient any sign of tampering. During the war a colleague officer came to me with another simple suggestion for detecting whether our own confidential letters had been subject to unauthorized opening. This was simply to seal a letter in the ordinary way, and then to run it several times through a sewing machine. For if the letter were subsequently opened by cutting the thread it would be almost impossible to replace the enclosed sheets in such a way that all the holes would line up with those in the envelope so accurately that the ensemble could be restitched exactly as the original. He asked me whether I thought that it would work, and on receiving my encouragement he said he would send a stitched letter over to some of our security experts to see if they would agree. "Just one more thing," I suggested. "Mark the cotton thread at intervals with a fluorescent dye, so that if they manage to replace the cotton we can identify that it is not what we used." Here I banked on a human weakness that I had seen several times before (and many since) which beguiles clever minds to concentrate on the difficult parts of a challenge to such an extent that they overlook the simpler ones. After three days the envelope came back to us immaculately restitched with no visible sign of tampering, but including a complimentary card from our friends to show that they had opened it. They were furious when we told them that we were certain it had been opened, and that they had failed to spot the simple trick of fluorescent marking in concentrating, otherwise so successfully, on the very difficult task of restitching.

In such an instance the contest between the men trying to protect their country's secrets and the men who are trying to pry them open can be a battle of wits in which each side is aiming to be cleverer than the other, with all the thrust and parry of a medieval joust. And while such chivalry as Lord De L'Isle showed in the *Sverdlovsk* visit is rare, the contest tends to develop its own rules. (Shortly before the Coronation in 1953, it was known that the Russians would be sending the new cruiser, *Sverdlovsk*, to the Coronation Review. We were of course by this time much aware of the electronic espionage by Russian "trawlers" around our coasts; and so when at a lunch they were giving me in Washington, the American Directors of Intelligence told me that they hoped we would have the *Sverdlovsk* "covered" electronically and photographically, I told them they could be sure that our Director of Naval Intelligence would have made all suitable arrangements. I was amazed on my return to find that no intelligence had been gathered. The DNI's arrangements had been canceled because permission for an aerial reconnaissance had been sought from the Secretary of State for Air, the Lord De L'Isle and Dudley, a descendant of Sir Philip Sidney and holder of the Victoria Cross. He ruled that since the Russian cruiser was on a courtesy mission to honor our Queen, it would be a discourteous act to conduct any intelligence operations against her. And so we did nothing. What the Americans may have done is a matter of speculation.)

Almost every power accepts that it is fair game to try and decrypt the signals of its potential opponents, even though there was the classic instance of the U.S. Secretary of State, Henry Stimson, who in 1929 closed down the famous Black Chamber, the American cryptographic center of World War I and afterward, because, as he said, "Gentlemen do not read each other's mail." But while there may be something sneaky and furtive in reading a private letter, cryptography need have neither of these aspects and can be a highly intellectual exercise even though we may regret the diversion of so much intellect to such an uncreative end.

OPEN SKIES

Much the same is true of both photographic and electronic reconnaissance. In pre-Sputnik days it could be argued that to fly a photographic aircraft over another country without its permission was an infringement of national sovereignty, and the Russians were prepared to shoot such aircraft down, as they showed in the U2 incident of 1960. This was after they had rejected President Eisenhower's offer of an "open skies" policy in which the Americans and the Russians would have been free to fly photographic aircraft over one another's territory. In retrospect the Russian rejection looks all the more unreasonable because within a few years both sides were able to orbit reconnaissance satellites over each other's territory with impunity. What the Russian attitude would be if it should become readily possible to destroy or blind reconnaissance satellites is a matter for conjecture, especially in the face of the Strategic Defense Initiative. There was much to be said for Eisenhower's offer, if only because good intelligence can be a stabilizing influence in international affairs: it can contribute to both mutual deterrence and mutual reassurance.

THE ESPIONAGE CONVENTION

There was another noteworthy aspect of the U2 incident, for Eisenhower himself confirmed that he had authorized the U2 flights. He was criticized for making such an official acknowledgment, which was almost unprecedented in intelligence affairs, where the convention was that a government did not acknowledge its intelligence activities, and, for example, gave no support to any of its agents who had been caught in espionage. Notably, as William Colby records in *Honorable Men*,[5] it was Khrushchev's annoyance with Eisenhower's acceptance of responsibility for the U2 flight that led him to cancel the Paris Summit. But it was time that such a bogus convention was abandoned.

Curiously, although the pre-1914 era was the heyday of the convention, the European powers were surprisingly ready to make statements of their expenditure on their secret services. In 1912 the British Foreign Secretary, Edward Grey, easily obtained from his ambassadors the published expenditures in the countries to which they were respectively credited. The figures were published as a parliamentary paper[6] and they still make interesting reading:

Austria-Hungary: £62,500
France: £40,000
Germany: £80,387
Great Britain: £50,000
Italy £120,800
Russia £380,000 (+ £335,000 for secret police)

The preoccupation with secret service, both external and internal, is a Russian characteristic older than the 1917 Revolution. In fact in *The Craft of Intelligence,* Allen Dulles, who was Director of the Central Intelligence Agency from 1953 to 1961, traces the "congenital suspicion" of the Russians at least as far back as the sixteenth century when, to resist the ravages of the Tartars and others, the inhabitants had to depend on the garrisons of walled stockades (kremlins) and cities in country that could easily be overrun. And since the Tartars sought to ascertain the strength of the defenses in advance by sending agents in (as did Joshua at Jericho), the inhabitants developed a suspicion of strangers.

SECRET SERVICES

While there are relatively few problems of ethics in the operation of photographic, communications, or electronic reconnaissance, it is otherwise with secret service. "Oh, where hath our Intelligence been drunk, where hath it slept?" demanded King John, and knowing two of the traditional temptations—alcohol and sex—he might well ask. To these must be added money and disaffection with a native land, or greater affection for a foreign one. The problem for a secret service, or at least for one in a democracy which values decency, is how far the ends of national security can justify these means, nearly all of them disreputable, by which valuable information can sometimes be obtained.

The Russians, for example, have been ruthlessly unscrupulous in exploiting sexual weaknesses of both the hetero- and homo- varieties, not only by tempting employees of foreign powers to provide information in return for gratification, but also by subsequent blackmail in threatening to bring such sexual indiscretions and treachery to the notice of an employee's superiors unless he (or she) continues to supply information. To any decent man such methods are thoroughly distasteful, even more so than the induction of an employee's treachery in return for money and material comforts; but the possibility that valuable information may thereby be obtained cannot be overlooked, although I for one would try to draw a borderline. This limit might be set at "No sex please, we're British!" or, rather shorter, at attempting to suborn an employee with money. I cannot conceive that a relationship based upon mutual respect could be built up between the suborner and the suborned in such instances, and all my own experience of successes in intelligence has suggested that these have been based on some degree of mutual respect between the various elements in an intelligence chain.

But while I would have little respect for a man who attempted to sell his country's secrets for money, I would have to admit that information of value may be obtained in this way. For an example, the German cryptographic employee in 1932 to whom the French military intelligence gave the code-name "Asche" (and whose real name may have been Hans-Thilo Schmidt) offered to sell them information connected with his employment in return for financial reward. When his offer was accepted, he provided among other items some operating instructions for the model of the "Enigma" machine then in use and tables of some current keys. These by themselves might not have been very helpful, but when the French gave them to the Polish cryptographers they greatly aided the latter's progress in solving the workings of Enigma. And, more recently, we saw the devastating Walker case in America. Not all such cases, though, end so brilliantly for either the accepter of the offer of treachery or its provider. Sometimes the offer is bogus, and ends in the accepter being duped; and sometimes the fear of being duped may lead the intended accepter to be suspicious and therefore to reject the offer, as appeared to be the case with Michael Bettany in 1983, whose treacherous overtures were treated so warily by the KGB that he was caught by his MI5 employers before his treachery could become effective.

The approach of Bettany to the KGB had some similarity to that of Oleg Penkovsky to the Americans in Moscow in 1960: to them his offer looked "too good to be true," although it turned out to be for no personal reward but arose instead from a genuine disillusion with the Soviet system. Fortunately, although rejected by the Americans he established six months later a contact with the British, and a most valuable flow of information passed between him and his contact, Greville Wynn. Here mutual respect and friendship easily grew up between the two men.

That kind of respect was at its height of sublimity in World War II among those of us in London who were working with agents in the many resistance networks in German-occupied territory. These agents were men and women who were risking themselves to help us and seeking no other reward than the liberation of their countries. On our side we were mainly amateurs who had been brought in to strengthen the previously slender organization, and one such was Jimmy Langley who so successfully headed the MI6 section responsible for helping our shot-down airmen and other service personnel to escape from the Continent. This effort was, of course, crucially dependent on specialized resistance chains whose sacrifices were such that Langley estimated that for each of the three thousand-odd men who were brought back, one resistance worker had lost his or her life. No wonder, therefore, that some of us, including Langley, became completely committed to their support. In his book, *Fight Another Day,* he records the reaction of a "professional" officer, Claude Dansey, the Vice-Chief of MI6, upon Langley's outburst at the directive that nothing could be done to help some workers in the famous Comet line who had been caught and condemned to death. "Your trouble is, Jimmy," said Dansey, "that you love your agents."[7] That cynical verdict would have applied to most of us.

CAN AGENTS (AND OTHERS)
BE EXPENDABLE?

Certainly we would not have countenanced any suggestion that one or more of our agents should be intentionally betrayed by another agent whom we aimed to ingratiate with the Germans as a double agent whose sympathies lay with them, and through whom we would subsequently feed false information about, for example, the coming landings in France. We were therefore concerned when the publication of Anthony Cave Brown's *Bodyguard of Lies* gave the impression in France that we had been prepared to do just that. One of the most gallant of French Resistance workers, the Vicomtesse de Clarens, wrote to me in 1981: "*Bodyguard of Lies* has stirred reactions and emotions, as you can well imagine, among those who have been led to think by Cave Brown that their lives and fates were considered of little value indeed when balanced with the dire necessity of avoiding the Germans finding out their Enigma was no longer secure." Appealing to me to write to one of the Resistance journals, she continued: "You will no doubt put things in their proper perspective, and publication in *Voix et Visages* could help to soothe some rather peeved feelings." Faced with so much trust I took every possible step with old colleagues throughout the wartime intelligence organizations to check whether anyone could recall an instance where an agent had been intentionally betrayed, or which might be so interpreted. In reporting to *Voix et Visages* the firmly negative result, I could only console the French Resistance with the fact that the same author had said that Churchill himself had sacrificed both Coventry in 1940, to preserve the Ultra secret of our breaking Enigma, and Bomber Command on the Nuremberg raid in 1944. He argued that the bogus agent who delivered such accurate information would be so entirely convincing that the Germans would believe the false information that he would subsequently provide about the coming D-Day landings. Neither the Coventry nor the Nuremberg claim has, to my knowledge, the slightest element of substance.

The Coventry story, though, for all its falsity has a widespread appeal because of the ethical problems that it illustrates for an operational commander and his intelligence officer. Let us suppose that the intelligence organization has established a source that can reveal the enemy's intentions, and so give notice of an impending attack in such detail that it can be parried by suitable preparation. The danger that then has to be faced is that this preparation may be so specific as to indicate to the enemy, either before or after his attack has been defeated, that information has been leaked, and that it has probably been leaked by a particular channel, for example, an insecure cipher or an agent in a key position. The enemy can then block the leak, and so valuable information on some future operation, or operations, will have been lost. Not only this, but the agent—if a human one—may have been caught and executed: an ungrateful reward for his work. Apart from this problem in ethics there are also the relative values to be assessed in the short-term advantage of acting on the information about an imminent threat and the long-term loss of information about later and possibly greater threats should the secret source be sacrificed.

Had Churchill in fact been faced with the Coventry dilemma, for example, a successful defense might have saved five hundred deaths in Coventry. But as the argument goes, if the necessary preparations could have led the Germans to realize that *we* were reading Enigma, and had they then changed the machine, some tens, or even hundreds, of thousands more lives might have been lost in the subsequent battles (the Atlantic, the Desert, and France) in which Enigma played a part. So Churchill must inevitably have had to decide on the sacrifice of Coventry. Actually, though, such decisions are rarely so clearcut: even in the hypothetical case of Coventry, for example, the Germans might have preferred to suspect that we had divined their intentions by some method other than breaking Enigma, such as observing the settings of their radio beams as they were lined up in the afternoon prior to the bombing. Indeed, this is what they actually did when, later in the Blitz, they realized that we were somehow anticipating their nightly targets. Similarly, in the Battle of the Atlantic, where the Enigma information was invaluable, we were able to lead the Germans to think (as we had also done in 1914–18) that the information about V-boat positions came not from cryptography but from accurate direction-finding on the signals transmitted by the U-boats. The possibility of creating such an alibi may therefore ease the discomfort of making a painful decision; but it will always be a matter of judgment, and sometimes this judgment will have to be stern.

"BLOCK 26"

As for whether it is ethical to risk sacrificing an agent as a result of using information he or she has provided, I am grateful never to have been confronted with the problem. But an instance has come to my notice where the agent himself took the decision for us, and it deserves to be placed on record. Pierre Julitte was an officer on the staff of General de Gaulle in London who volunteered to be parachuted back into France on intelligence missions. Captured by the Gestapo on his third mission in March 1943, he spent the next twenty-five months in prisons and concentration camps, including Buchenwald and Nordhausen (Dora). At the former, in early 1944 he and his fellow inmates of Block 26 were living in terrible conditions when they were set to work in a nearby factory making and assembling electronic components, gyroscopes, and control equipment. With their knowledge of engineering they considered ways in which they might subtly sabotage the components so that whatever these were to be used for would fail in operation. Gradually they realized that the "whatever" must be something new and important, and Julitte deduced that this could be "a self-propelled projectile, navigating in space, subject to vibration and remote-controlled by radio." A colleague returning from a stint in the works where the V2 (A4) rockets were being assembled confirmed Julitte's guess. And when they learned from the German radio that the VI campaign had opened on 13 June 1944, they decided to try to warn the British and American Air Forces about the production of the V2.

One of Julitte's colleagues was to attempt to escape with a message to Julitte's sister in Paris and his cousin in Neuilly. The message gave instructions that the information be forwarded to London with the advice that their factory should be bombed—even though Julitte and his colleagues might be killed if this advice were acted upon. When I wrote *Most Secret War* I was quite ignorant of this heroic episode; but Julitte himself then sent me a copy of his own book *Block 26* in which he had recounted his story, though with all the personal names changed. This gave the book the atmosphere of a novel, but so many of the details rang true that I was convinced. Later I was able to meet M. Julitte and ask him why he had falsified the names. His characteristic reply was that some of his colleagues had not shown up so well, and that if he had changed only their names and given credit to those to whom it was truly due, a reader might deduce those who had behaved badly, and so he decided to falsify all names.

The one remaining item in his story that puzzled me was his precise statement that the factory had been heavily bombed in daylight on 24 August 1944. The factory had been destroyed and five hundred of his coworkers had been killed, as he himself might have been. I could, though, find no mention of such a raid in the Official Histories of either Bomber Command or the Air Defense of Great Britain, although other raids to inhibit the development of the V-weapons had been faithfully listed. Ultimately the Air Historical Section found the answer for me: the factory had indeed been attacked by 128 Flying Fortresses on 24 August 1944, but the target had merely been described in the records as "an armaments factory at Weimar (Buchenwald)" and so the historians had failed to connect the factory with V2 production.[8] The air intelligence summary described the results of the subsequent photographic reconnaissance: "Smoke from extensive fires obscures the greater part of the armaments factory but in the southern and eastern parts which are visible it can be seen that the USAAF attack on 24 August has caused severe damage to almost every building. The radio factory to the north has been completely gutted and some barrack huts in the concentration camp have been severely damaged."[9] Through the lost production of V2s the lives of many must thereby have been saved in London and Antwerp who never knew what they owed to Julitte and his colleagues. Can anyone wonder that Langley and I "loved our agents"? Their sacrifice stands in sublime contrast to the hideous conditions under which they made it.

TORTURE (AND REPRISALS)

The German treatment of captured agents raises the question of how far a captor is entitled to go in forcing a prisoner to disclose information, and in discouraging intelligence activities in occupied territory by reprisals on the civilian population. The German treatment of prisoners of war was, with some exceptions, correct, but their attitude towards civilians was harsh and, often, brutal. They followed the doctrine of Clausewitz, that terror was justified as a way to shorten the war. They had employed it after Sedan in 1870, and again in 1914 in Belgium. Barbara Tuchman in *August 1914* gives the examples of 211 civilians shot at Andenne, 50 at Seilles, 400 at Tamines, 612 at Dinant, and uncounted numbers at Louvain.[10] In World War II they again used terrorism as a policy; the massacres at Oradour and Lidice were among the appalling results. While it may not be entirely fair to cite these examples as inhumanity specifically to intelligence agents, they do indicate the utter harshness of the German viewpoint during both wars. And the harshness undoubtedly had its effect on intelligence agents, of which there are two examples in two examples in *Most Secret War*. One was of the outstanding agent, Georges Lamarque, who gave himself up to the Germans when they surrounded the village from which they had detected his radio transmissions, sacrificing himself to protect the villagers who might otherwise have suffered the fate of those at Oradour. The other was of the agent Yves le Bitoux, who surrendered to the Gestapo at Treguier in 1944 because he feared that the Germans would savage the town if he succeeded in escaping. He later died in a concentration camp.[11]

Apart from the questions of the morality of reprisals and also of the extent to which they may be counterproductive by stimulating resistance rather than cowing it, we need to consider the morality of torture as a means of forcing a captive to reveal information. We in Britain eschewed it. From the interrogators whom I knew personally, I am sure that this was on the grounds of humanity, although it was also true with them that torture could produce misleading results because a person under torture is likely to tell his torturers what he thinks they would like to hear rather than what he truly knows. But we would have to admit that the Germans did achieve some successes by torturing captives, and we would also have to admit that the sadism from which we so firmly refrained has sometimes been exhibited in Britain.

I am personally grateful never to have been confronted with a problem of this type: Suppose you have captured a terrorist who has planted a bomb which has not yet exploded but which you have reason to think he has left in some place where its explosion will cause casualties and damage. In an extreme case it might be an atomic bomb. He refuses to tell you its location. To what limits are you justified in going to make him talk?

I would hate to resort to torture, all the more so if he has shown himself to be a brave man, but the same fundamental respect for human life and dignity that makes torture so repulsive would also justify driving him to the point of death if you could thereby save the many more lives that would perish if the bomb exploded. And then, if you admit the argument for torture in such an instance, where do you draw the line? A rationalist answer might be: at the point where you are reasonably certain that the total of human suffering will be less if the torture succeeds in extracting the information required. But while this argument may have been valid for the overall saving of human lives by the atomic bomb on Hiroshima, it also underlies Clausewitz's justification of terror tactics, and we have seen the depths into which we can so easily slide.

If we admit that torture might in some circumstances be justified, we have to return to the responsibility of an intelligence service toward its agents in the field who risk capture and torture by the opposing security service. They may also risk death. My own experience was almost entirely in the circumstances of war, where such considerations were much simpler. In peace, there are not only agents at risk but also foreign relations if an operation goes wrong. Such problems have been described by Admiral Stansfield Turner, who was Director of the CIA from 1977 to 1980, in *Secrecy and Democracy*.[12] Coming into intelligence after a distinguished career in the U.S. Navy the Admiral looked afresh at all such problems, and his conclusions have much in common with those that I myself formed in wartime. This might be partly due to the fact that even in peacetime an intelligence service is in effect engaged in a war with its opposing security service. One difference, though, that makes peacetime working more difficult is that intelligence operations are then regarded far less sympathetically by the public, and there is much more time for postmortems and recrimination if mistakes have been made.

COVERT ACTION

This last factor has dogged the CIA over the last thirty years, all the more so because the agency has been involved not only with intelligence but with the more aggressive forms of covert action. In Britain in World War II there was originally a section in MI6 concerned with sabotage, but in 1940 this was hived off into a completely new organization, the Special Operations Executive. On the whole this was beneficial to both activities, since the intelligence organization—if it had an agent placed in a good position to gather information—aimed to keep him there, even sometimes to the extent of not using his information if this might lead to his being discovered, and therefore to his inability to provide more valuable information in the future, whereas SOE tended to regard its sabotage agents more as elements in an active army where casualties were to be expected, and where the results of their work would be much more immediately obvious to the enemy.

Again, sabotage usually required greater numbers of personnel, and the organization had therefore to be larger; and so, although the same conflict between short- and long-term operations could arise in sabotage as well as in intelligence, there was much merit in separating the two activities as far as possible. They also attracted rather different types of officer—some who would be repelled by actions of the "dirty tricks" variety would have less hesitation in working for intelligence.

Admiral Turner, though, takes a differing view. While accepting that separating covert action from intelligence might solve some problems, he argues that it would create others: "The CIA's intelligence agents overseas are often the same people needed for covert action. It would be confusing, and at times dangerous, to have two agencies giving them orders and managing their activities. And if one agency did only covert action, what would it do during periods of slack demand?" This last consideration did not apply to us in war because there were continuous demands for both activities; but we certainly encountered problems in rivalries between the two types of organization operating in the same territory.

A further complication arises from the fact that an intelligence organization—if it is doing its job—will often be the first to realize, from its unique viewpoint, the vulnerability of an opponent, actual or potential. Therefore intelligence will know where and how the enemy can best be hindered by deception, sabotage, or—in war—overt military action. For example, I myself was sometimes in this position in World War II, as in the cases of "Window" (or "Chaff") and countermeasures to German radio bombing techniques: but it was clear that once I had made a technical or tactical suggestion for action, the responsibility for its implementation belonged to the operational staff.

Obviously action is facilitated if both intelligence and operations can be controlled under one organization, but an offsetting merit of separation is that an intelligence unit is more likely to be impartial in its assessment of the success of operations if it is independent of any attempt by the operational side to interpret the evidence regarding success or failure too favorably. For all these reasons I continue to stand for the independence of intelligence from operations, both covert and overt, to the highest possible level in government organization although of course recognizing the need for the greatest possible understanding between intelligence and operational staffs.

Returning then to America, it can be seen how the responsibility of the CIA for both intelligence and covert operations has created many problems for the Agency. Its involvement in, and part responsibility for, the Bay of Pigs disaster in 1961, which attempted to overthrow Castro, led to the resignation of the Director, Allen Dulles. Richard Helms, who had been Director from 1966, was fired by President Nixon in 1973 because, according to his biographer Thomas Powers, he refused to provide a CIA cover-up for Nixon in the Watergate affair.[13] These grounds would have been quite implausible if the CIA had always kept itself apart from covert operations concerned with internal security. William Colby, who became Director in 1973, was in his turn dismissed in 1975 by President Ford largely because of public outcry at the CIA's involvement in assassinations, over which Colby himself had been scrupulously honest—too honest, many of his staff thought—in exposing the Agency's past mistakes. His departure was finally precipitated by press and public indignation over his revelation to a Senate Committee of the existence of a dart gun and small quantities of virulent poisons that had come to light in an obscure storeroom which had been overlooked in his previous survey, conscientious though this had been. Colby welcomed me in his office shortly after his dismissal. When I expressed my regret he nobly told me that he did not mind how much he himself suffered from the episode if by "taking the rap" he could leave the Agency in a healthy condition. Finally, this story of the fates of CIA Directors might have had a further melancholy chapter over the arms for Iran affair, had not the death of William Casey early in 1987 intervened before the official inquiries into the affair could be completed—although Casey himself was convinced that he and the Agency would be vindicated.

ASSASSINATION

Helms himself observed that "war corrupts and secret war corrupts secretly"[14] So it is easy to slip toward the acceptance of assassination as one of its techniques. In 1940 there was a suggestion that there would be a special British clandestine operation to attack the aircrews of the German pathfinders who were causing us so much trouble in the Blitz. They were to be ambushed while being ferried by bus between their billets and the airfield at Vannes before taking off for an attack. This was vetoed by Sir Charles Portal, the Chief of Air Staff; but as the war progressed, feelings became less delicate. Later, at the time of the Suez crisis in 1956, there was even talk—it appears—of attempting to assassinate President Nasser.[15] In America, Allen Dulles, aware of the danger of the CIA slipping toward an acceptance of assassination, specifically forbade it when he was Director, and an embargo was included in presidential directives on three occasions. Nevertheless it was sometimes attempted, with disastrous results for the CIA when it came to light.

TORTURE AND DURESS

Torture, too, was officially barred—at least to the extent of a rule being formulated by Helms in 1955 under Dulles's directorship: "You may not use electrical, chemical, or physical duress," it read, although, as Powers then went on to point out, "psychological duress was okay."[16] We, in World War II, certainly tried to bluff prisoners of war into thinking we knew much more than we did in the hope that this would mislead them into giving away things about which we knew little or nothing. And it seemed not too unfair to "fence" psychologically with a prisoner and thus to trap him into saying more than he had originally intended. But there had to be a limit such as, for example, not playing on a man's emotions by encouraging him to worry about the safety of his family. I take it that no such restraint is likely to be widely observed today.

"CHARACTER ASSASSINATION"

Short of killing a key individual on the opposing side, his value to them may be destroyed if his colleagues or countrymen can be misled into suspecting that he is a secret agent for your own side, or has some other motive for working against his side's interests. This mischievous technique is only likely to succeed when the individual in question is working in an organization prone to mutual suspicion; but in so far as it exploits a moral weakness in that organization, so "hoisting the engineer with his own petard," it may be less repugnant than other measures.

INTERVENTION

In parallel with the ethical problem of the humane limits of conduct toward individuals, there is the problem of the extent to which any one state can be justified in attempting to interfere in the internal affairs of another. The "Irangate" affair and the clandestine mining of Nicaraguan harbors under CIA auspices are cases in point. In discussing such questions Stansfield Turner in *Secrecy and Democracy*[17] quotes John Stuart Mill's *A few words on non-intervention* (1859):

> The doctrine of non-intervention, to be a legitimate principle of morality, must be accepted by all governments. The despot must consent to be bound by it as well as the free state. Unless they do, the profession comes to this miserable issue—that the wrong side may help the wrong, but the right must not help the right.

Thus a Gresham's Law will tend to operate in international affairs, especially in any field of covert action where the operators think that their actions will be free from public scrutiny. All the more reason, therefore, to endorse Turner's specification for CIA personnel selection: "The CIA needs people not only with skills, but with high moral standards, with the confidence to be independent, and with the desire to be innovative."[18] He also stated that "there is one overall test of the ethics of human intelligence activities. That is whether those approving them feel they could defend their decisions before the public if the actions became public. This guideline does not say that the overseen should approve actions only if the public would approve them if they knew of them. Rather it says that the overseers should be so convinced of the importance of the actions that they would accept any criticism that might develop if the covert actions did become public, and could construct a convincing defense of their decisions."[19]

INTERNAL INTELLIGENCE

Besides the ethical questions concerning how a nation and its officials and agents should restrain their activities in gaining information about another nation's secrets, or in attempting to interfere in its internal affairs, there are other questions that will arise when a nation's officials have to seek out activities within its own borders that could jeopardize its security. In Britain these are the province of MI5, while MI6 covers intelligence about other nations. Although this is a neat division of functions, MI5 and MI6 at times have joint interests. For example, when foreign agents operating outside Britain attempt to organize sub-agents for espionage, sabotage, terrorism, or whatever inside it, the agents abroad are, strictly, targets for MI6 and the sub-agents in Britain for MIS. For such problems, liaison between MI5 and MI6 has to be very close: in 1939–45 this was largely effected by having a special section inside MI6—ironically, its head was Kim Philby.

In America a rather similar separation of functions is made between the Central Intelligence Agency and the Federal Bureau of Investigation, although the separation there is now more on a territorial basis; the CIA being responsible for all intelligence and counterintelligence activities abroad, and the FBI for all inside the United States. Much the same problems arise in America as in Britain respecting individual privacy, for example, in opening private correspondence, tapping telephone conversations, or breaking into private premises. According to Colby in *Honorable Men*,[20] the CIA in 1952 started a program of opening selected letters in the mail between the United States and Russia in the hope of detecting undesirable activity. This was "a direct violation of a criminal statute," and the practice was shelved in 1973. Admiral Turner records that the tapping of telephones and other forms of electronic communication in the United States have since 1978 been governed by the Foreign Intelligence Surveillance Act, which stipulates that if it has to be done it should be carried out using the least obtrusive technique that will do the job; every such operation should be certified as necessary before the Attorney General and reviewed by a special court of senior judges. Breaks into private premises presumably now require similar authorization, since the Watergate and Ellsberg (1971) cases brought such break-ins so embarrassingly to public notice.

Following disclosures by former MIS officers about break-ins by MI5 in Britain, the Government has introduced a Bill to put such operations—hitherto illegal—on a legitimate basis and subject to the safeguard that each operation must be authorized by the Home Secretary and "only when he was satisfied that the information was likely to be of substantial value and assistance to [the Security Service] . . . and . . . could not reasonably be obtained by other means."[21] An independent commissioner would be appointed to review the issuing of warrants and to make an annual report to the Prime Minister. There appear to be few reasonable alternatives to these proposals in a democratic society.

PRIVACY

While any decent individual instinctively reacts against break-ins and less violent infringements of privacy, a state legitimately requests some details about each of its individual citizens for a wide range of social purposes such as taxation, educational planning, transport facilities, and potential for military and other forms of public service. It might therefore be asked why we set so much store by a right to privacy. Apart from the nightmare of a "Big Brother" state, there is an instinctive dislike of surveillance, even parental surveillance; and there may well be an apprehension based deeply back in the evolutionary process arising from a feeling of vulnerability while executing bodily functions or in sickness, and of latent trouble from a stalking predator whose staring eyes betray his intentions. More rationally, I for one would have little objection to any authority having any information it wished about my actions—or even my thoughts—provided that I could be sure that it would not misinterpret the information to come to false conclusions about me.

Just as technology is tending to modify concepts of sovereignty (from a three-mile limit for territorial waters based on the range of a gun to a limit of 200 miles today, and the free movement of satellites over the territories of other nations, for example), so also it is tending to change the balance between the rights of individuals and the states of which they are members. The complex organization of a modem state needs to know more about its individuals for optimum functioning, and this is all the easier to achieve because of the technical advances in handling and storing information; and, unfortunately, it will be only too easy for zeal to replace judgment in the process.

OVERSIGHT

Some of the problems of internal intelligence, both in the United States and in Britain, have arisen from excessive zeal. Thirty years ago Percy Sillitoe's determination as head of MI5 to stop Britain from becoming a police state was all the safeguard that was needed; but today with the various exposures regarding both MI5 and the greater surveillance needed to protect against penetration, it is difficult to be so sure. The attempted remedy in America is "oversight," where the activities of the intelligence and security services are overseen by committees, one from the Senate and the other from the House of Representatives. Much obviously depends on the selection of members for these committees, but on balance Admiral Turner, in whose time as director of the CIA they first became effective, records a favorable impression. On the negative side, he found them restrictive: "We tend apply our new enthusiasm for oversight of the ethics of intelligence micro management by the Congress of the development of new intelligence technologies. . . . Another false economy that congressional oversight has fostered is the frugality in stockpiling intelligence collection systems. . . . One other dangerous hindrance is that the CIA's search branch is gradually losing out to the large and clever military bureaucracy at the Pentagon. . . . The espionage people also deserve better protection from the Congress and the White House."[22]

But on a positive side, he wrote, "oversight, especially by Congress, can give helpful guidance to the CIA as to what is and what is not acceptable conduct. In the pursuit of secrets . . . the better the oversight process is, the less concern there need be about concentrating too much authority the hands of the DCI. If we want good intelligence in the long run, our only option is to make oversight work."[23] At the same time, Admiral Turner would fuse the Senate and Congressional oversight committees into one with a membership limited to reduce the possibility of leaks.[24]

While, though, Admiral Turner so firmly supports oversight, the record in Washington since it was introduced has not been one of qualified success. It is now generally agreed that the CIA-sponsored mining of Nicaraguan harbors in 1983 was a mistake, and it was owed to go ahead despite nominal oversight by both the Senate Intelligence Committee under Barry Goldwater and the Congressional Intelligence Committee under Edward Boland. The latter had been so disturbed by earlier developments that in August 1982 he had succeeded moving that the CIA and the Defense Department should be prohibited from furnishing military equipment, training, or support to anyone "for the purpose of overthrowing the Government of Nicaragua."[25] Robert Woodward, who with Carl Bernstein exposed the Watergate affair, has described this episode at length in *Veil: The Secret Wars of the CIA, 1981–1987.*[26] Formally, the members of the oversight committee were in a difficult position. The law which established them stipulates that they must be informed of major intelligence activities, but appears not to have given them a right of veto; moreover, the individual members had been sworn to secrecy, and so they could be in trouble if they made a public disclosure.

It is not easy to see a way out of this difficulty. No intelligence organization can surrender its executive responsibility to an oversight committee, no matter how able, experienced, and responsible the individual members of the committee may be. Two reasons preclude any such procedure. The first is that an intelligence organization is constantly waging a war, and any operations in that war need a commander with full responsibility for their planning and execution. At times risks have to be taken, and a committee approach is likely to be inhibiting. Clive of India said that he had held a council of war but once, and had he heeded the advice of the council rather than his own judgment the British would never have been masters of India.

The second reason against the committee approach is allied to the first; it arises from the way in which intelligence appreciations have to be formed from the information that has been gained. Despite Napoleon's worry about the danger of "making a picture of the enemy," this is what an intelligence organization has to do in presenting its conclusions for assimilation by those who have then to undertake executive action. Just as an artist has to present as faithful an impression as possible, according to his lights, with the economy of detail of a painted portrait as contrasted with a photograph, so an intelligence officer has to convey a portrait of the opponent constructed to give the truest possible impression from the limited amount of detailed information that will be available even to a good intelligence service. An intelligence report therefore has much in common with a work of art, and my experiences on the Joint Intelligence Committee suggest that committees are hardly more likely to produce good intelligence reports than they would be to paint good pictures. When information is sparse it permits a multitude of explanations, and committees can lose much time over indecisive argument as to which is the correct one.

This was also the experience of General Eugene Tighe, head of the Defense Intelligence Agency in the Pentagon from 1977 to 1979. In thirty-six years of intelligence work, "he had seen administrations, Secretaries of Defense, and DCIs come and go, and the shape and tone of intelligence work change. But the real squabbles arose when they didn't have enough information. When U.S. intelligence had a lot of good data, there was rarely a fight."[27]

While not wishing to underrate the second of the foregoing reasons, I believe the first is decisive in determining that an intelligence service must have freedom to act as it thinks best, and to that extent oversight must have limits. The example of the mining of Nicaraguan harbors may suggest that these limits were too loosely drawn, or that an enterprising DCI could too easily find a way round them. The same example may also suggest that it is dangerous for an intelligence organization to have such autonomy, even though nominally subject to oversight. But, once again, intelligence is waging a war and risks sometimes have to be run. Churchill's delighted soldiers in the Royal Scots Fusiliers in 1916 told how he, as their commanding officer, was visited in the front line by a general from some rear headquarters. "If you would care, sir," said Churchill, "to step over the parapet, we could go for a walk in no-man's land." "Wouldn't that be dangerous?" asked the general. Churchill replied, "Sir, this is a dangerous war!" And that will always be true of war fought by intelligence agencies too, where the lines may be covertly drawn.

As for whether we in Britain should adopt oversight of the intelligence services on the American pattern, I would have said in the days of men like Percy Sillitoe that there was little need for it—at least as regards the danger of the services overstepping the limits of reasonable conduct. The oversight that was needed then was more in looking for inefficiencies in the system such as were all too evident in 1939 and, more recently, were the subject of the Franks inquiry over the Falklands. But moral standards have fallen from the days when an Englishman's word was his bond, as we have seen in other walks of public life, such as the City. It cannot be guaranteed that this is never likely to affect the conduct of intelligence affairs, with all the temptations that they may afford. Some measure of oversight is therefore desirable, if only to assure Parliament and the public that intelligence is being wisely and scrupulously conducted.

Successive prime ministers have strongly discouraged the discussion of intelligence affairs in Parliament, where obvious dangers could arise from disclosure. But, while it was easy to protect the intelligence services from scrutiny when these were small, it is less easy today when organizations like GCHQ are much larger. Besides the problems that thereby arise from trades unions, increases in numbers give rise to increased chances for treachery and for leaks that will sooner or later come to public notice and so lead to discussion in Parliament. There appears to be a body inside government itself that could provide oversight, the Ministerial Steering Committee on Intelligence. But whether this is the best body for the purpose, or whether a small inter-party body of senior politicians (and perhaps others of experience, discretion, and judgment) might be better, would itself be a fitting matter for Parliamentary discussion.

MINIMUM TRESPASS

Two final points on ethics are worth making. The first is that, despite all the opportunities—and temptations—that it offers for malpractice, intelligence can be an honorable pursuit. Indeed, by improving the assessment by one nation of another it can, on occasion, contribute to international stability. On less happy occasions, of course, the children of light will be at a disadvantage unless they know enough of the ways of the world to forestall or counter any unworthy exploitation of those ways by the children of this world. There need be absolutely no dishonor in trying to ascertain what a potential or actual opponent is likely to attempt, be it by external armed threat or by internal subversion. The risk of disrepute will depend on the extent to which the individual intelligence officer or his organization departs from the norms of morality in uncovering an opponent's activities.

The second point follows from the first. One of the canons governing military or police action is the doctrine of minimum force, and a parallel canon should govern intelligence: it should be conducted with the minimum trespass against national and individual human rights. This canon applies to all forms of intelligence, both external and internal, that a civilized state may find it necessary to undertake.

NOTES

1. Peter Wright and Paul Greengrass, *Spycatcher* (Heinemann Australia, 1987), 72–73.

2. Wright and Greengrass, 110–13.

3. R.V. Jones, *Most Secret War* (Hamish Hamilton Press, 1978; and Coronet Books, 1979), 262–3, 317, 496–7.

4. Wright and Greengrass, 45.

5. William Colby, *Honorable Men* (Simon & Schuster, 1978), 417.

6. Parliament Paper, Cmnd. 6144, 1912.

7. J.M. Langley, *Fight Another Day* (Collins, 1974), 202.

8. An example of the difficulty historians aiming to write a comprehensive account.

9. *Air Ministry Weekly Intelligence Summary*, No. 261, August 1944.

10. Barbara Tuchman, *August 1914* (Papermac, 1980) 173, 248, 307.

11. R.V. Jones, 354.

12. Admiral Stansfield Turner, *Secrecy and Democracy* (Sidgwick & Jackson, 1986), 175.

13. Thomas Powers, *The Man Who Kept the Secrets* (Simon & Schuster, 1979), 312.

14. Powers, 266.

15. Christopher Andrew, *Secret Service* (Heinemann, 1985), 690 in Sceptre edition.

16. Powers, 155.

17. Turner, 86.

18. Turner, 205.

19. Turner, 178.

20. Colby, 334.

21. *The Times,* "Parliamentary Report," November 1988.

22. Turner, 97–98, 219.

23. Turner, 264 and 270.

24. Turner, 276.

25. Turner, 168.

26. Robert Woodward, *Veil: The Secret Wars of the CIA, 1981–1987* (Simon & Schuster, 1987).

27. Woodward, 227.

3

Ethics and Morality in U.S. Secret Intelligence

Arthur S. Hulnick and Daniel W. Mattausch

Recent revelations surrounding the Iran-contra affair, as well as activities of United States intelligence agencies before the founding of the Central Intelligence Agency more than forty years ago, have raised questions about ethics and morality in American strategic intelligence.[1] Though several writers have discussed the morality of war and the ethics of the soldier,[2] few have specifically addressed the ethics of intelligence operations. Perhaps this void in the literature exists because such operations do not fit neatly within the more traditional forms of foreign policy operations—diplomacy and military force—but instead lie somewhere in between.

In this article, we seek to outline a moral structure that is appropriate for intelligence operations in a democratic and free society. Our discussion is divided into two parts: the first section focuses on the ethical dimensions of intelligence operations in general; the second explores the moral considerations that confront the individual intelligence officer. We assume that, much as military and diplomatic operations have codes of conduct, intelligence services have cultural and behavioral norms that constitute a body of ethics for the intelligence professional. Our discussion represents an interpretation of the existing intelligence system and an implicit belief that the philosophy behind this system ought to have an audience both inside and outside of the intelligence community.

For the purposes of this article, we define "intelligence services" to mean both (1) the collection and analysis of information about threats to the security and interests of the nation, and (2) the use of clandestine resources to carry out the foreign policy of the nation. The former category involves such activities as espionage and the use of intrusive technical sensors; the latter includes such activities as propaganda, psychological warfare, the use of agents of influence, deception, disinformation, and support for paramilitary or guerrilla forces. Throughout our analysis, we recognize the important distinction between mere information-gathering services, which most people consider to be acceptable intelligence activities, and covert activities that interfere with the internal affairs of other nations, which are more difficult to justify on moral grounds. Nevertheless, we contend that some forms of intelligence operations that may be considered immoral are nevertheless justifiable in particular circumstances.

ETHICAL DIMENSIONS FOR INTELLIGENCE OPERATIONS IN GENERAL

Spying as a form of statecraft is as old as recorded history. Babylonian tablets reportedly contain passages about spying,[3] and the Bible has several passages about the use of intelligence agents.[4] Modern times also are replete with spy sagas of all kinds.[5] This legacy of intelligence operations by nations throughout history is evidence of a long-standing acceptance of such activity by many diverse cultural groups.

However, while many people may feel intuitively that at least some form of intelligence activity is morally justifiable, it is somewhat difficult to articulate exactly what the ethical foundation is for such activity. We will approach this task first by presenting a set of guidelines that should define the morality of both open and clandestine information-gathering operations. Next we will discuss the more difficult subject of covert activities. Finally, we will consider the implications of just war theory and shared expectations theory for an ethical theory of intelligence operations.

Information-Gathering Activities

We submit that the following principles provide an ethical basis for the use of information-gathering services by a democratic government for foreign policy purposes. First, because a state has the responsibility to its citizens to protect their lives, welfare, and property, it must take steps to understand the foreign threats, if there are any, to those citizens as well as to the nation as a whole. In order to do this, the state must gather information—openly if possible, but by using secret methods if necessary. In a world in which many societies are closed, or in which information does not circulate completely freely, the state must engage in clandestine information-gathering to protect against foreign threats to its security. Historically, the notion that "Gentlemen do not read each others' mail" has proven dangerous when applied to a state's collection of information affecting national security.[6]

Our second principle is that the state should use the least intrusive means of collecting information. That is, one should not spy when information can be gathered in an open way. Further, the information to be gathered ought to be related to advancing the goals of the state as a whole rather than the private interests of individuals.

Third, intelligence data must be presented to policymakers without bias or political taint. Those who report the information must not manipulate it to drive policy or to justify further intrusive intelligence collection.

Finally, one should recognize the need for the state to employ counterintelligence to protect its own national security information from being stolen. All nations generally agree that the state has the right to punish those it catches in the act of spying. Thus, one country's hero is bound to be another's traitor; one country's intelligence success is, *ipso facto*, another's counterintelligence failure.

It is important to note here that what is morally acceptable behavior for the government in protecting the nation as a whole may not necessarily be acceptable for the individual; in fact, quite the opposite may be true. While nations may sometimes use intrusive measures to collect information, individuals may not. Thus, espionage as a form of acceptable statecraft would be considered mere theft if practiced by individuals.

Covert Activities

While most people recognize the state's need to possess the capability of gathering information by clandestine means, a significant number are troubled by the use of intelligence resources to interfere in the internal activities of another nation. In wartime, one might condone this interference as a preferred alternative to direct military action, and defining the enemy is easier in wartime. In peacetime, however, internal interference with other nations may seem less acceptable. Under what circumstances, then, does a nation, especially a free and open society that professes to follow the rule of law, have the right to interfere with a foreign government, or even to seek to change its nature, when that nation would find such activity totally unacceptable, even hostile, if done to it?

Given the adversarial relationship between East and West since the end of World War II, some pragmatists might argue that a government's foreign policy cannot function without some degree of covert activities with questionable ethical aspects.[7] This argument is similar to the one made by Niccolo Machiavelli that rulers must sometimes be immoral in establishing and maintaining the states.[8] While Machiavelli's counsels earned him one of the most unsavory reputations in the history of political philosophy, theorists find it difficult to refute him.[9] If one follows Machiavelli's line of reasoning, political action must be separated from individual moral considerations. For the "prince," morality is subsumed by the political responsibility of maintaining the power of the state.

While pragmatists may be content with the Machiavellian rationale, it has extreme results when the preservation of the state's power conflicts with other highly esteemed values. Can a nation espouse such moral positions on freedom, democracy, and human rights as does the United States and still support actions that contravene these ideals? Only the most extreme political or religious leaders would reject the pragmatic line in these areas. Yet these same leaders might argue that under certain circumstances a state may be justified in using convert activities to carry out foreign policy.

Just War Theory

Some authors have used the existing literature on just war theory to establish a moral basis for clandestine intelligence operations.[10] Although just war theory is concerned with permissible acts of the state during wartime, some aspects of the theory may indeed contribute to our understanding of the morality of peacetime covert intelligence activities.

Just war theory posits that there are times when conflict is morally justified. It painfully seeks to discern the difference between a just and an unjust cause. Simply defined, a just war is a conflict that is fought either in self-defense or in collective defense against an armed attack. There is an assumption that the opposing party is in the wrong and that its attack is unjustified. Of course, there are numerous examples of conflicts in which both sides claimed to be the morally correct party and accused the other of aggression.[11]

In constructing a middle ground between the Machiavellian position and the absolute view that no immoral act is justified, those who believe in the just war theory have allowed for measured resolute acts in the face of immorality. These rationales permit absolute values to be broken while still maintaining that the violated values remain absolute in a universal sense. For instance, even if we accept commandments such as "Thou shalt not kill" or "Thou shalt not steal" as deontological imperatives, in certain defined circumstances both such activities might be tolerated. They remain as absolute, however, because we agree that such acts are evil even when justified. Thus, a moral law is broken out of necessity. This philosophy forms the basis for the just war theory.

It is important to emphasize that the function of just war theory is not to justify warfare itself, but rather to judge conflicts. The standard method under the theory is to lay down common criteria by which to measure wars. The criteria encompass intentions as well as the actual acts and consequences of wars. The theory thus calls into question both deontological and utilitarian considerations.

Jacques Ellul has written that "as early as the year 314, at the Council of Arles the Church realized that to deny the state the right to go to war was to condemn it to extinction. But the state is ordained by God; therefore it must have the right to wage war."[12] St. Thomas Aquinas was one of the first philosophers to advocate standards for a just war. In his *Summa Theologica*,[13] he laid down three criteria for a just war.[14] Modern philosophers have expanded the list to seven necessary conditions:[15]

(1) *Just Cause*. All aggression is condemnable; only defensive war is legitimate.

(2) *Just Intention*. Nations must seek a just peace; they cannot justify revenge, conquest, economic gain, or ideological supremacy.

(3) *Last Resort*. War is acceptable only when nations have tried all possible negotiations and have failed.

(4) *Formal Declaration*. The use of force is the prerogative of governments, and not private individuals; legitimate authorities must officially declare a state of war.

(5) *Limited Objectives*. The goal of war is peace; unconditional surrender or the destruction of a nation's economic or political institutions is an unwarranted objective.

(6) *Proportionate Means*. Nations should limit the weaponry and force used to what is absolutely necessary to stop aggression and secure a just peace.

(7) *Noncombatant Immunity*. Only those who are official agents of government may fight; individuals not actively engaged in war should be immune from attack.

These conditions are obviously stringent. The just war theorist accepts conflict hesitantly and with great regret, concluding that participation in war is sometimes a lesser evil than allowing aggression and terror to go unchecked and unpunished. To the just war theorist, war is not a matter of choice, but rather one of necessity that arises from the need to control violence in a fallen world. In the words of Rev. Arthur F. Holmes, a proponent of the just war doctrine, "[w]ar is evil. It causes evil. . . . Its consequences are evil. . . . To call war anything less than evil would be self-deception. . . . The question that tears the Christian conscience is not whether war is good, but whether it is in all cases entirely avoidable."[16] This, then, is the paradox of just war theory: it advocates evil to stamp out an even greater evil.

One can successfully incorporate intelligence activity—both espionage and covert interference with internal affairs of foreign nations—under the penumbra of just war theory if one understands that governments use such activities as a means for government survival. Some intelligence professionals have argued that "there is . . . implied in Just War theory a basis for the right of one government to interfere in the affairs of an other, so long as the principles of just cause, just means, proportionality, etc. prevail."[17]

The element of formal declaration of conflict is missing, but because the deontological absolutes that are breached by intelligence activity are presumably less stringent than might exist for a declaration of war, we can reasonably assume that just war theory will proportionally relax its requirements when it is applied to intelligence operations.

Nevertheless, just war theory offers only nominal consolation to the conscientious intelligence professional involved in gathering intelligence or carrying out secret operations. The justifications for breaking deontological imperatives do not relieve those who violate them—those who commit evil—from all guilt.[18] One can thus view secret intelligence operations as a sphere of moral tension and even moral tragedy.

Shared Expectations Theory

If there is little solace in just war theory, perhaps other moral views merit examination. One such view has its basis in shared expectations theory. There are no deontological imperatives in this theory; rather, social institutions develop their absolutes over time by looking to what individuals within the institution expect. Professor Jeanne Kirkpatrick, former United States Ambassador to the United Nations, defines "institutions" as "stabilized patterns of interaction based upon reciprocal relations and expectations."[19] One can consider the intelligence community to be an "institution" by this definition.

The foundations of the intelligence institution are clear enough. The Byzantines first added the concept of reporting to the traditional diplomatic responsibilities of communication and negotiation.[20] Ithiel de Sola Pool has written that

> standards have . . . evolved for the collection of foreign information. The nations of the world have reached agreement that each is free to post a limited number of agents within the other; these are called diplomats. Ambassadors were defined by Diego de Saavedra Fajardo in 1640 as public spies and by Sir Henry Wotton as honorable spies.[21]

Sir Henry elsewhere described an ambassador as "an honest man, sent abroad to lie for the good of his country."[22]

In more recent times, states have accorded foreign diplomats the right to report home in secret dispatches or through the sacrosanct diplomatic pouch. Even military attaches are widely accepted, although it is understood that they collect tactical military data. It is generally agreed that spies, when captured, are not to be summarily executed without trial; spymasters are usually allowed diplomatic status; third-party relationships are protected; and technical collection systems, to the extent that they "spy," may be thwarted but not destroyed.

Thus, intelligence can be viewed as an extension of diplomacy, complete with rules that prevent certain forms of abuse, although these are largely unacknowledged parameters and conventions.[23] Intelligence in the United States' context, with American emphasis on freedom and human rights, means even further restrictions on the uses—and avoidance of the abuses of secret intelligence.[24]

While the considerations in the paragraphs above provide a basis for understanding the general collective view of espionage, there is less of a consensus regarding the more intrusive forms of secret operations known as covert actions. Here, the theory is less clear. Absent shared expectations, can there be a moral construct to justify the secret interference of one nation in the affairs of another in peacetime?

In the United States, justification of any covert action is contingent on a written presidential finding that a particular secret operation is vital to the security of the nation and, presumably, that the action of some other nation has threatened the United States.[25] Machiavelli would have no problem with this construct, although he might argue about the need to issue a written order. Henry Kissinger, as the President's National Security Adviser, is alleged to have said, with regard to efforts by the American government to overthrow the elected government of Salvador Allende in Chile, that the United States should not have to tolerate the inability of peoples of other countries to deal with incompetence when American interests are at stake.[26] Dr. Kissinger's statement aside, is there a moral position here that can be sustained?

Those who favor covert operations argue that the United States should not have to tolerate activities by other countries that we would find unacceptable if they were to take place here, when those activities directly threaten the security and interests of the United States. Thus, the proponents of covert operations contend that it is acceptable to help our friends and work against our adversaries. They see benefit in activities such as secret support for internal political groups, psychological warfare, propaganda, deception, and disinformation to discredit, embarrass, or reduce support for internal groups in other countries that appear to threaten American national security.[27]

On the opposite side are those who argue that our actions abroad should accord with our domestic standards of behavior. Interference in the internal affairs of other nations, the argument continues, is acceptable only when those nations do things that are direct threats to the United States, not just to the people where the activity is taking place. Thus, secret operations to stop terrorist acts against Americans might be acceptable; aid to a foreign political party or interference in a foreign election would not.[28]

Even in their most extreme forms, the opposing sides of the issue are not irreconcilable. The ardent Machiavellian strategist and the absolute pacifist may agree on a framework of four categories into which one would classify covert operations for the purpose of making judgments about their moral acceptability.

The first category includes those ideal covert operations that are both necessary and moral. Rescuing hostages, stopping the assassination of a world leader, and preventing a wanton act of terrorism would all fall within this category. Necessary and moral covert operations to preserve life secure a great benefit without causing any harm.

A second category of covert activity is that which is necessary, but immoral. Examples include aid to a democratically oriented, but beleaguered, illegal political group to prevent it from being crushed by a dictatorship, or similar aid to a newspaper or magazine operating without government permission. In this category, the covert action interferes with the affairs and policies of another state, and the benefit is political rather than moral. But if we espouse and defend democracy as an ethic at home, can we avoid aiding it abroad?

The third category—unnecessary and immoral covert operations—includes activities that are undertaken in secret to accomplish unnecessary, illegal, or perhaps foolish ends. Assassination and aid to criminals or terrorists fall in this category. The fact that other countries do such things to us does not justify similar activity on our part.[29] The Doolittle Committee, investigating similar activities in the 1950s, noted that the use of the same tactics as our adversaries was essentially a "repugnant philosophy."[30] If the United States stands for the protection of human rights, can it carry out, in secret, operations that violate that standard?

The fourth category—unnecessary but moral action—may exist, but there is scant evidence that a secret operation could fit within this definition.

It might appear to be an inappropriate restriction on a great power to argue that activities within category one would be acceptable, even encouraged, and those in category two might be justified under certain circumstances, but that those in category three ought not to be accepted. The opposing argument is that such restraints on power are necessary to ensure that the United States is a force for moral good in the world. Writing in the *New York Times* not long ago, columnist Tom Wicker said that "a democratic nation, supposedly devoted to the rule of law and the self-determination of peoples, has *no* right to destabilize or subvert even governments we disapprove, or try to change—much less kill or kidnap—even undesirable leaders."[31]

We have thus reached a point where the choices for action move outside the intelligence system and lie with policymakers—those chosen by the people (or appointed by those chosen by the people) to make policy. In a free and democratic society, one would hope that the people would send appropriate messages to their elected representatives. While some would argue that the people are unable to register their views when they are not consulted about secret operations, in fact such operations must form part of some larger scheme of foreign policy.[32] Once a public policy consensus has been achieved, it is hard to envision a circumstance in which voters would not be willing to support secret operations necessary to implement that policy.

MORAL CONSIDERATIONS CONFRONTING THE INDIVIDUAL INTELLIGENCE OFFICER

Having explored the moral constructs that support an intelligence system as a whole, we now examine the ethical considerations that confront the individual intelligence officer. Are these considerations different from what they would be for other civil servants, military officers, or members of the private sector?

Ethics are often defined as behavior relating to professional standards of conduct. As in any other profession, such standards exist in the field of intelligence, even if these standards require behavior that is unacceptable for private citizens. Dr. David Hunter has argued that "for intelligence professionals to disregard the national values they are committed to defend is to ignore the fundamental reason for being in the game."[33] Indeed, American intelligence agencies are required by executive order to collect information in a manner that is "respectful of the principles on which the United States was founded."[34]

There are several key differences between intelligence professionals and their counterparts in other areas of government service or private business. Professional standards require intelligence professionals to lie, hide information, or use covert tactics to protect their "cover," access, sources, and responsibilities. The Central Intelligence Agency expects, teaches, encourages, and controls these tactics so that the lies are consistent and supported ("backstopped"). The CIA expects intelligence officers to teach others to lie, deceive, steal, launder money, and perform a variety of other activities that would certainly be illegal if practiced in the United States. They call these tactics "tradecraft," and intelligence officers practice them in all the world's intelligence services.[35]

In other contexts, intelligence officers must be as honest and forthright as those who work in the private sector or other parts of government. Intelligence officers must *always* tell the truth about their activities to their superiors. Otherwise, they may find themselves suspected of betraying the organization to which they owe their loyalty. Honesty is especially important in intelligence because many officers operate in settings where their actions cannot be observed.[36]

Intelligence analysts must *never* alter intelligence judgments to fit the desires of policymakers who might prefer different conclusions. Forcing the facts to fit policy warps the purpose of intelligence operations.[37]

Intelligence officers must be scrupulous in managing funds or equipment with which they are entrusted. Care in this area is especially important because funds are often "unvouchered" (not subject to outside audit), and equipment is deliberately designed to prevent its identification with the officer or service concerned.[38]

Intelligence officers must give up certain rights of privacy so that they may be trusted with secrets. They are subject to examinations of their private and professional activities during their careers and must accept some restrictions on their behavior even after leaving the service: for example, they must continue to protect secrets they learned while on duty.[39]

The United States military has long recognized that individual soldiers are obligated to follow the lawful orders of their superiors; in fact, soldiers must swear that they will do so.[40]

The military also recognizes that following illegal or unlawful orders is not acceptable. The so-called Nuremberg defense—that one is not accountable for one's actions if merely following orders—is not acceptable. The question for intelligence professionals is whether they have the same kinds of obligations.

In the authors' view, government servants, whether military or civilian, have an obligation to tell their superiors about matters they consider illegal, immoral, or ill-conceived. If, in the judgment of the superior, the questionable order must stand, the junior official has the choice of carrying out the unacceptable order, appealing to a higher authority, or, ultimately, resigning.

What is not possible in the realm of intelligence—although it might be possible in other areas of United States government service—is to "go public" with the issue in question. Intelligence officials have the obligation to keep secret issues properly classified, and thus public discussion is not possible without a gross violation of classification rules and the professional ethics of the intelligence officer.[41]

In reality, such ethical disputes rarely arise. As in most enterprises, superiors want to develop the loyalty and trust of their juniors and also want to be advised when things seem to be going awry. Thus, strong disagreement often leads to compromise rather than confrontation.

CONCLUSION

Ethics and morality in intelligence are integral parts of operating a secret intelligence service in a free, democratic, and moral society. A free, democratic government has the obligation to protect the interests and security of the people it serves. If the world were perfect, intelligence operations would be unnecessary. Given the depravity of the world around us, however, free societies have no choice but to engage in intelligence activities if they are to remain free.

NOTES

1. Writings about the alleged and actual activities of the CIA are legion. One recent view of the controversy is contained in Miller & Robbins, "The CIA, Congress, Covert Operations, and the War on Terrorism," in *Intelligence And Intelligence Policy In A Democratic Society* 145–63 (S. Cimbala ed. 1987). For the view of a former intelligence professional, *see* H. Rositzke, *The CIA's Secret Operations: Espionage, Counterespionage, And Covert Action* (1977).

2. *See, e.g., War, Morality and the Military Profession* (M. Makin ed. 1986); B. Paskins & M. Dockrill, *The Ethics of War* (1979).

3. For a discussion of the early manifestations of espionage, *see* B. Innes, *The Book of Spies* 7–14 (1966).

4. *See, e.g., Joshua* 2:1–24 (recounting spy mission to Jericho); *see also* B. Innes, *supra* note 3, at 7–14.

5. N. Buranelli & V. Buranelli, *Spy/Counterspy: An Encyclopedia of Espionage* (1982). The prevalence of spying is also reflected "in popular culture by the fictional writings of such authors as Tom Clancy, Len Deighton, John LeCarre, and Ian Fleming.

6. G. Treverton. *Covert Action: The Limits of Intervention in the Postwar World* 11 (1987).

7. *See, e.g.,* W. Leary, *The Central Intelligence Agency* 64–65, 70 (1984) (discussion of the Doolittle Committee).

8. N. Machiavelli, *The Prince* (D. Donno trans. ed. 1981) (M. Bonafanti ed. 1954) (orig. ed. 1532).

9. *See* G. Tinder, *Political Thinking* 107 (1979) ('The chief works of political thought contain no argument, answering Machiavelli's, for the same uncompromising morality among rulers that is expected of private individuals").

10. *See, e.g.,* "Langan Just War Theory and Decisionmaking in a Democracy," *Naval War College Review*, 67 (July-Aug. 1985); J. Chomeau & A. Rudolph, *Ethical Need to Know for Intelligence Officers* (unpublished paper delivered at the Conference on Military Ethics and Education, Washington, D.C., 1986).

11. During World War I, for example, the Allies were sure that God was with them, but the Germans wore belt buckles that were inscribed "Gott Mit Uns." Military artifacts such as these can be seen in many military museums. The war between Iran and Iraq provides a more recent example of a conflict in which both sides believed they were fighting for a moral and just cause.

12. J. Ellul, Violence 5 (1969); *see also Romans* 13:1 ("[F]or there is no authority except from God, and those in authority are divinely constituted.").

13. *See* II-II T. Aquinas, *Summa Theologica*, q. XL, at art. I (J.Pickaby trans. 2d ed. 1896).

14. St. Thomas's three criteria were: (1) war had to be waged under the authority of a sovereign; (2) there had to be a just cause; and (3) belligerents had to have rightful intentions. *See id.*

15. *See, e.g.,* Holmes, *The Just War,* in War: Four Christian Views 120–21 (R. Clouse, ed. 1981).

16. *Id.* at 117.

17. J. Chomeau & A. Rudolph, *supra* note 10, at 14; *see also* E. Lefever & R. Godson, *The CIA and the American Ethic* 15–18 (1979).

18. Walzer, *Political Action: The Problem of Dirty Hands,* 2 PHIL. & PUB. AFF. 160–80 (1973).

19. Interview with Professor Jeanne Kirkpatrick, at Georgetown University (Jan. 21, 1988). Professor Kirkpatrick noted that the notion of shared expectations was first suggested by Harold Lasswell. *See* H. Lasswell, *Psychopathology And Politics* (1930).

20. D. Miller, *Studies in Byzantine Diplomacy: Sixth to Tenth Centuries* (1978).

21. de Sola Pool, "International Intelligence and Domestic Politics," in *Surveillance and Espionage in a Free Society* 274 (R. Blum ed. 1972).

22. "Legatus est vir bonus, peregre missus ad mentiendum Reipublicae causa," *quoted in* I. Walton, Life of Wotton (London 1651). The reader will note that the English "lie" is ambiguous, but the Latin "mentiendium" is not. Sir Henry was at the time (1604) English Ambassador to the Court of Venice.

23. W. Macomber, *The Angel's Games: A Handbook of Modern Diplomacy* 275 (1975).

24. R. Jefferys-Jones, *The CIA and American Democracy* 1–6 (1989).

25. G. Treverton, *supra* note 6, at 248–63.

26. *See id.* at II.

27. For a useful discussion involving proponents of covert action, see *Intelligence Requirements for the 1980s: Covert Action* (R. Godson ed., 1981).

28. For a good discussion of the ideas of those opposed to various forms of covert action, *see* G. Treverton. *supra* note 6; for a less rigorous approach, *see* J. Kwitny, *Endless Enemies* (1984).

29. Codevilla & Godson. "Intelligence: Covert Action and Counterintelligence as an Instrument of Policy," in *Intelligence Requirements for the 1980s: Intelligence and Policy* 87–118 (R. Godson ed. 1986).

30. W. Leary, *supra* note 7, at 65.

31. Wicker. *Not Covert, Not Smart, Not Right, N.Y. Times,* Aug. 2, 1988, A19.

32. Codevilla & Godson, *supra* note 29, at 89–96.

33. D. Hunter, *Intelligence: The Ethical Dimension* 195 (Ph.D. dissertation, University of Georgia, 1978). For a view from the professional side, *see* Godfrey, *Ethics and Intelligence,* 56 Foreign Affairs. 624–42 (1978).

34. Exec. Order No. 12,333, pt. 2.1, 3 C.F.R. 200, 210 (1981), reprinted in 50 U.S.C. § 501 app. at 44–51, 49 (1982).

35. S. Breckinridge, *The CIA and the United States Intelligence System* 120–25 (1986).

36. *See id.* at 286–99; *see also* Godfrey, *supra* note 33, at 642.

37. Hulnick, "Managing Analysis: Strategies for Playing the End Game," 2 *Intelligence & Counterintelligence* 32 I (1988).

38. This observation is based on Mr. Hulnick's experience of more than thirty-one years as an intelligence professional. These rules are embodied in CIA regulations, but most of them are classified and not available to the public.

39. The CIA maintains a Publications Review Board that reviews manuscripts prepared by former Agency officers to ensure that there is not inadvertent release of properly classified information. The regulation governing this process is not available to the public.

40. For a good discussion of the military code, *see* Dyck, *Ethical Bases of the Military Profession,* 10 Parameters:]. U.S. Army War College 39 (Mar. 1980); Taylor, "A Do-It-Yourself Professional Cork for the Military," 10 *Parameters*:]. U.S. Army War College 10 (Dec. 1980).

41. Employees of the intelligence agencies of the United States government enter into agreements with their employers to protect the secrecy of materials with which they are entrusted. The agreement continues in force even after their employment is terminated. Each agency maintains its own regulations in this regard.

4

The Need for Improvement
Integrity, Ethics, and the CIA

Kent Pekel

"People who have been here for a while cannot believe it when I say that being a case officer is just a job for me . . . for them, it has been a priesthood or something. There is just a big difference in what motivates us. We are committed to different things."

"It seems to me that one of the good things to come out of the Aldrich Ames mess is that now it is more possible to speak out around here when you see something that could mean trouble down the road."

"I think we often misdefine failure. If you ran the program correctly and it failed, it is a learning experience, not mismanagement."

"The best managers I have had have been the ones who stop to ask 'Is this the right thing to do?' They were willing to be questioned and sought to avoid the arrogance of certainty."

—Four Agency employees

While these diverse voices from across the CIA are addressing different issues from at times divergent perspectives, they are linked by a common concern for the integrity of the organization. This concern speaks both to effectiveness and to ethics, to how capably we achieve our mission and how honorably we go about doing it. The two, of course, are intimately linked; over time, even the most effective organization will be tripped up or eaten away by unethical behavior. At a moment when the Agency is engaged in numerous efforts to improve its effectiveness, ethical issues are also much on people's minds. In a series of conversations with people from throughout the Agency, it was the four broad issues addressed by the speakers quoted above—issues of ideology, dissent, failure, and management—that I heard about most often as challenges to our integrity as an organization, and as critical determinants of our ability to navigate the potential minefield of ethics.

ORIGINS AND OVERVIEW

This article grew out of my participation in an Office of Training and Education working group charged with looking at how ethics education is conducted at the CIA. At the group's initial meetings, there was agreement among the participants that approaching this subject exclusively from the standpoint of training and education was not enough, that regardless of how good the curriculum and the instructors might be, an organization cannot simply inoculate people with "good ethics" in the classroom and then send them out into an organizational environment that will profoundly shape the way they think and act in doing their work. We agreed with Lynn Sharp Paine, a Harvard Business School professor who specializes in management ethics, who wrote that:

> Ethics has everything to do with management. Rarely do the character flaws of a lone actor fully explain corporate misconduct. More typically, unethical business practice involves tacit, if not explicit, cooperation of others and reflects the values, attitudes, beliefs, language, and behavioral patterns that define an organization's operating culture. Ethics, then, is as much an organizational as a personal issue. Managers who fail to provide proper leadership and to institute systems that facilitate ethical conduct share responsibility with those who conceive, execute, and knowingly benefit from corporate misdeeds.[1]

Given our shared conviction that ethics is as much an organizational as a personal issue, the members of our working group decided that an "ethical inventory" of the Agency's operating culture might be useful in our effort to design a new Agency-wide program of ethics education. As we imagined it, the goal of this inventory would be to surface the major ethics-related issues on the minds of people throughout the organization. Such an effort would inevitably be anecdotal, unscientific, and incomplete, but our hope was that it might provoke thought and discussion among ourselves, among senior management, and among the Agency population at large.

This idea became a series of approximately 50 hour-long one-on-one interviews that took place between February and mid-March 1996. The Agency Information Staff selected a rough cross-section of the employee population for me to talk with, and provided invaluable help in setting up the interviews. Without exception, people were willing to engage the issue, and their candor with an outsider—albeit one possessing a blue badge for a one-year assignment to CIA as a White House Fellow—made for fascinating and productive conversations. Although no one requested anonymity, in an effort to facilitate frank and open discussion I informed them that my report would not attribute any statements or opinions to specific individuals. A copy of the questions I loosely followed during the interviews is included at the end of this article.

After the first few sessions, I found that these discussions yielded greater insight when they focused more broadly on integrity than on ethics. This was in part because the word "ethics" often invokes thoughts of compulsory annual briefings in the Agency auditorium, while "integrity" more clearly connotes commitment *without coercion* to deeply held priorities and values. Integrity also carries the idea that this commitment to values is maintained even when it goes against one's self-interest to do so. In this sense, being ethical implies doing the right thing; having integrity implies doing the right thing even when it hurts. As a result of this project, I have come to believe that alongside an effective program of ethics education, devoting management attention and resources to the task of defining, auditing, and inculcating organizational integrity is the best way the CIA can prepare itself for a future that is likely to be even more ethically challenging than the present.

An important caveat to this point: to call for a focus on integrity is not to suggest that the people of the CIA lack it. If one accepts the premise that ethical or unethical behavior most often reflects an organization's operating culture, then that culture has to be examined continually through the lens of integrity to check for faultlines and tensions that could lead to problems down the road. This approach is preventive medicine for organizations— trying to clarify values and improve systems before the storms hit.

It was this kind of forward-looking approach that left Johnson & Johnson Corporation well prepared to act quickly and with integrity in the 1982 Tylenol tampering case, a crisis that could have put the company out of business. In contrast, a narrow management approach to ethics, one based on trying to weed out the bad apples from the organization while providing a few compulsory ethics training sessions to remind everyone else to be ethical, is short-sighted and destined to fail. As recent history has shown, from the Exxon Valdez to insider trading on Wall Street to Iran-Contra, organizations that fail to monitor and adjust their operating cultures for integrity pay a high price for their mistaken assumption that good ethics "happen" without constant organizational effort.

Many people I interviewed felt that the CIA too has largely taken this passive approach to organizational integrity. While informal conversations about issues of ethics occur frequently throughout the Agency among friends and immediate colleagues, and while some parts of the CIA have developed codes of ethics and have run successful ethics education seminars, in general most of those I spoke with felt that the issue either has not been addressed or has been addressed only within the framework of legal compliance. Some suggested that this has been due to the mission-driven character of the Agency, which has necessitated an intense focus on external events rather than on internal organizational dynamics. Others thought the rigorous selection process that people go through before they join the CIA has generally guaranteed that Agency employees possess strong moral backgrounds, and has thus made a formal focus on integrity unnecessary.

Whatever their perception of the CIA's past attitude toward organizational integrity, most of those I interviewed saw a need to address the issue more explicitly at this moment in the Agency's history. Public tolerance for ethical lapses in all institutions is uniformly low and is likely to remain that way, particularly with regard to an organization charged with conducting espionage in the national interest. In addition, the availability of fewer financial resources with which to fulfill a difficult mission may increase the temptation to cut ethical corners in pursuit of that mission.

Given these constraints, almost everyone I spoke with pointed out the inadequacy of trying to deal with ethics as an issue primarily of legal compliance. While clearly stated rules are important, inherently there can never be enough of them to cover all potential scenarios. And, as Lynn Sharp Paine has written, "Even in the best cases, legal compliance is unlikely to unleash much moral imagination or commitment. The law does not generally seek to inspire human excellence or distinction."[2]

Similarly, the injunction that all ethical dilemmas must be reported up the chain for resolution at senior levels is neither practical nor respectful of the professional competence and "ground truth" knowledge of the people who actually face the problem. Perhaps most important, an ethics strategy founded primarily on legal compliance ignores the fact that what is neither illegal nor against the rules may still be ethically problematic. This is particularly true because, as Rushworth Kidder has written, it is more often the "right versus right" issues—the ones where core values come into conflict—than the "right versus wrong" ones that get organizations and individuals into trouble.[3]

THE ELEMENTS OF INTEGRITY

To avoid approaching the issue from the narrow confines of compliance, organizational integrity replaced ethics as the project's theme. This focus on integrity began with a central question: "What for us as an Agency and as a profession constitutes integrity?" Over the course of those 50 interviews, common themes from across the directorates merged into a working definition of integrity for the CIA, and perhaps by extension for intelligence as a profession. In considering this question, people identified four broad challenges the Agency faces in striving to be an integrity-driven organization.

While each Agency directorate has elements of integrity that are specific to its particular mission—protecting sources and methods in the Directorate of Operations (DO), avoiding politicization in the Directorate of Intelligence (DI), adherence to procurement ethics law in the Directorate of Science and Technology (DS&T), and total discretion with sensitive personnel information in the Directorate of Administration—the following seven themes were mentioned repeatedly regardless of directorate or other affiliation:

1. Belief in and awareness of the moral purpose of the Agency mission.
2. Always speaking truth to power, both within the Agency and with the policymakers we serve.
3. Doing our homework—knowing when we have enough information to make a decision and explaining with clarity and honesty what we cannot do or do not know.
4. Willingness to be held accountable for what we do, write, and say.
5. Taking calculated risks in obtaining and analyzing information.
6. Responsible use of the public's money and honor—knowing that we can always answer this question in the affirmative: "If the American people could know all the facts, would a clear majority agree that this is the right thing to do?"
7. Giving all employees an equal chance to achieve and be rewarded for excellence. Accepting and learning from failure as a means of continually improving who we are.

THE CHALLENGES TO INTEGRITY

The preceding seven-point definition of organizational integrity for the CIA is, of course, eminently debatable. In fact, having that debate is exactly the point of trying to arrive at a working definition of integrity; it is the best way to surface challenges and obstacles to integrity before they become problems and crises.

In the course of my discussions with people from across the CIA, four such broad challenges emerged: a sense that the Agency's guiding values have become clouded in the aftermath of the Cold War; a belief that within the Agency open discussion and dissent are often discouraged, making it less likely that people will speak out about ethical problems; a concern that an unwillingness to acknowledge failure as an acceptable outcome creates an incentive to cover up honest mistakes and to avoid risk; and a belief that promotions and performance appraisals regularly reward those who acted without integrity.

CLOUDY MORAL PURPOSE

Arthur Applbaum, a specialist on professional ethics at the Kennedy School of Government, has written, "If a claim of professionalism is to have any moral force, it has to refer to ideals and commitments."[4] This is particularly true, he suggests, when a professional role requires a person "to act in ways that, if not for the role, would be wrong." Applbaum cites law, business, politics, journalism, and the military as professions that depend upon "moral force" to legitimize actions that would be societally unacceptable outside the context of their professional roles. The conduct of espionage could certainly be added to Applbaum's list. One senior manager I interviewed underscored the importance of clear guiding principles for the profession of espionage when he told me, "In this business, you start to get soiled when you *want* to do the 'dirty' part of espionage rather than feeling that you *must* do it to achieve noble goals."

During the Cold War, there was universal clarity about the ideals and commitments to which the Agency was dedicated. Awareness of and commitment to shared values were the driving forces behind the CIA's operating culture. As the dust has settled from the fall of Communism, threats to the United States still remain. But for many I interviewed, these new threats lack the obvious moral dimension presented by the expansionist ideology of the Soviet Union, and are thus less compelling motivators for doing a difficult job with integrity. As one case officer told me, "Now the only thing that matters is: Is it good for the United States?"

Also during the Cold War, what was good for the United States was seen to be a matter of *principle*, while today it is often more clearly seen as an issue of national interest. Many people I interviewed felt that this shift has had significant implications for the intensity with which Agency personnel approach their jobs and also for the caliber of individual who will be attracted to a career in intelligence. Others suggested that this cloudier sense of moral purpose may in the future also have ethical implications. They worried that, if the DO case officers of tomorrow are less clear about the goals to which their profession is dedicated, they will be more likely to become "soiled" by the "dirty" aspects of their craft.

ENCOURAGING DISSENT AND
ACCEPTING BAD NEWS

Computer scientist and management theorist Jay Forrester of MIT once remarked that the hallmark of a great organization is how quickly bad news travels upward.[5] If an organization is to deal with problems effectively, they have to be brought out into the open before they become too serious to manage. For this to happen, employees must know that managers will respond to the bad news itself, rather than shoot the messenger. They also have to know that, although it may not result in management action, all thoughtful dissent will receive a fair and honest hearing. This kind of open environment is particularly crucial if an organization is to surface potential ethical dilemmas, which there is a great incentive to cover up.

The interviews I conducted suggest that the CIA's record on this score has been mixed. In the DO, one career officer told me, "There has never been a time when I felt I couldn't speak up," while another said that those who do speak up challenge the "most prized value" of the DO—loyalty. They are considered "wave makers" who are "not on the team" or "in revolt." A senior manager who spent his career in the DO related the story of a time when he reported a colleague for unethical conduct with a "floozy" and was criticized by Headquarters for not being "one of the boys."

Most DO officers I interviewed felt that willingness to accept dissent varies greatly from manager to manager. They pointed out that this is a particularly critical quality for a chief of station, who in large part sets the "ethical climate" for that unique environment. Some chiefs have genuine open-door policies and are committed to understanding the concerns of the officers below them, while others, I was told, are interested in "being told what they want to hear." A former case officer now working elsewhere in the Agency suggested that this dynamic exists between Headquarters and stations as well: "A chief of station's overriding goal," he said, "is to get through his watch without a flap. The name of the game is to deal with it within the station or to find a way to avoid telling Washington."

Some DO officers I talked to, particularly younger ones, felt that this lack of willingness to countenance dissent extends even to philosophical discussions of the ethical nature of espionage and the psychological difficulties of the life of a case officer. One related the story of an instructor in a Career Trainee class who refused a student's request to watch a tape of a national news program's interview with a former DO case officer who left the Agency because he came to the conclusion that espionage was immoral. The student had hoped to discuss the issue openly in class and pointed out to the instructor that "everyone was already thinking about these things and talking about them on their own." Despite this, the instructor refused to show the tape, reportedly because he feared that it would raise too many "doubts" in the minds of the new recruits and make them "soft."

Another former case officer told me that the first time in his career he ever engaged in a discussion of the ethical and moral dimensions of espionage with his managers and colleagues was when he was considering leaving the Agency for precisely those reasons. Although he praised his supervisor for ultimately supporting his decision to move to another position within the directorate, he wondered if an earlier discussion of ethical issues might have allowed him to work through his concerns and to continue as a case officer.

Dissent and discussion are the lifeblood of the DI. "Speaking truth to power" depends upon a vigorous effort to find the truth, and high-quality analysis is as much the product of open intellectual discourse as it is of diligent research. While none of the DI employees I interviewed suggested that there has been a conscious attempt to stifle debate within the directorate, a significant number did raise concerns about the unintended effects of the "constant need to please the customer" on the free flow of ideas. Their primary concern on this point was that the current emphasis on producing analysis that speaks with one voice and reflects consensus increasingly leads to "group think" and a watered-down analytic product.

Several analysts I spoke with lamented the "demise of the footnote" as a means of making dissent visible to the customer, thereby increasing his or her options for action or further inquiry. A number of others suggested that the relative absence of dissent in the directorate's analytic products reflects a decrease in dissent within the DI itself. As evidence of this, they pointed to the "drying up" of internal publications devoted to the expression of dissent and to the decreased use of competitive analysis. One young analyst suggested that this is chiefly a result of shortened production time lines. "You always have to fight the idea," he said, "that alternative views slow down the process."

A number of individuals in the DS&T pointed to the same muting of debate and reluctance to receive bad news in their directorate. One such individual, who defined scientific integrity as "a willingness to be challenged and a willingness to grow," felt particularly strongly about the subject. "Scientific integrity is bankrupt at CIA," he told me. "People do not like being challenged and consider a request to see the proof behind an assertion to be aggressive behavior." Another manager from the directorate echoed this concern when she told me that "some people in the S&T avoid challenges by hiding behind the excuse that 'you do not have enough information to challenge me on this.'"

Several DS&T employees suggested that this lack of vigorous debate leads to an overreliance on contractors' judgment in making crucial decisions about support for R&D programs. Another scientist in the directorate said the absence of debate leads to "a cultural arrogance that builds what is technologically neat but does not focus on customer needs."

MISDEFINING FAILURE AND THE FEAR OF TAKING RISKS

The CIA has long had a "can-do" approach to its mission, characterized in particular by a refusal to accept failure as an end result even in the most difficult of situations. Every employee I interviewed was justifiably proud of this tradition. A significant number of them, however, also suggested that this unwillingness to tolerate failure has a negative side as well. They argued that when people fear they will be blamed for anything short of an optimal outcome, pressure is created to do whatever it takes to achieve that outcome, including cutting ethical corners and covering up mistakes. By contrast, if it is understood and accepted that failure often results not from dereliction of duty or lack of effort, there is less chance that people will feel the need to compromise their integrity when things go badly. In this sense, they argued, failure should be seen as part of the normal cost of doing business. One senior DI manager put it this way: "If you have not been wrong lately, you are not doing your job."

The people who made this point were quick to note, however, that accepting failure does not mean there should be no accountability for negative results. They insisted that ethical lapses and poor performance must have very real consequences. But they believed that failure should be regarded primarily as an opportunity for learning and growth, rather than as cause for punishment and permanent stigmatization. Thus, even though failure must have consequences, it must finally be followed by forgiveness. In other words, it must be understood that, as management guru Peter Senge puts it, "Screwups will not always be hanging over the offender's head."[6] Many I interviewed pointed to fear of just such stigmatizing screwup as the force behind what they described as the "risk averse" environment that exists across the Agency today.

From people in the DI, I heard of a "tyranny of reputation," in which "a bad call can stay with you for three years," greatly influencing future work assignments and opportunities for advancement. Others suggested that at times potentially valuable lines of analysis do not reach policymakers because "today there is little willingness to dare to be wrong." They saw the same force behind changes in the language used in intelligence products, pointing to the increased reliance on what they describe as "fudge words" that allow analysts to hedge their bets in place of more direct phrases like "in our judgment" and "we believe."

In the DO, disciplinary actions recently taken by senior management regarding operations in Guatemala in the 1980s have clearly sent powerful but conflicting messages about what constitutes failure in the world of operations. Some saw the management decisions in the Guatemala case as an instance of people "finally being held appropriately accountable for horribly bad tradecraft." Many others, however, felt that the overriding lesson of the Guatemala episode is that "accountability is a codeword for political expediency"—that whatever displeases senior management can be deemed a failure and cause for disciplinary action. Many on both sides of the divide agreed that amidst this confusion about the real nature of accountability, as one manager put it, "Nobody is taking risks out there."

In the DS&T, I heard from several individuals that managers often seek a "guarantee of success" before committing resources to a project. The cost of this tendency, they argued, is that many of the most difficult projects with potentially the greatest payoffs do not receive serious consideration.

PROMOTION AND PERFORMANCE APPRAISAL

Almost without exception, the people I interviewed—including senior managers—agreed that it is in the area of promotion and performance appraisal that management most "walks the talk" on ethics and integrity. Are people actually rewarded for integrity, or chiefly for effectiveness more narrowly defined, such as the ability to get a job done quickly and without flaps? The best managers do both, and I heard numerous stories of such people at the CIA.

But many I interviewed also described a long tradition at the Agency of promoting people who have demonstrated effectiveness *at the expense of integrity*. Most suggested that this was because the system did not ask or encourage them to do otherwise. As one manager in the DS&T told me, "A manager's old role was to spend money fast. Getting the system done on cost and on schedule was everything. This is what you were rewarded for, and management ignored the piles of bodies left from someone's rise."

In the DO, I frequently heard about the legacy of the "numbers game" that led to "case officering other case officers" and "running ops" against each other because people had no incentive to work together against a target. Others shared stories of "management by intimidation" and "treating our employees like assets." This management style did not inspire much devotion or sincere commitment from those subjected to it. "We need people you want to follow out of the trench," a young DO officer told me. "A lot of the people I have worked for we wanted to *throw* out of the trench."

A significant number of those I spoke with suggested that, despite current efforts to improve the quality of Agency management, integrity and ethical behavior continue to receive too little emphasis in determining who will be promoted. One of the people I interviewed expressed this view more strongly than others: "People today are getting promoted who have done things I would never do," she said, "and everybody knows it."

When I raised this issue with senior managers, they acknowledged that it has been a problem, but pointed out that in making promotion decisions managers often have more information about an individual than the rest of the workforce. This allows them to look broadly at that individual's entire career, rather than "extrapolating from possibly isolated ethical lapses to decide that the person is fundamentally corrupt."

While this may be the case, to a certain extent perception is what matters here, as employees take their cues about what behavior is rewarded in the organization from their reading of how top managers got where they are. Given this, managers should understand that they cannot "start over" with integrity once they become managers; to a great extent, the most powerful message has already been sent.

Senior management may at times underestimate the symbolic power of promotion decisions, and several of those I interviewed recommended that an effort be made to measure the "hallway reputations" of people in order to make issues of integrity a larger factor in promotion decisions. Others, however, pointed out the difficulty of accurately measuring something so intangible. In both cases, people agreed on the need for management to send clear signals on the issue. "If people are going to be promoted based on integrity," one man argued, "you have got to tell them about it, and then you have to really do it."

Many I interviewed also spoke of a related failure to enforce adequate consequences for conduct *lacking* in integrity. They referred to a tradition of avoiding the task of holding people accountable for even the most egregious breaches of integrity, of "passing the trash," rather than forcing a change in behavior or separation from the organization. They pointed out that often there were good intentions behind this tradition: the Agency sought to protect its own and also had to weigh the troubling security implications of firing a disgruntled employee. Despite these good intentions, however, when managers failed to take action in such cases the wrong message was sent to employees about the organization's real commitment to integrity.

Many of those I interviewed cited this tradition as a welcome casualty of the Aldrich Ames affair, as well as of an era in which tighter budgets do not allow for keeping nonperformers on the payroll. Thus, while I did find widespread concern that integrity and ethical decisionmaking are not yet adequately rewarded at the CIA, I also found a general consensus that their absence is less tolerated than in the past.

A PROGRAM OF ETHICS EDUCATION

This inquiry began with the assertion that an organization should not think of ethics uniquely or even primarily as a problem of training and education. Broadening the issue from ethics to integrity leads to a more productive focus on the institutional structures and management practices that create ethical dilemmas or impede their efficient resolution. Without attention to the challenges to integrity presented by these structures and practices, even the best ethics program is destined to become irrelevant within the larger life of the organization.

That said, a quality program of ethics education is an essential element of an overall strategy for organizational integrity. Some of the lessons learned in the course of this project might serve to inform the development of such a program. In conclusion, I offer a few preliminary suggestions:

- The CIA should grow its own program of ethics education. Because intelligence is a unique field with particular ethical challenges and dilemmas, the use of outside consultants without full clearances will in general be of limited value. One possibility might be to develop a number of "intelligence ethicists," who would first spend several years studying approaches to ethics in the worlds of business, law, medicine, the military, and elsewhere, and who would thereafter be tasked with developing case studies and curriculums that incorporate the best thinking from other fields in ways that apply to the intelligence profession.
- CIA ethics education should present ethics as an evolving framework of values that requires continual thought and attention. It should creatively ask participants to consider the connection between their professional and personal ethics and should push them to think about reasons for differences between the two.
- Ethics education should be presented as something we pursue in our own self-interest, not as a matter of legal compliance or as "punishment" for past misdeeds. It should be discussed as something that makes us better colleagues and managers and more effective as an organization.
- Ethics education for all parts of the Agency should be corporate in nature. Despite the significant differences in mission among the four directorates, the Agency cannot afford to have four separate ethical subcultures.
- A CIA ethics program should encourage students to identify and debate the ideals upon which the Agency's mission is based. Ethics education should include courses in which managers consider the ethics of good management, among them fairness in performance evaluation and promotion, sensitivity to employee needs, openness to dissent, and the acceptance of failure and the commitment to learn from it.
- CIA's program of ethics education should be based on case studies specific to intelligence that illustrate the most difficult issues of right versus right, in which two or more deeply held values come into conflict. Among these conflicting values might be individual advancement versus teamwork; taking risks versus the cost of failure; and customer service versus telling truth to power. Taken together, a carefully prepared group of such studies could help create a framework for thinking about ethics

at the CIA that is based on actual experience and shared values instead of on rules and legal compliance.

- In addition to case studies that focus on the times when bad decisions were made, ethics education at the CIA should celebrate the "heroes of integrity" who have stood by the Agency's core values in the face of pressure. These heroes should include both those who prevailed in the end and those who failed honorably. Ethics education should remind us that our organizational heritage is an ethical one and should also call us to the same high standard.

ETHICS INTERVIEW FORMAT

1. Please agree or disagree with this statement by a career CIA officer: "Espionage is essentially amoral." How do you think about the ethical implications of your job?
2. What inputs shape your own sense of ethics and morality?
3. What are some examples of ethical dilemmas that you or your colleagues have faced?
4. To what degree do the Agency's standards and policies give you practical guidance on the ethical issues you face in the course of your work? Which specific policies would you be likely to look to for such guidance?
5. When confronted with an issue that has ethical implications, what decisionmaking process do you go through to reach a decision?
6. In what ways does the structure of this organization reward or hinder ethical decisionmaking?
7. In your experience, is raising ethical concerns or objections with supervisors about Agency policies or programs encouraged or discouraged?
8. Is making ethically sound decisions a factor in determining who is promoted and who receives performance awards?
9. How are we as an organization and as individual employees held accountable for ethical behavior? What could be done to improve such accountability?
10. What degree of importance would you say senior management places on ethics and integrity? What leads you to this conclusion?
11. Have we become more or less "ethical" as an organization during the time you have been with the Agency? If you have noticed a difference, what do you think has driven this change?
12. What, if anything, would you like to see done to improve or reinforce the ethical climate in the Agency today?

NOTES

1. Lynn Sharp Paine, "Managing for Organizational Integrity," *Harvard Business Review*, March-April 1994, p. 106.

2. Ibid.

3. Rushworth Kidder, *How Good People Make Tough Choices* (New York: William Morrow and Company, Inc., 1995).

4. Arthur Applbaum, "Professional Detachment: The Executioner of Paris," *Harvard Law Review* 109, No. 2 (1995), pp. 474–486.

5. Quoted in Peter Senge, *The Fifth Discipline: The Art and Practice of the Learning Organization* (New York: Doubleday/Currency, 1990), p. 226.

6. Ibid., p. 300.

5

Bungee Jumping off the Moral Highground
Ethics of Espionage in the Modern Age

Tony Pfaff

A fundamental tenet of American military training inculcated in our cadets from the various commissioning sources is the credo that we as serving officers are not allowed to lie, cheat, or steal, or tolerate those who do. Nonetheless, graduates of that and similar institutions have tolerated the presence of the intelligence community and the moral boundaries that it is perceived as crossing. In fact, not only have they tolerated it, they have valued the courage the members of the intelligence community have shown and the contributions they have made to ensuring national security in defense of American interests at home and abroad. But, since September 11th the boundaries of that community have been questioned and the effectiveness of their methods reassessed as the world comes to terms with the largest act of terrorism in modern history.

But not only has the effectiveness of the agencies been questioned, but also the ethics as well. There is a great deal of dissatisfaction within the various intelligence agencies, as well as the public it serves, that they have been restrained by well-intentioned but excessive policies. These policies, as the arguments go, may have prevented these agencies from doing much harm, but also, in light of recent events, prevented them from doing much good as well. Thus, these restraints are also being closely scrutinized. There is much talk that this it is now time to take the gloves off. Thus it is imperative as these agencies review their methods that they review their ethics as well. It makes no sense, in defense of justice, to do things that are unjust. When agents of a government which professes to champion justice ignore its demands they undermine the very enterprise they claim to undertake. Such bungee jumping off the moral high ground is nonsensical and self-defeating and needs to be resisted.

The purpose of this paper is to consider the ethical demands of the intelligence profession and then consider what it means to serve ethically as intelligence professionals. In order to limit its scope, I will focus exclusively on intelligence gathering as opposed to other elements of espionage such as assassination and political manipulation. There has been a great deal more written about the latter than the former, and since gathering intelligence is a precondition for many of these other activities, it makes sense to start there.

Like military professionals, intelligence professionals must sometimes do things that are morally prohibited outside the professional context. But just as there are moral boundaries on the kinds of activities military professionals are morally permitted to engage in, so too are there boundaries for intelligence professionals. Military professionals sometimes must kill people and destroy property to accomplish their mission. Intelligence professionals must sometimes deceive and harm in order to accomplish theirs. The boundary for these activities lies in their purpose. In defending human life it may be necessary to take it, but it makes no sense to devalue it. *Thus intelligence professionals, like military ones, must always take care not to act in such a way that disregards the notion that individual human life and dignity are valuable for their own sake and that people should be treated as an end in themselves and not merely a means.*

THE ETHICAL CHALLENGES OF INTELLIGENCE GATHERING

Is tolerance of the intelligence community—one that is perceived as crossing the moral barriers that constrain other military professionals—a case of hypocrisy? Some would categorically argue that it is not. Nevertheless it is worth noting that in recent years, evidence of disquiet within and outside the profession has been apparent particularly in relation to major debates regarding human rights discourse in a global age. In the wake of the ending of the Cold War the value of such an approach to national security was reassessed, and the intelligence community feared its days were numbered. The community was further undermined by the demands of the New World Order and economic primacy of U.S. interests rather than the ideological battles of the past. In addition, many intelligence agents have quit the profession because of moral objections they have not only to the *way* they were required to carry out their duties as a professional, but also sometimes to the profession itself. Not only have they felt that the deceiving and harming they have done in service to their country have corrupted their integrity, they feel this corruption is exacerbated by the "cloudy moral purpose" their agency serves.[1]

But taking the "high road" has its own share of difficulties. In 1929, an outraged Secretary of State Henry Stimson closed down the U.S. State Department's only crypt-analysis organization (known as the Black Chamber) that had provided invaluable service over the previous ten years, deciphering thousands of messages from dozens of nations. In his view, "gentlemen do not read each other's mail."[2] And while this action did not end American crypt-analysis efforts, it did much to cause them to become poorly organized and operated. One of the results of this was an otherwise avoidable surprise attack on Pearl Harbor, which claimed a number of lives which otherwise may not have been lost. In fact, the irony of the situation was that the same Henry Stimson, who had by then become Secretary of War, found himself ordering the reorganization and revitalization of the crypt-analysis organizations in an effort to make them more efficient.[3]

This suggests that answering ethical questions is just as important to the profession as answering the pragmatic ones. In fact, failure to come to some resolution on the former may make it difficult, if not impossible, to answer the latter. Thus, the thrust of my paper will focus on the nature of the ethical debate in a modern age—one shaped by dynamic shifts in global politics which impact on the American national interest with significant repercussions for the way in which we live. This is the challenge of any professional ethic, particularly in those rare professions where its members must sometimes harm others in the course of fulfilling their obligation to society. It should not be permissible to casually violate one moral principle in an attempt to uphold another. But in finding a place to draw that line we must be careful not to place it so high that the institution cannot function, nor so low that any course of action can be rationalized. Such a task is made more difficult in the post–September 11th environment where the moral debate surrounding such issues as proportionate response, the war on terror, and the inevitable civilian casualty cost dominate the American political agenda.

Service in the intelligence profession sometimes involves doing things that in other times and places most would agree would be horribly immoral. Sometimes intelligence officers must deceive, harm, steal from, and even kill (or cause to be killed) others in the course of doing their jobs. But good intelligence officers do not do so in such a way that treats the human targets of their operations merely as means, but in such a way that respects them as ends. But with these challenges in mind, we need to first consider whether this is, in fact, possible.

ETHICAL INTELLIGENCE WORK:
AN OLD-FASHIONED OXYMORON?

Perhaps one of the oldest, and most tiresome, jokes in the world is that military intelligence is an oxymoron. Perhaps not as old, but certainly as tiresome, is the observation that the same can be said of ethical espionage. The implication of this is that no matter how noble the cause there is no way to conduct espionage in a moral fashion. This perception is so widespread, a number of agents have left the service because they have problems with the "cloudy moral purpose" the institution serves.[4] Part of this perception arises from the fact that intelligence professionals, like military ones, have to do things that are, outside the professional context, morally repugnant. Intelligence professionals must sometime lie, cheat, steal, and harm others in order to fulfill their role as spies. But often the public fails to consider the demands of the profession when making moral judgments about its activities. So just as some of the public has expressed moral outrage at the deaths of civilians in Afghanistan as a result of military action, many have also expressed moral outrage at some of the activities of intelligence professionals. But just as not all civilians' deaths as a result of military action are unjustified, it is not the case that every time an intelligence professional harms or deceives someone he has committed a moral wrong, even though the public may deem it so.

Another part of this perception arises out of the fact that intelligence professionals, on occasion, do in fact do things that are morally repugnant even in the professional context. In the case of intelligence gathering, extreme forms of torture, betraying an informant, even in order to serve otherwise legitimate goals, serve as good examples.[5] While some of this disregard for morality can be dismissed as character flaws of individual agents, much of it can be traced back to misunderstandings regarding the nature of professional ethics which, as my former students clearly demonstrated, there are numerous ways to do. However these misunderstandings, though I am labeling them as such, represent viewpoints that are still widely accepted.

A first kind of misunderstanding can roughly be labeled "moral nihilism." This view holds that all moral claims are meaningless, even those that are supposed to hold between individuals. I do not propose to spend a great deal of time on this point since it does not in fact represent a misunderstanding of ethics, but rather a rejection of it. But, a misunderstanding arises when someone who holds this view argues that someone else has done him a moral harm. Thus someone who argues that activities designed to destabilize a democratically elected but unfriendly government are beyond moral discourse but the attacks of September 11 represent a great evil is practicing an extreme form of cognitive dissonance. One simply cannot reasonably hold both views. Given the rather extensive use of moral language by the President, as well as others, in pursuit of this new war, such a position seems to be untenable for those who wage it. The national security strategy itself underscores the U.S.'s commitment to protecting "basic human rights."[6]

A second kind of misunderstanding can be labeled "realism." Briefly stated, this position holds that ethics has no place in international affairs. This idea is most famously argued by Hans Morgenthau, who argued that the statesman's, and by extension the intelligence professional whose activities support the statesman's, highest duty is to ensure national survival. When national survival is really at stake, this may in fact be the correct view (see the section on Supreme Emergency). But in the world of international politics, survival is often conflated with being stronger than the opponent is—even if it is only a potential opponent. Thus anything that gives the nation an advantage is therefore necessary to survival and thus supersedes any obligation there might be between nations.[7] This is how words like "national survival" come to really mean "national security," which comes to mean "national interest."

In this view any advantage can be pursued against any target—ally or enemy—regardless of the moral harm done. Thus, if we placed the end of national security as our highest end, there would be no acts that would be intrinsically wrong, regardless of the harm caused. Furthermore, given that each state has the same moral obligation to provide for its citizens' security, then the actions of Aldrich Ames and Richard Hannsen, who betrayed friendly agents to a foreign government, would not be intrinsically immoral. Intrinsically inconvenient, perhaps, for Americans and some Russians at least, but because these actions enhanced the security of Russia, they would not be immoral in and of themselves. This view does offer some limitations as it does prohibit any activity that would not serve the national interest. But what it does not do is render any particular action as morally prohibited. Instead it introduces a sliding scale upon which to weigh moral judgments regarding the activities of intelligence professionals. The greater the threat, the fewer things that are prohibited in pursuit of defeating it.

In fact, this idea has been quite influential in the intelligence community for a long time. A report to President Eisenhower in 1954 urged the U.S. to employ "more ruthless methods" than its enemies in order to prevent the spread of communism, then the greatest threat America had ever confronted. Even though the report conceded this was a "repugnant philosophy" that violated the American concept of fair play, the authors of the report nonetheless felt these measures were warranted given the seriousness and immediacy of the threat.[8]

A third kind of misunderstanding is offered by R.V. Jones, an intelligence professional during World War II and following that a noted scholar of the profession. This approach represents a greater limitation than the two above in that it recognizes some kind of limit besides utility in the pursuit of national objectives. Jones offers the following test: "that is whether those approving them [acts deemed unethical] feel they could defend their decisions before the public."[9] This test is insufficient, however, in terms of offering any kind of comprehensive guidance for the intelligence community. For example, many colleagues praised Helms for lying to Congress regarding CIA activities in Chile in the 1970s. But even after his conviction many colleagues within the Agency as well as others hailed him as a hero.[10] Thus he felt he could defend himself before the public, and though he failed with some, he succeeded with others. Thus such an approach remains problematic, with decision-making remaining within the intelligence realm and other mechanisms of accountability and transparency vis-à-vis the decision-making process absent.

A fourth kind of misunderstanding that is offered by the same author is the idea of "minimum trespass." This criterion, roughly modeled after the military's concept of minimum force, states that intelligence operations "should be conducted with the minimum trespass against national and individual rights."[11] While this criterion may restrain some intelligence professionals in the pursuit of minor goals or less important information, it is again insufficient for a comprehensive professional ethic. The problem with this criterion is that the concept "minimum" is notoriously vague. Given the importance of any particular piece of information to national security, there is, in principle, no act that would be impermissible in the pursuit of it. Thus in the presence of a great enough threat, this position becomes indistinguishable from realism. For example, given the enormous destructiveness of the activities of Richard Hannsen and Aldrich Ames to U.S. national security, it would have been impermissible, under this criterion, to torture or threaten to torture members of their families—or families of their Russian handlers—in order to stop or minimize the damage they caused. But though this criterion does not, as written, rule out such activities, it is interesting to note that the author who offers it does.[12]

In these views of ethics, there is no meaningful place to draw the line. There are few, if any actions, policies, rules, or institutions that would be morally prohibited either because such claims are meaningless, too subjective, or too vague. It does no good to establish moral criteria if any kind of action may be permitted given a particular set of circumstances. But this is not sufficient to dismiss them. One may plausibly argue that there is in fact no such thing as morality. One may also plausibly argue that the national interest is the highest good, and there are no limits on the kinds of things that can be done in its pursuit. But for this to be plausible, someone who holds this view must reject the idea that human life, and any rights we may want to associate with it, are valuable in and of themselves.

Thus, the problem with these views of ethics is that reasonable people cannot hold them and hold that human life and liberty are fundamentally valuable for their own sake. Yet holding at least some of these things valuable is fundamental to any form of government reasonable people would consent to. So in pursuit of the defense of these values, it makes no sense to violate them. To do so is to make the claim that it is not human life that is valuable, but rather particular lives, by virtue of their membership of a particular state. It is arbitrary, however, to make such a claim given that such membership is an accident of birth. If this were the foundation of our moral approach, then we would be right back to the "anything goes" morality we presumably oppose in our defense of the values of a democratic state.

ETHICAL FOUNDATIONS OF INTELLIGENCE GATHERING

Fundamental to most moral approaches is the idea that human life has a special dignity and value that is worth preserving even at the expense of self-interest. From this belief it follows, as Charles Beitz notes in his classic work *Political Theory and International Relations*, "that there are occasions when we have reasons to override the demands of self interest by taking a moral point of view towards human affairs."[13] This requires, says Beitz, that we regard the world and our actions in it from the standpoint of one person among many rather than as a particular person with particular interests. This position, much like John Rawls' concept of *reflective equilibrium*, requires us to choose course of actions, policies, rules, and institutions on grounds that would be acceptable to any agent who was impartial among the competing interests involved.[14]

What this also means is that we cannot hold beliefs about these actions, policies, rules, and institutions that are mutually exclusive, that is they cannot be held at the same time in the same way. For example, I cannot rationally hold that the institution of a police force is necessary to protect me and my interests and then hold that I am not subject to the laws they enforce. It devalues others relative to me. Thus a necessary condition for any moral approach is that it is rational, that it is not possible to hold two mutually exclusive moral beliefs in the same way at the same time. This then underscores what is so objectionable about certain kinds of intelligence gathering operations. Few people will honestly admit that they like being blackmailed, extorted, betrayed, or even simply "monitored." No one likes to be *used*. But this is not quite true. In fact, we use people every day, often in ways they want to be used. Most teachers want and expect students to use them as teachers. Employees want and expect to be used in the roles for which they were hired. Thus it does not seem to be a violation of their dignity to do so.

Perhaps some teachers and employees do not want to be used as such, but it would be unreasonable for them not to expect it given that they have chosen, or at least accepted, these professions. Thus in resolving ethical problems in intelligence gathering we have to learn what it means to use people in a reasonable, as opposed to unreasonable way. But it is wrong for students to threaten teachers to give them good grades. It is wrong for employers not to pay a fair wage. Each of these examples involves treating people merely as things, affording them no more respect than one would any other tool. When we treat people this way, we are treating them merely as a means to an end, and not as ends in and of themselves. Now, most of what we do is a means to some ends. We go to work to make money, we make money to achieve a certain standard of living, and we achieve a certain standard of living to be happy. Happiness is, therefore, the end, and all of these actions are good or bad depending on whether and to what degree they make us happy, whatever that consists in.

According to German Philosopher Immanuel Kant, however, the ability of human beings to act morally is itself an end. Specifically, it is the end, or purpose, of morality. That ability is what gives us dignity, and to rob someone of it is wrong. So expressed simply, what it means to treat people as an end is to respect their dignity as human beings and, importantly, to not limit their capacity for rational thought and thus their capacity to act morally, which Kant saw as essentially synonymous.[15] It is of course true that not everyone acts morally, but this does not mean we are permitted to treat bad people merely as means. But what it does mean is that we hold people responsible for their actions. In fact, Kant saw punishing wrongdoing as a means of upholding human dignity rather than a way of undermining it. Furthermore, because we cannot know from its effects whether a will is good, we cannot be sure whether or not any particular will is good. Consequently, in order to not omit any beings with good wills, we must treat all rational beings and therefore all humans as an end in themselves.[16]

Because human life has a special dignity and value we afford it a special status by claiming that everyone has a right to it. Why this is the case is easy to understand, and hard to prove. Regarding rights, Walzer notes, "if they are not natural, then we have invented them, but natural or invented, they are a palpable feature of our moral world."[17] This is so because we value our life and the liberty to set for ourselves how we are going to live it. The fact that we value our lives in this way stands as a reason for anyone not to interfere with it. Since this reason applies to anyone, it applies to everyone and thus it applies to us since we are part of everyone.[18] Thus it does not matter if other individuals do not value their lives in this way, the fact that we do gives us reason to proceed as those others do. It is not that we simply hold our life and liberty to be intrinsically valuable—that is no better than self-interest and, if Beitz is right, not sufficient to count as an ethical approach. For this view to count as ethical it must be that we hold the rights of all persons to be intrinsically valuable. But rights entail obligations. Thus, if human life is so valuable that people have a right to it, then someone else has an obligation to preserve it. What is not so easy to see, however, is where this obligation falls. Certainly it is easy to see that this results in the negative obligation not to harm others, which clearly falls on everyone. But it also entails a positive obligation to prevent harm to others and it is not always clear where this should fall.

Sometimes, however, it is clear where it should fall. Parents, for example, have a positive obligation to preserve their children's lives even if that means taking special risks to do so. They incur this obligation by virtue of what it means to be a parent, an arrangement they voluntarily entered. This arrangement gives them authority over their children, but in addition to gaining this authority they incur the obligations commensurate with it. The purpose of this authority is so that they may raise healthy and happy children. Thus parents who use their authority to exploit and abuse their children are bad parents. But I am not arguing that the parent-state analogy be taken too far. The state does not always know best in the same way good parents usually do. Thus the legitimacy of policies, rules, and institutions a state creates depends to a great extent on the consent of its citizens. The policies and rules of parents on the other hand do not require the consent of the child for their legitimacy.

Thus I am not arguing that a state is some kind of parent with a broad mandate to do what it "thinks best" for (or to, for that matter) the citizenry. What I am arguing is that people who possess authority have obligations that come with that authority. What those obligations are depend on the kind of authority they have. I am also not arguing, as Walzer does, that states have necessarily rights by virtue of the fact that individuals do, but rather that by virtue of these individual rights, states have an obligation to preserve them.[19] This obligation of the state may roughly be labeled "national security" to distinguish it from "national interest." Things done in the interest of national security are things done so that the state may fulfill its moral obligations, things citizens have a right to expect; things done in the national interest are those things that benefit the citizens of a state without them necessarily having a right to such benefits.[20] Thus Morgenthau was partially right. Those who serve the state do have an obligation to ensure national security. But when that gets translated into specific action, it is not always in all circumstances the only thing they must consider.

This is because fulfilling this obligation can sometimes conflict with other persons' right to life and liberty. The current War on Terrorism serves as a good example. In an effort to render the Al-Qaeda network incapable of committing any further harm, the U.S. forces have harmed others who were innocent of the crimes of the terrorists. Additionally, in an effort to reduce the vulnerability of the American people to further terrorist attacks, Attorney General John Ashcroft has proposed using military tribunals, which may rely on secret evidence, to prosecute people suspected of being associated with terrorist organizations.

It is important to note that though the debate regarding these issues is framed as a tension between these competing obligations, few advocates of either side claim the other position should not be considered. On one side few people argue that the U.S. Government should do nothing. On the other, the U.S. military has taken great care to minimize the number of civilian casualties and the proponents of detaining noncitizens on secret evidence assure us that basic civil liberties will be upheld and that they will be prosecuted fairly, even if secretly.[21] Thus there are limits to how nations may go about fulfilling their obligation, of course, because nations also have obligations to people of other nations.[22]

To fulfil their obligation to their citizens, most states establish standing militaries in order to deter, and failing to deter, defeat, any attack against that nation. Militaries are permitted, in the course of fulfilling the state's obligation, to do things that outside this context would be immoral, like kill people and destroy property. But this is only permitted if the moral criteria of *jus ad bellum* are fulfilled, and typically this means that such force is permitted only in response to an act of aggression against one's nation or another nation.[23]

To fulfill their obligations to the state and its citizens, militaries require timely and accurate intelligence. Thus much of the justification for the deceiving and harming that intelligence professionals must do in the course of supporting a military at war will be justified by the same sets of reasons that justify the killing and destruction that militaries must do in the course of fighting the war. But it is also the case that much intelligence gathering is aimed at determining the nature of a threat before any act of aggression has been committed. To do this, intelligence professionals often cast a wide net, sometimes directed at people and nations which do not and never will represent any kind of threat. Thus, there is a dis-analogy between the activities of the military professional in war and the activities of the intelligence professional in peace—even if those activities are intended to support the future wartime activities of the military, which often they are not. The only just targets of military operations are those who have proven themselves a threat by committing an act of aggression. But to prepare for this, intelligence professionals must target people who may never be a threat. Thus, we are left with the question if intelligence professionals outside the context of war are permitted to engage in activities that are otherwise immoral.

For this to be the case, such intelligence activities would have to be essential to the nation's ability to provide for the defense of its citizens and their way of life. In some ways this point may seem trivial: by providing timely and accurate information on other nations' capabilities and intents, intelligence professionals give military leaders a greater capacity for developing weapons and strategies necessary for defeating any potential enemy. They also give political leaders and diplomats greater capacity for choosing courses of actions that promote peace and security—usually the best way to provide for a nation's defense.[24]

But this theoretical justification for peacetime intelligence activities has a practical limit. Espionage is itself a kind of act of aggression, and is thus a kind of double-edged sword. When one nation conducts espionage against another it may learn something of the other's intentions and capabilities, but it also signals distrust and suspicion. Distrust and suspicion, rather than fostering peace and security, fosters instability and conflict. One need only consider the case of Jonathan Pollard, the American intelligence officer who was convicted of spying for Israel, to see the dire effects of undermining trust among allies. After his conviction, relations between Israel and the U.S. became quite strained. When former President Clinton refused to release him, Netanyahu reneged on a promise he made at the Wye Accords and set 200 Palestinian criminals free—people the Palestinians themselves did not want free—as opposed to the political prisoners he promised to free during the negotiations.[25] This was a contributing factor to the failure of the Accords later on as it undermined the already very tenuous trust the Palestinians felt toward the Israelis.

The problem for the intelligence professional in peacetime is determining who may be a legitimate target against whom such activities may be directed. What justifies the actions of the military and its supporting intelligence activities in wartime is the fact that an act of aggression has occurred. In peacetime, however, such an act of aggression has not been committed (by definition). But absent an act of aggression, there is no justification for the destruction and killing the military does, much less the deceiving and harming by the intelligence profession. For intelligence gathering activities in peacetime to be justifiable, there needs to be an analogous "act of aggression" that would give the nation that seeks to obtain these secrets, in some sense, a "right" to them. When a nation withholds information that is important to the security of another nation, it is knowingly, if not intentionally putting that nation's citizens at risk. This, in effect, is an act of aggression (though certainly not an act of war) and thus they subject themselves to intelligence operations of other nations.[26]

Thus what gives a nation a right to this information is that if it did not possess it, its national security would be severely compromised and its citizens would be placed at great risk. Conversely, this means that it would be wrong to conduct intelligence operations to obtain secrets that do not enhance national security. Thus, as Drexel Godfrey points out in his 1978 article in *Foreign Affairs*, "Ethics and Intelligence," it is wrong to deceive and harm in order to obtain secrets from Ruritania simply to know more about Ruritania than the Ruritanians do.[27] But what intelligence professionals do not know in advance is where those secrets are or whether they are, in fact, essential to national security. Thus, intelligence professionals tend to cast a wide net in order to uncover this information. But just as wide net fishing does a lot more harm than good (most of a catch is often thrown back as waste) so to do intelligence gathering activities run the risk of doing a lot more moral harm than good. [28]

This then gives us a limit, as well as a justification, for peacetime espionage. Just as the law enforcement officials, for example, must conduct surveillance activities against some private citizens in order to protect the rest, so must intelligence professionals conduct intelligence operations against other nations. But just as it is wrong for the law enforcement officials to tap a private citizen's phones or otherwise pry into her personal life on the off chance she might commit a crime, it is wrong for intelligence professionals to conduct certain kinds of intelligence gathering activities against a nation, or individuals within that nation, on the off chance they might represent a threat.

However, just as a private citizen can engage in activities which legitimately make him a suspect and thus a legitimate target of surveillance by law enforcement officials; nations, and other organizations, can also engage in activities that make them legitimate targets of espionage. And just as the private citizen can be the legitimate subject of surveillance, but not arrest, states as well as certain other organizations can be the legitimate subjects of espionage, but not military action, because of the threat they may represent. Determining what kinds of activities make another nation a legitimate target of espionage is going to be a matter of judgment and will be very hard to list or codify. Such judgments will depend on a number of factors and require a great deal of experience to make. Fortunately, listing them is not necessary for the purposes of this paper. The point here is simply that not all kinds of espionage are permissible against any state. As the Pollard case suggests, disregarding this moral point may have bad practical consequences. This then gives us our first place to draw the line. It is wrong to conduct espionage against nations that give no indications of posing any threat. What may pass as an indication may be broadly or narrowly defined—again that is not the subject of this paper. But given evidence of a threat, what remains to be discussed is what kinds of things might be morally permitted, as well as prohibited, to uncover it.

DRAWING THE LINE: OPEN SOURCES

Not all intelligence gathering is morally objectionable. A great deal of intelligence gathering work is done by analyzing open source material and discovering connections that might enable intelligence professionals to draw conclusions about a particular nation's activities or intentions. Such intelligence gathering is no more objectionable than someone reading a newspaper and then drawing conclusions about how a politician will vote on the issue of raising taxes. When political leaders make speeches or issue press releases it is reasonable to conclude they expect, even desire, that others read them. If they place no restrictions on who has access to the information, then there is nothing wrong in obtaining it and then drawing conclusions based on it. The conclusions based on it could be wrong, but this is a pragmatic matter, not an ethical one.

Now it could be the case that someone "leaked" the information and that it is not something the politician would want made public. It may also be the case that the informant leaked the information for morally wrong reasons. For example, a politician's close friend may betray certain secrets about his campaign strategy to a journalist in exchange for money—an act I take to be immoral.[29] But though that information enters the public domain immorally, once it is "out there" there is nothing wrong with obtaining it. It may be wrong to betray a friend, but it is not wrong to read a paper. So once it is made public, one has done nothing wrong by knowing it even though the informant should not have divulged it, as long as one is not the person who encouraged the informant to do so.

Furthermore, depending on the information, I do nothing wrong by acting on it. It is possible to commit a moral wrong by voting for specious reasons. But assuming this information is relevant to the campaign then I do nothing wrong if I vote based on it, even though it entered the public domain by means of an act of betrayal. Thus intelligence professionals do nothing wrong by accepting and drawing conclusions based on information gained from open sources. Nor should these kinds of sources be easily dismissed. Furthermore, it suggests that there are alternatives to conducting espionage against illegitimate targets. Blackmail, extortion, or simple deception may be the most expedient ways to gain information, but not always the most moral. Thus while certain methods may serve short-term interests, when used in a morally inappropriate fashion, they will rarely serve long-term interests. Though interest is not the sole determinant of moral behavior, it is interesting to note that behaving badly rarely does anyone any good. There have to be good reasons to use people in a manner they should not reasonably expect to be used.

DRAWING THE LINE: THE MORAL
BOUNDARIES OF INTELLIGENCE GATHERING

What this analysis suggests is that the Kantian notion of treating people as ends and not merely as means will be an important part of the line to draw when considering ethical courses of actions in intelligence gathering. But as stated before, this is too vague to offer any meaningful practical guidance. It cannot be that it is wrong to treat people a certain way just because they do not expect it. Thus it remains to be shown what they should reasonably expect.

Here it is important to introduce the idea of *shared expectations*.[30] By holding secrets, especially secrets which affect the well-being of people in other nations, nations willfully (and arguably rationally—I'm not arguing that there is anything wrong in keeping secrets) engage in a form of low level conflict. When states engage in conflict with other states, it would be irrational for them to expect that other states not take actions to protect their interests. Certainly not all actions are permissible, but equally certainly some are.

To further explain the moral significance of "shared expectations," a sports analogy is useful. When football teams take the field they both expect the other to play as hard they can, taking what advantages they can as long as the rules are not broken.[31] Thus if one team has a weak quarterback, the other team is free to exploit that fact, even if the other team would prefer they did not. Furthermore, the teams are free to deceive or otherwise manipulate each other as to what their next play is even though this is clearly using them as a means. But because they agree to be on the field, both teams should expect such deceptions and manipulations. Thus they are also being respected as ends, since nothing interferes with their choice to play the game. But the opposing team would be remiss if it did not do all it could to limit or manipulate the choices the other team can make *during* the game. So the fact that one team is completely overwhelmed by some deception is not the fault of the deceiving team, but of the deceived team.

But the fact that an expectation is shared is not sufficient to justify it. In Bill Watterson's cartoon *Calvin and Hobbes*, the title characters play a game called "Calvin Ball" which is played by changing the shared expectations of the players. When someone has the ball, he makes a new rule. Thus changing shared expectations is a shared expectation of the game. But there is nothing that prevents the rules from being contradictory and self-defeating and as a result, the game quickly devolves into chaos. In one game, Calvin scores a point by changing sides three times only to have that point added to Hobbes's score; he then changed sides as soon as he got the ball. I have no idea who won.

Thus there must be a further limit of what can count as shared expectation. It must also be reasonable. What counts as reasonable is found in the nature of the game itself. In football, the nature and purpose of the game provide those limits. That there are only two sides, one field, a ball of a particular shape, limit the range of rules that may be imposed. Furthermore, the purpose of the game is to score points by crossing a line and thus there will be a natural limit on the different ways to go about this that are not self-defeating. For example, it would not be rational to allow a team to conceal the ball for an indeterminate period. If this were the case, then the team that scored first could do so and thus end the game—perhaps only minutes or seconds after it started. This makes the game much less of a contest than those who play it (and especially those who watch it) intend for it to be. Thus it would irrational for them to adopt such a rule, even if they both agreed to it in advance. *Thus what justifies a shared expectation is that it is rational for the members of that profession to hold it—that is it is not self-defeating.* If by holding the expectation one cannot play the game if the other side held that expectation, then one should not hold it. To do so and act on it is the very definition of cheating.

In the field of international relations, these shared expectations are found in treaties, conventions, agreements, and in some cases certain shared beliefs that different societies may hold. The importance of recognizing these is underscored by the following example. In the law of war, it is generally accepted that when one waves a white flag one has agreed to lay down one's arms and cease fighting. In exchange for this agreement, the other side agrees to grant "benevolent quarantine" to the soldiers surrendering. This limitation reduces the amount of misery caused by a war, which is the purpose of these laws in the first place. However, if one side waves the white flag as a means to deceive the other into a false sense of security so that they may get them out in the open in order to kill them, they completely undermine this rule. Often in conflicts where this has occurred even once, it becomes very difficult for other members of the deceiving side, even those who were not part of the original deception, to surrender. In this way, not only the rule but also the very purpose of the law of war is undermined.

Here we also need to introduce the concept of *good faith*.[32] Good faith that the standards will be met is essential to holding them rationally. As the case of false surrendering dramatically shows, if one side does not believe the other will uphold the rule, the rule ceases to be a meaningful part of the "game." Taken to extremes, it becomes impossible to play the game at all since failure makes it impossible for anyone to uphold the rules. In the case of intelligence gathering, failing to act in good faith makes it impossible to engage in such activities and rationally hold that human beings are ends in themselves.

Now of course in the world we are discussing the stakes are quite high and, unlike football, people's lives are at stake, as the Ames and Hannsen cases dramatically point out. But the basic analogy holds. By holding secrets that affect the ability of a state to fulfill its obligations to its citizens, such nations freely agree to "take the field." This, in effect, is an act of aggression (though certainly not an act of war), and thus they subject themselves to intelligence operations of other nations. Thus if they are deceived, for example, it is their fault, and not the fault of the deceiver.

LEGITIMATE TARGETS OF ESPIONAGE

Kinds of States: Espionage against Allies, Neutral, and Hostile States

Before turning to the specific activities associated with intelligence gathering, it is important first to discuss who and what may be legitimate targets of such activities. This analysis makes spying against friendly nations problematic. In fact, the tradition of not spying on allies is so strong that Churchill himself ordered that there would be no espionage against Russia once the German attack had brought them in alliance with Britain.[33] One might reasonably counter that there is no way to determine in advance if a particular nation is harboring secrets which threaten our national security or not without some sort of covert surveillance. Since this is true, this argument is probably sufficient to justify some level of surveillance in a variety of nations, even ones with which we enjoy good relations. But one can conduct many kinds of surveillance without overstepping any moral bounds. The real question is whether it can be permissible to conduct the kind of espionage that involves deceiving, stealing, and other forms of harming against friendly nations.

The problem with such activity is that it undermines the possibility of such friendships and alliances in the first place. It is difficult to maintain a friendship if you hold the expectation that your friend may lie, betray, or otherwise take advantage of you. The same can be said of nations, and the Jonathan Pollard case is a good case in point. Even though he was only passing information the Israelis were entitled to anyway, by virtue of an agreement signed by the two countries, he was convicted, and U.S.-Israeli relations suffered.[34] This sort of activity in turn undermines the conditions for a just peace, which presumably is the moral purpose the intelligence community serves.

A similar problem exists when considering espionage against neutral states. While the nature of this relationship does not make it self-defeating to conduct espionage, it is nonetheless problematic. Espionage is a double-edged sword as it can be considered an act of aggression itself. Thus it has the potential to turn neutral nations into hostile ones. Therefore, any such activity has to be weighed against this possibility. While this is inherently a pragmatic issue, because it has the potential to make the world a little more hostile there is a moral dimension that must be taken into account.

Nations that are openly hostile do not share any expectations that would make espionage, within limits, problematic. As such, considerations regarding whether to conduct such operations are pragmatic ones, though there will be moral considerations regarding how to go about conducting these operations. What remains to be done is to fully develop definitions of allied, neutral, and hostile states as well as what reasonable expectations these relationships entail. But while space does not exist to explore this area in great detail, it does seem that covert operations against even nominally friendly nations must be carefully considered. Thus we have another place to draw our line.

Kinds of Persons

As Nagel notes, it is not fair to target just anyone in war; there must be "something about that person" that justifies it.[35] Thus, just as it not "fair" to tackle a spectator in a football team (even though he is rooting for the opposing team), it is not justifiable to conduct intelligence operations against certain people, even if as citizens of unfriendly or even threatening nations they are legitimate targets of espionage. The football analogy does suggest that other intelligence professionals are legitimate targets of intelligence operations. By entering into the field of intelligence and by accepting the special training this affords they accept the risks associated with it. However, operations against such persons must be limited to that "something about them" that makes them legitimate targets in the first place. Thus, it is permissible to steal information about a weapons program from an enemy agent, but it is not permissible to steal his car (unless, of course, he keeps the information in the car).

But it is not only intelligence professionals who are legitimate objects of espionage. In fact, this analysis suggests that anyone who has information that could put other nations' citizens at risk is a legitimate target. Yet it also follows from this analysis that those who do not possess such secrets are not legitimate targets. Thus, the real question is how wide a net may intelligence professionals cast in order to discover who they are. Clearly there are some people who, by virtue of their profession or role, are likely to harbor such secrets. While who those people are exactly may depend on the nation involved, certain military personnel, scientists, and government officials are good examples of the kinds of people who fit in this category. It should be noted, however, that not any such person might fit into this category. For example, a military officer, because he likely knows about plans and weapons that may represent a threat to another nation, is a legitimate target. A scientist who works in a weapons laboratory or a member of Congress who is on an oversight committee for military or intelligence operations will also be a legitimate target. By knowing they hold such secrets, they have entered the "game."

But a scientist who works on cancer research or a postman, though he works for the government, is not. Nor are family members of people who possess vital information. None of these people are likely to know any secrets by virtue of their position that may represent a threat to the citizens of another nation, and are thus not legitimate targets.[36] But though the postman, scientist, or family member may not be likely to possess some vital piece of information, it is not logically possible that they cannot. This is particularly true of scientists and engineers who may be working on purely civilian projects, but which may have military uses. Similarly with family members and friends of those who do not possess vital information. Exploiting them may be the most expedient way to get information, but it is not the most moral because none of these groups have knowingly and intentionally entered the "game" in the way the other groups have. Because they have not entered the game, it will not be permissible to harm or deceive such people in order to find out if they possess such secrets, much less to discover what those secrets are.

This will not preclude, however, engaging in intelligence gathering activities that do not involve deceiving or harming and it will sometimes be the case that permissible surveillance activities—monitoring public sources of information such as newspapers or journals—will reveal that such a person does in fact know something vital to someone else's national security. In this case, we have a person who has not intentionally entered the game but who has nonetheless become an important source of information that intelligence professionals have an obligation to obtain. Here our football analogy will do us little good. If a fan finds herself somehow in the middle of a football field during a game holding the ball she does not become the legitimate target of a tackle. Instead the game will be suspended long enough for her to return the ball so that the game may be resumed. Furthermore, she is obligated to give the ball up unless it is hers, in which case the players will simply have to find another one.

But in the world of espionage one simply cannot suspend the game. Furthermore, once one has information vital to another nation's security it may not be possible or even prudent simply to give it up. For example, we can imagine a scientist who discovers a way to use lasers to aid in surgery. We can also imagine that this technology enables a nation to build a weapon that can destroy another nation's satellite network, thus disrupting normal communications and commerce—thus posing a grave threat to that nation. In order to discover a way to counter this threat, the vulnerable nation must first possess the technology.

If this technology remains in the public sphere, there is nothing wrong with going after it, for the same reasons that open sources are always "fair game." However, we can easily imagine a situation where the government under which this scientist lives classifies this information, but the scientist herself does not become a part of the project to turn the technology into an offensive weapon. Intelligence gathering operations against this person will likely be the easiest means to gather the required information, but we must reasonably ask if it is fair to make this scientist the subject of deception and harm in order gain the technology. Here the negative obligation not to use people merely as means comes into direct conflict with the positive obligation to preserve the lives and well-being of the citizens of one's nation. According to this analysis the answer to this question is no. One may be able to gain this information by blackmailing, extorting, or simply deceiving the scientist. But this scientist has not joined the game and is thus not a legitimate target of such operations. The fact, however, that this technology has been classified suggests that there are those who possess it, like the government scientists who may be using it to develop an offensive weapon, who are legitimate targets. *They* may be the subjects of operations that involve deception and harm, not the scientist. We will now turn our attention to some of these activities and to how the idea of respecting the dignity of individual human beings can provide practical limits to activities commonly associated with espionage.

DECEPTION AND THEFT

Imagine you are an intelligence professional and you must create a cover identity for yourself or for some other agent in order to convince someone to give you access to information you could not get any other way. Additionally, creating this cover story involves falsifying academic and professional records and credentials. In such cases it seems you are using the people who will hire or place you based on those credentials as a means to an end. Furthermore, it requires you to lie to family, friends, and employers about what you really do. Is this permissible? Deceiving and stealing are related activities that lie at the very heart of spying. These activities are related in that deception operations are often conducted in order to gain access to information or technology in order to steal it. As such, they are hard to separate from each other so it makes sense to treat these two kinds of activities together. Permissions and prohibitions that apply to one will, for the most part, apply to the other.

The job of the spy is to enhance national security by obtaining certain secrets that foreign governments and organizations would not otherwise willingly part with. Furthermore, spying is an activity that enjoys legal sanction, most notably in the Hague Convention, and is justified morally by the idea stated before: when one nation withholds secrets from other nations that threaten that nation's security, that nation may take steps to uncover those secrets.[37] Furthermore, because this activity enjoys such sanction, it is not a violation of shared expectations and good faith to engage in it.

This does not mean, however, that there will not be limits to how it can be conducted even against legitimate targets. It is interesting to note that Kant saw lying as inherently wrong, especially because it involved diminishing someone's capacity for acting morally. Nonetheless, we can draw a distinction between deceptions and lying. If we accept the Kantian model, then lying is going to be wrong because it is incompatible with respecting the inherent value and dignity of human beings. But this does not require that we accept all forms of deception as lying.[38]

With regard to lying, Kant explains it this way. Imagine you are poor and in need of money. You have a friend who has plenty of money, but who will only loan it to you if you promise to pay him back. You work for the government, and you know there is no way you are going to be able to do this. Nonetheless, you need to feed your kids. Do you lie? If you choose to lie, you are in effect acting under the maxim that "whenever I need money to feed my kids, and I can get it by lying, I shall do so." The problem arises when you make it universal, that it is when you understand it as a rule that would apply to everybody, the very possibility of doing it would be undermined.[39] This is because if your friend also believed that it was permissible to lie to get money, then he would have no reason to believe your promise and thus he would have no reason to give you the money. So one cannot believe that lying to a friend is morally permissible unless it is also true that the friend may believe this also. But if he believes this, then such lying is impossible. Otherwise, one is simply using his friend merely as a means. So lying is self-defeating—and thus irrational—in a way that truth telling is not. The same can be said of stealing. And as discussed above, the state has a right to information that puts its citizens at risk.

But as suggested above, not all deception is lying, nor is all taking stealing. Just as the quarterback may deceive the opposing team as to what the next play is or take the ball from them, intelligence professionals are free to deceive and steal from anyone who is a legitimate target. This is not cheating because the other "team" is supposed to expect it. Thus such deceptions and theft are not self-defeating in the way that lying in the example above is.

But some deceptions and stealing are. As noted above, deception and stealing of this sort is only permitted against those who are legitimate targets. But in much intelligence gathering activity there are those who may not be the direct target of deception, but who are subject to it anyway, such as family, friends, and employers. These people are innocent of the kinds of activities that would otherwise make them legitimate targets, and involving them would be self-defeating. Relationships with family members, friends, and employers rely on a great deal of trust. Deceptions, however, undermine this kind of trust and thus cannot be part of the shared expectations of people who have such relationships. This analysis suggests that deceiving them is not permissible and thus should be avoided. Most intelligence professionals will likely write off this conclusion as hopelessly naive. The information gained from these operations is too important for them not to occur, and for them to occur many people are going to have to be deceived. They may also plausibly argue that many of those subject to, but not targets of, the deception will never know they are deceived and thus experience any harm. "No harm, no foul," as the saying goes.

The problem with this argument is one that plagues all utilitarian arguments. One cannot predict the future and thus one will rarely know in advance what harms will arise from one's actions. Furthermore, even if one could it does not change the fact that such operations require an agent to use people who should not expect to be used. To partially resolve this tension it will be helpful to distinguish between lying and telling the truth. A commitment to the idea that it is wrong to use people merely as means requires that one observe the negative duty not to lie. It is not clear that this includes a positive duty to tell the truth. The difference is this: If my wife gains ten pounds I am under no obligation to point this fact out. However, if she asks me if she has gotten fat, I have a problem, though I may prefer to resolve it by redefining my conception of "fat." What I am not permitted to do is lie, as that will undermine the trust a husband and wife are supposed to have by virtue of their relationship.

Thus one is not obligated to divulge all the information about one's activities, but only that which is necessary to preserve the integrity of the relationship one has voluntarily entered into. If an agent or recruited foreign national who is a qualified accountant assumes this as a cover identity and performs the duties associated with it, then he has not lied. That he is also collecting information to pass on to an intelligence agency is not necessarily information the employer is "owed." This changes, as I will discuss later, if by withholding the information he puts the employer at risk. Furthermore, it is also the case that what information is in fact owed will depend on the nature of the relationship—things one should tell his wife are different than one should tell his employers.

But many times, maintaining one's cover and not lying about it is not possible. At some point, the agent will likely find himself in a situation where he has to tell a lie, where no answer at all will have the same effect as telling the truth. Consider, for example, the general who, on the eve of a major deployment, must respond to a journalist's question. If the journalist asks him if there is a major deployment tonight, he cannot say, "I am not at liberty to disclose that." The journalist will take that as a yes.[40] Similarly, if someone gets suspicious regarding the agent's activities and asks, "Why do you need that information?" he cannot simply answer, "I am not at liberty to disclose that." In such cases, he will have to tell a lie in order to maintain his cover.

When such a deception is directed at someone who is a legitimate target of espionage operations, it is not a lie. As discussed before, in this case the agent has not violated reasonably shared expectations and good faith by doing so. The problem is when the agent tells a lie to someone who is not a legitimate target. By lying to such a person he has involved him or her in his operation, a role he or she cannot willingly take on by virtue of the lie. In this situation, though in pursuit of a legitimate goal, the agent must knowingly engage in a course of action in which people who should not be involved are deceived and possibly harmed. The tough question then is, when and under what conditions, if any, is this permissible?

In war, the military is permitted to engage in courses of action in which non-combatants—people who should not reasonably expect to be targets of a military operation—may be harmed or killed. This is in part due to the fact that it is a harsh reality of modern warfare that the military cannot engage in war and do otherwise. Thus it is not reasonable for anyone to expect this to be the case. However, this is permissible only under certain limitations and these limitations are known collectively as the doctrine of double effect.[41] This doctrine results from the recognition that there is a moral difference between the consequences of our actions that we intend and those we do not intend but still foresee. Thus, according to this doctrine, it is permissible to perform a good act that has bad consequences, if certain other conditions hold. Those conditions are: 1) the bad effect is unintended; 2) the bad effect is proportional to the desired military objective; 3) the bad effect is not a direct means to the good effect; and 4) actions are taken to minimize the foreseeable bad effects, even if it means accepting an increased risk to soldiers.[42]

To the extent that the deception or theft is necessary for the intelligence professional to fulfill his role, and by extension the obligations of the state, it may be permitted. But these activities will be limited in the same way military operations are, by the restrictions imposed by the doctrine of double effect. Under these restrictions, it then may be permissible to involve innocents in intelligence collection activities. First, though, it would have to be the case that the activities are aimed at a legitimate target. As noted above, the fact a non-legitimate target may possess important information does not make it permissible to deceive or steal from her to get it. Thus the scientist engaged in purely medical research is still not a legitimate target, regardless of how important the information is.

Second, the value of the information must be greater than the harm done by the deception or theft. The fact that this information is vital is sufficient to fulfill this condition; however, this also means that the agent would have to know this information exists. It will not be permissible to involve non-legitimate targets on the off chance there may be some vital information. This would be like trawling in such a way that kills a lot of dolphins on the off chance you might catch a tuna or two. Given that living dolphins have a kind of value themselves, this just is not rational.

Third, this means the deception of non-legitimate targets is not the means by which the agent obtains the information, though it may be incidental to it. This may be, perhaps, the most restrictive of these conditions in terms of intelligence activity since this means an agent may not lie to or steal from a non-legitimate target in order to get the desired information. Thus, under this condition, it would not be permissible, for example, to forge credentials in order to get a job in an organization if that organization is not already a legitimate target.

Finally, this means that agents will have to minimize any risk this incidental involvement entails, even if that means taking additional risks upon themselves. In wartime,[43] the amount of risk that intelligence professionals must take is limited in the same way it is for soldiers. Soldiers are not required to take so much risk that their mission will fail or that it necessarily precludes their ability to conduct further missions. This means it will be permissible for soldiers, as well as intelligence professionals, to engage in activities in wartime in which non-combatants may knowingly, though not intentionally, be harmed. One of the harsh realities of modern war is that people who are not directly involved in fighting the war nonetheless reasonably expect not to be harmed by it. They do, though, have a reasonable expectation that combatants on both sides will minimize the chances and effects of this harm.

In peacetime, however, the calculation of risk changes. One is not permitted to engage in intelligence gathering activities if innocents will knowingly be harmed, as one is in war.[44] This is because such acts represent a breach of peace, and it never makes sense to breach the peace in order to preserve it. Thus for the intelligence professional, certain permissions which exist in wartime will not be present in peacetime. This means if infiltrating an organization that is not a legitimate target means putting the people in that organization at risk, then it is not permissible. This does not mean intelligence professionals will not be permitted to take any risks in this regard. But if in conducting such activities the agent knowingly sets innocent people up as a target for the other side—even if they are never in fact harmed—then that activity is not permitted. Thus the agent in peacetime may be able to conduct such activities but not in a way that he knowingly puts civilians at risk. Involving people in the "game" without their knowledge, especially when that puts them at risk, violates the limitations imposed by reasonable shared expectations and good faith and thus must be avoided.

Thus, while intelligence professionals are permitted to engage in deception and stealing in order to fulfill their roles, they must take great care when these activities involve innocent people, people who have no reason to expect to be targets or subjects of such activities. Thus when such operations involve innocents, they should be avoided and other means of gaining this information should be pursued. If this is not possible, and the information is vital, then limitations imposed by the doctrine of double effect must be observed.

HARMS: BLACKMAIL, EXTORTION, AND BETRAYAL

But spying is not solely the effort of the intelligence professional. Intelligence professionals also actively recruit sources to provide them with information. Sometimes such foreign nationals do so willingly. Sometimes intelligence professionals offer an incentive such as money to induce cooperation. Sometimes they coerce foreign nationals into cooperating by means of blackmail. This analysis suggests that it is not a problem to offer an incentive to a foreign national to become a controlled source. It does not matter if he does it because he loves our country, hates his, or just likes money; he willingly engaged in this activity. Thus he bears the risks that come with that. What is much more problematic is when an agent blackmails, but this is less so if the individual actually did the blackmail offense. If you possess a secret, then you are obligated to protect it, which includes keeping yourself free of the risk of blackmail. Thus, just as the football team is free to exploit the weakness of the quarterback, the professional intelligence officer is free to exploit the weaknesses of certain foreign nationals who possess secrets that pose a threat to our national security.

In cases such as these, it is important to remember that the foreign national can always refuse to give in to the blackmail and he is probably morally obligated to do so. But while it may be wrong for that foreign national to betray his country, it is not necessarily wrong for the intelligence professional to exploit his doing so. This can put the intelligence professional in the odd situation of being obligated (or at least permitted) to exploit, and perhaps even encourage, the wrongdoing of others. But because his obligation is to his society, it is not self-defeating in the same way making the lying promise is. One can accept the maxim "whenever someone in one nation presents an opportunity to enhance national security in your nation, you should exploit that" without having to accept that people in the first nation have an obligation to present such opportunities.[45] But you clearly cross that line when such exploitation does not serve the needs of national security.

This does beg the question regarding homosexuality or other behavior whose moral status is in dispute, but which may make someone at risk for blackmail. This is a complex question for which there is not enough space to discuss it in every detail. However, since anytime people have any information they would prefer to keep secret they open the door to blackmail, this analysis suggests that intelligence professionals will have a special obligation not to have any personal secrets they would not want to come to light. This means that they will have to live fairly transparent lives, at least to the extent that if any personal information did come to light, they would not care so much about it to betray their country to prevent its release. Thus, an agent who is homosexual is not a blackmail risk so long as he does not hide this information or care if it comes to light.

An agent also crosses the line when in some way he makes it impossible for the individual he is recruiting to choose otherwise. This is what it means to treat him merely as a means. Thus entrapping someone by manufacturing a blackmail offense in such a way that he faces the choice of revealing the offense and consequently suffering a severe sanction because no one will believe him, or of cooperating with you, you have crossed the line. Furthermore, this clearly rules out threatening his friends or members of his family in order to get him to cooperate. If these others did not freely enter the game, they are not subject to its rules. They do not represent a threat to national security and thus have no expectation to bear the risks of someone who does.

A related question to this is whether it can be morally permissible to intentionally treat agents, particularly foreign nationals, as expendable. According to Jones, it had been alleged that Allied intelligence professionals considered betraying a German double agent by letting another agent "sell him out." By betraying that agent the other agent would ingratiate himself to the Germans and be in a position to pass false information regarding the landings on D-day.[46] According to Jones, this did not happen and would have been viewed by the intelligence community at the time as unacceptable, whether the agent was a member of the organization or a foreign national working for it. Not only is there a practical downside to such a practice—it will be hard to recruit agents if they believe you would likely betray them—there is an obvious ethical downside as well.

For an intelligence agency to function, it must be able to trust the information it receives from its agents in the field. Thus the agency and agent have a set of shared expectations regarding the moral obligation each owes the other. Agents do not expect to be betrayed, regardless of the goal of such betrayal, and agencies expect to receive accurate information from the agent. Furthermore, the agent undertakes his assignments in good faith that the agency is not deceiving him regarding the actual nature and purpose of the operation. For the agency to do otherwise is clearly treating the agent merely as a means to an end. For an agent to be trustworthy, he must have no reason to betray the agency. If the agent believes that it is likely that any given assignment may lead to his betrayal by the agency, then he will have good reasons to betray the agency in turn.

Of course, any individual agent may have personal reasons for betraying the agency—money, power, avoid the consequences of blackmail, etc. He is, of course, wrong for acting on them. But if the agency gives him that reason then it is acting in an irrational and self-defeating manner. Thus, not only does such a practice in the short term treat agents as merely a means, in the long run it compromises the agency's ability to contribute to national security, thus undermining the agency's ability to fulfill the moral purpose which justifies its activities in the first place.

HARMS: TORTURE

Probably the most unambiguous way to use someone merely as a means is to torture him in order to get information he would not willingly give otherwise. In spite of this, the logic behind its practice is compelling. If you can make someone value his comfort or his life a lot more than his information, you stand a good chance of getting that information. When you can use that information to save the lives of innocent people, the logic becomes even more compelling. But, paradoxically, this is rarely the case. It is a well-established fact that information gained under the duress of torture is rarely reliable. In fact, its practical benefits are so few and its assault on our moral sense is so great that torture is almost universally condemned.[47]

Almost.

Israel, in its own war against terrorism, has debated the use of torture as a means to get information from suspected terrorists. A 1987 commission—the Landau Commission—formed to investigate the Israeli General Security Services practices in response to terrorist activity directed against it concluded that "a moderate measure of physical pressure" might be justified in certain circumstances.[48] The Israeli Supreme Court, in rendering its own judgment on the use of torture, underscored this point when it opened its judgment with the statement, "The State of Israel has been engaged in an unceasing struggle for both its very existence and security, from the day of its founding." Though it found that forms of interrogation that involved physical pressure, as well as cruel, inhumane, and degrading treatment, were prohibited, it did allow interrogators to claim a defense of necessity in "ticking time-bomb" scenarios.[49]

Furthermore, in the United States, the FBI in its efforts to extract information about terrorist activities is reported to be considering using torture and drugs.[50] According to a *Washington Post* report, they have tried all of the conventional and humane means of obtaining information, such as offering lighter sentences, immunity, new identities, etc., but no one is cooperating. According to one FBI agent, "We are known for humanitarian treatment, so basically we are stuck. . . . Usually there is some angle to play, what you can do for them. But it could get to that spot where we could go to pressure . . . where we won't have a choice, and we are probably getting there."[51] What justifies considering these measures, according to the Landau Report, is the "vital need to preserve the very existence of the State and its citizens." But the conclusions of this report are not simple realist or utilitarian arguments. Included in its findings was the idea that there are limits to the kinds of things a state can do in order to preserve the lives and well-being of its citizens if it is to maintain its character as a law-abiding state which believes in basic moral principles.[52] Thus the report does not conclude that anything goes, just some things under some circumstances.

But this recognition is in spite of the fact that Israel and the United States are signatories to the Geneva Convention[53] as well as the Convention against Torture and Other Cruel, Inhuman or Degrading Treatment or Punishment[54] that prohibit any kind of torture under any circumstances. Given the importance of these kinds of documents in the forming of reasonable shared expectations, it will take very good reasons to permit setting them aside. The question, then, is whether the limitations that reasonably shared expectations and good faith impose can include disregarding an international treaty to which one's nation is a signatory as well as general commitment to humanitarian principles. That this can seem plausible is illustrated by the following example. In philosophy class, professors often pose the following problem: Suppose you find yourself in a country where a local government official has lined twenty people up against a wall. He threatens to shoot all of them as a disincentive for guerrillas with whom his government is engaged in conflict. Now the twenty people may or not be involved with the guerrillas, but he is trying to send a message and turn the people against the opposition by making their struggle too costly for the populace to bear. When you walk by this scene the official, because you are a guest, offers you a choice: shoot just one and he will let the rest go free. A caveat in this story is that you, somehow, know that the government official will keep his word. The students must then tell what they would do and why. While this story is usually told to test a student's commitment to utilitarian or deontological approaches, it also highlights just how compelling purely utilitarian arguments can sometimes be. It is telling that very few students ever say they would not shoot the one person in exchange for the others' lives.

Certainly someone can do something that puts him in a position where it is justifiable to do things he would prefer did not happen. Our criminal justice system would collapse overnight if this were not true. Furthermore, we can imagine a situation where government authorities have detained a known terrorist who they know has planted a bomb that will go off soon. It would be a callous investigator indeed who did not at least want to apply "physical pressure" to this person to get him to divulge the location of the bomb. Most of us would regard as morally deficient the public servant who would say to the victims of the impending attack that he would have liked to have prevented it, but there was this rule that prohibited him from doing so.

I will take it as uncontroversial that terrorism, that is, attacks aimed exclusively at civilians with the intent to create fear in a general population, is immoral.[55] By wilfully engaging in such activity the terrorist is a criminal and thus there are no legitimate moral arguments he can reasonable invoke to justify withholding this information, as can the prisoner of war. In such cases, it would not be reasonable to expect that the terrorist enjoy the protections of international law. It defeats the very purpose of such laws in the first place. A primary purpose of laws and treaties like the Geneva Convention and the Convention against Torture is to protect the innocent from abuse.[56] When applied in such a way that they fail to do so, they become nonsensical and self-defeating. The problem here is not with the laws themselves, but the way they are applied.

But this will not mean any form of torture will be permissible, a fact the *Landau Report* recognized. Space does not exist here to give a complete discussion of what a proper sense of "moderate physical pressure" would consist in. But it does suggest interrogators should apply a "minimum harm" rule and not inflict more than is necessary to get the information. Any pain inflicted to "teach a lesson" or after the interrogator has determined torture will not bear fruit would be morally wrong. But in the case of torture in Israel and the United States it is not always, or even often, the case that the GSS and FBI investigators know if their suspect actually has the information they are seeking. This can put the victim of the torture in an impossible position. There is nothing he can say to prove he does not have the information. Thus we have a case of competing logic: for the torturer the only thing the subject can give to get the torture to stop is the information the torturer is looking for. But the victim of the torture, or anyone else for that matter, cannot prove a negative. There is nothing he can say, if he does not in fact possess the sought-for information, to make the torturer stop. This is why torture is so problematic in the first place. Often people will say anything, even make something up, to get it to stop. Thus, information gained under this kind of duress is extraordinarily unreliable.

In fact, these situations are like the hostage example, except that in this case you do not know if the government official is going to keep his word. You can violate the moral principle for the greater good, but in this case you do not know if there is going to be any greater good. Here the utilitarian calculation that was once so compelling is less so. It now is important to ask, if you are not certain of the outcome, are you willing to sacrifice your integrity? How certain do you need to be in order to justify sacrificing your commitment to moral principle in exchange for consequences that may benefit a great number of people.

But this is somewhat dis-analogous to the situations in Israel and the United States. Central to this argument is that the forced detentions and torture can save (and some citing the Israeli example will argue have saved) hundreds of lives, lives that would not have been saved otherwise. Central to the U.S. argument is that the more we know about how the terrorist networks operate, the better able we will be to prevent future acts. That a number of innocent people, or people who may not be innocent but who do not have any relevant information, are tortured is not as important as the fact that a number of guilty or knowledgeable ones are, and the information they give has saved a great many lives. The GSS and FBI investigators are certain that many of their detainees have information that will save lives. They are just not always sure which ones those are.

But this utilitarian argument cannot be justified in light of international law and treaty and the impossible position in which such practices put a large number of people. One reason stems from the utilitarian ethic itself: given the unreliability of information obtained this way, the benefits rarely outweigh the harms. Furthermore, it may be the case some useful information will be uncovered, but one has to use people to get it. Thus, when the practice of torture is aimed at a specific population, members of which may or may not have relevant information, it cannot be justified. It does not make sense to commit oneself to the principle that such acts are wrong and then disregard that fact when threatened. This, in effect, says that one set of lives (one's group) is more valuable than another set (the other group), and this is inconsistent with the idea that all human life has special value and dignity.

However, the purpose of international humanitarian laws regarding torture is to protect human lives and dignity. But when they are applied in such a way that prevents an interrogator from doing just that, it does make sense to reconsider this application. Furthermore, sometimes there are ways to tell if the information gained is reliable. If an interrogator knows that a terrorist has planted a bomb that will soon go off but does not know where, he can test the answer he gets by going to where the terrorist indicates. If there is no bomb, then the information was unreliable. Thus the objection that information gained from torture is usually unreliable does not hold up in this kind of situation.

Thus, when a terrorist has done or knows something that puts other peoples' lives in danger AND it is still possible to save those lives, then an interrogator may be permitted to use some forms of torture to obtain that information. When someone wilfully puts innocent lives at risk, he loses the shared expectations he may otherwise reasonably possess. If an interrogator knows this person has such information, he then knows he has a means to save lives. It is not reasonable for an interrogator to know he has means to save innocent lives but not use them simply because a rule exists. But I am not arguing that this is an occasion when it is permissible to disregard the limitations that shared expectations and good faith impose, but rather that they are changed.

When pushing the boundaries of any moral approach, as questions about torture do, it is important to be clear about what question we are asking. Sometimes we want to know what should be a matter of moral principle and sometimes we want to know if there are circumstances in which it can be justified to violate these principles. As noted above, this ethical approach is based on the idea that all human life has an inherent value that all people are rationally obligated to respect. The next question then is, is it ever permissible to disregard this foundational belief?

SUPREME EMERGENCY

In the end, many may find this analysis to be naive. They will insist that when pursuing important enough national security goals, it is foolish to insist that agents concern themselves with moral principle at the expense of mission accomplishment. To those who believe this based on the idea that there are no moral obligations between nations or that the ends of national security can justify any means, those arguments have been already addressed. There may be no moral obligations between nations, but there are between people. Only someone who rejects that their own life and liberty have value may reject the same for others.

Still, there are many who reject the realist arguments addressed above who may still argue that some threats are so grave that they may still justify any course of action. This seems to be the spirit behind the conclusions of the 1954 Doolittle Commission's report. It recognized that some moral claims, like those of fair play, had some weight, but were outweighed by the need to defeat the threat of Communism. Today, in view of the War against Terrorism, many also argue now is the time for the "gloves to come off." This problem has been an important feature of just war theory for many years. It seems wrong, even callous, to uphold a moral principle, even a well-founded one, at the expense of innocent people's lives. Here the demands of good character and moral principle clash.[57] Our integrity may be important, but it may not be that important.

In just war theory, the doctrine that addresses this most directly is the doctrine of Supreme Emergency. As Walzer notes, sometimes the evil the enemy represents is so great, almost anything is justified to prevent their victory.[58] But not all conflicts are with such an enemy, and even when they are there is a difference between preventing their victory and ensuring their defeat. Thus for it to be permissible to disregard the morality of war, two conditions must hold: 1) the threat must be grave—it must represent the enslavement or genocide of a people, or some other like catastrophe; and 2) the threat must be immediate, that is defeat must be imminent—which implies that the morally legitimate means at one's disposal to fight the threat are insufficient. When these conditions are met, only then may one disregard fundamental moral claims in favor of claims of necessity.[59]

This argument, though controversial, may justify allowing necessity and the idea that the "ends justify the means" to supersede other moral considerations in wartime. Presumably, this could apply to intelligence as well as military operations. But this would not be the case with intelligence operations in peacetime. And it follows from this argument that in peacetime the threat, while possibly grave, is not imminent, so breaches of moral principle, in this case treating people merely as means, are justified. But the "War on Terrorism" has changed the calculation to some degree. Before the events of September 11, it would be hard to make the case that it would be permissible to invoke Supreme Emergency. The threat the terrorists represented was just not grave enough to warrant it. Before then, terrorists were more like criminals than like enemies. However, on that day certain terrorists demonstrated that they could represent a grave threat to the lives and well-being of large numbers of people. Given that these terrorists are known to at least be pursuing nuclear and radiological weapons and other weapons of mass destruction (WMD), this threat may not just be grave, but in fact catastrophic.

To the extent the use of the weapons of mass destruction represent a grave threat to civilization, it is permissible to disregard moral norms to prevent their use. Like in the case of torture, it would be unconscionable for a government official to know he could have prevented the use of weapon of mass destruction but failed to do so because other moral considerations would not have permitted it. But this is only the case if the threat of their use is imminent. Information like this, however, is very hard to obtain. We know, for example that they want to develop such weapons. We also know they have tried to obtain the information and material necessary to do so. We also know that if they did develop them, they would likely use them.

But we do not know if they have them. Thus we cannot know if their use is imminent. This being the case, it is impermissible to wage this war in a way that disregards the fundamental value of human life, that violates restrictions that otherwise should be there. But this should not be conflated with leaving the "gloves on." In this approach, and as noted above, when pursuing information about terrorist activity, intelligence professionals are permitted to do what it necessary in order to obtain it. This is not because of utilitarian considerations, but rather that terrorists who possess this kind of information have no reasonable expectation not to be harmed, deceived, or otherwise exploited in order for the intelligence professional to obtain it. What it does mean, however, is that restrictions on involving non-legitimate targets would still apply. But because this is a war, at least in the relevant sense, agents would not be required to minimize risk to non-legitimate targets in the same way they must in peacetime.

Furthermore, it is not the case that Supreme Emergency could never be invoked in this conflict. Though tragic as the events of September 11 were, they failed to represent the catastrophe to our civilization that the terrorists intended it to be. However, these events did underscore to what extent the terrorists are willing to go in order to create such a disaster. In order to do this, the terrorists are attempting to create and use weapons of mass destruction. But as noted before, knowing that someone wants to do something or is trying to do something is not the same as knowing they can do something. However, if one knows that someone wants to do something AND that they can do this thing, then one can safely conclude this thing is imminent. Once there is information that the terrorists have weapons of mass destruction, it will be permissible to invoke Supreme Emergency and disregard—to the smallest extent possible—the moral norms associated with the law and morality of war.

This conflict is much different than the conventional conflicts from which the doctrine of Supreme Emergency emerged. Sometimes it is like a war, as in the operations in Afghanistan, and sometimes it is like a criminal investigation, as in much of the operations in the United States. There is not space here to discuss these operations in detail or develop a comprehensive theory for such conflicts; however, it is not the case that the doctrine of Supreme Emergency would justify disregarding moral norms in its pursuit at this point. The threat, while grave, is not immediate in the sense meant under the doctrine of Supreme Emergency. The terrorists may be developing weapons of mass destruction, but there is no evidence they have them yet. Thus the terrorists, at this point at least, do not represent the "utter catastrophe to civilization" that Supreme Emergency requires.[60] Our lives and well-being are threatened, but there are still a number of more moral means to pursue our goals in this conflict. This argument does not entail, however, that we "keep the gloves on." It simply entails that when pursuing the terrorists and those who support them that we keep in mind the fundamental value of human life. Such is the risk good people must take if they are to remain good people.

ECONOMIC ESPIONAGE: NATIONAL SECURITY VS. NATIONAL INTEREST

Previous arguments imply that deceiving and harming—whatever actual activity consists in—may be legitimate in pursuit of certain national security goals. But not all such activity directly impacts national security. In the mid-nineties, the National Security Agency uncovered the fact that agents for the French aircraft manufacturer Airbus had bribed Saudi officials in an effort to beat the American companies McDonnell Douglas and Boeing to a contact worth $6 billion. Based on this information, President Clinton called King Fahd to complain, and the Saudis subsequently awarded the contract to the American companies.[61] Clearly, the act of bribery by Airbus personnel was immoral. It fundamentally violates the conditions of shared expectations and good faith in regard to the competition. Further, it undermines the ability of the nation making the purchase to make a rational decision in the matter since those influenced by the bribe will likely fail to consider certain relevant information or will cause others to fail to consider this information. Otherwise, what would have been the purpose of the bribery in the first place? What is not so clear is whether it was morally permissible to use National Security Agency assets to uncover this fact.

As stated at the outset of this paper, the moral justification for the practices of the intelligence profession, particularly where such practices involve committing acts that would be immoral outside the professional context, is that such acts must aim at promoting national security, not simply national interests, and especially not simply the interests of some nationals. However, sometimes issues of national security get conflated with these other concerns. Some things are good for the nation, or even a number of citizens of that nation, without being necessary in order to fulfill its obligations. Recently, it has become fashionable for intelligence agencies to conduct operations that support the welfare of corporations operating in that nation presumably with the intent of preserving or enhancing, by extension, the standard of living in that country. In fact, last year the Association of Former Intelligence Officers held a convention in Washington, DC, specifically to discuss aspects of economic espionage. Speakers and attendees came from both governmental and nongovernmental agencies and groups to discuss all aspects of such operations. Such developments are worrying in the context of the ethical debate.

Thus when intelligence agencies engage in activities which specifically promote the welfare of organizations—whether they are governmental organizations, non-governmental organizations, or corporations—which do not directly enhance national security, they have crossed the line. This also precludes corporations from hiring intelligence professionals to do their "dirty" work for them. Unless narrowly pursuing the requirements of national security, it is wrong to steal industrial secrets or otherwise pursue unfair advantage over one's competition.

A counterargument to this may be that some corporate sales are, in fact, vital to national security. If the Airbus sale were military aircraft, it might be plausibly argued that robust sales of a nation's defense products directly contribute to the health of the defense industry, which directly contributes to national security. Thus, the NSA's intervention in this matter would have served national security. However, in this view, so would the activities of the Airbus Corporation. What separates the activities of the NSA from that of Airbus was that Airbus's actions aimed at gaining an unfair advantage over the competition. The acts of the NSA aimed at preventing the competition from gaining an unfair advantage. Thus given the logical connection between the health of the defense industry to the ability of a nation to defend itself, it follows that it is permissible to use any intelligence asset or method to prevent competition from other nations from gaining an unfair advantage.

But the line is crossed when such information is used to take unfair advantage. Additionally, what is not immoral is the use of intelligence assets to obtain information through open and other legal sources. While there are certainly important issues to raise regarding the use of government assets, and thus taxpayer dollars, to aid corporations, to the extent they are used exclusively for national security reasons, and as long as there are no competing obligations, their use is moral. Thus, to the extent the operations of a corporation are essential to national security it may be permissible to use government assets to assist them in conducting those specific operations. But where this is not the case, the use of taxpayer dollars will likely not be permissible.

There is certainly much more to be said on this point, but that is not essential to our argument. Neither public nor private intelligence professionals are permitted to deceive or harm to pursue things that are simply in the interest of a particular corporation. The interest of the corporation and national security intelligence professionals may be permitted to conduct surveillance, but only to prevent other corporations and nations from taking an unfair advantage, never to gain one.

CONCLUSION

A committed moral nihilist or realist may still reject every claim set forth in this paper. There is nothing that logically requires that one sees all human life as inherently valuable other than that one sees his own life as inherently valuable. Even then, this is only the case if one expects the fact that he values his life and liberty to stand as a reason for someone else to value, at least to some degree, his life and liberty. The only real problem with being a moral nihilist is if you are right, then there is no good reason not to kill you so that we more morally minded folks can get some sleep at night.

But what is difficult to do is to accept any moral claims, and then reject that they apply to you in the same way they apply to others. This formulation of the Golden Rule, one of the most ubiquitous and ultimately rational features of nearly every moral system, requires that when we disregard the dignity and rights of others there need to be good reasons, reasons we would accept if the same were done to us.

But it is not sufficient for a reason to be good that we accept it, or expect others to accept it. Thus what emerges from this analysis is that the nature of the activity, to a large degree, determines the kinds of things that may be reasonably expected from people who engage in it. Intelligence professionals must often deceive and harm others in order to fulfill their role, and thus the state's obligations to its citizens. But even so, intelligence professionals need to have good compelling reasons to justify some of their more "repugnant" activities.

These reasons begin with the obligation of every state to preserve the lives and well-being of its citizens. In fulfilling those obligations, people acting on behalf of the state must sometimes deceive and harm citizens of other nations. When intelligence professionals conduct such operations, they are limited by the respect all persons owe each other by virtue of the special dignity and value of human life. This means it may be permissible to deceive and harm, but not in such a way that treats people merely as means and not ends in themselves.

In practical terms this means intelligence professionals must take care in determining the nature as well as the targets of their operations. In terms of the nature of their operations, these are limited by those sets of shared expectations that make it possible to play the game in the first place, while still respecting the fundamental dignity of human life. In terms of the targets of their operations, this means they may only target those who have voluntarily entered the game and avoid involving people who may be useful, but who have not, by any choice they have made, entered the game.

The work of the professional intelligence officer, because it is indispensable to national security, which is a moral obligation of the state, is thus itself a moral obligation. Thus we can dispense with the idea that somehow the work of the intelligence professional is not compatible with the dictates of morality. But the road to hell is paved with good intentions, and lines get crossed. Thus it becomes imperative to establish such a line so intelligence professionals can execute their duties in clear conscience. This is not only good for the professional, it is good for the profession, and given the profession's importance, the nation as well.[62]

NOTES

1. Kent Pekel, *Integrity, Ethics, and the CIA*, in Studies in Intelligence (Spring 1998) p. 87–89.

2. James Bamford, *The Puzzle Palace*, New York: Penguin Books, 1982, p. 34.

3. Ibid., pp. 33–62.

4. Pekel, p. 88.

5. *The National Security Strategy of the United States*, September 2002, http://www.whitehouse.gov/nsc.nsall.html

6. R.V. Jones, *Reflections on Intelligence*, London: William Heinemann Ltd, 1989, p. 42. Jones, an intelligence professional in WWII and noted scholar on the subject, considers betraying an agent immoral under any but the most extreme examples.

7. David A. Welch, "Morality and the National Interest," in *Ethics and International Affairs*, Andrew Valls, ed. New York: Rowman and Littlefield Publishers, Inc, 2000, p. 8.

8. James Doolittle et al., "Report on the Covert Activities of the Central Intelligence Agency," pp. 143–145, quoted in Dr David L. Perry, "Repugnant Philosophy: Ethics, Espionage, and Covert Action" *Journal of Conflict Studies*, Spring 1995.

9. Jones, p. 50.

10. Bamford, p. 35.

11. Jones, p. 56.

12. Ibid., pp. 49–50.

13. Charles R. Beitz, *Political Theory and International Relations*, 2d ed, Princeton: Princeton University Press, 1999, p. 58.

14. Ibid. See also John Rawls, *Theory of Justice*, Revised Edition, Boston: Harvard University Press, 1999.

15. Immanuel Kant, *Foundations of the Metaphysics of Morals* (1785) Lewis Beck, trans. Indianapolis, Indiana: Bobbs-Merrill Educational Publishing, 1959, Preface.

16. Ibid.

17. Michael Walzer, *Just and Unjust Wars*, New York: Basic Books, Inc, 1977, p. 54.

18. Thomas Nagel, *What Does it All Mean*, Oxford: Oxford University Press, 1987, pp. 59–61.

19. I am sidestepping this debate. There are numerous problems with this view that I do not wish to address here. Whether or not states themselves have rights—whether they are derivative of individual rights or not—is not as important to this discussion as is the nature of the obligations states possess by virtue of the special value with which we hold human life. I am also sidestepping the issue of exactly which rights people possess. But what I am suggesting is that any rights you consider yourself to have you must also grant to others.

20. Welch, p. 8.

21. CNN 6 December 2001. http://www.cnn.com/2001/US/12/06/inv.ashcroft .hearing/index.html. In this article Ashcroft is quoted as saying "Our efforts have been crafted carefully to avoid fringing on constitutional rights, while saving American lives."

22. In the context of Just War Theory, the obligation not to commit an act of aggression against another sovereign state serves as an example. See Walzer, chapter 4, for a complete argument.

23. While there is some disagreement on exactly what the criteria of *jus ad bellum* (the justice of war) consist of, most agree on the following: just cause, right authority, right intention, proportionality of ends, last resort, reasonable chance of success. Only when all of these criteria are fulfilled is it permissible to go to war.

24. Jones, *Reflections on Intelligence*, p. 38. Jones makes the point that had either the U.S. or the USSR been able to obtain reliable information regarding each other's nuclear weapons programs, arms control talks aimed at reducing nuclear arsenals would have been much more effective. One of the chief obstacles to many of the proposed treaties was that there was no way to verify compliance except by taking the word of the other side.

25. Rabbi Berel Wein, "Jonathan Pollard," *Jerusalem Post*, June 30, 2000. http:www/rabbi.wein.com/

26. Walzer argues that the only kind of act of aggression that justifies going to war

is a violation of political sovereignty and territorial integrity of a particular nation since these are essential if the state is to fulfill its obligations to its citizens (see Chapter 4). While I agree that this is true, there are other lesser "acts of aggression" that though they do not justify war, do justify surveillance.

27. E. Drexel Godfrey, "Ethics and Intelligence," *Foreign Affairs* 56, no. 3, April 1978, p. 624.

28. Source: Monterey Bay Aquarium.

29. I am not arguing that all betrayal is wrong. Certainly "whistle blowing" is a kind of betrayal, where someone divulges about the wrongdoing of a particular person or organization that they would prefer remain secret. But when done to prevent a moral wrong, it is not immoral.

30. Major Mark Mattox, *The Moral Status of Military Deception,* paper presented at the Joint Services Conference on Professional Ethics, 28–30 January 2000. http://www.usafa.af.mil/jscope/JSCOPE00/ Mattox00.html, p. 2.

31. Ibid., p. 3.

32. Ibid.

33. Jones, p. 35.

34. David Hoffman, "Betrayal vs. Loyalty," *Jerusalem Post*, March 19, 1993, http://www.shamash.org/lists/jpollard/post/jq930319.htm. See also the Association for the Liberation of Jonathan Pollard website: http://www/shamash.org/lists/jpollard/pollard.htm.

35. Thomas Nagel, "War and Massacre," in *Philosophy and Public Affairs,* Princeton: Princeton University Press, quoted in *Ethics*, Timothy Challans, ed. New York: McGraw Hill, 2000, p. 210.

36. Walzer, p. 201. Walzer makes this distinction in discussing who may legitimately be targets of "freedom fighters" in pursuit of a just cause. Jones also agrees that it is morally offensive to target family and friends in order to obtain information. Jones, p. 49.

37. *An Encyclopedia of War and Ethics,* Donald A. Wells, ed. Westport, CT: Greenwood Press, 1996, p. 434.

38. Mattox, p. 5.

39. Kant, p. 40.

40. I am grateful to Colonel Anthony Hartle for this example.

41. Paul Christopher, *The Ethics of War and Peace: An Introduction to Legal and Moral Issues,* 2d ed. New Jersey: Prentice Hall, 1999, p. 52. This doctrine was developed in response to Augustine's prohibition against self-defense. Augustine held that self-defense was inherently selfish and that acts motivated by selfishness were not morally justifiable since selfishness is not morally justifiable.

42. Ibid., p. 93.

43. War, in this case, is to be taken in a literal rather than legal sense. Thus wartime permissions would be present in the Korean War that would not be present against, for example, North Korea today.

44. For a detailed argument regarding why it is wrong to put the lives of innocent people at risk in peacetime, see Tony Pfaff, *Peacekeeping and the Just War Tradition*, Carlisle, Pennsylvania: Strategic Studies Institute, 2000.

45. This statement is undoubtedly controversial, but I will take a military example

to illustrate my point. It may be cowardly, and thus immoral, for an enemy soldier to surrender in some circumstances, but that does not make it wrong for the other side to accept or encourage that surrender. So in environments of conflict, I think you can end up in situations where an action by one side is immoral, but taking advantage of that act by the other side is not.

46. Jones, p. 43.

47. Geneva Convention, pt I-IV quoted in *Documents on the Law of War*, Adam Roberts and Richard Guelff, eds. Oxford: Clarendon Press, 1989, pp. 172, 175, 188, 195, 223, 273, 323, 431.

48. Report of the Commission of Inquiry into the Methods of Investigation of the General Security Service Regarding Hostile Terrorist Activity, p. 80, quoted in *The Israeli Law Review*, p. 2. http://unixware.mscc.huji.ac.il/~law1/ilr/ilr23_2.htm.

49. Amnesty International, *Israel: High Court Should End the Shame of Torture*, http://web.amnesty.org/ai.nsf/Index/MDE1500519999?OpenDocuments&of = THEMESTORTURE%5CILL-TREATMENT. See also http://62.90.71.124/eng/verdict/framesetSrch.html

50. Walter Pincus," Silence of 4 Terror Probe Suspects Poses Dilemma," *Washington Post*, 21 October 2001. Online at http://www.washingtonpost.com/ac2/wp-dyn?pagename = article&node = &contentID; eqA27748–2001Oct20.

51. Ibid.

52. Amnesty International, p. 1.

53. Roberts and Guelff, p. 328.

54. Amnesty International, p. 2.

55. There are numerous definitions of terrorism, up to 109 by some counts. For our purposes I will define terrorism as violence intentionally directed at noncombatants in order to achieve desired political ends. What makes such activity morally objectionable is that the deaths of the noncombatants are the means to the desired ends and not incidental to them.

56. Roughly speaking, soldiers are protected from torture even if they likely possess information that will help the other side, because they are innocent of the cause of the war. Civilians are protected to the extent they are suspects. This point will be developed in the next paragraph.

57. For a detailed discussion of how they clash, see Tony Pfaff, *Virtue Ethics and Leadership*, http:www.usafa.af.mil/jscope/JSCOPE98/PFAFF98.htm. In this paper I argue that there are circumstances in which good people may have good moral reasons for doing something that is morally repugnant, but this does not mean they should not be held accountable for such action.

58. Walzer, chapter 16.

59. Ibid., p. 252.

60. Ibid., pp. 252–254.

61. Thomas Pickering, *Mr. Diplomat*, interview by *Foreign Policy* (July/August 2001), p. 40.

62. I would like to thank Dr Beverly Milton Edwards of Queens University, Belfast, Northern Ireland, and Dr Sandra Visser, Valparaiso University, for their invaluable help in preparing and reviewing this paper. I am also grateful for the efforts of Captain Eric Larson, U.S. Special Forces, and Captain James Dickey, Military Intelligence Branch, who were instrumental in helping develop and articulate this argument.

6

Moral Damage and the Justification of Intelligence Collection from Human Sources

John P. Langan, S. J.

One of the most serious charges brought against intelligence agencies is that those who work for them become morally corrupt. This argument is advanced specifically with regard to case officers who recruit and handle agents to collect intelligence. The duties required of case officers can be judged repugnant on other moral grounds, for instance, that they normally involve violations of binding moral rules or that they involve the manipulation or coercion of other persons and hence are incompatible with our moral duty to treat other persons as ends worthy of respect in themselves and not as means to further our own projects and desires. Such objections lead quickly into larger issues of moral theory. Are there exceptionless moral rules? Are we obliged always to treat other rational beings as ends in themselves? This paper will not resolve these central and difficult issues but will rather offer some reflections, partly philosophical and partly practical, which will show not only why the moral damage argument taken by itself is unsatisfactory, but also why it points to something that should concern officers and leaders of an intelligence agency.

The moral damage argument figures explicitly in the article by Drexel Godfrey, "Ethics and Intelligence" in *Foreign Affairs* (April 1978). He writes:

> A fundamental ethical issue concerning clandestine human collection remains, that issue is the impact on the clandestine officer of his relationship with his

source. . . . Whatever the chemistry between the two individuals, collector and source, or perhaps more pointedly, dominant and dominated, the biggest loser is the one whose ethical scruples are most damaged in the process. Depending on the techniques he may have to use to bring the source under control and maintain that relationship, the biggest loser may be the clandestine officer."[1]

Most of us have conflicting beliefs about the general relationship between a person's social environment and his or her moral character. On the one hand, we think that bad companions and what an older Moral Theology spoke of as occasions of sin do contribute to the corruption of persons and result in evil deeds. On the other hand, we also commonly think that strength of character is shown precisely in the person's ability to resist the pressures of the environment and to transcend the limits it seems to set.

One way to reconcile these beliefs is to affirm that the social environment has important effects on personality and the range of choices open to the person but does not determine choice and character ultimately. This reconciliation underlies traditional philosophical and theological disputes about free will and determinism. On the practical side we should recognize the likely, even if not necessary, consequences of a social environment in which there has been a deterioration of ethical standards. Neither a government nor an intelligence agency can afford to be complacent about the development of an environment in which morally right action would routinely require heroic virtue or would be perceived as abnormal. (Both leaders and critics of an intelligence agency should acknowledge both the importance of the free and responsible individual as subject of moral choice as well as the general human need for a social environment that will be supportive of moral values.)

But the moral damage argument actually cuts closer to the bone than general considerations about the moral aspects of the environment within an intelligence agency. It raises the question of the effect of the officer's actions on the officer himself—rather than his social environment. The issue is really the moral damage which the intelligence officer inflicts on himself or suffers as a result of actions that contravene common moral standards. The claim that immoral action, while it may bring certain nonmoral gains to the person who performs it, actually leaves him worse off is at least as old as Plato.[2] Kant is particularly emphatic in maintaining that the person who advances his interests by immoral means fails to respect himself "as a moral person and violates his nature as a rational being."[3] The Biblical tradition suggests similar views when it insists on the unworthiness of the prosperity of the evil and unscrupulous man.[4] Any theory, whether theological or philosophical, which allows for transcendent sanctions for immoral conduct may be developed in such a way that punishment is not so much an extrinsic penalty for wrongdoing but a manifestation of the harm already inflicted on the soul of the individual by his own decisions.[5]

In assessing claims that immoral activity damages the perpetrator, we have to recognize the distinction between two fundamentally different types of actions. The first type is the choice of actions which the individual believes to be morally wrong; the second type is the choice of actions which the individual believes to be justifiable even if they are in violation of recognized moral norms. The grounds for the justification of deviant actions may be various, e.g., the avoidance of greater harm (especially important in the utilitarian moral tradition) or the requirement of one's mission or task or role. Thus, we find that in intelligence agencies there is a general recognition that the acquisition of intelligence from human sources requires deception and manipulation. Foreign nationals are encouraged to violate the laws of their countries, which is likely to involve them in conflicts of conscience, but it is believed that such practices are "necessary means" to the preservation of our national security.

Preserving national security is regarded as a morally worthy goal, at least when the nation in question constitutes a free political community[6] that observes certain general standards of justice both internally (the requirements of the Rule of Law) and externally (refraining from aggression and subversion against its neighbors). Furthermore, the task of preserving national security through the provision of accurate intelligence through the chain of command is a task to which the officers of the agency have a commitment. This task gives rise to role-specific obligations and responsibilities[7] to which members of that agency have freely bound themselves.

*   *   *

This framework of task and obligation provides the basis for an argument justifying exceptions to certain moral norms, particularly in the area of truth-telling and deception. Three things should be stressed about the intent of the following line or argument.

First, it attempts to justify systematic departures from accepted moral norms because we are dealing with practices which, it is argued, are inherently necessary for an agency that aims at gathering intelligence from human sources. We are not dealing with exceptions to moral rules on an emergency basis or as a way of handling isolated cases of exceptional difficulty. Thus, we are dealing with something more analogous to the rules of war than to the spontaneous measures one improvises to protect himself from unexpected assault.

Second, it is not intended that even repeated departures from moral norms should overturn the moral system in general or even the specific norms which are being broken. The departures from moral norms are meant to be discriminating. The internal standards of accountability for one's actions are upheld with a rigor that surpasses what is customarily found in many areas of public and private life. Deception is to be used against the nation's adversaries or against those who might consort with those adversaries—but not against colleagues (except possibly in some counterintelligence activities) or against constitutionally established authority.

Finally, the mission of intelligence is to gather information in as reliable a manner as possible and to communicate that information to those charged with making decisions in matters of national security. Clearly, this mission would be gravely compromised if deception on the part of Agency officers were to be undiscriminating, that is, if they were to become liars, cheats, or persons in whom others could not have confidence. Thus, the requirements of the intelligence mission itself demand that those who fulfill it not be corrupted.

The justifying argument may be put briefly as follows:

1. The defense of the security of a just political community is a morally worthy end.
2. Intelligence is necessary to the protection of that just political community.
3. The gathering from human sources of information that is otherwise unobtainable is in at least some cases a necessary means for acquiring insights into the intentions, capabilities, and activities of actual or potential adversaries.
4. The effective gathering of such information from human sources may require both the use of deception and other actions that deviate from generally accepted moral norms.
5. The protection of the security of a just political community then provides moral justifications for the use of deception and for other actions that deviate from generally accepted moral norms.

This reasoning exemplifies a rather common type of argument in which an appeal to the worth of the end serves to justify the means proposed. The means are not commended for themselves, though it need not be supposed that they are always objectionable in themselves. This particular argument does grant that there is a prima facie moral case against deception and other practices that are part of intelligence work, but maintains that there are other considerations some of which (such as the protection of a free society) have a certain moral weight that overrides the moral objections.

In examining the argument step by step, the following points should be borne in mind. *The protection of a just political community is a morally worthy end.* This principle is not highly controversial when the community to be defended meets certain minimum moral standards. It would not hold for such regimes as Nazi Germany. Some morally unsatisfactory regimes may be defended on the ground that the likely alternative is worse—but the force of the argument is materially weakened. This principle would not be acceptable to anarchists, but could even be accepted by many pacifists, who actually direct their objections to the means commonly used to defend the political community. It is a principle that can be used to justify a wide range of actions—some of them violent and some deceptive, but many neither. But it is not a fundamental principle itself; for, as we have already seen, the application of it requires prior judgments about the moral character of the regime to be defended. These judgments are complex since they involve both the adoption of certain normative standards for assessing the justice of political societies and empirical information about the performance of the government to be assessed. Such judgments need not involve sophisticated theories from philosophy or await recondite information from the social sciences. Usually, they are broad summary judgments which allow for the possibility of contrary tendencies in a regime that is generally committed to the rule of law but at the same time acquiesces in miscarriages of justice and in the denial of rights to certain minority groups. Also, such judgments can be changed in the light of new information and developments. The intent is not to accord an absolute value to the security of the nation but to affirm its moral worth because (a) it satisfies significant human needs and (b) it conforms to moral standards. Also, it should be remembered that like most of the considerations advanced in this paper, it can be appealed to by citizens of different nations.

I observed earlier that this principle is not highly controversial in itself, but we have to recognize as a political fact that it can be affirmed by different people at different times with varying degrees of conviction and force. Thus, in the case of certain sections of our society during the period of American involvement in Vietnam, especially after 1965, there came to be a weakening of the readiness to affirm it; this was relevant to changes in the public's acceptance of the legitimacy of intelligence activities.

The second principle, that *the provision of accurate information on actual or potential adversaries is a necessary part of the protection of a just political community,* is not controversial in itself, although obviously there can be disagreements about what foreign governments or political movements are to be counted as actual or potential adversaries. This principle affirms that information is a "necessary part" of the protection of national security. In contrast to "the necessary means" discussed later, it is intended to highlight the essential part that information plays in protecting the national security. The link is not merely contingent. There may well be disagreements about the effectiveness or reliability or precision or moral justifiability of particular ways of gathering the relevant information, but one cannot conceive a rational program for protecting national security in which accurate information does not play a central role.

The third principle—that *collection from human sources of otherwise unobtainable information is in at least some cases a necessary means for acquiring insights into the intentions, capabilities, and actions of actual or potential adversaries*—is a claim of a different character. It has been disputed recently, notably by Godfrey and by those people who accept our second principle but hold that American intelligence should rely exclusively on such technological means of getting information as satellite photography and electronic monitoring. The question of whether American intelligence should rely primarily on technological means or human sources is irrelevant for the present, since the problem of moral justification arises from any systematic use of human sources. In assessing our third principle we are dealing with an empirical or factual necessity. The issue in dispute is whether, given both the general facts about an adversarial situation and about the capabilities and costs of various system for gathering information and given agreement about the objective to be attained, a specific kind of means is necessary for the attainment of the objective. This is the sort of issue that cannot be resolved without extensive familiarity both with the work of gathering and assessing intelligence and with comparative evaluations of different types of collection systems. A priori considerations of the sort dear to philosophers have a relatively small part to play in such an assessment, with one exception. To the extent that social and political events are shaped by the choices of individuals or relatively small groups, then there will be a corresponding place for the gathering of information from human sources on the intentions, decisions, and activities of these individuals and groups.

While we admit that acceptance of a principle such as this depends in a decisive way on expert judgment, it may be worthwhile to offer a layman's impression. Intelligence is an inherently open-ended task. Possession of information by an intelligence agency does not actually contribute to the defense of national security unless that information is communicated to responsible authorities in a form suitable to guide and inform their decisions. Hence, both analytic judgment in the preparation of the intelligence product and confidence in the reliability of the product on the part of those using it are crucial factors if the information is actually to contribute to the morally significant objective of protecting national security. This points two ways with regard to the use of human sources. On the one hand, simply gathering more information is neither necessary nor sufficient to ensure that objective. In certain cases, that can be done by improving the intelligence product or by cooperation among agencies or with foreign services—and not by gathering more data. Confidence in the product is, however, likely to be significantly increased if end-users are aware that all sources are being used to the fullest practicable extent. This would in itself constitute a significant reason for the use of human sources.

A further point to bear in mind is that this principle asserts that the gathering of information from human sources particularly with respect to an adversary's intentions is a necessary means in some cases. This claim constitutes an effective reply to the argument that the practice is to be rejected in all cases. The line of argument that we are considering is not intended to constitute a blank-check justification for any and every form of deception and morally problematic activity that may be connected with human source collection. Judgments about the necessity and, hence, the justifiability of such collection efforts and morally problematic activities have to be made on a more specific basis. They have to be made with a view to devising alternative means for collecting the information that is likely to be gained, and the unavoidable costs and risks inherent in a particular operation. In many situations these can be estimated only in a very rough way, since much of what one would have to know to make a more precise judgment is hidden at the time.

The prudent assignment of missions—a responsible delegation sensitive to the capacities and vulnerabilities of the personnel involved—can resolve the question of moral justification. But to do so, it must confront in a serious and honest way the question of whether collection of intelligence from human sources is really necessary. That decision normally is the responsibility of those who hold executive authority within and over a particular intelligence agency. It cannot realistically be taken by subordinates or on a case-by-case basis. Subordinates, however, may well be able to surmise that the wrong answer has been given and that alternative means are being overlooked or that information of peripheral value is being pursued by questionable means. It then becomes their responsibility to call this to the attention of appropriate authorities.

Our fourth principle—that *the use of human sources requires the use of deception and other activities that deviate from generally accepted moral norms*—does not seem to be controversial. The important point to remember for anyone who would argue for the moral justifiability of deception and other problematic activities on the ground of necessity is that the requirement that the questionable means must be genuinely necessary still holds.

The final principle is that *the protection of the security of a just political community provides moral justification for practices that deviate from generally accepted moral norms*. It is offered as a conclusion from the conjunction of the previous four principles. This argument has significant similarities to arguments advanced to justify the use of violence in self-defense and in defense of the nation or political community. In arguments advanced to justify the use of violence there is a similar appeal to necessity, i.e., to preserve goods that are in some sense one's own in a situation of conflict. Hence, these lines of argument are usually unpersuasive to people who are more drawn to altruistic and utopian forms of moral discourse. On the other hand, they are likely to seem irrelevant to those who take the legitimacy of self-defense for granted, whose only concern is to find the most effective means to that end. Nonetheless, arguments and considerations of this general type serve to remind us that the struggles in which we engage as political and human beings are against adversaries who, however malevolent their intent, share with us both the grandeur and the misery of the human condition. However wrongheaded or even wicked they may be, evil is not to be done to them without serious justification. A readiness to inflict evil without sufficient reason is indeed a sign of moral corruption and is not acceptable within any of the major Western ethical traditions. The mere fact of an adversary relationship, even one of open conflict, does not itself justify the infliction either by violence or by deception of injury beyond that needed to protect the security and the rights of those individuals or groups that the officer or the organization is defending. This constitutes the foundation for limiting the activities of combatants in war through what Michael Walzer refers to as "the war convention."[8] It should also constitute a foundation for bringing espionage activities under certain limitations.

The need to justify the questionable practices inherent in collecting from human sources and the possibility of providing such justification by an appeal to the protection of national security should leave the intelligence officer both cautious and resolute. The need for justification should make the collector cautious about gathering information from human sources; the provision of that justification should make him resolute in carrying on his work, though also sensitive to the possibility that greater evils than had been foreseen may result.

*   *   *

Having considered at length one way of providing moral justification for the questionable activities inherent in human source collection, we are now in a position to assess the claim by Godfrey and others that participation in such activities is likely to result in moral damage to officers of an intelligence agency. We must begin by considering the individual officer's attitude to the considerations advanced in the argument we have been presenting and in similar arguments that may be offered to make the same point. An officer who accepts this argument and has some sense (which need not be fully explicit) that he or she is engaged in a morally justifiable work will be in a very different position from one who finds that he or she is not able to make such an affirmation. Here we are talking about a reasonable affirmation on the basis of one's experience after a general consideration of the issues—not about the ability to construct a decisive argument or "proof" for one's position.

This reasonable affirmation can be made even when one feels some emotional discomfort about some aspects of the work or a reluctance to have one's own activities brought to the light of publicity or to the knowledge of innocent acquaintances. An inability to make such affirmation would suggest that should serious moral issues surface the officer is very likely to experience a crisis of conscience. If he or she then continues, such perseverance will involve either a violation of conscience or at least a response to the situation that is a flight from decision. The officer then is likely to develop a form of moral schizophrenia, perhaps thinking of himself as a good officer (loyal, obedient, diligent) and a bad person (because of the immoral things he does or thinks he has to do). An officer in such a frame of mind is indeed a likely candidate for moral damage. He is also likely to be of diminished usefulness to any agency that employs him. It should also be pointed out that he will be aware of the moral damage that he is suffering.

What of the officer who affirms that engaging in deception and the other questionable practices inherent in gathering information from human sources is justified? As we have already indicated, there may well be psychological burdens imposed on him. But these burdens are not a sufficient indication of moral damage. After all, we recognize that heart surgeons, air traffic controllers, and some construction workers may bear psychological burdens as a result of their work, without concluding that their work is morally wrong. (It may be morally wrong to encourage or to allow vulnerable persons to accept unnecessary risks, but that is another matter.)

The person who engages in questionable practices in the belief that they are justifiable will not suffer a crisis of conscience except when he confronts an activity which oversteps a legal constraint or moral limit. Overstepping a legal constraint on intelligence activities normally should raise a moral problem because limits may well have been designed to protect certain moral values and prevent wrongdoing, because respect for the common good in a substantially just society imposes a prima facie: a reasonable affirmation based on experience obligation on all citizens to obey laws that are not manifestly unjust, and because the officer has voluntarily assumed an obligation to defend and uphold those laws.

Now the line of argument advanced in the second part of this essay presupposes the possibility that collection activities may exceed the limits of what can be justified by the need to protect national security. These limits may shift, depending on the situation, but limits must always remain and must be acknowledged, even while they bring with them the possibility of crises of conscience. The recognition that crises can arise itself is a sign that the intelligence officer has not suffered the ultimate moral damage of becoming incapable of perceiving the implications of his actions or of preferring the more moral course. There remains, however, the possibility of lesser degrees of moral damage. Certain patterns of action can become habitual and can affect a person's sense of values and general way of dealing with the world. A sign that the intelligence officer may be suffering moral damage is a tendency to apply morally problematic or questionable practices beyond the realm in which the person's assignment demands them, for instance, in managing one's personal affairs, or in dealings with one's colleagues. Tendencies to use deceptive or manipulative techniques to resolve the problems of ordinary life, to advance one's career, or to further a particular point of view are likely in the long run to bring harm to the individual, his associates, and to the agency, even if they offer some short-term benefits. They should be treated as a serious problem.

Another sign of possible moral damage would be preoccupation with questionable practices for their own sake. The point that should be uppermost, both in the psychological awareness of the officer and in the logic of moral argument is the contribution to national security that his work is to make. He may carry this work forward with a distaste for certain of its aspects or with cool resolution or with professional composure, but there is no way to combine moral integrity with a positive enthusiasm for deception, manipulation, and "dirty tricks." (This needs to be distinguished from understandable feelings of satisfaction arising out of a difficult task successfully accomplished or from the immature enthusiasm of a junior officer, which he may well outgrow with experience.)

An officer's continued performance of his duties when they involve questionable practices does not serve as a sign of moral damage, if the argument of this paper or something like it is right. If such practices can be given moral justification as a means of protecting national security and if the officer forms a good faith judgment that they are justified in his situation, then he does not suffer moral damage by following his conscience. Outside observers may feel regret that he does what he does, and we may all feel regret that the world is such that his actions are necessary and useful. But we should also recognize that the doing of these things can be an expression of clear conscience, of devotion to duty, of concern for the common good, and of civil courage in difficult circumstances.

NOTES

1. Drexel Godfrey, Jr., "Ethics and Intelligence," *Foreign Affairs* 56 (1978), p. 631.

2. Plato, *Republic* I, 353 c–e.

3. Immanuel Kant, *Groundwork of the Metaphysic of Morals*, tr. H. J. Paton (New York: Harper & Row, date?), pp. 102–103.

4. Cf. 1 Kings 21; Psalm 1.4–6; Psalm 37; Amos 5:7–1:3; Isaiah 29:13–21.

5. Immanuel Kant, *Religion Within the Limits of Reasons Alone*, tr. Theodore M. Greene and Hoyt H. Hudson (New York: Harper & Row, 1960), pp. 63–64. See also S. I. Thomas Aquinas, *Summa contra Gentiles III*, pp. 140–144.

6. Michael Walzer, *Just and Unjust Wars* (New York: Basic Books, 1977), pp. 54–55, bases the right of national defense on the character of the communal life.

7. A stimulating treatment of role-specific moral obligations can be found in David Hollenbach's "Plural Loyalties and Moral Agency Government," in *Personal Values in Public Policy*, ed. John C. Haughey (New York: Paulist Press, 1979), pp. 77–82.

8. Walzer, pp. 44–47, where Walzer gives an account of this notion.

7

Intelligence Collection and Analysis
Dilemmas and Decisions

John B. Chomeau and Anne C. Rudolph

Editor's note: Chomeau and Rudolph consider the requirement for clandestine operations and covert operations, observing that these operations routinely involve deception and other activities which would in most contexts be considered both illegal and immoral. The authors argue that "just war" principles provide an appropriate ethical framework for such activities.

To establish a consensus for discussion of the intelligence profession as similar to or distinct from other professions, and to assist us in arguing for the importance of a professional ethic, we define profession as an honorific title founded on a unique competence in the performance of special tasks or services with a commitment to community-related services which establishes a professional-client relationship.

The intelligence officer is a highly trained professional with strict standards for performance, conduct, and promotion within the profession. Through additional training and overseas travel the intelligence professional is obligated to improve skills in the clandestine collection and analysis of secret information, while always mindful of the responsibility of being a public servant. We assert that the source of an ethical dilemma of keeping secrets in an open, democratic society resides in an unclear notion of who is our client, particularly if circumstances merit security classification of intelligence information.

Therefore, we must ponder whether the need to maintain secrecy overrides the right of the American public for an accounting of our activities. As professional intelligence officers we must know for whom we are acting as a moral agent and what secrecy does to change the nature of the professional-client relationship in the sphere of national security affairs?

It is the view of the professional intelligence officer that our clients are ultimately the American people, but in the day-to-day effort to get our jobs done, few have an opportunity to reflect upon this. Under our system of government the congressional oversight panels and the existence of a free press serve as protectors of the public's interest. Accountability for intelligence operations should be ensured through this reflection on the nation's conscience. We must also consider the special responsibility of the intelligence officer as one who is obliged to work in secret, obliged to perfect the skills of the profession, and to employ these skills solely for the benefit of the American society or client. Some of the skills of the professional intelligence officer if exercised outside of their proper purpose or place would be both illegal and immoral. Moreover, the purpose and unique expertise of the intelligence officer is not too dissimilar from the military officer. Both professionals employ skills that have little direct application outside of government. Both support policy makers by managing the use of force in an effort to ensure peace by protecting information and operations vital to our national security. In a sentence, the intelligence professional, like the military officer, protects innocents against aggression.

The fundamental question remains, how does ethics relate to the intelligence profession? After all, it is clear that intelligence officers are supposed to be ethical. That the Intelligence Community has an ethically responsible task is also clear. However, how ethics relates to the specifics of their work and what an individual officer needs to know about ethics is not clear. This issue is not talked about much in the Intelligence Community, probably because the "business" of intelligence is shrouded by secrecy, need-to-know, distrust, and deception. Perhaps some prefer the role of ethics in international affairs to be "as little as possible."

When attempting to set forth a body of principles for the conduct of intelligence operations and the inculcation of these principles for officers serving in the collection and analysis components of organizations such as the CIA, one is faced almost immediately with several key questions.

Are there general moral principles governing the conduct of professional intelligence officers? Do we have a code of ethics similar to those which apply to other professions such as law, medicine, and the military? If so, whence do they come, how well are they understood by intelligence officers, and how do we teach them to those involved in collection, analysis, covert action, and the management of intelligence operations? If there is not a recognized code governing the conduct of intelligence operations, in what manner are limits set on what is acceptable and needed, and how do we prevent our profession from accepting guidelines such as "the end does justify the means" or "everything goes, just so you don't get caught"? Our intent is to present the nature of this question, to describe the moral vitality and bankruptcy of various theoretical approaches to this problem, and to devise a systematic means of processing an ethical question which can be taught to the practitioners of this profession. We assume the intelligence profession possesses power in the form of secret information, and this represents a kind of force that can be used to protect our nation's interests. We therefore advocate the application of just war theory as a way of establishing certain prima facie evidence against the use of force in secret intelligence operations until such an act of force may be justified under these criteria. We therefore assert deontological principles against intervention and the use of secrecy except in justifiable cases. Hence the burden of proof is on the consequentialist who must reasonably justify a divergence from the deontological principles by applying the Just War criteria. Where possible and within the limits of security we will provide case studies representative of the types of dilemmas that may confront the intelligence professional.

ARGUMENTS

There are several hypothetical arguments that can be made on the issues of whether there exists a body of ethics governing intelligence operations. These arguments will provide a structure for further discussion of the dilemmas.

Our actions are first governed by U.S. law, although some of these statutes were written in such a way that they are subject to a broad interpretation. To deal with these statutes, CIA seeks assistance from its own legal staff, as well as from the Department of Justice and other governmental bodies. A review of intelligence law indicates, however, that it is difficult to derive a moral standard from this source. Many situations are deliberately left fuzzy. Where there are specific requirements or prohibitions, these usually have been placed on the books as the result of an executive or legislative judgment that a situation or practice needed correction or regulation. We also operate under Executive Orders which have the force of law, but which can be changed by the president without reference to Congress and the courts. These are a little more specific than the U.S. Code, but may not provide guidance in all cases. Executive orders issued by Presidents Ford, Carter, and Reagan all specifically prohibit the use of assassination. This structure was established as the result of congressional investigations that uncovered efforts, albeit unsuccessful, to murder specific foreign political figures. Despite this guidance, questions continue to be raised in the press about CIA practices in this regard, and some observers do not see the presidential order as guidance which has universal applicability.

If laws and regulations do not provide adequate moral guidance, what can you fall back on? And what is customary and proper in intelligence operations is hard to codify and particularly hard to provide to new employees. We all have a personal sense of what is right and proper, but how do we evolve an institutional sense—what are the traditions within our profession, and how do these correspond with what this nation, through its citizens and their elected representatives, considers to be justifiable and moral options?

Here we find the crux of the dilemma. In an open, democratic system of government, "We the People" govern, and each federal official is ultimately responsible to the people. But how can you keep the people adequately informed about sensitive intelligence operations? Even if they knew the details, they frequently would not comprehend the whys and wherefores of the conduct of clandestine operations. The principal question, therefore, is whether public sentiment can serve as an adequate judge of the ethics of our profession. We have tried to formalize this through the use of congressional oversight. This has provided for collective responsibility on the part of both the executive and legislative branches of government, but recent press reports indicate that there remains considerable skepticism in public about the effectiveness of this system.

It is necessary at this time to outline some of the types of intelligence activities considered in this essay, so that we can discuss the ethical principles which apply to each of them. The first category involves clandestine intelligence collection operations which are meant to be secret. We are attempting to obtain information denied to us through normal means. In fact, other governments, especially in closed societies, use specific methods to prevent us from learning information they wish to restrict. We use various methods, including the use of human agents, and spies, whom we recruit to obtain the information using clandestine methods. This, by its very nature, requires a certain amount of deception.

Our officers serving overseas need to have cover stories to protect their clandestine operations. Because every nation considers spying to be illegal and those who get caught are subject to severe penalties, cover stories are important not only for the safety of intelligence officers, but also to protect our agents and our very ability to conduct espionage. The deception is not intended to be malicious; it is used to hide the true identity and purpose of those involved in what we consider to be legitimate aspects of espionage. In moral terms, a certain amount of operational deception is proper if used to protect the clandestine operation and those involved in it. It is not proper if used to hide embarrassing outcomes from the American people.

There is clearly a requirement for a certain amount of deception in clandestine operations. At times we must make others believe that we are doing something that is plausibly innocent when in fact we are conducting secret operations. This is an extension of the principle of cover and provides the clandestine officer a means to open a door or peek through a window so that a secret operation can be undertaken. Clandestine operations to gather information inevitably involve human relationships as well. A recruitment is frequently made on the basis of personal friendship and mutual trust. Nevertheless, the intelligence officer must have some measure of control. Thus, these relationships may involve manipulation or deception. To what extent are the practices needed to maintain control "honorable"? Does this create a moral dilemma for the intelligence officer involved in such operations?

Clandestine operations are considered to be correct and morally justifiable as long as they are conducted on the basis that they are needed to protect the state. But they would not be morally justifiable if they violated the basic principles for which we stand and the institutional traditions of this intelligence service.

That is easily said, but how do we, as professional intelligence officers, know what is morally justifiable and what is not? Under what standard do we operate? Who sets the rules and how do we apply them in a given situation? It certainly encompasses more than the intelligence laws, and the ethics of this institution and profession do differ markedly from any other body of personal or professional ethics. (In fact, we come closer to those ethics which apply to the military profession than most intelligence officers recognize.)

In order to provide some kind of guideline, we have developed what we call the Chomeau-Rudolph proposal. It holds that:

- We follow the guidelines for duty, honor, and country.
- We upgrade these principles using Just War theory as a systematic approach to ethical problems inherent in intelligence operations and analysis.

The goal of the Chomeau-Rudolph proposal is to increase the morally appropriate options available to professional intelligence officers.

Duty. Duty is the obligation not only to do the job, but within ethical norms. Therefore, one needs a knowledge of the moral principles and a facility developed through practice in applying them.

Honor. Honor emphasizes moral development to be as important as physical, intellectual, tradecraft, and other criteria of professional competence.

Country. By country, we mean seeking to uphold the Constitution, but this should extend beyond the strictly legal underpinnings to cover other criteria of professional competence.

We have determined that the most sensible basis for justifying the use of intelligence operations corresponds with the general principles for the use of military power in the protection of the nation-state. Thus, we have turned to the Just War theory to provide a framework for establishing moral principles for intelligence. Making moral assessments on complex matters requires applying universal principles and making prudent judgments. The variables involved in these moral assessments include (1) the type of logic involved, (2) the perceptions of the facts as they apply to the case at hand, and (3) the values of the judges.

The logic we have employed starts with the basic deontological principles favoring nonintervention, honesty, and trust in another country until such time that holding such values can cause more harm than good. In other words, the burden is put on the consequentialist who must argue a case for a departure from the absolute moral principles. A consequentialist may be justified in recommending a clandestine operation to counter the hostile actions of another country against us or the use of deception to protect U.S. interests or operations.

The accurate perception of facts, in a mass of noise and attempts on the parts of others to confuse us, is a critical part of our profession. Knowledge is our product. We endeavor to maintain analytical objectivity, for it is key to the integrity of our work. Analytical perceptions which have been distorted by policy preferences, political ideologies, and personal bias may obscure the facts. We must ever be cognizant of these pressures and potential dilemmas created when policy skews analytical judgments.

Finally, the values of the judges—our policy level consumers and the American public—become the true arbiter of the activities of the intelligence system. Frequently we must consider what projects will look like to the public when (not if) exposed. But people who are basically moral can reach quite different conclusions about what is right or wrong. In intelligence operations there is no truly objective right or wrong which is universally understood. We must attempt to operate within a scheme of ethical norms which is commonly understood and applicable to our profession. We believe that this scheme is contained in Just War theory.

The Just War principles have evolved over the centuries and are well understood to apply to the ethical standards to be followed by a nation at war. Since the major function of intelligence is to provide early and adequate warning of an attack by forces inimical to the nation, one can derive an extension of the Just War principles to intelligence. The CIA was formed in 1947 primarily to protect the United States against a growing Soviet threat and to ensure that we would suffer no more Pearl Harbors. Initial focus was almost exclusively on the USSR and its allies, but recent threats to this nation have taken so many other forms that we have come to use intelligence to provide timely and accurate information on a whole host of issues that affect the security of the U.S. and its people, including economic and agricultural problems overseas, as well as problems such as terrorism and narcotics. To review briefly the *jus ad bellum* requirements:

- just cause—defend one's state, citizens, allies.
- just intent—restoration of peace, freedom.
- probability of success—can we pull it off?
- proportional objectives—counterintervention, preserve secrecy of operation.
- last resort—all options considered, exploited.
- ordered by competent authority—president, DCI, etc.

The *jus in bello* requirements are:

- discrimination—no assassination, invoke double effect principle.
- proportionality—cause limited damage, undertake "acceptable risk."

A reasonable explanation for intelligence capability is the argument of the consequentialist who remains true to the value of Duty, Country, and Honor but can justify a departure from the prohibition on the use of force.

The consequentialist is justified for arguing for a use of force given that the superpower nature of the U.S. places such an obligation on it that not acting in a certain situation could be more evil than acting. Policymakers as well as intelligence officers must consider the right thing to do in the context of the real, rather than the ideal or hoped for situation . . . and the price of neglect may be too high. In many instances the instrument of choice in the conduct of foreign affairs is the quiet and deniable use of intelligence resources instead of the more forceful and overt means, such as military force. But there are some serious considerations, including the ability of political leaders to develop a consensus that the non-war options are viable and acceptable. How does one integrate the wishes of the American people and to what extent should their intentions control the planning and execution of intelligence operations? If secrecy is an executive privilege in our society, how we do protect our secrets from other components of our own society? Some effort must be made to weigh the moral imperatives against the possibility of damage to the nation if secret operations are not used.

Staying for the moment within the rubric of clandestine intelligence collection, the principles outlined above suggest that you must seek information in which this government has a legitimate interest. Operations simply for their own sake are not justifiable. The officer seeking approval for a particular collection effort needs to have a specific goal in mind in order to gain approval. The CIA has an internal review mechanism to assure this is the case. The principle of "just means" is a little more murky, but there are well-understood professional standards included in what we call tradecraft, or the proper conduct of clandestine operations. These principles are taught to all clandestine service officers. An officer who departs from the norm or uses unethical means to gain information runs the risk of criticism, reprimand,

and endangering future operations. The principles of last resort and proportionality come together in the conduct of clandestine operations. Our officers understand that they should be working to collect only that type of information which cannot be collected overtly by State Department officers, or through clandestine technical means; then the case officer should question whether the use of an agent is proper. Sometimes the agent will be asked to provide reporting in order to verify or amplify data from other sources, but that would still meet the criteria of last resort and proportionality.

The last criterion, likelihood of success, is one of the most troublesome. Sometimes the information desired is so valuable that extremely high risks and costs in an attempt to gain it are justifiable. In every operation the key questions to be asked are how much risk can be accepted, what is the potential payoff, and what penalties would have to be paid if the operation failed. As with the rest of clandestine operations, these principles are taught in training programs for clandestine service officers and are part of the review process undertaken before CIA Headquarters approval is given.

Let us review a few illustrations of the types of dilemmas faced by clandestine officers. All would agree that it is wrong for government officials to accept a bribe. Is it wrong for an intelligence officer to give a bribe in the course of operations to accomplish the task? There are many areas of the world where bribery is an accepted norm. Another interesting situation might involve a cover story that is starting to unravel. The basic principle in the use of cover is deniability. Should an officer deny association with intelligence—that is, lie—to maintain cover? Intelligence officers are taught to maintain cover even if taken prisoner and there is ample evidence about the activity in question. Is it a lie and immoral to persist in a cover story at that time? A good example is the U-2 incident in which Francis Gary Powers was shot down over the Soviet Union. His cover story was that he was on a weather reconnaissance flight and had gotten lost. President Eisenhower stuck with the cover story despite clear evidence that, first, Powers was alive and, second, that the Soviets had recovered part of the aircraft. When Khrushchev paraded the evidence out in front of Soviet television cameras, however, deniability was gone. At that point, President Eisenhower came forward and assumed complete responsibility for the operation. This was proper, for to continue in the denial was no longer justifiable in an attempt to protect sources and methods. They had been totally compromised. To continue to deny would be to lie without purpose or effect.

A totally different set of problems arises in the area of intelligence analysis. These problems may result in part from the separation between operations and analysis. While there is good communication between the officers involved in both activities, the functions are quite distinct, and because of compartmentation—or "need-to-know"—analysts and operations officers carry out their tasks in what might seem to be two different cultures. Nevertheless, they must understand their collective responsibility to the system as a whole. One of the points we attempt to inculcate in training is that all agency officers are collectively responsible for whatever the CIA does. An analyst cannot distance himself or herself from operations and say "that is not part of my business and I don't know what is really going on in the clandestine side of the agency anyhow."

In the business of intelligence analysis, principles of business ethics may provide better guidelines than the Just War principles which we have applied to clandestine operations. The CIA analytical function was set up to provide to the DCI and to the White House a truly independent group of country and technical experts who could determine the threats to the U.S. as they saw them. Intelligence analysts must not get involved in the formulation and implementation of policy, nor can they construct their analysis so as to favor one particular policy position over another. This means that the CIA analyst must walk a very fine line in order to provide information which is both objective and policy or program relevant without taking sides in the internal fights within the administration which frequently evolve over these issues. In addition to providing intelligence to the executive branch, CIA also provides intelligence analysis to the Congress. In the U.S. system, that inevitably means that the agency will be providing information to a legislative body that may seek to overturn, stop, or alter the policies of the executive. That raises the question of "For whom are we really working?" Former DCI William Colby, just prior to his testimony before a Senate committee, responded to that question by saying that our obligation is to the truth.

All analysts have personal opinions and biases. It is hard to write a truly objective article which does not in some way reflect how the analyst feels about the issue. We used to say, when training analysts, "are you starting with the premise that the glass is half full or half empty?" If an analyst believes that the administration is off on the wrong track, is it proper to attempt to steer or change policy through analysis? Some analysts believe that they should try to change the views of policymakers through their analysis—not understanding that high-level policy decisions are based on many other factors than just the "objective" facts and interpretations provided by intelligence specialists.

The most serious ethical problem faced by intelligence analysts is the attempt by others to politicize their product. The CIA by and large has been able to stand back from policy and program squabbles, but it is very possible to state what is considered to be a nonpolitical view and discover that the analyst has lined up on the side of one of the principal policymakers and has perhaps alienated others. Sometimes, then, what is perceived as politicization is only an association of our analysis with a specific policy position. Most intelligence analysts jealously guard their position as guardians of the truth and resist strenuously any attempts to co-opt them. Sometimes, however, we go so far in an attempt to maintain our independence and objectivity that we find ourselves taking a line of reasoning which argues a position which is in opposition to a policy which has been espoused by the administration. There are enough checks and balances built into the system so that the view of any one analyst does not get out until it has been reviewed and coordinated with all the other analysts who have an interest in the subject. There is also a very cumbersome, but necessary, mechanism for editorial and managerial review of papers before they are published. If an individual analyst believes that he or she is not being adequately heard on a key issue or that his or her analysis has been politicized, there are several avenues of appeal. There have been a few analysts who have resigned in protest and taken their case to the American people (as did Sam Adams over the differences in counts of enemy forces in Vietnam), but these cases are quite rare.

Covert action, which can be quite controversial, is the type of intelligence issue most frequently discussed in the media. It accounts for only a small fraction of CIA's overall effort and does not relate either to the collection of secret information or the production of intelligence analysis. It does provide a covert means to the administration for the execution of U.S. policy overseas. That the CIA is the executive agent for most covert activity on behalf of the U.S. Government is almost an accident of history. When the national security apparatus (including the National Security Council, the Department of Defense and the Central Intelligence Agency) was being created in 1947, the logical place to put the responsibility for covert action was in the CIA. These kinds of operations had been performed well by the OSS in World War II. It seemed to make sense to continue to use those methods as the Cold War began in earnest; and although we can not brag about our successes, covert action has made a positive impact in many instances.

The major feature of covert action is that it is deniable, i.e., that the hand of the U.S. Government is hidden and deniable. It is designed, in part, to head off nasty situations overseas which could harm the United States and its interests and secretly to favor those who are most likely to support us. Many of the recipients of U.S. covert assistance would be seriously compromised should the fact of the covert action be known. For this reason, it is necessary to take extraordinary measures to protect these relationships. Unfortunately, in recent years thanks to investigative work on the part of some journalists and because of leaks of sensitive information, the details of many of these covert activities have been compromised. Such revelations force the intelligence and policy communities into even greater secrecy and can set up great pressures on those charged with the protection of intelligence sources and methods. This creates a dilemma which has been faced by every DCI since Richard Helms. The DCI must balance the need to protect the viability of clandestine assets against the obligation to keep both the Executive and the Congress informed about intelligence operations.

There are no clear principles which apply in the use of clandestine or covert action. Each case must be judged on its own merits. There is once again implied in Just War theory a basis for the right of one government to interfere in the affairs of another, so long as the principles of just cause, just means, proportionality, etc., prevail. It is where they are exceeded or ignored that we run the risk of conducting a covert operation which violates both the principles of the agency and the nation.

The major moral principle we would set for the conduct of covert action is that it should be the sort of thing that would be acceptable to the American people, if its details were revealed—remember what we said earlier about "We the People." The final judge in these matters appears to be American public opinion as reported in our public media and pressed through our elected representatives. The problem is that we are not dealing with an informed public in most instances relating to espionage and covert actions. Does the public appear to trust either officials of the administration or their elected representatives to do what is right and proper? Just mention the name CIA in some circles in this country and you conjure visions of agents working the back alleys of the world doing things that Americans would not approve of. To make our system of checks and balances work, someone must do a more effective job explaining the why of what we are doing without revealing any of the secret specifics. In that sense, the intelligence system is dependent on the White House to explain its use of intelligence resources within the bounds of secrecy, and it is also dependent on the Congress which must learn not only what is going on, but also keep in mind what the American people would think about such operations.

If the American people are truly the final arbiters of policy in this country, and of what is ethical and moral, they need to have enough of an understanding of what is at stake to make informed judgments on these matters.

So what ethical construct do we have and how do we teach it in the classroom? First, it is patently clear that despite the problems of defining, in a universal sense, what is ethical, the CIA needs to have a commitment to teaching ethics to its employees. The nature of our work is such that it is not sufficient merely to depend upon hiring the right people. Loyalty to the agency as well as an understanding of what is appropriate in various situations can be taught in the classroom and handed down from one generation of intelligence officers to the next. Each CIA employee comes to us with a strong personal set of moral values. We are very careful to screen for these and to hire "honorable men." In our training and orientation programs, we strive to inform our officers of laws and regulations relating to our profession as well as to instill in them some of the ethos of the CIA and our traditions. Old hands usually take the newer officers under their wings and help them develop an understanding of the sensitive nature of our work and some of the principles which govern our behavior. In training classes, we frequently resort to case studies and a discussion of the pros and cons of some of the more sticky operations. It is necessary that every CIA officer has an adequate understanding of what the other components are doing—without revealing even to other CIA employees the details of the more sensitive operations. Nevertheless, the bottom line is that there is no code, no universally understood set of principles. In our work, the end does not justify the means, but it frequently charts the course which must be taken. It is up to the professional intelligence officer to choose the right and proper course of action to obtain the proper results. Just War principles can help, but the final judge does appear to be what the American people and their elected representative would hold to be necessary and proper.

8

An Ethical Defense of Torture in Interrogation

Fritz Allhoff

After the events of 9/11, the concept of torture has emerged as one that is both pertinent and provoking. National polls have shown that some Americans support torture in some situations, though the majority still stands opposed. Torture has not received a tremendous amount of discussion in the philosophical literature, though I suspect that the leftward slant of academia would, for the most part, ensure limited support for torture. In this paper, I would like to first discuss why torture is an important issue and then advance an argument that supports torture in limited cases.

The *Encyclopedia of Ethics* defines torture as "the deliberate infliction of violence, and through violence, severe mental and/or physical suffering upon individuals. It may be inflicted by individuals or groups and for diverse ends, ranging from extracting information, confession, admission of culpability or liability, and self-incrimination to general persuasion, intimidation, and amusement."[1] I think that this is a good definition. Notably, torture is not necessarily a form of punishment, though it could be—both deterrence and retribution theorists could advance arguments in its support. Rather, torture can also be used instrumentally in order to achieve important aims, such as the acquisition of important information.

It is of course worth noting that torture is illegal in the United States and that no United States agency can legally engage in torture abroad.[2] As absolute as this policy stance seems, there are important questions regarding its implications. For example, if an American intelligence official is standing quietly in the corner of a room while a foreign government subjugates a terrorist suspect to torture, has the American government violated its mandate? Less hypothetically, American officials have admitted that the United States has transferred prisoners to the intelligence agencies of Jordan, Egypt, and/ or Morocco, all of which are known for using torture as a method of interrogation. Reportedly, some of these prisoners have even been handed over along with lists of questions to which they might know the answers and whose answers would be valuable to the United States.[3] While the transfer might not always be accompanied by a list of questions, it would be very naive to think that the United States would not welcome and has not accepted the information that resulted from interrogations by hostile interrogators, whether that information has been actively solicited by our government or not.

A related concern has to do with the definition of "torture"; while some practices might clearly violate our anti-torture stance, there are others whose standing is less clear. A recent *Washington Post* article detailed American interrogation methods and quoted American officials who admit to the beating of prisoners, the withholding of medical treatment, and "stress and duress" techniques, such as sleep deprivation, hooding, and forcing prisoners to hold awkward positions for hours. Prisoners may be placed in environments which resemble those of hostile countries (e.g., Arabs may be distraught to observe an Israeli flag flying overhead), or they may be subjugated to interrogations by female agents—this is psychologically traumatic for men raised in conservative Muslim cultures. The officials have maintained that these practices, while certainly unpleasant, have nevertheless fallen short of torture; they maintain that all treatment of prisoners is consistent with the Third Geneva Convention of 1949 which delineated acceptable practices of confinement and interrogation.[4] Despite the interesting legal and policy questions inherent in a debate regarding torture, I am more concerned with the morality of torture than the legality but, insofar as legality tracks morality, if torture could be shown to be morally permissible then there might be cause for legal reform.[5]

THE CONFLICT BETWEEN UTILITARIAN AND DEONTOLOGICAL APPROACHES

One reason that makes the questions as to the moral permissibility of torture so interesting is that the two leading schools of moral thought, utilitarianism and deontology, seem to disagree as to the moral status of torture. For all of the talk made as to the great differences between these programs, they seem to, at the end of the day, agree on most substantive moral questions. Torture is, I think, an interesting dilemma because the two groups would give different answers to the problem.

First, consider utilitarianism. The utilitarian argues that the right action is the one, out of those available to the agent, that maximizes total aggregate happiness. We could quite easily imagine a scenario wherein the disutility of torturing a captive (his pain, the discomfort of the torturer, expense, permanent effects to both, chance of negative events causally connected to torture, etc.) is outweighed, or even dramatically outweighed, by the utility of torture (information is provided that saves many lives and therefore garners all of the associative utilities). This utilitarian approach is most conspicuously displayed in the so-called "ticking time-bomb" cases which have been discussed by Michael Levin and Alan Dershowitz; they have both argued that torture is *obviously* justified when it is the only way to prevent a serious and imminent threat.[6]

The utilitarian might not welcome this consequence and argue that, as an empirical fact, such conditions as would be required to ensure these utility forecasts will never transpire (and thus his theory is not actually committed to torture). This is, of course, irrelevant since the point is merely that utilitarianism would, in some cases, support torture. It makes no difference whether cases are real or imagined; all that matters is the theory's commitment to the moral obligation to torture in some cases. The cautious utilitarian could also argue that I have presupposed act-utilitarianism when in actuality we should be rule-utilitarians (the right action is the one, out of those available to the agent, that accords with a rule that, when generally followed, maximizes happiness). Perhaps the general adherence to the rule "torture is wrong" is more likely than its negation to maximize happiness. Unfortunately, the problems with rule-utilitarianism are well documented; one only needs to ask whether rules have exceptions. Then, if the answer is yes, rule-utilitarianism collapses to act-utilitarianism and, if the answer is no, rule-utilitarianism really is not very utilitarian at all. I therefore find neither of these responses very effective and take it to be fairly straightforward that utilitarianism is, in some cases, committed to the moral permissibility and even moral obligation to torture.

On the other hand, deontology would seem to prohibit torture in all cases. Invoking Kant as the traditional torchbearer of this approach, we can see that torture would fail the categorical imperative test (whether applied to the first or second formulations). Perhaps the easiest way to see this is by applying the humanity form which states that we may only treat humanity, whether ourselves or others, as an end and never as a means only. By torturing a captive, we are treating him as a means *only* (toward the acquisition of information, e.g.); he is certainly not being treated in a manner to which he would consent. Torture fails to respect him as an autonomous agent and constitutes an attack on his dignity.[7, 8]

I think that because utilitarianism would, in some cases, support torture and that because Kantian deontologists would, in all cases, reject it, torture has the position of being a very interesting concept for ethical inquiry. People no doubt have their allegiances to utilitarianism or deontology but, given the conflict, there is at least something to talk about and some forum within which to advance arguments to support one conclusion or the other.

WHAT ABOUT RIGHTS?

One way to try to quickly end the debate is to assert that people have rights and that torturing them violates their rights.[9] Insofar as these two claims are true, torture could be argued to be morally impermissible. Are they true? As a descriptive claim, people certainly do have rights; in the United States these are most overtly delineated in the Bill of Rights. Even as a normative claim, most everyone agrees that people have rights, though the justifications for rights are certainly debatable.[10] Even John Stuart Mill recognized that utilitarianism needed to be able to accommodate a system of rights,[11] though many rights theorists would be unhappy with the derivative value that utilitarianism would assign to rights.

But does torture actually violate any right? Some people might think not. It could be argued that we forfeit whatever rights might protect us against torture once we engage in certain activities, such as terrorism.[12] The suggestion might be that through our complicity in terrorist activities, we give up certain protections (both legal and moral) that we might otherwise have had and, consequently, there exist no remaining rights which torture could be said to violate.[13] If this is true, that rights are the kinds of things that can be forfeited through certain circumstances, then torture would be substantially easier to defend since, given those circumstances, there would be no rights violations. Absent rights violations, appeals to the greater good could easily justify torture. There are, of course, questions as to what kinds of circumstances lead to forfeiture of rights, whether such forfeiture is partial or absolute (i.e., consists in forfeiture in some or all rights) and, if partial, which rights are the ones that are forfeited. These would be substantive questions that are certainly worth pursuing. But it is unnecessary to answer any of these questions if torture can be justified *even if* it violates rights—then the conditions and details of rights forfeiture are largely irrelevant.

So let us now presume that torture does, in fact, violate some right. I am not sure that this is always true (especially given complicity in terrorist activities), but if torture can be defended given its violation of rights, then it can certainly be defended when it does not violate rights. Thus it seems to me that this is the position that one wishing to argue for torture must consider; if successful in this endeavor then everyone should be persuaded, but if torture can only be successfully defended by supposing that it does not violate rights, then those who suppose that it does violate rights will not be convinced. The question then to answer is, supposing that rights are inalienable and are therefore never forfeited, regardless of the atrocities committed, can torture be justified?

I think that the answer is yes. The existence of a right, particularly a claim-right, provides a reason for someone not to commit a certain act against the possessor of the right. For example, if Smith has a right to life, then this right provides a reason for Jones not to kill him. For him to do so would be wrong because it would constitute a violation of Smith's right to life. But this reason is stronger than, or even incommensurable with, other reasons. For example, Jones could not justifiably say that, though he recognized that Smith had a right to life, he elected to kill Smith because of the tremendous pleasure that he would derive from the murder. The fact that Smith's death would bring Jones pleasure no doubt gives Jones a reason to pursue Smith's death, but this reason is rendered inoperative in virtue of Smith's having a right to life. To deny this would be to completely misunderstand the notion of a right.[14] In this sense, Ronald Dworkin has argued that rights are trumps because, regardless of what end Jones could realize from Smith's death, the fact that Smith has a right to life will always ensure that Jones cannot justifiably kill Smith.[15] Thus when the interests of one person come into conflict with the rights of another, the adjudication must always be decided in favor of the possessor of rights.

But what happens when rights come into conflict with each other? In this case, some right will necessarily be violated (recall, for the sake of argument, that we are now assuming rights to be inalienable, so it will not do to suggest that, dependent upon circumstances, one of the two conflicting rights goes away). Imagine that a policeman comes across a gangster who is preparing to execute five people who witnessed the gangster's latest crime. The five victims are about to have their rights violated and the policeman can prevent these rights violations by shooting the gangster, though doing so would violate the gangster's rights. This situation yields a rights conflict: either the gangster will have his rights violated or else the five witnesses will have their rights violated. I take it to be fairly obvious that, in this situation, the policeman is morally justified in shooting the gangster (and moreover that he is morally blameworthy if he does not).[16]

What this shows is that there can be cases involving rights conflicts where one right has to be violated in order to prevent further rights from being violated. Now the application to torture should be apparent. Assume that a captive has knowledge that could prevent the deaths of innocent lives. Further assume that he is unwilling to divulge his information but could be coerced through torture. By violating his right not to be tortured, we can therefore ensure that the innocents' rights to not be killed unjustly are not violated. Even if all rights violations were equally undesirable (which is most likely not true) it certainly seems appropriate to torture the captive to obtain the information; not only are the innocents' lives saved, but rights violations are minimized. Even if you are not a utilitarian, this minimization of rights violations should seem attractive.[17]

Some people, most notably Robert Nozick, have nevertheless objected to this "utilitarianism of rights." Nozick has argued that rights violations are always unjustifiable, even if they are necessary to prevent further rights violations. Nozick thus conceives of rights as "side constraints," which is to say that rights are absolute and inviolable; no considerations or circumstances can warrant intentional assault on anyone's rights, regardless of the end being pursued (including minimization of rights violations overall).[18] This is certainly a controversial thesis—many people think that if we really value rights, then the minimization of rights violations is more attractive than rights fetishism.

Nevertheless, two points can be made in response to Nozick's position. First, Dworkin has suggested that, in cases of rights conflict, we should look not at the explicit formulation of the right but rather to the values that suggested the right in the first place.[19] So, if individuals have a right to life, it is because life itself is something that is valuable and worth preserving. Given a conflict then, where the violation of one person's right (to life, let's say), could prevent the violation of five other persons' right to life, the values that led to the creation of the right to life would suggest violating the one in order to prevent violation of the five.[20] By considering why we would endorse rights in the first place (because we value the objects of those rights), it seems permissible to act such that the underlying values (and their associative objects) are preserved to the highest degree possible.

The second response that could be made to Nozick is more on his own terms. He asks "why . . . hold that some persons have to bear some costs that benefit other persons more, for the sake of the overall social good?"[21] This question is indicative of a concern about certain theories of rights, including utilitarianism, which would advocate violating the rights of certain (innocent) people so that others may benefit. I think that Nozick is certainly right in that this conclusion, if drawn, is at least *prima facie* undesirable. But, insofar as we are discussing whether or not to torture terrorists (among others), we do not have innocent people! I think that we can allay Nozick's concern by agreeing that we should not torture innocent people such that others may benefit, but by saying that complicity in terrorist activities constitutes a forfeiture of innocence. We certainly must admit that there is an important moral difference between torturing an innocent girl so that the sadist frees his hostage and torturing a terrorist who, through his own actions, has created a situation wherein someone's rights are being or will be violated. I think that this distinction is enough to allow torture of terrorists while still being responsive to the spirit of Nozick's concern.

As a final remark, it should also be noted that even Nozick, in a footnote, admits that it is an open question whether these side constraints are "absolute or may be violated in order to avoid catastrophic moral horror."[22] While it certainly seems to me that this admission compromises Nozick's stance, I could nevertheless grant that rights, in normal situations, could (or should) be understood as side constraints. However, many of the cases that I am interested in are precisely those in which rights would be violated in order to prevent catastrophic moral horror! So, while either of the two above responses might allay Nozick's concern, it is not altogether clear that his opposition would be very strong in the cases that I am considering.

Therefore, I think that a strong case can be made for the idea that torture can be justified, even if it entails rights violations, so long as we find ourselves in such a quandary that rights will end up being broken whether torture occurs or not. In these situations, some rights violation is bound to occur regardless, so we might as well either serve the greater good or else aim to minimize the overall violation of rights (even in a way sensitive to Nozick's concern). Either goal suggests the permissibility of torture.

UNDER WHAT CONDITIONS IS TORTURE MORALLY PERMISSIBLE?

In this section, I would like to try to lay out specific guidelines for when I think that torture is warranted. I propose four conditions, all of which must be satisfied to justify torture. Before listing these, I take it to be obvious that the captive should be allowed the opportunity to voluntarily disclose information (perhaps after worrying about the possibility of torture for a while) before torture is initiated.

First, I think that torture should only be used to retrieve information that could be used to prevent future threats from occurring. This restricts the scope of torture by eliminating two other commonly suggested potential usages: to force confessions and to deter crime.[23] There are, I think, good reasons to object to these usages. Forced confessions are highly unreliable; under severe duress people will often give false confessions (e.g., during the Spanish Inquisition). So there are not good reasons to believe that forced confessions are true. If the authorities are highly confident about the involvement, then a conviction in court should be easy and the confession would almost be superfluous (though perhaps expedient).[24] So it seems tortured confessions are, at worst, likely untrue and, at best, unnecessary!

Another option would be to torture criminals for the deterrent value—if prospective criminals knew that they might be tortured, then they might abstain from crime. First, it seems quite unfair to torture one man so that another may not commit a crime. But, second, it is unnecessary. If deterrence was all that mattered, then we could accomplish the same effect by creating a myth that criminals are tortured without actually torturing any of them. The results would be the same and nobody would have to endure the hardship. Assuming that the myth could be sustained and that there would not be risks for leakage (which I think to be reasonable assumptions), there is no need to actually torture anybody to accomplish a deterrent effect!

Information, however, seems to be an appropriate aim. The acquisition of information differs from both forced confessions and deterrence in a relevant way: torture may well be the only way to realize the goal. Forced confessions are unnecessary insofar as we have a judicial system that should be able to render the appropriate convictions. Deterrence merely requires the perception of torture, not actual torture. So the torture, in either of those cases, is unnecessary. But, it is very plausible that the only way to obtain the information that would lead to the prevention of some future crime would be through torture; there exists no redundancy program in the sense that we have in the other cases. Perhaps the suggestion could be made that intelligence should pursue leads and might be able to thwart the crimes without anyone ever needing to be tortured. But empirically, especially once time constraints are considered, this reliance on intelligence is unwarranted and imprudent. Thus torture may, in fact, be the only way to acquire the important information, which is a reason to endorse its practice.

Second, there needs to be a reasonable expectation that the captive has knowledge of the relevant information. Torture cannot be permissibly used to "fish" for information. If, for example, we know that the captive worked in a building where terrorists were known to conspire, but that he was only a janitor and was therefore highly unlikely to have had access to any information that might be used to thwart terrorist activities, it would not be permissible to torture him. But if, on the other hand, reliable intelligence reveals the captive to have been intimately associated with those who likely planned a threat, torture would be appropriate. If the association is unclear or dubious, then torture should not be exercised (at least until further intelligence is forthcoming). Furthermore, there are pragmatic reasons for not torturing someone who is not thought to have the information—he may produce misinformation.

Third, there must be a reasonable expectation that the information that the captive has knowledge of corresponds to an imminent and significant threat. If the threat is temporally distant, there is no reason to pursue torture now. Between the present and the time that the threat becomes imminent, developments might take place that would render torture (in the present) unnecessary. For example, it is possible that the captive will have an ideological shift and no longer wishes to contribute to the terrorist act. If this is the case, he may voluntarily provide the information needed to stop the act. Also, it is possible that the threat is revealed through some other means (e.g., intelligence, confession of someone else, etc.). It would certainly be better to wait for these further developments than to needlessly engage in torture. Similarly, the threat must be significant. A "terrorist act" that involves the destruction of an unidentified dog house certainly does not warrant a torture-laden inquiry to discern the location of the bomb. But, if we can reasonably assume that the captive knows the location of a bomb that is going to explode in some building at noon tomorrow, thus killing thousands of people, there would be both an imminent and significant threat and, given satisfaction of the other criteria, torture would be acceptable.

Fourth, there needs to be a reasonable expectation that acquisition of the information can lead to prevention of the terrorist act. If it is thought that the situation cannot be disarmed, even if the details are forthcoming, there is no reason to torture. For example, imagine that we know the captive has details concerning a bomb that will detonate an unoccupied building tomorrow, but all of our bomb squads are already assigned to important projects (expensive, occupied buildings, let's say), then there is no reason to pursue the information. Similarly, if we know that the bomb will detonate in thirty minutes but we do not know where, there is no reason to start torture that will give us the answer too late.

So, I think that the conditions necessary to justify torture are: the use of torture aims at acquisition of information, the captive is reasonably thought to have the relevant information, the information corresponds to a significant and imminent threat, and the information could likely lead to the prevention of the threat. If all four of these conditions are satisfied, then torture would be morally permissible. For example, imagine that we have just captured a high-ranking official with an internationally known terrorist group and that our intelligence has revealed that this group has planted a bomb in a crowded office building that will likely explode tomorrow. This explosion will generate excessive civilian casualties and economic expense. We have a bomb squad prepared to move on the location when it is given, and there is plenty of time for them to disarm the bomb before its explosion tomorrow. We have asked this official for the location of the bomb, and he has refused to give it. Given these circumstances (which satisfy all four of my criteria), I think that it would be justifiable to torture the official in order to obtain the location of the bomb.

WHAT FORMS OF TORTURE
ARE PERMISSIBLE?

After arguing for the permissibility of torture under certain circumstances, something should be said as to which forms of torture should be allowed. There is certainly a wide range of (historically) practiced techniques, which can range from the mundane (e.g., food deprivation) to the creative (e.g., removal of fingernails). Perhaps some forms of torture are more permissible than others? Or maybe there are some that should be avoided altogether? The first obvious remark is that the inflicted torture should never inflict more than the minimum trauma necessary to obtain the desired compliance. For example, if someone would be willing to divulge important information after being deprived of his lunch, there is no reason to remove all his fingernails. So torture programs would necessarily be tailored to both the physical and psychological constitutions of the captives. These assessments no doubt present some epistemic burdens, but psychological profiling should reveal to within a reasonable margin what would be the minimum necessary.

Generally, I think that torture can be broken down into three categories: physical, psychological, and other-directed.[25] Physical torture involves an infliction of physical pain (or discomfort) with the intention of surpassing the threshold of the captive. Examples of this form would be electroshock or drowning/suffocating. There is no doubt a psychological element to these forms (e.g., it is incredibly disconcerting to find oneself in the process of being drowned), but the primary assault here is on the physical constitution of the captive—the physical elements *lead* to the psychological elements. Psychological torture consists in assaulting the psychology of the captive. Bright lights, sleep deprivation, and harassment are all examples of this form. These techniques inflict a tremendous amount of psychological pressure without attempting to harm the body in any way; the psyche is targeted directly. I think that both physical and psychological torture in all their forms should be allowed, though I reiterate that only the minimum necessary to extract the information is allowed. This rejoinder, for all intents and purposes, effectively eliminates *any* uses of many of the so-called inhumane and brutal forms of torture.

The third category of torture, other-directed, occurs when someone other than the (primary) captive is tortured in order to coerce his cooperation. In the aforementioned discussions of both physical and psychological torture, it was assumed that the recipient of the torture would be the same person in whose compliance we were interested. We could certainly imagine cases, however, where an effective way to reach the desired goal would be to torture someone close to the captive, most likely in plain view. Examples of this would be raping a terrorist's daughter or burning his mother. It is possible that such techniques would be highly effective, and that they might also be supported by considerations of prudence—if the bomb will explode soon, it would not do to go through a physical torture process wherein the captive continuously loses consciousness because of the pain.

I do not think that other-directed torture is morally permissible for two reasons. First, we return to Nozick's question: Why should some people bear the costs so that others may receive the benefits? I argued earlier that the complicity of the former would be a good reason—they *created* the risk (or were party to its creation) and therefore are obviously not innocent bystanders. This complicity is certainly morally relevant! There are good reasons to think, however, that the innocent bystander should not have to endure torture so that we can coerce the terrorist. This bystander has not done anything to deserve the treatment, whereas the terrorist has.[26]

Secondly, and more satisfyingly, I think that it is highly unlikely that other-directed torture will ever be necessary. Given the availability of other forms of torture, and given the proviso that we should never torture more than the minimum necessary, other-directed forms will not need to be used. If the options are psychological torture by other-directed torture or direct psychological torture, the latter is certainly more desirable (why involve the extra person?), and I see no reason to think that it would be any less efficacious. Insofar as other-directed torture targets the psyche of the terrorist, and therein presupposes some likelihood of loss of resistance, I think that there must be some other path to this goal through some other form of psychological torture through less controversial practices.[27]

FINAL REMARKS

Though, in some cases, I have argued that torture would be appropriate, there are several reasons for caution. The only aim for which I have endorsed torture, retrieval of information, resupposes that torture could be employed to successfully retrieve information. As a matter of empirical concern, is this true? I have found no indication to think that it is not. Some people, particularly terrorist operatives, are trained to withstand torture, particularly as pertains to information extraction. Nevertheless, there is no evidence that anyone can resist torture-laden interrogations indefinitely; the psychological trauma and the degree of confusion are simply too severe. Two of the more famous torture cases, those of Guy Fawkes during the Gunpowder Plot of 1605 and of Abdul Hakim Murad, a Pakistani terrorist suspect captured in the Philippines in 1995, are illustrative. Fawkes endured many treatments, ranging from hanging by his wrists to the rack, and, within four days, gave up the names of his conspirators. Murad, however, lasted longer; despite having cigarettes extinguished on his genitals, sitting on ice cubes, and being nearly drowned, he remained mostly silent. But, when interrogators told him that he was being sent to Israel, he started talking out of fear of even worse treatments from Israeli interrogators.[28] Everyone has a limit and, given time, any information can be extracted. Experience seems to show that not even that much time is required—many prisoners disclose quickly. Obviously the interrogators need to know what the most effective techniques would be; this would allow them to extract the information more quickly and allow them to minimize the suffering of the prisoner—psychological profiling can go a long way toward addressing these concerns.

But there is a more substantial problem: misinformation. While we might be confident that there are ways to extract the necessary information, a greater concern has to do with the relevant information being masked by irrelevant, or false, information, some of which the terrorists have been trained to weave into their disclosures. This undoubtedly presents a serious problem, particularly as terrorists from the same cells might have the same misinformation which could serve to corroborate itself. Nevertheless, I do not think that this is a reason not to torture, just that there will be higher demands placed upon the intelligence community to filter through the acquired information. By checking interviews against other facts, they can hopefully go a long way toward figuring out what to trust and what to reject. However, the prospect of misinformation does complicate the situation.

In this paper, I have argued that torture is, under some circumstances, morally permissible. In doing so, I have not presupposed utilitarianism to be correct, but have argued that even other normative approaches would be able to accommodate this conclusion. The conditions that I have suggested to be met in order to allow torture are: pursuit of information, reasonable expectation that captive has the information, reasonable expectation that the information corresponds to an imminent and significant threat, and reasonable expectation that the information can be used to disarm the threat. There are, of course, substantive issues as to what constitutes reasonable expectation, but I think that we could settle these ostensively, or else be confident that we have made progress on the formal account. I have also stressed that, though I would support torture if these conditions were met, we should still be prudent to administer the minimum amount of torture necessary (measured both in terms of intensity and quality) that is necessary to achieve the desired goal. Hopefully this moderate position has both intuitive appeal and is theoretically attractive.

NOTES

1. L.C. Becker and C.B. Becker, eds., *Encyclopedia of Ethics* (New York: Routledge, 2001), 1719–20.

2. This is due in no small part to interpretations of the 8th Amendment and its prohibition against "cruel and unusual punishment." I certainly have little to contribute to the legal interpretations, but it is worth noting from the outset that the forms of torture that I will end up endorsing are *not* ones that involve torture as punishment. Thus we may be able to quickly slide past this (legal) hurdle.

3. "Ends, Means, and Barbarity," *The Economist*, January 11, 2003. While officials have claimed that fewer than one hundred prisoners have been involved in such

transfers, thousands have been held with "American assistance" in countries which are known for brutal treatment of prisoners.

4. Dana Priest and Barton Gellman, "U.S. Decries Abuse but Defends Interrogations: 'Stress and Duress' Tactics Used on Terrorism Suspects Held in Secret Overseas Facilities," *Washington Post,* December 26, 2002.

5. For example, Alan Dershowitz has argued for the legal sanctions of torture though "torture warrants" which would be issued by judges. See his "Is There a Torturous Road to Justice?" *Los Angeles Times,* November 8, 2001. There may, however, be reasons to think that even if torture were morally permissible, it should not be legally sanctioned. See, for example, Tibor Machan's "Exploring Extreme Violence (Torture)," *Journal of Social Philosophy* 1990: 92–97.

6. See Levin's "The Case for Torture," *Newsweek,* June 7, 1982, which is a nice (albeit nontechnical) article that presents this view in somewhat more detail. See also Dershowitz (2001).

7. We could also see that torture would fail the law form of the categorical imperative. The maxim "I torture the captive" would yield a contradiction in will when universalized and compared with my standing intention, which would entail the desire that I, the torturer, not be tortured.

8. Stephen Kershnar has argued that this appeal to Kant's second formulation is not enough to "override" the warrant to torture on the grounds of desert. If this is true, it would not affect my conclusion. However, the true Kantian would see dignity as an incommensurable value, and not one that merely provides a value which can be outweighed by competing considerations. Therefore I do not think that Kershnar's argument is likely to convince a Kantian; thus the tension with which I am concerned still remains. See his "Objections to the Systematic Imposition of Punitive Torture," *International Journal of Applied Philosophy* 13.1 (1999): 47–56.

9. Following Wesley Hohfeld's classic distinction, rights are typically broken down into four categories: claim-rights, liberties, powers, and immunities. A claim-right imposes duties on others. For example, if someone has a right not to be killed, then everyone else has a duty not to kill him. Someone has a liberty to do x if nobody has a claim-right against him doing x. But, unlike claim-rights, liberties do not confer duties on others. For example, I have the liberty to win a footrace; nobody has a claim-right against me winning the race but, at the same time, nobody (particularly the other racers) has a duty to let me win the race. Powers are abilities to change someone's rights status. Ministers, for example, can change the rights of a couple by marrying them—once married, their legal rights have changed. Immunities exempt one from certain powers. Thus someone may be given an immunity such that a judge (who has powers) cannot change that person's rights, such as through restrictions of liberties. Torture, if it violates rights, would violate claim-rights; the most sensible interpretation of torture would be that people have a right not to be tortured, which means that others have duties not to torture them. I suppose that torture could, in some senses, restrict liberties in that, while someone is being tortured, they lack the ability to pursue some ends that they would otherwise be able to. But violation of liberties seems to me to be a nonessential part of torture. We could, for example, imagine torturing someone in such a way that they were still free to exercise their liberties (or at least the majority), such as torturing while, at the same time, allowing

the recipient the ability to walk around, talk to his friends, etc. Thus I take the substantial purported rights violation in torture to involve violation of claim-rights.

10. See, for example, Jeremy Waldron, ed., *Theories of Rights* (Oxford: Oxford University Press, 1984).

11. John Stuart Mill, *Utilitarianism* (Indianapolis: Hackett, 1979), Chapter 5.

12. I will consider fighting terrorism (whether domestic or international) as the prototypical application of torture. The reason for this is that terrorist activity frequently consists in broad networks and derives from advance planning. The situations where I shall argue that torture is most appropriate involve these sorts of features. There are certainly non-terrorist situations wherein I would also support torture, and the choice to discuss terrorism should not be viewed as evidencing any ideological bent; I choose it merely for convenience and simplicity.

13. There could be also be a more moderate position, one that I see instantiated in our legal system, that complicity leads to forfeiture of some, but not all, rights (such as the right to freedom, but not the rights to legal representation and due process).

14. Unless, of course, one were a utilitarian. Given that torture can easily be defended on utilitarian grounds, let us consider instead the (more traditional) non-utilitarian notion of rights.

15. Ronald Dworkin, *Taking Rights Seriously* (Cambridge: Harvard University Press, 1977), ix.

16. It would be very hard to argue with someone who wanted to dispute this conclusion, which I think that very few people would. Perhaps some deontologists would still maintain the wrongness of this act; I make some comments on the plausibility of this position below.

17. Appealing to a minimizing of rights violations is not utilitarian, but is probably still consequentialist (though I do think that deontologists could find some merit to this approach, or even that it could be directly accommodated by their theories). This idea is worked out nicely in Amartya Sen's "Rights and Agency," *Consequentialism and its Critics*, ed. Samuel Scheffler (Oxford: Oxford University Press, 1988), 187–223.

18. Robert Nozick, *Anarchy, State, Utopia* (New York: Basic Books, 1974), 28–35. Alan Gewirth argues for a similar position in "Are There Any Absolute Rights?" *Philosophical Quarterly* 31 (1981): 1–16.

19. Dworkin, 191.

20. This is, of course, much different from assuming that we should kill innocent people in order to harvest their organs to save the dying. Those who are already dying are not having any rights violated and therefore we could not violate the rights of the innocent "donor" in order to minimize overall rights violations (we would end up with one rather than zero). The case I discuss above closely approximates Bernard Williams' famous Jim and the Indians case wherein the journalist is given the option of executing one Indian so that all of the Indians are not executed. (Williams even agrees that Jim should accept the offer, though uses this thought experiment as evidence against utilitarianism since he thinks the decision is not obvious, even though choosing to execute obviously maximizes utility). See J.J.C. Smart and Bernard Williams, *Utilitarianism: For and Against* (Cambridge: Cambridge University Press, 1973).

21. Nozick, 33.

22. Nozick, 30. I would like to thank Michael Levin for directing me to this point.

23. The *Encyclopedia of Ethics* also listed intimidation and amusement as purposes of torture. I take these to be obviously impermissible. A less common suggestion is that torture should be used for retribution. I do not really have any comments on this idea other than to point out that it hinges upon the plausibility of retributive theories of punishment, which I find to be lacking. However, if retribution can be defended, then torture on retributivist grounds would readily follow.

24. If the evidence from which the authorities derive their certainty of the involvement is inadmissible in court, then perhaps the confession really is needed. Even in these cases, I think that forced confessions should be disallowed and, minus this alternative, I think that the authorities would work more diligently and prudently in obtaining the incriminating evidence.

25. There are surely other useful ways to categorize forms of torture, but I find these to be intuitive and helpful for future discussion. We could also discuss tortures as acts (e.g., electroshock) versus omissions (e.g., food deprivations), but I think that most of the interesting questions fall under which acts are permissible, so this distinction would be unilluminating. If one thought that the problem with torture was that it violated a sphere of independence that all rational beings have, we might want to talk of tortures as being invasive (e.g., sodium pentothal and other "truth drugs") versus non-invasive (e.g., bright lights). There is nothing wrong with any of these approaches; I just choose mine for ease and intuitive appeal.

26. The utilitarian, of course, might not care at all who is tortured, so long as the ends justify the means. I think this attitude is problematic, though I do not propose here to launch into a critique of utilitarianism. At a minimum, such a response would fail to respect the "separateness of persons" (John Rawls' famous phrase) by treating people as utility containers rather than distinct beings worthy of respect. See John Rawls, *A Theory of Justice* (Cambridge: Harvard University Press, 1971).

27. We could, of course, lie to the terrorist and tell him that his daughter will be or is being raped in an attempt to gain disclosure.

28. Peter Maass, "If a Terror Suspect Won't Talk, Should He Be Made To?" *New York Times*, March 9, 2003.

9

Interrogation Ethics in the Context of Intelligence Collection

Michael Skerker

The horrible pictures from Abu Ghraib prison in Iraq have brought the subject of interrogation into public view. There is a distinct divide in descriptive works about interrogation and torture: there are practical works written by and for security personnel emphasizing the efficacy of various methods, and there are victim-based accounts of torture. These two genres tend to correspond to attitudes both academics and nonacademics have toward the subject. One group loudly condemns torture or lesser infringements of rights, but begs the question of how authorities should fight terrorism or insurgencies. Another group emphasizes public authorities' protective obligation, and glosses over moral concerns with dismissive comments about the cruelty of war or incredulously posed thought experiments involving darling children held hostage. This all tends to be greeted by the sullen silence of security personnel, who rightly or wrongly may feel that force is required in some circumstances; that it has fallen to them to do the dirty work; and that their critics hypocritically benefit from the security such work assures.

Unless legitimate security concerns can be addressed, talk of human rights will be dismissed by some as naive and irresponsible. Yet unless human rights are respected by the state, the security it achieves will be in service of a state deformed by its agents' excesses. This chapter is an attempt to develop an ethic of interrogation in the context of intelligence collection that does justice to both concerns. It addresses both non-coercive and coercive interrogation. My intention here is not necessarily to promote coercive interrogation, but stimulate discussion among intelligence professionals as to coercion's efficacy and morality by starting with the strongest argument for it I can contrive—better than a straw man whose flaws would leave some to cynically revert to their received opinions.

NON-COERCIVE INTERROGATION

For the purposes of this discussion I will assume four classes of interrogatee: enemy soldiers, unlawful or irregular combatants, enemy intelligence officers, and civilians unaffiliated with the intelligence community. Further, at the risk of drawing too blunt a distinction, I will mostly assume "adversarial" interrogations with uncooperative interrogatees or interrogatees of uncertain motives, as opposed to "friendly" debriefing of assets whose intentions are not in doubt.

Police, military, and CIA manuals overlap considerably in their recommendations for what the latter two refer to as non-coercive interrogations.[1] Non-coercive interrogations do not rely on force external to the detainee; they usually involve oral gambits instead of physical pressure. Apparently, direct questioning—simply asking the detainee what the interrogator wants to know—is extremely successful in certain contexts.[2] The Army manuals cite a rate of 85 to 90 percent effectiveness for the direct approach in questioning of German soldiers during World War II.[3] Direct questioning raises relatively few moral concerns. The detainee can ostensibly remain silent and can attempt to derail the interrogator. True, his detention is inherently coercive. The detainee may be more or less anxious as a direct result of his arrest or capture; he is alone with the interrogator and other authorities in an unfamiliar place; he is uncertain about what will happen to him if he cooperates and if he refuses; and he is in the stressful position of having to alone conceal information the interrogator desires.[4] Nonetheless, the detainee's faculties are intact; he still has his wits about him and can make decisions according to what he sees as his best interest.

Further, the interrogation is structured to be self-testing—it is designed to elicit the truth—such that it should end if the detainee is not of intelligence value.[5] Error on the part of the interrogator is certainly possible, such that he mistakenly suspects a person has valuable information. There is inadequate empirical data on error rates in interrogations in police settings and no publicly available material to my knowledge on interrogations performed by American intelligence officers. The widely used police manual by Inbau and Reid says that good police interrogators get confessions 80 percent of the time—significant because the advocated "Reid technique" is only employed following the interrogator's discernment of the detainee's likely guilt—and the "Reid technique" does not produce false confessions.[6] Gudjonsson notes that the authors do not back up their claims with any data; there are no comprehensive studies of false confession rates in police interrogations. There are however, numerous anecdotal cases of false confessions, including criminal convictions thrown out on appeal on this account.[7] Presumably, interrogation by intelligence officers is similarly imperfect.[8]

It is therefore significant that interrogation limited to direct questioning has few negative effects on the detainee and probably little to no long-term ill effects. That a well-structured interrogation is self-correcting—capable of discharging innocent detainees or detainees of little intelligence value— would be morally insignificant if the process innocent and guilty alike had to endure were terrible and effectively punitive. That said, there is a profound need for detailed empirical studies of the false confession rate of various interrogation methods.

A captured soldier who is questioned in the direct manner (whether by an interrogator affiliated with military or civilian intelligence) has no rights violated, though he is under no obligation to answer the questions and the interrogator is prohibited by international law and the tenets of just war theory from causing the POW any mental or physical duress to get him to answer. Pfaff and Tiel argue that foreign intelligence officers have implicitly consented to having their liberties (e.g., of movement, and to privacy) infringed by participating in the "game" of espionage.[9] Like lawful combatants and spies, terrorists and guerillas expose themselves to their enemy's less than full respect of their rights by threatening rights violations themselves.

The major rights of a civilian unaffiliated with an intelligence agency that are infringed during direct questioning are freedom of movement and the right to privacy, and the former, only in custodial situations when the civilian has been forcibly detained. In a domestic law enforcement setting, the infringement of detained citizens' liberty is mitigated by the rule-governed nature of formal detention; the rules are structured to respect citizens' rights to due process and against arbitrary imprisonment. Arrest is open to eventual contestation, is carried out by specially trained personnel answerable for their decisions, and is pursuant to public order so is presumably something to which all citizens could consent. The situation is different in intelligence settings inasmuch as the assets intelligence officers might have occasion to interrogate do not necessarily have *de jure* or *de facto* access to full legal appeal. Enemy spies and unlawful combatants detained overseas are not covered by the international laws of war nor domestic U.S. law prior to the commencement of legal proceedings against them. The only relevant legal backstops to their treatment in overseas custody are the International Declaration on Human Rights and the Convention Against Torture. It is unlikely that spies or unlawful combatants would wish to invite the publicity associated with charges brought in the International Criminal Court or European Court of Human Rights. Even foreign civilians unaffiliated with intelligence agencies who might be more interested in bringing suit would likely be hampered due to the probably secret identity of their interrogators and interrogating agency.

In an intelligence setting, more of a burden is necessarily placed on ethics and prudence than law, because the secret nature of operations often precludes legal oversight. Morally, intelligence officers should follow the spirit of the laws their colleagues in law enforcement follow. People can only be deprived of their liberty of movement and their right to privacy given probable cause that they are a threat to the intelligence officer's nation. Intelligence officers are only entitled to treat others prudentially, i.e., as means, when doing so is pursuant to the officers' protective duty toward their home nation, and the target asset has done something "triggering" that protective role: knowingly or unknowingly threatening the home nation. Wearing a uniform or engaging in counter-force or political (i.e., terrorist) violence is obviously cause, as is working for a defense contractor. Barring some evidence of security-threatening behavior though, foreign civilians cannot be detained and questioned, whether in a dragnet operation or as a preventative measure. A possible exception would be questioning done in liaison with local law enforcement so that the foreign citizen has recourse to the local legal system if offended. Local law enforcement officials would then be accountable for the facilitating role they have played to a foreign intelligence agency. If local laws have nothing comparable to U.S. laws concerning due process, or the local judiciary is corrupt or ineffective, there is more of a burden on intelligence officials to not unduly harass foreign citizens with even the relatively mild rights infringements associated with detention and direct questioning.

Another interrogation method that does not raise too many moral problems may be particularly effective with religiously-motivated interrogatees. There are reports that some of the terror suspects recently "rendered" by the U.S. to Saudi Arabian authorities have been interrogated in a way that made special use of the kingdom's religious resources. The detainee was first visited by a radical mullah who seconded the detainee's worldview and buoyed his spirits. He was then visited by progressively more moderate clerics who showed the detainee the error of his former doctrine according to Islamic principles; these clerics effectively "deprogrammed" the detainee, to the point that he voluntarily confessed all of his previous associations.[10] This method non-coercively elicits a full confession, and does so in a manner that not only respects the detainee's autonomy, but leaves him better off, positively reconciled with his betrayal. Such a method deserves serious consideration, particularly in cases where cultural and religious differences may leave frustrated interrogators more apt to use coercive means.[11]

The manuals indicate that more recalcitrant detainees are to be cajoled, manipulated, frightened, lied to, and sometimes threatened. The interrogator is encouraged to display great confidence; whether he does so or not, he should act as though he knows everything the detainee has done, to give the detainee the sense that there is no point in denying the crime or action.[12] Then, based on whether the detainee seems an "emotional" or "non-emotional type" the interrogator adopts either a more empathetic or rationalistic approach, respectively. With emotional detainees, the interrogator aims at building rapport, and giving the detainee emotional reassurance regarding his misdeed as well as a rational pretext for his confession.[13] The CIA manual stresses that ". . . the effort to make the subject feel that his questioner is a sympathetic figure should not be abandoned until all reasonable resources have been exhausted . . ."[14]

There is a general moral presumption against lying and manipulation, as such behavior treats other humans as means to one's own purpose rather than as autonomous and free individuals (who depend on a true account of the world to judge the course of action they wish to elect). Yet the criminal (e.g., the terrorist) does not have the right to his criminal secrets, nor is the liar (e.g., the foreign intelligence officer or double-agent) owed the truth.[15] Both as plotter and liar, he exempts himself from the reciprocal web of deontological (i.e., rights and duties) obligations by plotting rights violations and through deceit. By violating his duties toward others, he looses others from an obligation to fully defer to his rights. Yet this does not necessarily imply that others have no obligation to rule-breakers, as David Hume suggests, in the license he grants soldiers fighting barbarians.[16] While the two questions are related, what someone deserves is distinct from how one should treat him.[17] The proposition that barbarians—who do not obey the rules of war—do not deserve the chivalric restraint owed other soldiers, makes one wonder about the purpose of dealing barbarously with barbarians.

Dealing barbarously with barbarians will not make them less barbarous. If they were barbarians before, and experience barbarism now (from non-barbarians), barbarism is all they know. But of course, Hume's point is the one his fellow philosopher John Locke makes more explicitly.[18] By resorting to "the rule of force," and treating the attacker/barbarian like a wild beast rather than a person with rights, the defender is not trying to *correct*, or punish the attacker, but just to make him go away. If this argument applies for someone acting in self-defense, it also applies to those professionally obliged to protect others. An interrogator's manipulation of a detainee is not for the sake of punishment, not to "show the detainee what it feels like," but to neutralize the threat he poses to society—by extracting actionable intelligence—and to restore the social order the detainee's presumed crime or plot disrupted.[19] Yet to disrespect the detainee's rights more than is necessary to neutralize the threat he poses is unjustified. The interrogator therefore ought not to lie or manipulate if being honest (the direct approach) will do, nor lie or manipulate more than necessary to reveal the truth and protect others (e.g., it may be acceptable to deceitfully tell a man his wife implicated him in espionage or crime, to trick him into confessing, but not, as he is confessing, add "and she's sleeping with the pool boy").

The preceding argument justifies manipulative treatment only of the detainee who actually is concealing threatening information. The argument—based on the detainee's status as a rights violator—is not able to justify authorities' use of deceit or manipulation in cases where they *suspect* but are not sure the detainee is concealing illicit knowledge. This in fact describes the context of many intelligence-gathering interrogations, where the detainee's identity and role are uncertain. In a domestic law enforcement context, the authorities' infringement on persons' right to privacy based on suspicion of wrongdoing is justified by the presumed consent citizens give authorities to so act when there is probable cause and the authorities' aim is only the prevention or solving of crimes. Interrogation involving deceit and trickery (what I will call "manipulative interrogation") is harder to justify than straightforward questioning, but it seems that manipulative interrogations are justifiable by presumed consent if they are mostly effective at revealing the truth; the authorities have cause for using these methods with a particular suspect; and the methods' effect on the detainee are not so terrible that no one would consent based on the chance that innocent people would be subjected to them. Foreign civilians who are not in the employ of intelligence agencies cannot be said to have implicitly consented to manipulative badgering by foreign intelligence operatives on mere suspicion. Therefore, prior to beginning a manipulative interrogation with a foreign citizen, there needs to be a higher standard of proof that he is in the relatively unprotected class of unlawful combatants or intelligence agents than there needs to be for treating a domestic citizen as a criminal suspect.

Lawful and unlawful enemy combatants, intelligence officers, intelligence informants, and military contractors lose the right not to be treated prudentially—as means to another's end—by engaging in activity that threatens the security of another nation. They are acceptable targets of intelligence collection, including manipulative interrogation, if the opportunity arises and prudence allows (intelligence officers or agencies may wish to forgo certain opportunities so that their symmetrical assets in the other state are not also interrogated). It would be immoral however, to subject the innocent neighbor or spouse of a foreign intelligence target to manipulation, deceit, or blackmail in the context of an interrogation. (They can however, be offered rational incentives for producing information, ranging from monetary to altruistic, e.g., "Did you know your neighbor is a terrorist?").

Enemy POWs have a special status among those mentioned above. Even though they engage in counter-force violence—assuming they have obeyed the laws of war—they have done nothing morally wrong. Once disarmed, they are no longer combatants and so no longer members of a class vulnerable to physical force. Moreover, since they are morally innocent, they cannot be punished in detention; the purpose of detention is merely to keep them from returning to the battlefield. Acceptable interrogation tactics are then properly limited to non-coercive measures. Since POWs do potentially have intelligence regarding the capturing power's national security, they are liable to manipulative and deceitful stratagems. They cannot however be threatened with physical violence or deprivation of privileges. These soldiers' being in enemy uniform is sufficient "probable cause" to treat them as POWs and to non-coercive interrogation.

The same restrictions on interrogation practices are not necessarily deserved by spies and unlawful enemy combatants, whether non-uniformed enemy soldiers (e.g., engaged in espionage, sabotage, or other covert operations), non-uniformed guerillas, or terrorists. A spy or enemy combatant dressed as an allied combatant or as a civilian is not owed the same deference owed a POW, in part because he has not taken the same risks as a combatant.[20] The disguised operator has essentially a criminal profile to the target nation, even if trained as a soldier and when acting under orders from the military representative of a nation-state. This is not to say that all these actors are morally the same, but all take advantage of the relative openness of their enemy's homeland, or the relative relaxed posture of warfighters behind their own lines to spy or do military-level damage. That said, prudence may advise against using force in interrogations for fear of reciprocal behavior by the enemy against irregular allied assets.

COERCIVE INTERROGATION

Historically, non-coercive interrogatory methods including deceit and trickery have perhaps been less obvious modus operandi for security and juridical officers striving to elicit a subject's true testimony from behind his tightly sealed lips. In ancient Greece, freemen's juridical testimony was taken as true on its face, according to the respect paid to the gentry, but a slave's testimony could only be entered if the slave had confirmed the account under torture.[21] The 3rd century Roman historian Ulpian defined *quaestio*, torture, as the "torment and suffering of the body in order to elicit truth."[22] Torture was largely replaced by combat between the legal contestants—the belief being that God would preserve the innocent party—in the period between the fall of the Roman Empire and the 12th century.[23]

By the late Middle Ages in Europe, new legal procedures demanded proof—the word of a gentleman no longer sufficed—and confession was considered "queen of proofs."[24] Ironically, the triumph of reason over superstition led to the return of juridical torture.[25] Enlightenment ideas largely led to the disappearance of torture in Europe in the 18th and 19th centuries, but wide-scale use of interrogatory torture returned under the

Nazi and Soviet regimes, and during the French anti-guerilla campaigns in Algeria and Indochina.

Intense research on sensory deprivation and sensory bombardment in the 1950s–1970s was spurred by accounts of Soviet and Chinese brainwashing of gulag internees, and American POWs in Korea, respectively, and apparently led to the development of psychological modes of coercion among some Western intelligence agencies. It seems appropriate to discuss these methods in greater detail as they appear to be currently in use by at least American, British, and Israeli agencies, and were widely taught to Central and South American intelligence agencies by the U.S. in the 1980s.[26] Further, it has been suggested by some, including the bench of the European Court of Human Rights that these psychologically oriented methods are less harmful than other methods of coercion and may be acceptable forms of interrogation.[27]

Contrary to popular imagination, the manuals do not present pain as the immediate objective of coercive interrogation, but instead, disorientation, anxiety, dread, and physical discomfort pursuant to "regression":

> Relatively small degrees of homeostatic derangement, fatigue, pain, sleep loss, or anxiety may impair . . . [those defenses most recently acquired by civilized man . . . the capacity to carry out the highest creative activities, to meet new, challenging, and complex situations, to deal with trying interpersonal relations, and to cope with repeated frustrations.] The interrogatee's mature defenses crumble as he becomes more childlike.[28]

The CIA manuals continue that regression is the aim of all coercive techniques:[29]

> As the interrogatee slips back from maturity toward a more infantile state, his learned or structured personality traits fall away in a reversed chronological order, so that the characteristics most recently acquired—which are also the characteristics drawn upon by the interrogatee in his own defense—are the first to go. . . . [R]egression is basically a loss of autonomy.[30]

The interrogator attempts to peel away the rationalist overlays immediately standing in his way of a confession, the conscious part of the suspect which seeks to maintain his cover story, and which links his silence or deceptive claims to his group identity and loyalty to his cause. The interrogator wants the core of the suspect's faculties to remain intact, such that the man still knows who he (truly) is and what he has done. As best I can gather, the point is not to make a person gasp out information in a moment of pain, but to get him to a pliable enough state where he answers questions honestly, too disoriented and drained to maintain a deceitful or recalcitrant façade. In such a state, the interrogatee is much more susceptible to the rationalization for capitulation which his interrogator then offers like a palliative cigarette (e.g., "You've done your best. No one lasts forever. You fought us longer than anyone else.")[31] What is assaulted is not bodily integrity as much as psychological or moral integrity: autonomy, which perhaps makes it seem at once both better and worse than less "sophisticated" torture.

Interrogators aim to affect regression proximately through disorientation and the creation of anxiety. The manuals stress that people can adapt to nearly any environment they confront with regularity, no matter how unpleasant. With that in mind, interrogators are counseled to constantly change interrogatees' routines and physical environment: bedtimes, meal-times (including the amount and type of food), interrogation times, the temperature and amount of light in his cell. They ought to manipulate his sense of time, including his sense of day and night. Doing so keeps the interrogatee anxious, his mind racing; the anxiety drains him emotionally.

All these changes—and all the mental scenarios they portend for the inter-rogatee—are harder to process and endure when coupled with sleep and sensory deprivation. The manuals indicate that the lack of external stimuli leads one's thoughts to turn inward: one's fears and anxieties magnify and become debilitating without external context to serve as a check, an orienting point to separate reality from fantasy.[32] The sensorily-deprived person becomes desperate for any kind of human contact and will feel overwhelming relief and dependence on anyone who breaks his isolation; in such a situation, the interrogatee will be loathe to upset the interrogator who is his only human contact, and who has assumed a kind of parental authority over him.[33] The interrogatee's will is more readily sapped by the debility incurred by stress positions than that inflicted externally, because brutality from the interroga-tor or guards tends to focus the interrogatee's will against the attacker. In a stress position, he is his own source of discomfort, and the interrogator, who releases him from the position, the source of comfort.[34]

In contemplating the moral status of coercion in the interrogation of ter-ror suspects, we first need to address coercion's efficacy. Ineffectiveness would imply the absence of any good effects which could potentially justify coercion. We will then discuss coercion's moral status. There are two main questions philosophers tend to ask in order to judge an action. First, the phi-losopher asks if the action is *deontologically* permissible, that is, if there are universal rules banning or permitting it. For example, most would argue that rape is deontologically impermissible: it is never allowed, for any reason, by anybody. It makes no sense to ask if a given situation makes rape more or less justified, or more or less rape is appropriate for the situation, because rape is never allowed. If, on the other hand, an action is permissible, the phi-losopher next asks if it is *appropriate* in a particular situation, usually by ask-ing if it is *proportional*—not an overreaction, not underreaction—to a particular situation. For example, a police officer is in principle allowed to use deadly force, but there are many situations in which shooting a suspect would be disproportional, or excessive, given the suspect's offense (e.g., spitting on the sidewalk, cursing at the officer, etc.). I will ask these two questions regarding coercive interrogation and then address some practical concerns in an effort to make what is at stake in the proportionality judgment clearer.

Parallel to the history of torture is one questioning the efficacy (though not until the 18th century, the morality) of interrogatory torture. The efficacy of coercive interrogations is relevant to ethicists because an ineffective technique is not proportional to any proposed good. To put this last point more exactly, to say a (morally questionable) technique is ineffective is to say it does not have any positive outcomes, only negative ones. To elect it then, is evil. The Roman emperor Augustus warned "confidence should not be unreservedly placed in torture . . . the evidence obtained is weak and dangerous and inimical to truth."[35] In many legal settings, torture was only indicated when there was already proof, or probable cause, of a suspect's guilt, in which case a confession was sought to "fill out the proof" or to implicate co-conspirators—which would seem to recognize both torture's blindly punitive and unreliable character.[36] In fact, part of a judge's skill was thought to be his ability to formulate questions that could winnow true from false coerced testimony. The problem, obviously, is there is no necessary connection between pain and truth. As many commentators point out, and as the manuals concede, a person put to torture will often say whatever he or she believes will make the torture stop.[37] Without corroborating evidence, coerced testimony is nearly useless, and practically undesirable in that it would presumably waste investigators' time pursuing errant leads.[38] Time is particularly relevant in cases where tactical exigencies pressed interrogators to use physical coercion in the first place.

Further, the inherent ambiguity of all interrogations—the interrogator can never be certain the suspect has disclosed all the relevant information— implies that coercive interrogations cannot be applied in a clinical manner.[39] Innocent people will be caught up in security sweeps, and with a given suspect, there would be a constant temptation for the interrogator to use more force than is (retrospectively) required to elicit the desired information, to make certain that there is not another kernel of precious intelligence being withheld.[40] Further, not everyone succumbs to physical pressure. Religiously or ideologically motivated suspects in particular will be less likely to succumb; for many, their torture plays into a drama in which they star as martyr, steeling their resolve.[41] It follows then, that those high-ranking members of terrorist organizations, who presumably have the best information about terror plots, will also likely be the least apt to break under pressure.[42] Further, under extreme stress some people mentally disassociate from their reality and cognitively withdraw; the very force creating duress for the suspects—meant to give them a rational incentive to cooperate, or to break down their conscious ability to dissemble—also saps their ability to coherently answer the interrogator's questions.[43]

The use of interrogatory torture has systemic problems apart from the interrogation itself, including the corruption of governmental and social institutions.[44] The argument has been made by some that it is better to professionalize and legalize torture so that courts could specify acceptable methods and circumstances for its application.[45] There are modern precedents in addition to those from the late medieval and Renaissance periods. French counter-insurgency forces sought approval from French courts for coercive interrogations in Algeria, the Israeli Supreme Court allowed "moderate physical pressure" to be used in the interrogation of Palestinian terror suspects, and infamously, U.S. Department of Justice lawyers issued memoranda in 2003 outlining an understanding of acceptable interrogation techniques to include anything up to those which created pain like that unto organ failure.[46]

With or without legal approval, recent regimes have responded to security threats by pushing for the regularization of what is often initially haphazard competence in coercive interrogation amongst its security forces. Practices which had previously been conducted ad hoc by a handful of intelligence officers come to be taught in special branches of service academies; foreign experts are flown in; whole corps specializing in coercive interrogation get trained. Once operational, the new intelligence wing must, like all parts of government, justify its budget by producing successes in the field and by identifying new threats.[47] What begins as an operation targeting actual terrorists or guerillas, then sometimes expands to pursue political dissenters, intellectuals, etc., or devolves to broad dragnets where all males of age are hauled in. Particularly when the terrorist or guerilla threat comes from a disenfranchised minority, legitimate security operations can turn into repressive campaigns, as regime leaders conflate military opposition with political opposition, and then political affiliation with mere ethnic, religious, or class identity.[48]

Meanwhile, the torturers themselves are often psychologically blighted, treated as pariahs by the regular security branches, either deviant to begin with, or more often not, but brutalized and morally deformed in the intelligence academies and in the course of their work.[49] The torturers are unstable forces in the government, as their ranks constitute a lawless and outcome-oriented cell within the legal framework of the state.[50] The necessary secrecy that accompanies intelligence operations creates massive opportunities for criminal corruption. Since the acts of the security forces are often extralegal, making torture routine requires the corroding of the professional standards and behavior of various branches of society: police are needed to help in the secret arrests, doctors to falsify medical reports or dispense drugs, judges and journalists are pressured to look the other way, etc.[51] The victims of torture often become willing recruits for terrorists or other criminals; others remain shattered, withdrawn, unable to participate in social and familial life.[52] It sum, it is argued that torture is fundamentally at odds with the principles of a democratic society, and this is reflected in the character of the institutions necessary for the perpetuation of torture. In resorting to its use in times of crisis, a democratic nation destroys what it means to protect.[53]

Yet if there are very strong practical arguments against using interrogatory torture, on account of its suspect efficacy and danger to social institutions, there are rumors of successful coercive interrogations which perhaps prompt security and intelligence officials to desire the retention of coercive interrogation as an option. It has been argued that there is nothing in principle that coercive interrogation can reveal that skillful, non-coercive interrogation cannot,[54] and that non-coercive interrogations are vastly more likely to reveal accurate information than coercive interrogations.[55] Yet it has also been argued that with respect to certain kinds of suspects (e.g., those trained to resist non-coercive measures), coercion can succeed where non-coercive methods fail.[56]

Israel's General Security Service, or Shabak, says that its coercive interrogation of Palestinian suspects (including beatings, shaking, sensory deprivation, sexual humiliation, and blackmail) has thwarted hundreds of planned terrorist plots and led to accurate information pursuant to the assassinations of scores of terrorist leaders.[57] Britain defended the Royal Ulster Constabulary's use of the "five techniques of interrogation in depth" (hooding, wall-standing, subjection to loud noise, temperature and meal manipulation, and sleep deprivation) in the European Court of Human Rights with claims that the six-day interrogation of 14 IRA suspects in the fall of 1971 elicited identifications of 700 IRA members and confessions to 85 terrorist incidents.[58] The financier of the 1982 Marine barracks bombing refused to cooperate with Lebanese interrogators until a CIA operative kept him soaking for 24 hours in freezing water.[59] A 1995 Al Qaeda plot to bomb 11 planes over the Pacific was thwarted with information allegedly tortured out of a Pakistani suspect by Philippine authorities.[60] The whereabouts of Ramzi bin al-Shibh were allegedly elicited from Al Qaeda leader Abu Zubaydah by withholding pain medication (he had been shot during arrest).[61] Bin al-Shibh led authorities to 9/11 mastermind Khalid Sheikh Muhammed, who in turned revealed the identities of other Al Qaeda figures after being mock-drowned by his CIA interrogators.[62]

Evaluating the significance of these and other anecdotes is difficult. It is possible that some of these above figures falsely confessed, or would have confessed eventually with non-coercive means. It is possible that in some cases, the interrogators telling these tales embellished the significance of the information revealed. Evaluating the efficacy of coercive techniques in the abstract is also difficult because of the indeterminacy of what some of the authors referenced above mean by "torture." There may be a significant difference in efficacy among various types of coercive methods. In deploying the above arguments regarding practical efficacy and the impact on social institutions, many authors seem to have in mind the most brutal coercive methods, those designed to cause intense, immediate pain, and an interrogatory logic that presumes the victim will either rationally decide to confess rather than endure more pain, or react in an automatic/animalistic manner, seizing on the one ameliorative path which the interrogator allows: confession. However, it seems significant to note that the manuals stress a different methodological logic, for their part also advising against the infliction of severe pain or severe debilitation of a suspect, precisely because of many of the practical concerns mentioned above: false confessions, bolstering the "martyr's" resolve, apathetic withdrawal, or severe cognitive impairment.

Given that their coercive recommendations are consciously meant to circumvent the other practical limitations, and that there are anecdotal instances of successful coercive interrogation (which security personnel have heard about too), the temptation is to identify the two, and characterize these anecdotes as the fruit of a rational, consistent approach used by some intelligence services, rather than random luck. I wish not to identify the map of the manuals with the territory they imagine of trained interrogators carefully using coercion on actual terrorists to successfully elicit their plots.[63] As Tindale points out, justificatory arguments for interrogatory torture involving dispassionate interrogators, known terrorists, and ticking bombs are unrealistic.[64] There is also perhaps a trap in assuming that developed nations can sustain the employment of the more scientific methods of coercion the manuals describe just because the nations are developed enough to contrive them. Civilian intelligence officers in particular need to be wary of an institutional arrogance—often noted by their FBI and military counterparts—assumed by "morally special" experts whose special training and quasi-legal powers are implicitly self-justifying. To a man with a hammer, the world seems to be full of nails.

However, barring definitive evidence that the above anecdotes represent successes amidst a majority of failures, and that the capitulations described were *not* a product of the coercion, it is likely that those authorities with the profound responsibility for preventing terrorist and other attacks will likely believe in some degree of efficacy for coercive techniques. In the abstract, the "new" psychologically oriented coercive methods described below and apparently more often utilized by developed nations strike me as more plausibly efficacious, and possibly less damaging to the interrogator. At least by the measure of one national poll, they also meet with the approval of a majority of Americans for use in the interrogation of *known* terrorists, suggesting that their use need not occasion the secrecy that so often brings corruption. As these points may mitigate for some the force of the practical arguments against coercive interrogation, it does seem appropriate to turn to a moral discussion of the matter.

Forming any sort of responsible normative argument about coercive interrogation is very difficult because of the lack of reliable data regarding its efficacy. Intelligence officers reading this article need to consider whether the following argument is supported or weakened by classified studies that may exist. Such officials need to carefully consider whether coercion can ever be seen as legitimate if there are *no* reliable studies about its efficacy, beyond institutional anecdotes that are uncritically repeated and may be inflated to aggrandize the narrator.

The following argument is meant to be taken in the conditional. *If* a method of coercion is reasonably effective; and *if* non-coercive methods have failed on a *known*, high-value intelligence asset; and *if* the leap in considering an asset's plot as dangerous as a soldier's weapon is granted (see below); and *if* the damage to be done to the interogatee can be reasonably judged proportional to the good likely to accrue, then coercion *may* be justifiable. Writing as a professional ethicist to non-professionals, I want to make clear that as rational moral arguments go, the *strongest* argument for allowing coercive interrogation is a relatively weak argument. Each element that will always or sometimes be uncertain—and therefore must be assessed in terms of probability—weakens the argument's power to justify coercion. These uncertain elements are: the status of the detainee as an intelligence asset, the exhaustion of non-coercive means, the efficacy of coercion, the threatening nature of the detainee's presumed plot, and the weight of the non-quantifiable variables of the interogatee's suffering versus the non-quantifiable variables of the good achieved by interrogation.

It is justifiable for public authorities with the duty of protecting their citizens to use force against those who expose themselves to it by illicitly using force themselves. The public authorities' actions are bounded by what it required to restrain and neutralize the threat rights violators pose. This entails using no more force than necessary to stop the violators' forcible actions and neutralize the threat of them in the near term. Therefore, if force can be justified by public authorities in a coercive interrogation, it must be because the interrogatee, while physically controlled by the authorities, is still an active threat to civilian society because of the secrets he is hiding. Neither the detained lawful combatant (POW) nor the domestic criminal (in most cases) is an active threat in these cases and therefore cannot be justifiably made the subject of force.

If the proposition that the detained terrorist is still presenting an active threat to society is granted, does the force the state is entitled to use include coercion targeting the interrogatee's rational autonomy? Using force to unravel the interrogatee's personality is presumptively a gross rights violation. However, force that risks violating a person's autonomy is normally justified when that person has legitimately exposed himself to force by threatening or attacking others. Yet in the cases of using force to restrain a violent person, disperse a rioter, or incapacitate a soldier, the loss of the autonomy (in the sense of rational control of one's actions) is collateral—a side-effect—to the aim of threat neutralization which is achieved through bodily control. The violent person (e.g., someone in the process of assaulting another) who is tackled and handcuffed by a police officer is still sapient and rational, but whatever decisions and plans he may be making are irrelevant because his body is controlled by the officer. In a way similar in kind, the killed or incapacitated soldier loses consciousness, or at least the ability to fully control his body, so the ability to reason is either irrelevant, or ceases at the same time his body is brought under external control. Though it usually serves no purpose to mention, the soldier's autonomy is intact at the moment of his death or incapacitation.

A soldier's autonomy is not intact in instances when he is so overcome by fear or combat exhaustion that he reacts to enemy action in an automatic, animalistic manner and flees, freezes, or surrenders. In these cases, however, the soldier's mental incapacitation is largely collateral to his surrender or retreat. The opposing side wants him to leave the battlefield; it does not matter whether it is in a panic or as the product of a rational decision.

In the context of a coercive interrogation, the interrogatee's autonomy is assaulted, but not in a way collateral to the physical control of his body, as in the above examples. If non-coercive means were exhausted, then the interrogator already tried reaching his goal while respecting the interrogatee's reasoning and self-control. In cases of coercive interrogation, it is the information in the interrogatee's mind that is (still) a threat to society; the interrogatee's rational autonomy the impediment to the interrogator learning what he needs to know; and so, the (at least temporary) disintegration of that autonomy is the direct aim of the interrogator's methods. If authorities are justified in partly controlling that which is threatening about a person (usually his body), it seems that they should also be justified in partly and temporarily controlling his mind, in the case of a terrorist or spy, *if* the good of preventing terrorist attacks or intelligence failures is judged important enough to outweigh the badness of regression, the effects on the interrogator, and the society that fosters the coercive interrogation.

Forcing regression would appear to be a significant evil, a perverse reversal of nature. However, the temporary loss of autonomy is not evil in the context of therapeutic hypnosis, nor is the mutilation of the body evil in the case of therapeutic amputation. In these cases, the mind and body, in a sense, are mutilated, but for the sake of the health of the whole, presumably with the affected person's consent, making the act justifiable. Actions in violation of a natural order may be acceptable in non-consensual, nontherapeutic instances (still in natural law terms) if performed by public authorities for the sake of the common good. St. Thomas Aquinas, for instance, justifies capital punishment using an amputation metaphor in which the criminal, as infected limb, is sacrificed for the good of society; the criminal has made himself vulnerable to prudential manipulation by the authorities by departing from rational behavior.[65] Even though the prime natural good of life is violated, a just execution is consistent with the natural order of things, because the criminal has effectively made himself bestial, and it is proper for rational creatures (humans) to prudentially manipulate irrational beasts.[66] One might justify authorities' deliberate infliction of pain on rioters, or the chemical castration of recidivist pedophiles in similar fashion.

That coercive interrogation is a tool of the public authorities pursuant to the public good may also suffice to meet concerns related to *the way* in which regression is induced. Henry Shue writes that what is most offensive about torture is the unilateral character of the force inflicted.[67] The victim is defenseless against whatever depravation his torturer can contrive. Shue surely is right that the unfairness of the situation is offensive, though I would argue the physical one-sidedness of the situation alone is not sufficient to prohibit force in interrogation if the interrogatee is judged to be a constant threat. There is no tenet in just war theory mandating belligerents be evenly matched. Combatants are always liable to lethal force if they themselves possess lethal capabilities, almost no matter how insignificant they are in comparison to their rival's. The notion of chivalry once addressed the intuition that fights should be fair in addition to just, but the notion has little currency regarding tactical operations today given the differences between contemporary combat and the face-to-face duels chivalry presupposes.[68] The relevant principle instead, is proportionality, and directs a belligerent party to not cause more damage than is needed and justified by the good done.

Yet if some force is warranted against certain detained intelligence assets, perhaps it is the degree of force used to cause regression, rather than regression itself, that is objectionable. Coercion usually involves a steady application of measures causing disorientation and discomfort rather than an immediate assault as in combat violence. It just seems worse to slowly, calculatingly discomfort someone than hurt them all at once. It is permissible to kill enemy combatants in war, though not with means causing more pain than is necessary for their incapacitation or death. The combatants' pain in being maimed or killed is collateral to their incapacitation—it is usually not integral to their incapacitation—and so considered cruelly inflicted if by weapons the design of which causes more pain than caused by readily available alternatives. Yet if the infliction of discomfort, pain, and disorientation is the only means to extract information regarding a plot, i.e., it is the only weapon available, it seems such infliction could then be proportionate.

Having dealt with concerns regarding the right to use force, the autonomy-attacking nature of the force, its unilateral application as well as its degree and duration, we can conclude coercion is sometimes permissible, at least in the abstract. The two main leaps we had to make, vital to the argument, were: 1) some forms of coercion may be efficacious and 2) some interrogatees' secrets are as threatening as a soldier's pointed gun. The argument fails if either one is invalid.

In practice, it might be judged that the severity and duration of the discomfort and disorientation is disproportionate to any actual good achieved. A comparable judgment would be acknowledging that one had grounds for a lawsuit against a company, but deciding that the expense and difficulty of a trial were not worth the possible award. This is a powerful argument with similar practical consequences to the *rule-utilitarian* argument I will discuss below: no good potentially achieved is worth the suffering of the interrogatee, so one cannot use force, or some level of force, even if one has exhausted all other options and one is certain that the interrogatee is a high-level intelligence asset. It is hard to make the worth of the good and bad effects of coercion more definite, as only one, if any, of the values to be weighed is quantifiable—the number of innocents saved from, say, a terror plot, as opposed to the level of discomfort and disorientation suffered by the interrogatee.[69] Proportionality arguments are inherently ambiguous (and to my mind, less than rationally satisfying), because the criteria for assessing and for balancing goods and evils can be massively weighted by the balancer's subjective interests, biases, and habits. Inevitably, the possible deaths of one's fellow citizens will seem more important to avert than the suffering of a foreign terrorist or spy. Were the detainee asked though, he would probably have a different point of view.

Acceptance of another's suffering for the sake of some good often depends on the justice and unavoidability of the act causing the suffering, as when collateral damage is deemed proportional to the good done in a legitimate military action in a just war. Sufficiently important goods justifying coercive interrogation *might* include the prevention of terrorist attacks on civilians, and perhaps the exposure of a double-agent, but perhaps not attacks against combatants in the field, knowledge of an enemy's technical expertise, the location of valuables, and revelation of commercial secrets. To the extent the reader may disagree with this hierarchy rather confirms my point about the ambiguity of proportionality arguments.

It has been explained how *an instance* of coercive interrogations may be just. The practical and institutional critiques of interrogatory torture, outlined above, argue that a *regime* of torture is disproportionate to any information a given interrogation might actually reveal, because the routine practice of coercion involves too many broad social evils and its desired output of actionable intelligence is rarely achieved. As Tindale and others argue, even if in principle, interrogatory torture could be justified (e.g., in the highly contrived "ticking bomb" thought experiment), real life instances meeting the relevant theoretical criteria—including having effective coercive measures and being certain of an intelligence asset's identity—are so rare as to suggest a practical ban on torture.[70] In other words, if the only occasion that justifies torture is almost nonexistent, and the likelihood of success on that occasion is remote, it is illegitimate to use such an occasion as the basis for a broad justification of the practice, particularly given the historical problems associated with having a standing corps of interrogators specializing in coercive methods.

Yet it is not clear if all coercive methods are equally hit-or-miss, nor if it is so difficult, at least in some contexts, to determine whether a detainee has had terrorist training. For instance, interrogators dealing with detainees captured in Afghanistan have said that fairly obvious counter-interrogation training as well as the characteristic abrasion a Kalishnikov trigger leaves on the index finger belied some non-Afghans' claims that they were merely peaceful religious students.[71] It seems appropriate therefore, to directly address these two major variables of *coercion's efficacy* and *detainee identity* to see if there are practical factors that could make the benefits and deficits of a regime of coercive interrogation definite enough to be proportionally compared. The following comments will then assume the permissibility of coercive interrogation in abstract (i.e., in at least one conceivable circumstance), and are activity-specific comments geared toward maximizing its desired outcome and minimizing associated evils. This efficiency analysis is of moral significance because given the prospect of two permitted actions with the same cost to the actor aimed at the same good end, it is immoral to choose the action with the greater number of negative effects to others.

Regarding the efficacy of coercion, it was argued above that coercive interrogations are useless without corroborating information, be it with respect to the interrogatee's guilt or the specifics of a plot, because the interrogatee's testimony has a direct relation only to his desire to stop the pain, not to the truth. Coerced testimony is inherently untrustworthy, and so is without intelligence value barring some external account with which to compare it or some means of rapidly corroborating it. This argument rules out coercive interrogations for the purposes of self-incrimination. A confession would presumably not be sought if there was enough evidence to implicate the interrogatee; the investigation now hinges on what is hidden to outsiders, the interrogatee's thoughts and memories. Yet his coerced testimony about that private store is inherently unreliable, so his "confession" adds nothing substantive to those insufficient external factors. Given that there are only two possible answers to the question "did you do X?" and that the interrogatee's response is unreliable, the interrogator has the same margin of error in judging the testimony as in *guessing* whether the interrogatee is guilty. If guessing is as good as *judging* the fruits of interrogation, there is no intelligence purpose to the interrogation. This argument would then also rule out using coercive interrogations in dragnet operations where citizens are hauled in at random, be it to determine their guilt with respect to particular past events or their knowledge of terror plots.

Confessions produced in interrogations aimed at eliciting actionable intelligence offer more opportunities for verification than the bare admission to membership in a terrorist organization or foreign intelligence service, or involvement in some incident. However, without corroborating evidence or some means of rapidly checking claims, coercive interrogations should be ruled out for the purpose of garnering actionable intelligence for the same reasons precluding interrogation aimed at self-incrimination. Without corroborating information, the interrogatee's testimony is the only foundation for the information, and his coerced testimony is inherently unreliable. Authorities have undertaken wide-scale coercive interrogations in dragnets aimed at composing mosaics of minor bits of intelligence that in relief described the enemy. Coercion on a wide scale is effectively a reign of terror, and is unacceptable for any liberal state domestically; colonially, the tactic could risk creating as many terrorists as it reveals. While evidence from Algeria and the Palestinian territories suggests that while it is tactically possible to cow dissent, there is no returning to the peaceful and unilaterally beneficial pre-terror situation.

This prohibition applies even if the interrogatee is not a random citizen but a suspected intelligence asset. Barring outside information, his admission of an alleged plot is no different than his compelled affirmation to the question "are you a terrorist?" Corroborating information or the ability to quickly check testimony provides a rational feedback into the interrogation process to help mitigate the unreliability of coerced testimony. The concern to gain time-sensitive intelligence, proposed by some to justify coercion, may be somewhat of a canard, unless there is very specific corroborating information (e.g., we know there's a bomb in one of the financial district buildings), as the time to check coerced revelations may well encompass the time taken to extract information in a non-coercive interrogation.

Coercive methods may be indicated for known, positively identified intelligence assets, even without corroborating information, though still as a last resort (e.g., if he refuses to respond or is clearly lying in non-coercive interrogation, or if the information he provides proves to be bogus). The risk of false testimony is real, but if time is to be wasted on erroneous leads, better it be confined to a person who can reasonably be suspected to have relevant information than to someone who may or may not have information.

The concern over systemic damage indicates that torture should not be legalized and routinely employed by a state. The concern over the self-perpetuating momentum of bureaucracies, mentioned above, is particularly well-founded. The smaller number of ad hoc actors performing coercive interrogations, as opposed to a corps of them, would, in itself work to contain the spread of whatever corruption might occur.[72] The suggestions some have made that coercive interrogation be the exception rather than the legal rule are well-taken. If coercive interrogation is legal, the temptation would be to employ it for increasingly slight reasons. As the *Miranda Court* warned, authorities are apt to become lazy and corrupt if they can prove a man's guilt by "the simple expedient of forcing it from his mouth." If revelations came to light, the interrogators would be subject to legal penalty, and would need to justify their actions in light of extraordinarily exigent circumstances. Various jurists have suggested there may be circumstances in which penalties would be set aside.

I am less sure that efforts beyond those taken to preserve operational discretion in other military and intelligence matters should be observed to conceal the coercive interrogation of a known terrorist. The check on the overly cavalier use of coercion in the previous argument is its illegality. An interrogator would need to think very carefully if the situation is so dire that it is worth risking "20 years in Leavenworth" by using force against an interrogatee. That an interrogator does judge a particular situation so dire implies his willingness to defend his actions before others. An official is less likely to become corrupt if trying, at least, to act in a way he expects would withstand publicity.[73] In contrast, the patronizingly arrogant attitude that "I alone know what needs to be done" that seems a constant risk for security personnel seems ready-made for corruption.

The challenge for a law-based society is to allow goal-oriented operators, be they businessmen or spies, to pursue their socially beneficial ends without those goals so singularly consuming their motivation that they become detached from their moral obligations toward others. Accepting possible publicity is a way of keeping security personnel's sensibilities in line with those of the society they mean to protect. By the same token, the risk of national and international publicity seems less of a problem if coercion has occurred in situations minimizing the risks of false confessions described here, particularly if it's of the sort designed to induce regression rather than intense pain.[74]

Regarding the identity variable, it seems appropriate to include with those individuals positively identified as intelligence assets (i.e., those particular individuals sought out by operators in raids and positively identifiable by appearance, distinguishing feature, or documentation on his person) those with the known asset who are armed or actively fighting at the time of the known asset's capture. Coercion would not be justified on suspected assets who do not meet the preceding criteria (and there will always be far more suspected assets, particularly suspected terrorists, in custody than positively identified assets). Non-coercive means must be used in a screening process; there are indications that such interrogation is fairly effective at determining whether a detainee has had counter-intelligence training. An interrogator may risk using more force than retrospectively would be considered necessary if he knows the interrogatee is an intelligence asset, but cannot use force at all if not reasonably certain the interrogatee is an asset. Again, the limitation is indexed to what the interrogator can know: the interrogatee's status, rather than the exact level of force required to elicit actionable intelligence. I am arguing a certain amount of force is proportional to the extraction of actionable intelligence, not to a certain number of tortured innocents.

Given its risks, coercive interrogation would have to be utilized as a last resort even with known terrorists or other high-value intelligence assets, following sincere attempts at non-coercive interrogation, and concurrent with attempts to garner intelligence through non-interrogatory means. In the first year of Operation Enduring Freedom, U.S. interrogators were most successful when working in teams and collating information gathered from a number of detainees using basic gumshoe reasoning.[75] As mentioned above, the religious deprogramming approach reportedly used in Saudi Arabia garnered full and complete confessions because the deprogrammed interrogatee *wanted* to come clean. Coercive interrogation should be the last resort in a spectrum of interrogatory practices, and interrogation should not be the first or sole means of garnering intelligence. This is because corroborating information is needed for coercive interrogation to be truly efficacious; coercion produces unreliable information; and a sole reliance on interrogation can both be a symptom and a cause of laziness and incompetence among security and intelligence services.

By the same proportionality argument described above, minimally discomforting techniques should be used before more discomforting techniques are employed. If the interrogatee is presenting lethal force in the form of his secrets, there is no amount of force in principle disproportionate to the extraction of information. Yet the interrogator has failed if he kills or renders delusional the interrogatee before extracting the desired information. Since the level of force inducing derangement or death is not necessarily known ahead of time, more damaging forms of coercion are disproportionate to use in the first instance when coercion is employed. It seems the only measures not potentially justified by this proportionality argument are those affecting people other than the interrogatee (e.g., threats to, or abuse of his relatives), and less certainly, those measures not involving force (e.g., those aimed at humiliating the interrogatee).[76]

If coercive interrogation is efficacious with any regularity, it can perhaps be justified for the interrogation of terrorists and some other high-value intelligence assets. If coercion can ever be justified for the interrogation of terrorists in principle, then the above restrictions describe the practical circumstances in which coercion may be more likely to be just. Interrogators using force in situations meeting the above restrictions can be understood as not personally doing evil, because they are acting on behalf of the state, and the state's directives are just. The terrorists or foreign intelligence operatives have made themselves vulnerable to force, and so to a prudential, or proportional calculation on the part of the state as to whether their suffering is outweighed by the value of the secrets they may hold. The team of intelligence officers who have custody of the interrogatee, as agents of the state, are then only liable for that proportionate reasoning, e.g., whether they judge this man to be a significant intelligence asset and whether it is likely he possesses actionable intelligence worth his suffering (that, in addition to the ordinary virtues of state agents: honesty in dealing with superiors, respect toward co-workers, integrity in dealing with state resources, etc.).

Even if the interrogator's task is justifiable, and in particular instances, justified, it is not an easy or pleasant job and some if not all interrogators will suffer adverse psychological effects as a result.[77] However, there are many unpleasant, but morally justifiable occupations, and few major vocations that do not typically impress its actors with particular personality traits, many of them socially deleterious to a greater or lesser extent. As a society, we have much more to do in every field addressing the integration and balance of professional imperatives with ordinary social morality.

With respect to their particular training and professional experience, interrogators who might employ coercive methods are not very different from military or intelligence personnel in special operations (e.g., anti-terrorist or counterinsurgency operations). Training for the various special operation branches is brutal and psychologically taxing not in the least because of the many measures trainers employ to induce gratuitous suffering—sleep deprivation, exposure to extreme temperatures, little food, and stress positions—measures that are often identical to those used in coercive interrogations.[78] Moreover, a portion of special operations training, geared presumably toward expected missions, involves close-up, stealthy killing, far closer in feel to murder than ordinary combat violence. State violence is often expressed in forms that serve to depersonalize it: soldiers, prison guards, and police officers wear uniforms which efface their individual personalities and replace them with a homogenous identity of "state actor." Their tasks are often highly choreographed, and performed in a group, again, reducing their individuality, and rendering them parts of a machine-like whole. To the extent that state violence is removed from this corporate, diffuse manifestation, it *feels* more like a personal action—and may have greater associated psychological effects for some actors—but I do not see a moral reason to make a distinction between distant and close-up violence. The relative indirectness of much of modern combat killing is an exigency of the weapons systems involved, and does not entail a moral reform from medieval close-quarter combat. If the training and deployment of special operations troops is judged to be a legitimate part of the state's protective function, the concerns associated with the training and intimate nature of interrogators' work ought not necessarily to be prejudicial to coercive interrogations. This said, operators in both the military and intelligence community deserve better after-action counseling than the sort the DOD now ham-handedly dispenses. The best sort of counseling appears to be mandatory, peer to peer, and non-prejudicial to the operator's career.[79]

Having said all this, the rule-utilitarian argument against the use of coercive interrogations is still compelling. Such an argument reasons that the possible benefits that might accrue from rare breaches of a well-founded rule are not worth the good achieved by strict compliance with the rule. Such an argument applies as well to a practice that can be morally justified in theory, but which may have too many practical side-effects when put into practice. For example, St. Augustine believed prostitution to be immoral, but advocated that it remain legal, lest the greater crime of adultery grow in prostitution's absence. Even if coercive interrogation can be justified under certain circumstances, and even if there are skilled, upright interrogators who can employ force selectively, it can be expected that the press of practical exigencies in any given campaign will contribute to coercion's increasingly broad, extreme, and undisciplined use. Coercive interrogations justified only to elicit actionable intelligence will be used by lazy investigators to secure self-incriminating statements. Doctors, psychologists, scientific researchers, lawyers, and military personnel will be forced to violate their professional standards and to participate in cover-ups. Innocents will be tortured; force will be used in domestic criminal cases; fear of scandal will lead to secrecy, and secrecy to corruption. Reports or rumors of the use of coercion will leak, bringing ill-repute to the intelligence services and bolstering the nation's enemies. Interrogators will be abandoned by their agencies and left alone with their grief. Unhappily, to say something is potentially morally justified is not to say it is without moral and practical risk.

In writing this article, I've borne in mind a bogeyman story I came across somewhere in my research; it has served as a caution, a kind of spectrum endpoint that represents both utter ruthless efficacy in counterterrorism tactics and the moral abyss those tactics presuppose. It has been said that decades ago, radicals in some outpost of Soviet influence seized Soviet embassy staff and held them hostage while communicating terms to the Kremlin. In turn, the KGB found and kidnapped the radicals' children. Prior to any further negotiation, the KGB sent one of the hostage-takers his son, in pieces. The Soviet hostages were released.

NOTES

1. The 1983 CIA "Human Resource Exploitation Training Manual" [HRETM] (reportedly used at the U.S. School of the Americas, where Central and South Ameri-

can officers are trained, though apparently not at Ft. Huachuca, where U.S. Army intelligence officers are trained) largely repeats the CIA KUBARK manual's section on coercion verbatim, though with inserted emendations (presumably added prior to its public release under force of an FOIA lawsuit), crossing out the most controversial sections and including provisos couching in the passive voice what had been directly recommended to interrogators in the original. HRETM opens with a statement that "[t]he use of force, mental torture, threats, insults, or exposure to unpleasant and inhumane treatment of any kind as an aid to interrogation is prohibited by law, both international and domestic; it is neither authorized nor condoned." p. 1. The corrected edition still has introductions to methods of the "we won't talk about when you stopped beating your wife" variety: e.g., "While we do not stress the use of coercive techniques, we do want to make you aware of them and the proper way to use them," was changed to "While we deplore the use of coercive techniques, we do want to make you aware of them so that you may avoid them." HRETM, p. 2. HRETM includes manipulation of time, meal times, sleep schedules, and interrogation schedules as non-coercive while the CIA manual includes those methods in the chapter on coercive techniques. HRETM, p. 9. The Army's standard interrogation manual, FM-34-52, used at the military intelligence training school at Ft. Huachuca, Arizona, does not have a section on coercive techniques. Such techniques would be illegal in the context of POW interrogation.

2. This varies with culture. Peter Watson, *War on the Mind* (New York: Basic Books, 1978), p. 280.

3. Further, military intelligence officers were taught in the early '90s that it was expected that 95% of (presumably Soviet) POWs would quickly respond to the direct approach, yielding the basic information of their unit designation that was nonetheless useful in determining Soviet force structure. Chris Mackay & Greg Miller, *The Interrogators* (New York: Little, Brown, and Co., 2004), p. 45.

4. *Miranda v. Arizona*, 384 U.S. 436; 86 S. Ct. 1602 (1966), p. 12 of electronic version.

5. As one Brazilian torturer put it, you only have to raise your voice to make an honest citizen talk. Wolfgang Heinz, "The Military, Torture, and Human Rights," in *The Politics of Pain: Torturers and Their Masters,* ed. Ronald Crelinsten & Alex Schmid (Boulder: Westview Press, 1995), pp. 65–98, p. 82.

6. F.E. Inbau, J.E. Reid, J.P Buckley, & B.C. Jayne, *Criminal Interrogation and Confessions,* 4th ed. (Gaithersburg, MD: Aspen, 2001), p. 364.

7. Gisli H. Gudjonsson, *The Psychology of Interrogations and Confessions* (London: Wiley, 2003), p. 12.

8. Some interrogators insist they can tell when people are lying; others admit to the difficulty of discerning when a person has revealed all that he knows. cf. Edwin J. Delattre, *Character and Cops: Ethics in Policing,* 2nd ed. (Washington, D.C.: the AEI Press, 1994), p. 200; Inbau, et al., p. 364. Arrigo has found that professional interrogators had only 40–60% accuracy in detecting lies (note that guessing should yield 50% accuracy with a random sample of subjects). Polygraphs are, at best, 85% accurate. Jean Maria Arrigo, "A Utilitarian Argument against Torture Interrogation of Terrorists," *Science and Engineering Ethics* (2004) 10, pp. 1–30, p. 14. An experienced U.S. Army interrogator told me that she could not necessarily tell when a

detainee was lying, but could tell if he had had counter-intelligence training. Personal correspondence, 2/4/05.

9. Tony Pfaff & Jeffrey Tiel, "The Ethics of Espionage," *Journal of Military Ethics*, vol. 3(1) (2004): pp. 1–15, p. 9.

10. Dana Priest & Joe Stephens, "Secret World of U.S. Interrogation," *Washington Post*, 5/11/04, p. A1.

11. The Shabak general considered Israel's best interrogator claims he never used coercion, but instead relied on excellent linguistic and cultural knowledge to know his enemy. Mark Bowden, "The Dark Art of Interrogation," *The Atlantic Monthly*, 10/03, p. 20 of electronic version.

12. KUBARK Counterintelligence Manual, [KUBARK was a code name for the CIA]. Available at www.parascope.com/articles/0397.htm, p. 52, 66; FM 34–52, ch. 3, p. 6.

13. FM 34–52, ch. 3, p. 6; William R. Johnson, "Tricks of the Trade: Counterintelligence Interrogation," *International Journal of Intelligence and Counterintelligence*, vol. 1, no. 2, 1986, pp. 103–112, p. 107.

14. KUBARK, p. 56.

15. Sissela Bok, *Lying* (New York: Pantheon, 1978), p. 126.

16. David Hume, *Enquiry Concerning the Principles of Morals*, sec. 3, pt. 1, ed. Henry Aiken (New York: Hafner Press, 1948), p. 188–9. Cf. Jan Narveson, "Terrorism and Morality," in *Violence, Terrorism, and Morality*, ed. R. G. Frey and Christopher Morris (Cambridge: University Press, 1991), pp. 116–169, p. 161. Brazilian Col. Erasmus Dias is quoted by Heinz: "These were fanatic terrorists. We had to use the same methods they used," Heinz, p. 82. The brutality of the Cheka, the precursor to the KGB, was once justified by Stalin along the following lines: Why should we treat bourgeois agents differently than they treat us? Edward Peters, *Torture* (New York: Basil Blackwell, 1985), p. 129.

17. Bok, p. 126.

18. John Locke, *Two Treatises of Government*, Second Part, ch. II, sec. 11.

19. See Christine M. Korsgaard, "Kant on Dealing with Evil," in *Ethics: The Big Questions*, ed. James P. Sterba (Malden, MA: Blackwell Publishers, 1998), pp. 199–211, p. 205.

20. Michael Walzer, *Just and Unjust Wars*, 2nd ed. (New York: Basic Books, 1992), p. 183.

21. Peters, p. 13. Torture is one of the five "extrinsic proofs" mentioned by Aristotle in his *Rhetoric*. Ibid., p. 14.

22. Ulpian, *Digest*, 47.10.15.41. *Quaestio* had once referred to the investigative process and the court itself and *qaestio tormentum*, forms of punishment applied for interrogatory purposes, but by Ulpian's day, *quaestio* was simply taken to mean interrogatory torture. Peters, p. 28.

23. Ibid., p. 42.

24. Ibid., p. 41.

25. Ibid., p. 43.

26. U.S. Department of Defense, *Improper Material in Spanish-Language Intelligence Manuals*, 10 March 1992. Available at www.gwu.edu/~nsarchiv/NSAEBB/NSAEBB122/

27. *Ireland v. UK*, European Court of Human Rights, Series A, no. 25, 41, (1978).

28. KUBARK, p. 82. The bracketed text replaces "these functions" and is taken from the preceding sentence.

29. KUBARK, p. 82; HRETM, p. 2.

30. KUBARK, p. 40; HRETM, p. 2.

31. KUBARK, p. 90.

32. KUBARK, p. 89. This stage was reached in Soviet gulags after 4–6 weeks of isolation in a featureless cell. Cutting out more stimuli hastens the effect, e.g., sound-proofing the cell, eliminating light, immobilizing the interrogatee. Modern interrogators have produced the desired effect within hours to days by hooding the interrogatee. The British (if not others) found the most efficient means of incurring regression was by combining sensory deprivation with sensory overload and sleep deprivation, hence the "five techniques" (employed with IRA suspects who could be held only six days without charge) involved hooding prisoners dressed in rubber suits, blasting music at them, and forcing them to stand in a stress position (the KGB-favored "stoika" position: the interrogatee on his toes, legs spread, hands over his head, and leaning against a wall with the weight on his fingertips) for long periods of time (days, in some cases). Timothy Shallice, "The Ulster Depth Interrogation Technique and their Relation to Sensory Deprivation Research," *Cognition* 1(4) (1972), pp. 385–405, pp. 387–390.

33. KUBARK, p. 83; HRETM, p. 5.

34. KUBARK, p. 93; Alfred W. McCoy, "Torture at Abu Ghraib Followed CIA's Manual," *The Boston Globe*, May 14, 2004, p. 101. Various agencies have used what the Romans called "mala mansion" to induce stress positions, a tiny closet in which the interrogatee has neither the room to stand nor lie down. The Shabak favored a tiny stool contrived for the occasion, to which a person would be tied with his hands at disparate and awkward angles and tipped forward so the weight of his body was supported by his bound hands. The Israeli Supreme Court expressly outlawed the stool in 1999.

35. Ulpian, *Digest*, 48.18.1.23.

36. See Moglen, p. 1101–2; Peters, p. 81.

37. William R. Johnson, "Tricks of the Trade: Counterintelligence Interrogation," *International Journal of Intelligence and Counterintelligence*, vol. 1, no. 2, 1986, pp. 103–113, p. 103; Michael Ignatieff, "Lesser Evils," *The New York Times Magazine*, May 2, 2004, pp. 46–86, p. 93; Arrigo, p. 16; Mackey, p. 32; FM 34–52, ch. 1 (p. 2 of electronic version).

38. KUBARK, p. 93. In cases of widespread interrogatory torture, intelligence agencies can be overwhelmed by the sure volume of false information proffered by suspects desperate to placate the interrogators. Alistair Horne, *A Savage War of Peace: Algeria 1954–1962* (London: Macmillan, 1977), p. 204.

39. Cf. Alan Dershowitz, "Want to Torture? Get a Warrant," *San Francisco Chronicle*, p. A19 (Jan. 22, 2002).

40. Henry Shue, "Torture," Philosophy and Public Affairs 7, no. 2 (1978), pp. 124–143, p. 135. The KUBARK manual warns against using coercion to the point that the subject is delusional, at which point his statements are unreliable; rather, interrogators are to relent (at least temporarily) once the subject has made an initial confession (e.g., to membership in a terrorist organization), p. 83.

41. Arrigo, p. 7; Christopher Tindale, "The Logic of Torture," *Social Theory and Practice*, vol. 22, no. 3, fall 1996, pp. 349–370, p. 369; KUBARK, p. 93. Mackey reports that interrogators in Afghanistan had to walk a delicate balance in creating fear and anxiety among detainees with respect to the possible consequences of their recalcitrance without going too far and triggering "that Muslim fatalism" which caused them to fully withdraw.

42. Arrigo, pp. 7–8.

43. Arrigo, p. 5; HRETM, p. 3; KUBARK, p. 83. Though the CIA manual stresses that the stage of disorientation desired by the interrogation is not so great as to render the suspect unsure of basic facts about himself, e.g., whether or not he is a spy, it grants once the suspect has been driven to the point where he is delusional, he is no longer reliable.

44. Douglas Lackey, *The Ethics of War and Peace* (Englewood Cliffs, NJ: Prentice Hall, 1989), p. 80; Shue, p. 138, 141, 143; Nigel S. Rodley, *The Treatment of Prisoners Under International Law* (Paris: UNESCO, 1987), p. 76.

45. Dershowitz, p. A19.

46. Tindale, p. 350.

47. Ronald Crelinsten, "In Their Own Words: The World of the Torturer," in *Violence, Terrorism, and Morality*, ed. R. G. Frey and Christopher Morris (Cambridge: Cambridge University Press, 1991), pp. 35–64, p. 53.

48. 30–40% of the male population of Algiers was arrested and interrogated (often under torture) from 1955–1957. Between 5 and 10% of the Soviet population was arrested and interrogated (usually with sensory deprivation and forced standing) between 1936 and 1939, resulting in nearly 100% confession rates. Between 1987 and 1994, 23,000 Palestinians (roughly 2% of the population) were interrogated by the Shabak, 94% of whom were tortured or abused. The Russian military has been accused of essentially operating a depopulation campaign in Chechnya. In 1990, torture occurred in 84% of countries categorized as "not free" by Freedom House and in 25% of countries categorized as free. Herbert Kelma, in *Violence, Terrorism, and Morality*, ed. R. G. Frey and Christopher Morris (Cambridge: Cambridge University Press, 1991), pp. 24–32, p. 24.

49. Lackey, p. 80; Heinz, p. 84; Crelinsten, p. 59; *Miranda*, p. 447; Arrigo, p. 11; HRETM, p. 2.

50. Arrigo, p. 17.

51. Arrigo, p. 5, pp. 14–16.

52. Ignatieff, p. 93; *Miranda*, p. 447.

53. Ignatieff, p. 93, 86; Bowden, p. 38; *Miranda*, p. 447; *Public Committee Against Torture in Israel v. State of Israel*, H.C. 5100/94 et al., (Sup. Ct. Israel, 9/9/99), para. 39. In an anecdote that seems to undercut and support this point at the same time, Mackey relates how one relatively high value detainee "broke" after 29 straight hours of questioning (the same interrogator was awake for the same amount of time). When asked why he finally capitulated, the detainee said he realized that if this was the worst that America would do to him, he was fighting for the wrong side. Mackey, p. 426.

54. See Arrigo, p. 9, for bibliography; Delattre, p. 202.

55. Ronald Kessler, *The CIA at War* (New York: St. Martin's Press, 2003), p. 277; Mackey, p. 477.

56. The original text of the 1983 CIA manual (apparently crossed out by hand, but not expunged in the actual document released under FOIA lawsuit) states it pertly: Under the heading "Justification for coercive techniques," it reads "These techniques should be reserved for those subjects who have been trained or who have developed the ability to resist non-coercive techniques." HR p. 4. Part of this resistance ability may stem from the confidence on the part of the detainee, that he is justified in his actions. "It should be equally clear that if the person does not feel guilt he is not in his own mind guilty and will not confess to an act which others may regard as evil or wrong and he, in fact, considers correct. Confession in such a case can come only with duress even where all other conditions previously mentioned may prevail." KUBARK, p. 38.

57. John Schmertz & Mike Meier, "Citing International Human Rights Conventions, Supreme Court of Israel . . ." *Human Rights*, vol. 6, no. 3 (Mar. 2000), p. 2 of electronic version.

58. *Ireland v. UK*, para. 98.

59. Bowden, p. 33.

60. David Luban, "The War on Terrorism and the End of Human Rights," in *War After September 11*, ed. Verna Gehring (Lanham: Rowman & Littlefield, 2003), pp. 51–62, p. 58.

61. Don Van Natta, Jr., "Interrogation Methods in Iraq Aren't All Found in Manual," *The New York Times*, May 7, 2004, p. 2 of web version.

62. James Risen et al., "Harsh C.I.A. Methods Cited in Top Qaeda Interrogations," *The New York Times*, 5/13/04, p. A1.

63. Peters notes that there is even a French term for the associated argument that torturers can be the responsible servants of the state (which is naïve at best, he feels), *massuisme*. It is a reference to the brutal Gen. Jacque Massu, who credited his wide-scale use of interrogatory torture for ending the Algerian uprising. Peters, p. 177. Wide-scale French revulsion with its security service's behavior led to an abandonment of the colony five years later.

64. Justifiers circularly conflate the success of an imagined instance of interrogatory torture with the conditions justifying interrogatory torture. In the classic "ticking bomb" scenario, imagined interrogators *know* they have a terrorist and *know* he's planted a huge bomb in a city and *know* that hundreds of thousands will die unless they torture the truth out of him. In reality, interrogators usually have a detainee who they *think* is a terrorist but do not know if he's planted a bomb, its size, and whether torture will reveal the bomb's location in time to deactivate it. Tindale, p. 366. Mackey writes that special operators or CIA officers would drop off detainees for interrogation without saying anything about the circumstances in which they were detained, or whom they were thought to be. p. 115.

65. St. Thomas Aquinas, *Summa Theologiae*, II-II 64.2. The Vatican currently justifies capital punishment only in the case of escape-prone sociopaths, suggesting justifiable cases of capital punishment are now deemed so by analysis utilizing the doctrine of double effect (inclusive of the elements of "least harm done" and "last resort") as opposed to Aquinas's purely proportional analysis. Aquinas's public authorities are given blanket power to prudentially compare public good with private loss when dealing with sinners whose actions have made them bestial, and so, subject

to prudential manipulation. Acting on behalf of the state in this proportional or prudential judgment, executioners can intend the deaths of sinners without danger to their souls.

66. Ibid., II-II 64.3.

67. Shue, p. 130.

68. This is not to say the dispositional side of chivalry—respecting your enemy as someone who is similarly risking his life and so not hating him, treating POWs honorably, not desecrating corpses, etc.—has not nor should fall away.

69. There do not seem to be very good ways of finely distinguishing levels of discomfort or disorientation associated with interrogation. The severity of pain suggested in the Department of Justice's March 2003 "torture memo" suggests a mode of discernment linked to the way in which the pain is inflicted—all at once in a blow vs. developing over time, as in a stress position—but the method of delivery does not seem to have any necessary connection to the level of pain induced. Whether or not the pain leads to lasting damage is also not necessarily related to the level of pain induced, but would be relevant to a natural law index of value (e.g., disfigurement is worse than non-disfigurement). The European Court of Human Rights (1978), the French Wuilhume Report (1955), and the British Compton Commission (1971) judged the distinction between psychologically and physically oriented forms of pressure salient enough to deem only the latter "torture." I agree with Anthony Storr that the distinction does not seem relevant to the level of suffering caused. Cited in Tindale, pp. 352–354. It should also be noted that the 1984 UN Convention on Torture and the Third Geneva Convention define torture as severe physical or mental pain or suffering. The short- and medium-term effects of psychological torture (sensory deprivation, sleep deprivation, isolation, environmental manipulation, etc.) in some cases appear to be significant, including nightmares, insomnia, compulsive shaking, constant dread, depression, and social withdrawal. See Shallice, and accompanying bibliography.

70. Tindale, p. 367.

71. Mackey, p. 179, 458; U.S. Army interrogator, 2/3/05, personal correspondence.

72. Professionals do, to a large extent, as they are trained, be it to torture or not to torture, but it also seems plausible that individuals, for instance, trained not to use physical coercion, might with experience judge it to be indicated in certain situations. Toward the end of his tour, which he spent admonishing his interrogators to scrupulously follow the Geneva Conventions, Mackey comes to suspect that physical coercion is probably necessary and warranted for hardened Al Qaeda members trained to resist non-coercive methods. p. 477.

73. See Immanuel Kant, *To Perpetual Peace*, Appendix II. Rawls develops this idea in both of his major works.

74. See Richard Morin & Claudia Deane, "Americans Split on How to Interrogate," *The Washington Post*, 5/28/04, p. A20.

75. Mackey, p. 461.

76. This is relevant to the discussion because of the frequent reports of the use of sexual humiliation to break interrogatees. Richard Rubenstein, "The Bureaucratization of Torture," *Journal of Social Philosophy*, Vol. XIII, no. 3, Sept. 1982, pp. 31–49,

p. 43, 44. The distinction between humiliation and force may seem picayune if sensory deprivation is considered an act of force. There does seem to be a difference though, in that humiliating tactics require the interrogatee to be lucid, ego intact, in order to feel shame. In contrast, sensory and sleep deprivation, stress positions, and the rest are direct attacks on that lucidity. The full regime of coercive techniques probably robs humiliating tactics of their efficacy. If the argument is that forms of force can be proportionally justified to neutralize a lethal threat, a different (e.g., utilitarian) argument needs to be used to justify humiliation. Also, as relevant to the next section, it just seems worse to humiliate someone than to exhaust, disorient, or hurt him—it seems to require a more perverse frame of mind.

77. Johnson, p. 104.

78. I assume, in many instances, coercive interrogation techniques are indirectly taught in the course of subjecting elite military and intelligence operatives to survival/evasion and counter-interrogation training.

79. Maj. Pete Kilner, "Military Ethicists' Role in Preventing and Treating Perpetration-Induced Traumatic Syndrome in Combat Veterans," JSCOPE 2005 website.

10

Guarding against Politicization
A Message to Analysts

Robert M. Gates

Editor's note: The following remarks by the Director of Central Intelligence were made on 16 March 1992 in the CIA auditorium.

Bourne Cockran wrote to Winston Churchill in 1895 that, "What the people really want to hear is the truth—it is the exciting thing—speak the simple truth." Twenty years later, Churchill himself wrote, "The truth is incontrovertible; panic may resent it; ignorance may deride it; malice may destroy it, but there it is." Truth, insofar as we can determine it, is what our work is all about. Indeed our own main entrance is dominated by the chiseled words, "And ye shall know the truth and the truth shall make you free." And because seeking truth is what we are all about as an institution, as professionals, and as individuals, the possibility—even the perception—that that quest may be tainted deeply troubles us, as it long has and as it should.

The problem of politicization is as old as the intelligence business. The missile gap in the late 1950s, the disputes over our work on Vietnam in the 1960s, the criticisms of pandering to Nixon and Kissinger on detente in the early 1970s, that we were foils for the Carter administration on energy in the late 1970s—all these controversies and more—predated the 1980s. For as long as intelligence data has been collected and analyzed by human beings, it has been susceptible to their biases.

Politicization can manifest itself in many ways, but in each case it boils down to the same essential elements: "Almost all agree that it involves deliberately distorting analysis or judgments to favor a preferred line of thinking irrespective of evidence. Most consider 'classic' politicization to be only that which occurs if products are forced to conform to policymakers' views. A number believe politicization also results from management pressures to define and drive certain lines of analysis and substantive viewpoints. Still others believe that changes in tone or emphasis made during the normal review or coordination process, and limited means for expressing alternative viewpoints, also constitute forms of politicization."

This has been an issue with which all of us have long grappled, but never as publicly, or as pointedly, as in my confirmation hearings last fall. I know that for many of you, the segments devoted to politicization were wrenching, embarrassing, and even humiliating at times. They pitted friends and colleagues against one another. I know too that there were strong views on all sides of the debate back here in the ranks. While I believed, and argued, that the specific allegations were unfair and untrue, I came away from that experience determined not only to find better ways to prevent the reality of policy-driven bias, but also to reexamine how we deal with perceptions of politicization.

I also came away with a renewed belief that, by dealing forthrightly with the politicization issue, we will also be strengthening our ability to fulfill our purpose—to provide the highest quality intelligence, accurate and relevant intelligence, to policymakers.

As a result of those hearings, one of my first moves upon becoming Director of Central Intelligence [DCI] was to instruct the Deputy Director for Intelligence [DDI] to form a task force to address politicization and to work with members of the Directorate of Intelligence to come up with recommendations for future action. In my view, the report provided valuable insights into the issue and prescribed a variety of measures to address many of the concerns associated with politicization. I thank the task force members for their effort and encourage those of you who have not yet read the report or my resulting decision memorandum to do so.

In their report, the task force found a persistent and impressive commitment to objectivity, high ethical standards, and professionalism in the [Directorate of Intelligence] DI. They found that most analysts and managers remain determined to resist direct or indirect pressures from policy officials for products that conform to their views. Moreover, they concluded that politicization is not perceived to be a pervasive problem by most in the DI. Indeed, it is not a problem at all in some areas.

But the task force did find that concerns about politicization are serious enough to warrant action. Furthermore, most of these concerns relate to internally generated distortions. Over half the respondents to the task force's survey said that forcing a product to conform to a view thought to be held by a manager higher up the chain of command occurs often enough to be of concern. Most of the charges raised in discussions with the task force revolved around internal distortions generated during the review and coordination process.

I agree with the task force that this level of concern is disturbing, that it goes beyond the degree of frustration that is inherent to the review process, and that it demands the immediate attention of Agency management at all levels.

While my comments to you today fulfill a promise I made to Congress several months ago and respond in part to the task force's recommendations, I believe I would have scheduled this address regardless. In the short time that I have been back at the Agency, I have become more aware of the profound impact the issue of politicization has had on the morale of analysts and managers alike. It is not a concern to be dismissed with token gestures. Politicization is a serious matter, and it has no place at CIA or in the Intelligence Community.

As best we can, we must engage in a candid discussion of the issue, devise effective measures to prevent it from occurring, and resolve to deal decisively with any circumstances that may foster distortions in our analysis. I hope that our encounter today will launch a process of greater openness and dialogue.

The DDI and I have accepted the task force recommendations in their totality, but before I discuss the specifics, I would like to talk with you further about politicization and the challenge it poses for us as intelligence analysts. The issue of politicization has dogged American intelligence for years and reflects the fact that although we belong to an institution with established norms and procedures, we are all human and prone to make mistakes and errors in judgment.

Although the task force study focused on the DI, I believe we must include the National Intelligence Officers [NIO] and the National Intelligence Council [NIC] in the discussion of politicization. They, too, are engaged in analysis and—given their frequent contact with high-level policymakers—their work is also vulnerable to distortion.

Let's start by defining the policymakers' proper role in the intelligence process. I believe that most of you would agree that policymakers should be able to request intelligence products that address the issues they are dealing with on a daily basis. Such tasking is an integral part of the intelligence process. If we ignore policymaker interests, then our products become irrelevant in the formulation of our government's foreign policies. I think we also all would concur that a policymaker should not dictate the line of march that he or she expects our analysis to take. Nor should we withhold our assessments because they convey bad news or may not be well received.

The challenge for us as analysts, then, is to produce intelligence that objectively assesses relevant policy issues—whether it supports or undermines current policy trends—and to ensure that our product is read and valued by the policymakers concerned. Ensuring objectivity means that we explore the issue fully, looking at and vetting all the available evidence and identifying where gaps, blindspots, or alternative scenarios exist. Our task is to facilitate an understanding of the realities of a particular situation and its implications for U.S. policy.

Getting the policymaker to read our product should not jeopardize our objectivity; it does not mean sugarcoating our analysis. On the contrary, it means providing a frank, evenhanded discussion of the issues. If we know that a policymaker holds a certain viewpoint on an issue that is different from our analysis, we ought not lightly dismiss that view but rather address its strengths and weaknesses and then provide the evidence and reasoning behind our own judgment. I believe such an approach enhances our credibility and value. I realize, however, that in many cases the issues may not be clear-cut. In such situations, we owe it to ourselves to discuss fully how best to approach the subject before we even set pen to paper. In no instance should we alter our judgments to make a product more palatable to a policymaker.

In dealing with policymakers, we also need to keep in mind our role as intelligence analysts. Managers and analysts alike should meet with policymakers on a regular basis to exchange views and explore new ideas. In today's changing world, however, we must guard against taking on tasks that do not deal with intelligence topics and may be intended instead to drive a specific policy agenda. Managers and analysts need to discuss such situations candidly and design products that address only the intelligence issues at hand.

This brings me to the second aspect of politicization identified by the task force—the apparent lack of understanding and confidence between a number of DI analysts and managers. Somehow some seem to have lost the ability to discuss the substantive or structural aspects of an intelligence product frankly and in an atmosphere of trust. The task force report indicates that such circumstances exist in enough offices to be of concern. Apparently we have lost a sense of professional collegiality and find ourselves, in many instances, adopting a them-against-us mentality which fosters perceptions of distortions in the intelligence process. No one has a monopoly on the truth; we are all learning new things every day. Although some may be more experienced than others, no one person should impose his or her view on another. Dialogue must take place, each participant must be open to new ideas, and well-grounded alternative views must be represented. There are many managers and analysts who understand this; unfortunately, many do not.

If an analyst and manager or two analytical groups interpret information differently and can't come to a common understanding, the situation can degenerate into a perception of politicization. If one group or one person forces his or her line of analysis out over another, whether by force of his or her position in the management structure or through control of dissemination channels, it can leave the perception that that person or group has politicized the process.

I believe the first line of defense against politicization and analytic distortions is our own personal integrity; I want to spend some time talking about how each of us must work to ensure the highest integrity in our work.

Let me talk for a moment to our managers. I believe that managers are in a special position, particularly branch chiefs, because they are the ultimate arbiters in any analytical disagreements. They are also the ones who are charged with teaching and counseling our analysts.

As I see it, managers have three critical responsibilities to prevent distortions and corruptions of our products. First, managers have to challenge all of the analysis that comes through them to ensure its basic analytic soundness, logical validity, and clarity. As part of this, managers should always require analysts to defend their work.

Second, managers must strive to be open to new ideas and new lines of analysis from any source. We cannot simply stick with our previous conceptions and hope to keep pace with our rapidly changing environment. In the past year, many of the old assumptions that helped us in our analysis have been invalidated.

Third, I would also strongly concur with the task force in its conclusion that poor communication is the key source of the widespread concern within the community about politicization.

Managers must strive in every interaction they have with analysts and managers to ensure all communications are clear. Managers must be able to state clearly why they disagree with a judgment, or how they want a logical argument reconstructed. We cannot simply say we don't like it and we'll know what we want when we see it. That is more than a cop-out, that is a prescription for trouble.

Let me emphasize this last responsibility. Managers, particularly those who are teaching our less-experienced analysts how to do basic intelligence analysis, cannot afford poor communications. Managers should be showing analysts the hows and whys behind their decisions, not just telling them to change words. If you can't tell an analyst why you don't believe his or her arguments, or if you can't offer a logical counterargument, then you should take more time to construct your own analysis.

Most managers in the DI face difficult and highly stressful demands on their time. In a directorate in which, at each level, the manager is expected to be part expert, part editor, and part bureaucrat, they are sometimes tempted to give the people-management side of their jobs short shrift. Frequently, the result is that suspicions of base motives arise when there are simply differences of view:

- This happens when a division chief is too timid or thinks he or she is too busy to sit down with the analyst and go over comments on a paper.
- It happens when a senior manager makes cryptic or offensive comments on drafts.
- It happens when the office director sits on a paper indefinitely because he or she lacks the courage to tell an analyst and his or her management that it is simply unworkable or irrelevant.
- It happens when an analyst responds to a reviewer with legitimate questions or counterarguments, only to discover he or she has been branded as uncooperative and unwilling to take criticism.
- It happens when subordinate managers are afraid to give bad news, or to admit to their own mistakes, and instead pin everything unpleasant on someone higher up the chain.
- It happens when there are so many layers of excessive review that some kind of misunderstanding somewhere along the way is inevitable.
- It happens when any manager becomes so intent on "making a call" or "sharpening the judgments" or "defining the office view" that he or she oversimplifies the argument or fails to provide alternative views.

I think you get the idea. Perceptions of politicization or other kinds of intentional distortion tend to arise in the absence of an open, creative environment that encourages give-and-take. The manager who allows the press of business and the frequent need to push and prod for the best possible product to cause him or her to behave rudely, abruptly, or imperiously does so at considerable peril to his or her reputation for objectivity. I know also that what is necessary is not the practice of some awkward, feel-good management technique. It is simply a matter of treating people the right way—with professional respect, civility, and confidence in their integrity and capabilities.

Managers must create an environment in which analysts feel comfortable airing substantive differences. Managers must listen; they must talk; they must erode some of the hierarchy. And they must create a sense of joint ownership of ideas. Managers need to create an atmosphere in which people can approach them without fear of retribution. Managers must—I repeat, must—create a barrier-free environment for ideas.

Now let me address our analysts. Analysts have their own responsibilities to prevent distortions and politicization from creeping into our analysis. First and foremost, analysts must be able to construct clearly a logical analysis of an issue. This includes not only the ability to write a clear argument, but also an ability to examine one's own biases, assumptions, and limitations.

Second, when an analyst sends forward a work to management, he or she should be prepared and expect to defend that analysis.

Third, every analyst must approach editing, coordination, and review as a process to improve a piece. An analyst must see the process as a team effort, with coordinating analysts and managers as team members who will offer input that must be considered and dealt with. No analyst should think that his or her view of the world is the only correct view, or that the opinions and arguments of others are not worthy of consideration. We must always keep our minds open. As Judge Learned Hand wrote, "Opinions are at best provisional hypotheses, incompletely tested. The more they are tested, after the tests are well scrutinized, the more assurance we may assume, but they are never absolutes. So, we must be tolerant of opposite opinions or varying opinions by the very fact of our incredulity of our own."

Last, and this is an important point, analysts must always challenge the arguments and opinions of others, including their managers. An analyst should not expect his or her analysis to go unchallenged, and he or she should not be willing to accept the analysis of others without challenge. By questioning managers and other analysts on the reasons underlying their comments and judgments, especially those in conflict with our own, we learn to look at issues in new ways, sometimes ways that are better. You should rightly question anyone who cannot defend or explain the reasons behind disagreements with your analysis.

Also, unwarranted concerns about politicization can arise when analysts themselves fail to understand their role in the process. We do produce a corporate product. If the policymaker wants the opinion of a single individual, he or she can (and frequently does) consult any one of a dozen outside experts on any given issue. Your work, on the other hand, counts because it represents the well-considered view of an entire directorate and, in the case of National Estimates, the entire Intelligence Community. Analysts themselves must play a critical role in making the system work. They must do their part to help foster an open environment. Analysts must understand and practice the corporate concept. They must discard the academic mindset that says their work is their own, and they must take into account the views of others during the coordination process.

What, then, can we do together to counter both real and perceived distortion of the analytical product? For starters, we can all recommit ourselves to a solid professional ethic and a high degree of collegiality. Distortion of analysis is much less likely, and much easier to spot, if there is a concerted effort at all levels to observe basic standards:

- We must make explicit what is not known and clearly distinguish between fact, inference, and judgment.
- We must recommit ourselves to the good old-fashioned scientific method—the testing of alternative hypotheses against the evidence.
- We should provide an outlet for different interpretations, theories, or

predictions in our mainline publications, not just in a staff note or a piece at the back of a monthly.
- While we strive for sharp and focused judgments for a clear assessment of likelihood, we must not dismiss alternatives or exaggerate our certainty under the guise of making the "tough calls." We are analysts, not umpires, and the game does not depend on our providing a single judgment. As Oliver Wendell Holmes wrote, "Certitude is not the test of certainty. We have been cocksure of many things that were not so."
- We must protect ourselves from groupthink, an institutional mind-set, or personal bias. We must also avoid the temptation to weight our arguments or our case as a corrective to the perceived failings of others.
- We must view coordination as an important step in ensuring that all views have been considered. Indeed, the task force found that refusal to alter a view or take into account the views of others during the coordination process frequently leads to charges of distortion or politicization.

But, above all, we must build an atmosphere of confidence and trust between analysts and managers. This requires a renewed commitment to accountability, expertise, and intellectual honesty. Accountability means standing behind the intelligence that one sends forward and being held responsible for any distortions that have been imposed upon it. It is not producing analysis designed to please one's superiors; nor does it mean that a branch, division, or office's analysis must always be right. Accountability requires that analysts and managers understand each other's viewpoints and work together in producing the best analysis they can.

In doing so, we rely on expertise. Managers should ensure that analysts are given opportunities to build and hone their substantive expertise and analytic skills. Managers are chosen to manage their analysts, not to become superanalysts themselves. In helping their analysts develop, managers can build a reserve of trust. Analysts, for their part, must dedicate themselves to becoming experts on their subject and sharpening their critical-thinking skills. This takes talent; this takes hard work; this takes dedication; and, not least, this takes time! It follows that managers will demonstrate increased confidence in analysts of such proven expertise.

Finally, we all need to recognize biases and blindspots in ourselves and in others—viewing them not as weaknesses but as opportunities to grow. Such an approach would allow us to deal more openly with others and foster a more collegial give-and-take among analysts and managers. Greater intellectual honesty on everyone's part can make the process less bureaucratic, less hierarchical, and less of a win-lose situation.

By improving analyst-manager trust, I believe that concerns about the review process skewing intelligence can be lessened. Moreover, in the scope of a more collegial relationship, a manager challenging assumptions should not be seen as a threat by analysts. On balance, it is the managers who bear the greater burden of responsibility in the review process, and they need to have a sound basis for their actions. In editing and revising intelligence products, I expect managers to explain their changes in face-to-face exchanges with their analysts and to be willing to admit when a revision is unwarranted. In turn, I expect analysts to use evidence and logic when arguing against proposed revisions in substance, to be open to new approaches and ideas, and to guard against purely defensive reactions. Expertise is a requirement, but analysts must not become so wedded to their views that they exclude well-grounded, alternative arguments.

The issue of analyst-manager communications is paralleled in the DI-NIC relationship, where NIOs review drafts submitted by DI analysts. A majority of the time, the process works smoothly. In some instances, however, tensions have flared over disagreements on substantive changes. Both sides must endeavor to communicate openly to resolve differences in views or outline alternative scenarios. Moreover, the NIOs' access to the DCI is not exclusive; analysts are welcome to bring their concerns about the estimative process directly to me.

I would like also to address the special obligations and responsibilities that fall on the Directorate of Intelligence and Directorate of Operations [DO] when CIA is involved in a covert action. For the DO, a covert action activity does not absolve it of its foreign intelligence reporting responsibilities. It must meet its professional obligation to report as accurately and as fully on an area or problem in which a covert action is under way as on any other subject. The DO's task is made harder and scrutiny will be all the more intense because inevitably the DO will be working against the perception that its reporting is skewed by involvement in a covert action. And, in truth, it is only human nature to expect that those who are trying to implement a policy will develop strong opinions about, and even attachments to, that policy. We would be fooling ourselves if we tried to deny that reality. But all the more reason for the DO, as professional intelligence officers, to assert their own first obligation to seek and report the truth. And all the more reason that we must reaffirm that those who are responsible for covert action must not be in a position to produce, coordinate, or disseminate anything that is, or looks like, finished intelligence. At the same time, DI analysts must seek out the expertise in the DO, including in areas where covert action is involved, where operations and reports officers have great experience, expertise, and day-to-day working insights. And a special burden falls on the leaders of joint DO-DI Centers, who must ensure that neither the perception nor the reality of politicization gets a toehold.

There is one other potential problem that I need to talk about. As we all know, the DO frequently has information that for one reason or another is not formally disseminated. This may be especially true in cases involving covert action. The DO, in those cases, must make sure that the relevant analysts are made privy to the information they need to strengthen their analytical understanding and work.

In discussing this topic, I would be remiss in not stating that, with a few exceptions, we have a long history of effectively making this partnership between the DO and the DI work—where the DI has earned a well-deserved reputation for independence and insight and the DO for reporting unblinkingly and accurately even when involved in covert action.

In its examination of politicization, the task force concluded that the solution to the problem of politicization, broadly defined, is not so much a matter of mechanisms as it is confidence in the integrity and capabilities of our people. For our recommendations to yield positive results, every Agency employee from the DI on down must demonstrate adherence to the principles of integrity on which objective analysis rests, and civility, which fosters a trusting, creative environment.

While I agree that, first and foremost, attitudes must change to help us overcome the unease that politicization has produced among Agency employees, steps should be taken to set a process of reconciliation and dialogue in motion. As I noted earlier, I fully endorse the task force's recommended actions. At the risk of reciting a laundry list of new initiatives, I would like to outline for you the measures that I have undertaken in an effort to address the problem of politicization.

As a first step, I pledge to you today my firm commitment to ensure that analytic objectivity is at the core of every finished intelligence product and that the importance of people-oriented management is instilled at every supervisory level. I want to see this Agency excel in its mission; but to do so, its personnel must have a sense of value and feel that their contribution matters. I expect every manager in this organization to echo my commitment and foster an atmosphere of confidence and trust.

To strengthen management skills and enforce accountability for good management, I have directed the DDI to initiate a zero-based study of DI management practices, to mandate that performance appraisal reports explicitly cite deficiencies in management related to charges of politicization, and to support initiatives to secure better feedback from personnel such as the evaluation forms being developed by the DI/MAG.

In an effort to assist managers in cultivating the analytic talent of the people under their supervision, I have asked the DDI to ensure that DI managers devote greater attention and resources to practical on-the-job training of analysts—showing them how to gather evidence, assess sources, make judgments, and write up or brief their analysis, our so-called tradecraft. The DDI also should develop a DI tradecraft manual and work with the Office of Training and Education to enhance the tradecraft training that analysts receive in formal courses. In addition, managers should rely more frequently on the expertise and experience of senior analysts to assist in developing new analysts. As a means of minimizing the chances for distortions and misperceptions caused by the review process, I have directed the OOI to institute practical measures to reduce layers of review, encourage greater flexibility and variety of formatting, and encourage fuller debate of substantive issues. To achieve these goals, a DI task force will be established to study the directorate's review and coordination process. At the risk of prejudging the task force's findings, I expect to see a noticeable reduction in the layers of review. In addition, I have asked the OOI to reserve his own substantive review to sensitive products intended for high-level consumers. I have not and will not become involved in the review process.

To ensure that our consumers get the benefit of differing analytic perspectives and to demonstrate the directorate's openness to new ideas and thoughtful alternative viewpoints, I have asked the DDI to restate his support for the inclusion of well-reasoned, relevant, and factually supported alternative views in mainline products, and to appoint a committee to develop practical means to accomplish this goal.

In an effort to remain vigilant to future instances of politicization, I have directed all major analytic components to establish and publicize procedures within the chain of command—to deal with allegations of politicization. I also asked the DOI to appoint a full-time ombudsman to serve as an independent informal counselor for those with complaints about politicization, and he has asked Dave Peterson to take on that job. Dave will have access to me, the DDCI, the DDI, and all DI analytic products; he will counsel, arbitrate, or offer recommendations and have the authority to initiate inquiries into real or perceived problem areas. While Dave will be administratively located in the DI he will be responsible for dealing with concerns about or allegations of politicization from throughout the Agency, as well as the NIC and estimative process. He will also publish an annual report that includes an assessment of the current level of concern and the effectiveness of measures being taken to alleviate it.

I have directed that several other measures be taken to guard against politicization becoming a problem in the future. IG studies of analytic components shall specifically consider the effectiveness of the review and coordination processes, and the DDI should make relevant portions of IG [Inspector General] studies of DI components available to a wider audience within the DI. The DDI should also mandate wider dissemination of studies by the Product Evaluation Staff, as well as increase the studies' emphasis on distortions of the product and process and on the use of alternative analysis.

As a follow-up to the task force's efforts, a survey of DI analysts and managers should be conducted a year from now on the issue of politicization.

Finally, the DDI and I are committed to encouraging open and continuing discussion throughout the DI and the NIC of politicization and will promptly take steps when allegations of problems arise, particularly in centers and task forces involved with DO operations. Specifically, I have asked the DDI to encourage all components to discuss politicization in general, and as it pertains to specific substantive issues, and to mandate that officers engaged in the conduct of covert action in areas where policy implementation and analytic functions are integrated shall not be involved in the formal coordination of finished analytic products. The DDI, the NIC Chairman, and the Deputy Director for Operations currently are developing guidelines to ensure that the entire intelligence production process, including the preparation of regular intelligence analysis, National Intelligence Estimates, briefings, etc., including in the DCI centers, are insulated from the influence of those with responsibility for implementing and supervising covert action.

I, better than anyone, know that this directorate lives and breathes skepticism. It is, after all, our stock in trade. And no area is so subject to skepticism—even cynicism—as senior-level rhetoric. "Show me" is the watchword. And so it should be. I intend to monitor closely the implementation of these instructions and ensure that they are carried out. This will be no paper exercise. Actions at every level and a sustained commitment will be required and, as we go along, the DDI and I will continue to welcome ideas in implementing the recommendations.

At the same time, you and I both know that this kind of problem cannot be directed away. You cannot order integrity, you cannot demand that a culture preserve its ethics. In the end, preventing distortion of our analysis depends on where all of us draw the line day in and day out. We must draw a line:

- Between producing a corporate product and suppressing different views.
- Between adjusting stylistic presentation to anticipate your consumer's predilections and changing the analysis to pander to them.
- Between making order out of chaos and suppressing legitimate debate.
- Between viewing reporting critically and using evidence selectively.
- Between avoiding wishy-washiness and pretending to be more certain than we are.
- Between being a team player and being a careerist.
- Between maintaining efficiency and suppressing legitimate debate.
- Between providing leadership and fostering a fearful, oppressive climate.

I wish I could look back on my career in the DI—from analyst to DDI—and say that in each and every case over 25 years I have always drawn all these lines in all the right places. I can tell you, however, that as DCI I intend to do everything in my power to guarantee that analytic objectivity remains the most important of the core values of the Central Intelligence Agency.

It is my sincere hope that the steps I have outlined will help alleviate the underlying causes of and concerns about politicization. Let me reiterate. In our efforts to be policy-relevant, we should not allow our analysis to become skewed in favor of one policy option or another. Nor should the views of one individual—manager or analyst—prevail when well-sourced, well-reasoned arguments support a different set of judgments. We must improve the analyst-manager relationship, and the burden is largely on those who lead. Collegiality and honesty should be two key watchwords in our dealings. We must also avoid ascribing base motives to those with whom we disagree. Moreover, the analytic process should vigorously scrutinize all available evidence, including clandestine reporting, to ensure that underlying policy goals are not distorting our analysis.

In closing, I want to emphasize that the underlying key to dealing with this issue of politicization is respect for individuals, trust in their judgment, confidence in their capabilities, and concern for their well-being. Managers must tell employees what is expected of them, and they must hold them responsible for following through. At the same time, however, managers must give employees the trust and confidence, as well as the training and control, they need to carry out the task. And they must reward employees for their competence, creativity, and commitment to the analytic process.

I want respect for the employee to again become a central value of this organization, and I want that value to run deep. Many managers pay lip service to this. I want all of us to deliver, and I think we should be held accountable for doing so. Because trust begets trust, I am certain perceptions of politicization would be reduced in the process.

I will make a commitment to you today. My door is always open to discuss this issue with you. If you believe your work is being distorted and you are not satisfied your managers are seriously addressing your concerns, I want to hear from you.

I am very proud of the Directorate of Intelligence. I served in it; I led it; and I used its analysis to frame policy. I want to see it—and the people in it—prosper. I have always been greatly impressed with the breadth and depth of expertise in the DI. And I do not want anybody—inside or outside the Agency—to believe this expertise is tarnished by political considerations.

I was uncertain how to present my message today, how exactly to say what I wanted to convey. So, I did what I have often done for years. I turned to the DI for help. I asked two members of the politicization task force each to give me a draft of what they thought I should say, and I asked them to choose two analysts—unknown to me—to do the same. My remarks today are an amalgam of those four drafts and my own views. Though many of the words today originally were not mine, I believe wholeheartedly in what they express. The sentiments, the views, are mine, if not every word. Those who helped me know who they are, and I thank them.

Let me conclude then by simply reiterating that the absolute integrity of our analysis is the most important of the core values of the Central Intelligence Agency. Policymakers, the Congress, and the American people must know that our views—right or wrong—represent our best and most objective possible effort to describe the threats and opportunities facing the United States. They must know our assessments are the product of the highest quality and the most honest intelligence analysis available anywhere in the world. Thank you.

11

Memorandum: One Person Can Make a Difference

Veteran Intelligence Professionals for Sanity (VIPS)

Our most recent open appeal to you, "Now It's Your Turn," was made on August 22, 2003. On that same day, it turns out, former Australian intelligence analyst Andrew Wilkie testified before a parliamentary committee examining the justification given by Prime Minister John Howard for Australia's decision to join the war in Iraq. Wilkie had been a senior analyst in Australia's premier intelligence agency, the Office of National Assessments (ONA). Of all the Australian, British, and American intelligence analysts with direct knowledge of how intelligence was abused in the run-up to the war, Wilkie was the only one to resign in protest and speak truth to power.

Those who dismiss such efforts as an exercise in futility should know that on October 7 the Australian Senate, in a rare move, censured Howard for misleading the public in justifying sending Australian troops off to war. The Senate statement of censure noted that Howard had produced no evidence to justify his claims last March that Iraq had stockpiles of biological and chemical weapons, and castigated him for suppressing Australian intelligence warnings that war with Iraq would increase the likelihood of terrorist attacks. One senator accused Howard of "unprecedented deceit."

This important story received little attention in the U.S. media. We call it to your attention as a reminder of what one honest person can do. Thanks to the courage and determination of Andrew Wilkie, much of the Australian populace understands much better that the reasons adduced for war on Iraq were cooked in Washington and served up by Australian leaders all too willing to give unquestioning support to the Bush administration. Those Australian leaders are now being held accountable.

185

As some of you know, VIPS invited Andrew Wilkie here to Washington in July to speak at a briefing in the House Rayburn Building. (Wilkie, of course, is out of a job; so mutual Australian friends paid for his flight, and we in VIPS passed the hat to cover his expenses here.) After his well-received presentation on July 14, we strongly encouraged him to keep throwing light on this dark chapter of history. We also voiced our hope that U.S. intelligence analysts who have also watched the deceit close-up would soon join him in speaking out. With a wan smile Wilkie shook his head and pointed to the cost—including the character assassination to which he had already been subjected at the hands of his government. Integrity and thick skin are what it takes, but a little outside encouragement helps. The month after Wilkie was here, he laid out his case before parliament.

Wilkie testified that the attack on Iraq had little to do with weapons of mass destruction (WMD) or terrorism. We single out one particularly telling paragraph:

> Please remember the Government was also receiving detailed assessments on the U.S. in which it was made very clear the U.S. was intent on invading Iraq for more important reasons than WMD and terrorism. Hence all this talk about WMD and terrorism was hollow. Much more likely is the proposition the Government deliberately exaggerated the Iraq WMD threat so as to stay in step with the U.S.

In the wake of Wilkie's testimony, Australian pundits have become more critical of Australia's current leaders' continuing refusal to acknowledge that, as one journalist put it, they were "conned by master manipulators masquerading as purveyors of objective intelligence." We include Wilkie's testimony below, with a reminder that . . . you too can make a difference.

OPENING REMARKS TO THE PARLIAMENTARY JOINT COMMITTEE ON AUSTRALIAN SECURITY INTELLIGENCE ORGANIZATION (ASIO), AUSTRALIAN SECRET INTELLIGENCE SERVICE (ASIS), AND DEFENSE SIGNALS DIRECTORATE (DSD), 22 AUGUST 2003, BY ANDREW WILKIE

Mr. Chairman, thank you for inviting me to appear before the Committee. You would be well aware that I resigned from the Office of National Assessments, before the Iraq war, because I assessed that invading Iraq would not be the most sensible and ethical way to resolve the Iraq issue. I chose resignation, specifically, because compromise or seeking to create change from within ONA were not realistic options.

At the time I resigned I put on the public record three fundamental concerns. Firstly, that Iraq did not pose a serious enough security threat to justify a war. Secondly, that too many things could go wrong. And, thirdly, that war was still totally unnecessary because options short of war were yet to be exhausted.

My first concern is especially relevant today. It was based on my assessment that Iraq's conventional armed forces were weak, that Iraq's Weapons of Mass Destruction program was disjointed and contained, and that there was no hard evidence of any active cooperation between Iraq and al Qaida.

Now the government has claimed repeatedly I was not close enough to the Iraq issue to know what I'm talking about. Such statements have misled the public and have been exceptionally hurtful to me.

I was a Senior Analyst with a top-secret positive vet security clearance. I'd been awarded a Superior rating in my last performance appraisal, and not long before I resigned I'd been informed by the Deputy Director-General that thought was being given to my being promoted.

Because of my military background (I had been a regular army infantry Lieutenant Colonel), I was required to be familiar with war-related issues . . . and was on standby to cover Iraq once the war began.

I've also worked specifically on WMD issues. In 1999 I prepared the assessment on WMD and terrorism, and represented ONA at the WMD working group held in the UK. In 2001 I helped prepare the update on my 1998 assessment, and I represented ONA at the Australian WMD working group.

I was involved also in covering global terrorism issues. In fact, on two occasions I provided the relevant brief for the Standing Advisory Committee for the Protection Against Violence. Finally, as the Senior ONA Transnational Issues Analyst, I was involved routinely in matters relating to Iraq. This provided me with almost unrestricted access to intelligence on that country. In particular, my December 2002 assessment on the possible humanitarian implications of a war required me to research in detail the strategic threat posed by Saddam Hussein.

If I could now turn more directly to the Committee's Terms of Reference. When I said that Iraq's WMD program was "disjointed and contained," I was describing a limited chemical and biological program focused on developing a break-out capability, in part by reliance on dual-use facilities. Weapons production was possible, though only on a small scale. My view was broadly consistent with ONA's position, maybe a little more moderate. I still believe evidence of such a program may be found eventually, if not already.

Now, in fairness to Australian and Allied intelligence agencies, Iraq was a tough target. From time to time there were shortages of human intelligence on the country. At other times the preponderance of anti-Saddam sources desperate for U.S. intervention ensured a flood of disinformation. Collecting technical intelligence was equally challenging.

A problem for Australian agencies was their reliance on Allies. We had virtually no influence on foreign intelligence collection planning, and the raw intelligence seldom arrived with adequate notes on sources or reliability. More problematic was the way in which Australia's tiny agencies needed to rely on the sometimes weak and skewed views contained in the assessments prepared in Washington.

A few problems were inevitable. For instance, intelligence gaps were sometimes backfilled with the disinformation. Worst-case sometimes took primacy over most-likely. The threat was sometimes overestimated as a result of the fairy tales coming out of the U.S. And sometimes Government pressure, as well as politically correct intelligence officers themselves, resulted in its own bias.

But, overall, Australian agencies did, I believe, an acceptable job reporting on the existence of, the capacity and willingness to use, and immediacy of the threat, posed by Iraq. Assessments were OK, not least because they were always heavily qualified to reflect the ambiguous intelligence picture. How then to explain the big gap between the Government's pre-war claims about Iraq possessing a massive arsenal of WMD and cooperating actively with al Qaida and the reality that no arsenal of weapons or evidence of substantive links have yet been found?

Well, most often the Government deliberately skewed the truth by taking the ambiguity out of the issue. Key intelligence assessment qualifications like "probably," "could," and "uncorroborated evidence suggests" were frequently dropped. Much more useful words like "massive" and "mammoth" were included, even though such words had not been offered to the government by the intelligence agencies. Before we knew it, the Government had created a mythical Iraq, one where every factory was up to no good and weaponization was continuing apace.

Equally misleading was the way in which the Government misrepresented the truth. For example, when the Government spoke of Iraq having form (being up to no good), it cited pre-1991 Gulf War examples, like the use of chemical weapons against Iran and the Kurds. Mind you, the Government needed to be creative, because 12 years of sanctions, inspections, and air strikes had virtually disarmed modern Iraq.

The Government also chose to use the truth selectively. For instance, much was said about the risk of WMD terrorism. But what was not made clear was that the risk of WMD terrorism is low, that leakage of weapons from a state arsenal is unlikely, and that the weapon most likely to be used will be crude. That is, the chemical, biological, or radiological device most likely to be used will not be a WMD.

The Government even went so far as to fabricate the truth. The claims about Iraq cooperating actively with al Qaida were obviously nonsense. As was the Government's reference to Iraq seeking uranium in Africa, despite the fact that ONA, the Department of Defense, and the Department of Foreign Affairs and Trade all knew the Niger story was fraudulent. This was critical information. It beggars belief that ONA knew it was discredited but didn't advise the Prime Minister, Defense knew but didn't tell the Defense Minister, and Foreign Affairs knew but didn't tell the Foreign Minister.

Please remember the Government was also receiving detailed assessments on the U.S. in which it was made very clear the U.S. was intent on invading Iraq for more important reasons than WMD and terrorism. Hence all this talk about WMD and terrorism was hollow. Much more likely is the proposition the Government deliberately exaggerated the Iraq WMD threat so as to stay in step with the U.S.

In closing, I wish to make it clear that I do not apologize for, or withdraw from, my accusation that the Howard government misled the Australian public over Iraq, both through its own public statements, as well as through its endorsement of Allied statements.

The government lied every time it said or implied that I was not senior enough or appropriately placed in ONA to know what I was talking about. And the government lied every time it skewed, misrepresented, used selectively, and fabricated the Iraq story.

But these examples are just the tip of the iceberg. For instance, the government lied when the Prime Minister's Office told the media I was mentally unstable. The government lied when it associated Iraq with the Bali bombing. And the government lied every time it linked Iraq to the War on Terror.

The Prime Minister and the Foreign Minister in particular have a lot to answer for. After all, they were the chief cheerleaders for the invasion of another country, without UN endorsement, for reasons that have now been discredited.

Mr. Chairman, I've skimmed over a lot of important issues here. Of course I'd now welcome the opportunity to discuss any particular aspect in more detail.

12

The Ethics of War, Spying, and Compulsory Training

J. E. Roscoe, Rev.

Editor's note: This selection is a chapter from a 1914 publication, reprinted in its original form. The 33-page booklet includes the following chapter headings: War Cleanses or Creates Channels of Peace; War Introduces New Ideas and Helps Form Civilization; War Fosters Such Virtues as Courage, Patience, Watchfulness, and Self-Sacrifice; War Acts as a Stimulus to Patriotism and Unity; War Has an Educative Value; The Ethics of Spying; and The Ethics of Compulsory Training. The penultimate chapter has been chosen for inclusion.

In the first place, it would be well for us to point out that the Bible does contain passages which for the moment seem to encourage secret spying. Firstly, Numbers xiii, 1–2: "And the Lord spoke unto Moses, saying, Send thou men, that they may search the land of Canaan, which I give unto the children of Israel." Secondly, in Joshua ii, 1: "And Joshua the son of Nun sent out of Shittim two men to *spy secretly,* saying Go view the land, even Jericho." We cannot imagine God giving or approving such commands unless there were some good purpose in them.

We cannot go farther without relating briefly the circumstances which gave rise to these injunctions. Of the former text, as the children of Israel were on their journey to Canaan, on arriving at Rithmah, or Kadesh-barnen, which was situated in the wilderness of Paran and close to the southern border of Canaan, eight leagues south of Hebron, Moses sent twelve men to "spy the land" and report upon its strength and riches. They returned in forty days and reported the land to be "flowing with milk and honey," but ten of them gave a formidable account of the inhabitants and walled cities.

The second text refers to the fact that Joshua had succeeded to the leadership of the people and had led the Israelites to the shores of the Jordan, on the eastern side of Canaan. As recorded in the text, he sent two spies into Jericho to view the land and ascertain the strength of the city. Their presence being discovered, they were sheltered in the house of Rahab, who, having concealed them on the roof of her house by covering them over with stalks of flax, afterward let them down from a window over the city walls, by which they escaped. In return for the women's kindness, they promised her and her family protection when taking the city, and directed her "to bind a line of scarlet thread in the window" that they might recognize the house.

In the Epistle of S. James ii, 25, she is commended for sheltering those spies. The question that at once confronts us is, was Rahab traitorous to the King of Jericho, under whose protection she was living? Whether loyalty to king or loyalty to righteousness is the problem to be solved before dealing with spies? It is right to state at once that in Scripture it is her faith and not her falsehood that is commended. God had given command that Jericho must be taken, and she had to decide whether she must obey God rather than man. She reasoned within herself, basing this reason on facts. From these facts she argued that the God of Israel must be mightier than the gods whom she worshipped, and ultimately found ample evidence of a power that maketh for righteousness. Rahab, fully convinced of the righteousness of their cause, threw in her lot on their side. "Your God shall be my God." Her falsehood is pardonable, because she had not known the God of truth previous to this event. To all intents and purposes she was a heathen, and why should we be so unwilling to allow falsehood in a heathen ages ago, when we extend our pity to the falsehood of the heathen of today? We have no intention of extolling her falsehood, but under the circumstances it was pardonable, and more so when she had not yet known Him who is "the way, the truth, and the life."

Now as to spies. The gravest accusation that can be brought against war is, that for the efficient conduct of it man finds that he must suspend the great moral laws; that to turn the other cheek to the enemy would mean destruction, and the triumph of perhaps a military despotism and barbarism. Things may be necessary for the ordering of society and for the abnormal relations of nations which cannot be permitted in private life. War, serious evil as it is, may be used by God for His great purposes, just as He uses other evil things, viz., plague, famine, pestilence, and the wrongdoings of men. So the employment of spies, the arrangement of ambushes, and stratagems serve their purpose, viz., forethought and prudence.

Christ indirectly enjoins these two virtues in His words recorded in S. Luke xiv, 31: "Or what king, going to make war against another king, sitteth not down first and consulteth whether he be able with ten thousand to meet him that cometh against him with twenty thousand?" How is it possible to gain this information as to the strength of another king's army without the aid of spies and the exercise of forethought and prudence?

Lango writes: "The use of human prudence, with all trust in Divine Providence, is not only allowable, but often also a binding duty. Joshua ought not, in his position as a General, to enter into a strange and hostile land without having explored it first." A little thought, a little care, a little preparation, "a look before you leap" policy.

Another quotation to prove the necessity of such action: "Man is an animal that knows what's o'clock, i.e., that take note of time. It is perhaps only an amplification of this last idea to add, man is an animal that thinks of tomorrow. The vegetable, in its vocabulary of time, knows only the word today; the animal knows yesterday and today; man alone lives in a yesterday, today and tomorrow. He belongs to tomorrow just as much as to today. . . . From tomorrow springs hope, fear, rest, and distress. 'Man never is—but always to be blest.' This instinct of anticipation is natural because it is necessary. We forecast what is coming; we cannot prepare for it, enjoy it, or secure it. If we advance without forecasting we find ourselves perplexed in the simplest circumstances, helpless though possessed of abundant sources."

The difference between a man who sends out the spies of forethought and prudence, and the man who doesn't, is that the one is more or less prepared, while the other is taken by surprise and perhaps blunders along, to a great degree relying on fate. We are well aware of a statement such as this: "Sufficient unto the day is the evil thereof." That does not forbid calm forethought, but anxious worry, which is a different thing. A blind rush policy would in most cases spell disaster. Napoleon, on being congratulated on his great victories by Las Casas, replied: "The victory of today was instantly forgotten in preparation for the battle which was to be fought on the morrow."

One cannot forget one of the greatest battles being won in English history by the aid of a spy, and that "spy" was no less a personage than Alfred the Great. In 878 he was defeated by the Danes and driven from his kingdom. He sought refuge in Somersetshire. Here he waited and watched for the right moment to attack his enemies. Disguised as a minstrel, he went into the Danish camp as a spy, where his music and drollery obtained him so favorable a reception. He noted their careless security, and after leaving the camp called his army together and defeated the Danes, the outcome of which was the peace of Wedmore.

Warfare dements this policy of caution or spying, to keep a sharp watch on fortification and movements of the enemy and bring back intelligence which may encourage, guide, and help those who are actually directing such warfare. The "Secret Service" is an established institution in most countries.

13

Legitimacy of Covert Action
Sorting out the Moral Responsibilities

Lincoln P. Bloomfield Jr.

The United States needs to have the mechanisms and ability to conduct activities in support of national foreign policy objectives on a secret, nonattributable basis. This does not mean that covert action has or should become a "principal" instrument of foreign policy, only that it is necessary as an "available" instrument. This does not mean that the United States government has incorporated immoral or illegal activities into its portfolio, nor that the American public may become the target of federal manipulation.

These aspects are not synonymous with covert action; in fact, all are prohibited by law or directive. Rather, the ability to conduct covert action allows the president to execute his constitutionally mandated charter in foreign affairs, and provides a mechanism to act in support of the national interest by working with foreign entities whose cause would suffer if U.S. support to them were to become common knowledge.

The key question, then, is not whether the United States should have the capability, but how to ensure that the Executive branch executes covert actions in a manner consistent with the Constitution. An important part of the answer lies in the constitutional role played by the Congress in exercising its proper oversight functions. A lack of oversight can weaken the process of good government; so can an excess of that oversight.

These issues are best explained by examining the roles of the Executive, the Congress, and the citizen as the American public seeks reassurance in the aftermath of the Iran-contra affair that its government is pursuing a role internationally that is both effective and morally sound.

THE ISSUES RAISED BY IRAN-CONTRA

Since the people of America declared their independence from the British crown, they have exhibited a strong anti-authoritarian streak. Every U.S. president has, undoubtedly, puzzled over the conflicting emotions of a people who love their elected leader when he looks strong but often recoil when he acts that way. The American public is quick to humble its elected leaders and representatives whenever they seem to be exceeding their popular mandate. The Watergate hearings were, for many Americans, cathartic in bringing officials who had secretly abused the public trust before the court of public opinion. Congress's standing with the public was enhanced.

When the Congress organized the Iran-contra hearings held in 1987, comparisons with Watergate were inescapable, if only because of the televised format. But the differences were profound. Whereas the Watergate participants had been motivated by the advancement of their personal political fortunes, those involved in the Iran-contra affair were pursuing designated or implied national policy objectives in the Middle East and Central America. Whereas President Richard Nixon had been named as an unindicted co-conspirator for his actions, President Ronald Reagan's actions were said to have fallen within the scope of his authority. Whereas President Nixon was faulted for covering up the facts, President Reagan opened up his administration's files and instructed all officials to testify fully and truthfully. He initiated the nonpartisan Tower Commission investigation, and pledged full cooperation with the Independent Counsel named to probe possible violations of the law. When procedures were found to have been wanting, the president reformed them. Clearly, President Reagan's response to the Iran-contra revelations was to restore the public's confidence in the Executive, whatever the political cost to him.

Some who closely followed the Iran-contra investigations recognized these basic differences between Iran-contra and Watergate; others appeared content to let similarities stand. Congress took particular umbrage at not having been told about either the president's initiative to sell arms to Iran or the extent of the NSC staff's actions in support of the Nicaraguan resistance. For some Americans, the spectacle of the Congress publicly berating the administration for its secret endeavors gave vent to feelings of frustration, tapping once again into the popular sentiment that resists entrusting power to anyone—even the nation's chief executive.

What the unfavorable national reaction to Iran-contra obscured, however, was that those powers had indeed been delegated by the people to their president, in Article II of the Constitution. In the United States, a most dynamic and open democracy, there is an unavoidable tension between the citizen's deeply felt need to control his representatives, and the recognition that the well-being of the state requires the capability to cooperate confidentially with other states in a dangerous world, and to act secretly in defense of those interests.

Covert actions—whose sponsorship by the United States is deniable and intended to be kept secret forever—confront the citizen with the uncomfortable thought that, in these instances at least, he is trusting his representatives completely to act on his behalf. This trust is severely tested by sensational public revelations of alleged covert action failures or misdeeds, particularly since the government does not usually address the subject in public.

Covert action has an anomalous but necessary role in the functioning of an open democracy. The world does not permit the United States the luxury of forswearing a capability to act secretly. What might surprise disillusioned citizens is how much the system is receptive to their values and policy preferences.

THE LIMITS ON COVERT ACTION

Covert action, a very limited tool of statecraft, is not a substitute for any other instrument of national policy or influence. The secrecy involved is as perishable as it is essential, so that only activities of modest scope and duration can reasonably be expected to remain secret. Other than circumstantial constraints, the most significant limits on covert action are the limits on covert actors.

The American system of government affords several protections against the exercise of absolute power of the sort that Lord Acton deplored, without negating the power itself. Some examples:

- The president is popularly elected, serves a term of office, and exercises only those powers enumerated in the Constitution.
- The Congress has the constitutionally based power of the purse, and an intelligence oversight role which includes being informed of covert actions. Should Congress ever conclude that the president is abusing the powers of his office and that regular checks and balances are not adequately safeguarding the national interest against these abuses, procedures exist for Congress to remove the president.
- Statutes impose discipline on Executive branch participants in the covert action process, including the Counsel to the President and the NSC General Counsel, who review covert action findings before they are signed by the president.
- The personal integrity of public servants, beginning with the president, and including appointed officials, career civil servants, and military personnel, serves as a factor in the policy process. Because equal opportunity exists for any qualified citizen to gain employment with the

government, the system incorporates the values of a broad cross-section of Americans.

Reciting basic civics tenets may seem out of place when discussing covert action, a realm of activity more frequently portrayed by its critics as anti-democratic, unrepresentative of the popular will, and therefore illegitimate. Precisely because of these factors, however, U.S. covert actions meet any test of legitimacy that can reasonably be applied to a state. What remains is the theoretical case of a covert action in which public servants break the law or otherwise act dishonorably, and their misdeeds are kept secret from the Congress and the public. What safeguard is available to the country against secret abuse of the public trust?

THE QUEST FOR PERFECTION—THE ENEMY OF GOOD GOVERNMENT?

Combined power and secrecy can, theoretically, beget corruption. Those who object to the present statutory framework for covert action propose denying the president the discretion to exercise secret, unilateral power in this area under any circumstances, thereby—again, theoretically—eliminating the potential for unchecked corruption and abuse.

That is the essence of the proposed House and Senate legislation to require presidential notification of covert actions to the Congress within 48 hours. The president's unilateral power to conduct a covert action and control authoritative knowledge of it within the government would, no matter what the circumstances, be eliminated. Among the problems with this approach:

- It would purport to "remove" powers that are vested in the president by Article II of the Constitution. Even if the CIA were abolished, the president would still have the sworn responsibility to preserve, protect, and defend the Constitution—by whatever means he chose to fulfill that task.
- It would not add one iota of protection against a theoretical secret abuser of the public trust as described above. New laws are no defense against lawbreakers.
- Leaving aside the merits of either side of the constitutional debate, the very fact of such a disagreement between the branches would have adverse implications for the covert action process if Congress were to pass such legislation over the president's veto.
- An intelligence statute which the president and Congress viewed as an arena of contention over constitutional "turf" would undermine the very atmosphere of trust and candor between the branches which

responsible officials in both branches agree is essential to a successful national intelligence program. Indeed, such an atmosphere of mistrust appears to have led the president to withhold notification of the Iran initiative, and the NSC staff to conceal some of its Central America efforts from the Congress.

- When a constitutional disagreement is incorporated into the law, as happened with the War Powers Resolution, the legal counsels in the Executive branch have two jobs: while advising policymakers on how to keep their actions consistent with statutes, they are expected to exert no less effort in preserving the prerogatives of the Executive in recommending courses of action and in drafting reports to Congress which reflect the president's view of the law. This has been the experience with military deployments since the Congress passed the War Powers Resolution in 1973 over President Nixon's veto.

Notwithstanding the president's constitutional prerogatives, sponsors of the proposed new intelligence oversight legislation appear unsatisfied with the idea of trusting a president not to abuse his secret power. At a December 1987 public hearing held by the Senate Select Committee on Intelligence to consider S. 1721, the then-proposed Senate legislation, Secretary of Defense Frank Carlucci described the extensive changes in personnel and procedures—including President Ronald Reagan's willingness to notify the Congress of covert action findings no later than 48 hours after they are signed—which had been undertaken with respect to covert action in the aftermath of the Iran-contra affair.

The Committee vice chairman, Senator William S. Cohen (R., Maine), indicated his satisfaction with these new procedures, but noted that they were merely expressed as presidential policy, not codified in the law. The Senator told Secretary Carlucci, "You may no longer be here next year, and so we have no guarantee in terms of the continuity of those procedures, personnel, atmosphere, [and] environment. . . . It seems to me that this is an appropriate thing for us to pursue to make sure that we try to maintain the same line of propriety."

Carlucci responded by cautioning the members to be careful about the boundary between necessary legislative action and appropriate administrative action, saying, "We have to allow our presidents to administer." Referring to a National Security Decision Directive (NSDD) on covert action procedures that President Reagan had promulgated in 1987, Senator Cohen said he thought the NSDD had gone "a long way in the right direction; but the next president might totally change it, might decide to throw it out the window."

Secretary Carlucci, noting that the NSDD was very detailed, specifying which interagency groups were to work on particular problems, reiterated his commitment to proper Executive branch procedures and close Executive consultation with the intelligence committees regarding covert actions; but he drew a line beyond which Congress should not reach into the Executive policy process, telling the Senator, "if you are saying that you have to have absolute and total unrestricted knowledge into every president's internal management processes, that is just an impossible order." Senator Cohen responded that "no one on this Committee is asking for that."

Carlucci was emphasizing the point that one branch of government cannot try to put another branch on "auto-pilot," as it were, by taking one president's preferred management practices and imposing them on all future presidents. The Tower Commission, headed by former Senator John G. Tower, recommended "that each administration formulate precise procedures for restricted consideration of covert actions and that, once formulated, those procedures be strictly adhered to."[1] But the proposed Senate and House legislation would have imposed President Reagan's procedures on his successors. Additionally, it would have mandated sweeping congressional access to Executive Branch information, where access had heretofore been granted consensually.

Here the question arises as to whether one branch of government should attempt to "chaperone" another; at what point does oversight become intrusive to the point of inhibiting good work in the name of preventing bad? The medical profession may offer some insight. In certain states where courts have consistently ruled in favor of patients and awarded them large claims in medical malpractice suits, an increasing number of surgeons are reportedly refusing to operate on needy patients, for fear of facing costly recriminations. In considering new intelligence oversight legislation, the Congress must consider the practical effect of the oversight system on the functioning of the intelligence community itself.

A new statute would effectively end the president's traditional control over his intelligence bureaucracy. While the Congress has not claimed a share of the president's authority over covert actions, the effects of sweeping access to the Executive branch would be the same. Like the surgeon unwilling to risk a malpractice suit, intelligence professionals could be expected to avoid actions in the field—however essential to their missions—where time did not permit full-scale review and congressional consultations in Washington. A recriminatory environment would discourage initiative and innovation in the intelligence bureaucracy.

In Congress, as well, a statute suggesting that certain members of Congress always know the details of every covert action could place those members in the position of appearing to have supported the president's actions, should the actions be revealed publicly. Fear of political "guilt by association" could inhibit the smooth functioning of intelligence operations. This may not be the intent of the Congress—far from it. Yet members of the Iran-contra and Senate Intelligence committees have stated repeatedly that, had the president advised the Congress of his covert action finding to sell arms to Iran, the American people would have been spared this difficult problem. What these members would have done to stop the president is unclear, since the president had the authority to sell arms to Iran (and indeed, has the authority to do it again). In exercising its oversight responsibilities, Congress should welcome a modicum of political "deniability," since it does not control these operations.

To summarize: no one in either branch is dissatisfied with the present covert action review and reporting procedures authorized by President Reagan, but the intelligence committees are not content to trust future presidents to implement satisfactory procedures of their own. Under the U.S. system of government, however, the voters—not the Congress—make the decision to entrust their elected presidents with constitutional Article II powers; and the powers of one branch of government may not be taken away by another branch.

Injecting this constitutional disagreement into the law governing intelligence activities is an invitation for trouble, given that the country must live with the same Constitution. In seeking to make the system abuse-proof, sponsors of the new legislation court the risk of immobilizing the system with a perpetual atmosphere of confrontation over prerogatives between leaders in both branches, as well as fear of unreasonable legal recrimination in the intelligence bureaucracy and fear of misplaced political responsibility in the intelligence committees. This is not a prescription for good government.

Those not content with the present state of affairs—notwithstanding the president's post–Iran-contra reforms—would do well to contemplate yet another fact of life in Washington: just because a mistake is made in the Executive Branch does not guarantee that subsequent congressional actions undertaken in the name of oversight will further the public interest. They often are salutary, but Congress claims no special exemption from the laws of human nature.

ACCOUNTABILITY—WHEN OVERSEERS OVERREACH

When the Iran arms sales and the probable diversion of funds to the Nicaraguan resistance became public in late 1986, President Reagan appointed former Senator John Tower, former Secretary of State Edmund Muskie, and former National Security Adviser (and retired Air Force Lieutenant General) Brent Scowcroft to conduct a full investigation of the affair. Their *Report,* issued on 26 February 1987, offered the public a comprehensive narrative of

what had transpired. Subsequently, the congressional Iran-contra committees conducted their own investigation and issued a report in November
1987.

The conclusions and recommendations of the Tower Commission and
congressional reports were, by nature, subjective; observers could agree or
disagree about the significance of the events under investigation, the correctness of the role of each participant, whether any changes were warranted in
the processes of government as a consequence, and if so, what changes. But
with respect to the factual narratives themselves, important qualitative differences between the two reports existed. The Tower Commission narrative
represents the more dispassionate search for the truth of the two. How so?

The congressional Iran-contra committees, for reasons of their own, set
up their investigation quite differently from the Tower Commission inquiry,
in two main respects:

1. The Congress Set out to Expose Lawbreaking.

The Tower Commission, consisting of three of the most experienced public servants in America, spanning Republican and Democratic parties and the
Executive and Legislative branches, set out to investigate the matter. These
principal commission members conducted most or all of the interviews. In
contrast, the congressional panels imported attorneys from the private sector—in the case of the Senate committee, a Wall Street attorney whose excellent reputation had been earned not in the Washington policy community,
but in the area of securities fraud, embezzlement, and other white-collar
financial crimes.

Whereas the Tower Commission examined how the policy process had
functioned in the Iran-contra matters, the congressional committees "were
charged by their Houses with reporting violations of law and 'illegal' or
'unethical' conduct."[2] During the latter's hearings, when attorneys for witnesses under simultaneous investigation by the Independent Counsel pro-
tested that the committees were prejudging criminality at the expense of their
clients' rights to due process, the committees (now disclaiming any such
purpose) redirected the focus of their questions toward the bureaucratic
process. From this point on, the counsels' unfamiliarity with the policy
process in Washington was manifest. As a consequence, the congressional
report's treatment of the policy process was less focused, and ultimately carried less weight, than that of the Tower Commission.

2. The Congress Televised Its Proceedings.

Once the Congress chose to hold open hearings, to include televised
broadcast to over 100 countries around the world, the purpose of the investi-

gation became wed to two not necessarily reconcilable goals: seeking the truth and "telling the story" to the public. What appeared on the television screen was genuine as far as it went. But because of public interest in the hearings, the investigators themselves inevitably developed a personal stake in generating favorable public perceptions of their own performances. Having promoted widespread interest in the hearings, the legislators were, understandably, eager to demonstrate that such an extraordinary public tribunal was justified.

This approach satisfied many citizens in the sense that the Congress served as a surrogate for the venting of popular emotions aroused by the Iran-contra revelations. Had Congress held its inquiry behind closed doors and concealed its findings, public confidence in the integrity of the process would probably have suffered. In several respects the highly publicized hearings were affected by considerations which detracted from a dispassionate search for the truth:

- Important parts of the story were never told. Viewers were left with the odd impression that the administration and the Congress communicate only by mail or in formal hearings when, in fact, the much-discussed Boland Amendment formulations were far more the product of close, informal collaboration between officials in both branches than of careless draftsmanship.
- The Congress's deep and abiding interest in supporting U.S. relations with Israel—while perfectly legitimate—nevertheless led it to avert its gaze from Israel's key role in this matter, other than as an adjunct to the actions of other participants in the affair. In the congressional report, a chronology provided by the government of Israel to the committees was used as the sole source for significant assertions of fact—even when officials of the United States government had provided evidence to the contrary. This overriding consideration on the investigators' part may have had a misleading effect.
- A standard of "entertainment value" appears to have been applied to the choice of testimony to be taken before the television cameras. If a staff counsel assigned to cover a particular Executive branch agency persuaded the senior counsels that he had turned up "sexy" testimony, his reward was to conduct the questioning himself on international television.
- What was particularly misleading about this concern for media interest was the near-total failure of the committees to show the viewing public the backdrop against which the Iran-contra actions occurred—namely, a national security, intelligence, and diplomatic apparatus that functioned correctly, competently, and productively, for the most part, in the service of the national interest during this same period. Viewers

might have been less likely to question the inability of senior officials to recall certain statements, documents, or activities if the hearings had also given the public some appreciation of the enormous scope and pace of the daily activities of the nation's most senior national security executives.

- In particularly sharp contrast to the Tower Commission, the congressional committees seem not to have given a high priority to weighing conflicting information and rendering a considered collective judgment on what they believed to be the truth in each instance. Undoubtedly, the large membership of the committees (26, compared to three Tower Commission members) made consensus more elusive. The publicity of the hearings and the strong public reactions feeding back to members' offices throughout the proceedings also magnified the members' mutual disagreements, at the expense of consensus.

- As a result, not only did the committees submit two reports—a majority and a minority report—reflecting different analyses and conclusions, but the factual narrative of the majority report lacked authority. After prefacing the report with the statement that four primary witnesses had "all told conforming false stories" about U.S. involvement in arms shipments to Iran, the report's authors relied exclusively on the testimony of three of them to support a substantial portion of the narrative (see the majority report's footnotes), with no corroborative sources or any apparent hesitancy to accept their testimony as fact. Numerous investigative loose ends highlighted in the Tower Report were not acknowledged, much less pursued, in the congressional report

Without demeaning the efforts of the Congress, its Iran-contra proceedings arguably turned into more of a surrogate national debate than an authoritative factual inquiry. Reflecting the wide spectrum of public opinion and ideology, the hearings provided an outlet for tensions between the branches, and perhaps within them, which may initially have contributed to the great secrecy with which the Iran-contra activities were undertaken. Indeed, officials in both branches have remarked on the improved atmosphere of mutual cooperation in recent months.

The recommendations of the congressional report derive less from the facts of the Iran-contra affair than from other, more subjective factors, including the Congress's understandable desire to appear to have "fixed" the "problems" of the Executive branch. In the case of the proposed intelligence oversight legislation, this recommendation does not even flow from the report's own conclusions. Referring to the existing body of "laws and procedures to control secret intelligence activities, including covert actions," the report says, "Experience has shown that these laws and procedures, if respected, are adequate to the task. In the Iran-contra Affair, however, they were often disregarded."[3] The Tower Commission's only recommended change to the system of intelligence oversight was that the House and Senate Intelligence Committees be replaced by a smaller joint committee with a reduced staff, to enhance confidence within both branches that secrets would be safe and could be shared.[4]

In sum, those familiar with the Iran-contra affair and intelligence oversight issues should recognize that the statutory changes now under consideration in the Congress do not conform to the findings of either the Tower Commission or the Congress's own investigation; and that the net effect of such legislation upon the workings of the intelligence community might be to render it less effective while affording the nation no new protection against an unscrupulous operator willing to disregard the law and proper procedure.

As for the fear that future presidents might misuse any freedom of action (what Congress might term "loopholes") left to them in the laws relating to covert action, the tremendous political repercussions of the Iran-contra affair will undoubtedly give future decision-makers pause as they consider how the public might react to prospective initiatives, if revealed. The lesson that covert actions must reflect purposes and methods that would be understood and accepted by the public, if revealed, has come through loud and clear, and is now a cardinal tenet of the formal review process.

CONCLUSION: PROBLEMS WITH THE ENDS/MEANS DEBATE

Sissela Bok has written: "When linked, secrecy and political power are dangerous in the extreme. For all individuals, secrecy courts some risk of corruption and irrationality; if they dispose of greater than ordinary power over others, and if this power is exercised in secret, with no accountability to those whom it affects, the invitation to abuse is great. . . . In the absence of accountability and safeguards, the presumption against secrecy when it is linked with power is very strong."[5]

These words do not apply to the system of managing covert actions in place today in Washington. By virtue of existing statutes and presidentially-directed procedures, secrecy is not absolute, and accountability to the Congress is maintained in practice, notwithstanding the president's unwillingness to yield the constitutionally-based prerogatives of his office. Even in the theoretical instance wherein the president believed his unique executive responsibilities required him to act in total secrecy, Bok's "strong" presumption against secret power would be mitigated by two important facts: those powers are willingly given by the citizen to the Executive under the

Constitution, and the president is chosen by the citizens to execute those powers.

Quite naturally, many Americans are suspicious of what their government will not tell them; disenchanted when actions taken secretly on their behalf turn out, in retrospect, to be mistakes; and supportive of any suggested remedial measures that would appear to strengthen the oversight of secret power. All of these sentiments reflect strong, and proudly held, character traits common to Americans.

A periodic national self-examination such as has occurred in the aftermath of the Iran-contra revelations calls for more than the instinctive venting of the democratic bias against secrecy, however. Perspective—circumstantial as well as moral (indeed, the two are inseparable)—is required on the purposes of government, the duties of those who serve in government, and the responsibilities of the citizen.

"Selling arms to terrorists," as the Iran arms sales have so often been characterized, sounds immoral; and critics have said that the objective of obtaining the freedom of captive Americans and creating an official U.S. channel to elements of the government in Iran did not justify the sale of arms to Iran. Yet a president's military alliance with a foreign leader who, by his successor government's own recent admission, killed over sixteen million of his citizens, was universally supported by the American people, as was his successor's dropping of atomic weapons on two foreign cities.

Clearly, the "means" used in pursuit of the national interest cannot be morally examined in isolation. The "ends" of national survival as a secure and independent republic justify measures in some circumstances which would be unjustified in others. Secrecy can be a condition sine qua non of good government, just as it can be an instrument of bad government. Passing a negative moral judgment on the tools of covert operations—the use of untraceable funds, deception, selective violence on occasion, and the like—is tempting, but utterly meaningless when detached from the circumstances on which basis national leaders decide whether such steps are warranted.

The frustrating reality for citizens, of course, is that the totality of those explanatory circumstances can never be shared with the public, because they include information gained through classified methods and the confidences of foreign sources. Regardless of how much information is revealed to the public by the president or the Congress, as in the Iran-contra hearings, entire categories of information remain which no official on either end of the investigatory process would see fit to place in the public realm. The fact is that citizens can never gain a complete appreciation of the judgments which their leaders must render and the choices they must make in matters of national security.

Members of Congress are frequently heard giving voice to the public's frustration at the Executive's perceived hoarding of information and guarding of prerogative in sensitive foreign affairs. They regularly invoke the American people's right to know about these matters and to share in the process of reaching important policy decisions. To the extent that foreign confidences will not be betrayed by public discussion of the issues, they are absolutely justified in seeking open policy debate.

Under Articles I and II of the Constitution, however, the American people do not hold either the Legislative or Executive powers; their elected representatives do. Not far into the future, technology might make it feasible for every citizen, sitting by his television set, to watch congressional debates, identify himself and vote on resolutions as they are introduced, thereby substituting a national referenda for congressional votes. This will never happen because citizens do not elect presidents and legislators to follow their every dictate, but to lead and to exercise moral responsibility by reflecting their values and bringing sound judgment to bear on their behalf.

Good government strives to meet the objective that citizens will continue to enjoy "life, liberty, and the pursuit of happiness." While this end is greatly served by a vigorous free press and an interested, informed public, it is no less served by the ability to act effectively to protect the national interest. This may mean acting secretly, quickly, and even violently—and keeping it secret, if possible, forever.

Where does the citizen exercise his control over the most secret, and, thus elusive, aspect of his government? The answer is: at the ballot box. Making the laws on intelligence oversight more restrictive in order to assuage moral self-doubts about the United States will be for nought if leaders are elected who disregard them. Greater oversight could, in fact, turn out to be counterproductive if exigent circumstances undermined a future president's confidence in his ability to fulfill his constitutional duties working within the existing statutory framework.

Rather than seeking to curtail the ability of the U.S. government to act in service of the national interest, the citizenry should impose an electoral test which elevates men and women of the highest probity and judgment to assume these burdens of constitutionally based power. Not only does such an approach have the advantage of bringing the best out of public servants: it is the way the founding fathers intended the U.S. system to work.

NOTES

1. *Report of the President's Special Review Board,* 26 February 1987, p. V-6.

2. *Report of the Congressional Committees Investigating the Iran-contra Affair, with Supplemental, Minority and Additional Views,* November 1987, p. 411.

3. *Report of the Congressional Committee,* p. 375.

4. *Report of the President's Board,* op. cit., p. V-6.

5. Bok, Sissela, 1982, *Secrets—On the Ethics of Concealment and Revelation,* New York: Pantheon Books, p. 106.

14

Covert Intervention as a Moral Problem

Charles R. Beitz

Covert operations have come to prominence in public debate twice in our recent history—in the mid-1970s and in the mid-1980s—prompted each time by disclosures of scandalous misuse of executive authority.[1] More than a decade ago, the Church committee investigations provided the impetus for a closer look at covert action considered as an instrument of foreign policy. It is fair to say that we understand its historical and political features much better today than before.[2] One might have thought that inquiry into the moral questions would have been stimulated as well, particularly in view of the resurgence of interest in more general issues about ethics in international affairs. Oddly enough, however, the literature of international political theory is virtually silent about covert intervention regarded as a moral problem. In this paper I will take a first step toward filling this gap, mainly by trying to distinguish between several of the questions of ethical significance that tend to be confused when the moral dimension of covert action is discussed. I will also advance some thoughts about some substantive issues, but with the caveat that these are tentative observations by a newcomer to the subject.

IDENTIFYING CATEGORIES

"Covert action" has been used to describe many different kinds of activities in U.S. foreign policy since World War II. The most controversial of these include the U.S.-backed coups d'etat in Iran and Guatemala in the 1950s, the

CIA assassination plots against foreign leaders such as Fidel Castro and Patrice Lumumba in the 1960s, the attempts to prevent the election of Salvador Allende as president of Chile in 1970 and then to subvert his government after he was elected anyway, the shipment of arms and supplies to the FNL and UNITA in Angola beginning in the mid-1970s, and, of course, the contra war in Nicaragua during this decade.[3] A larger number of covert operations have met with general, if not unanimous, public approval—for example, financial and political support for moderate parties and labor organizations in Italy and France in the late 1940s and 1950s, financial aid for the socialists in Portugal in the mid-1970s, and military aid for the anti-Soviet guerrillas in Afghanistan in the 1980s.[4] The various congressional investigations have left no doubt that more numerous instances of covert action still remain undisclosed.

These operations had certain elements in common. Each involved interference in the internal affairs of another state. In each case, efforts were made to conceal the involvement of the United States. Each was carried out without public congressional scrutiny or review.

Yet it is the differences among the cases that are more striking. They vary in at least four significant dimensions. First, these cases encompass many different kinds of activity: advising foreign leaders and other political influentials; propaganda; manipulation of foreign news media; financial support of private organizations such as labor unions; financial and logistical support of political parties; economic and military aid to friendly governments facing internal challenges (or to forces mounting challenges to unfriendly governments); corruption of domestic political processes (rigging elections, bribing public officials); paramilitary or counterinsurgency training for friendly forces; participation in assassination plots aimed at foreign leaders; and paramilitary operations designed to subvert or overthrow, or alternatively to defend, foreign regimes.

Second, they were undertaken in pursuit of disparate political objectives: to influence the climate of political opinion in another state; to strengthen the positions of social forces seen as friendly to the United States; and to destabilize a government or to induce it to adopt specific changes in policy.[5] Nor do these aims exhaust the possibilities; covert action might aim at noninterventionist objectives as well, such as the release of hostages or the thwarting of terrorists.

Third, the environment of covert action has varied from case to case. For example, there were differences in the character of domestic political institutions in the target countries, and in some cases there had been prior interference by other powers. Finally, political action was undertaken covertly rather than overtly for several different reasons: to avoid embarrassment to the government of the target country; to circumvent political procedures in the target country; to avoid delay; or to maintain the credibility of intelligence personnel or other agents of the United States who were already on the scene. Each of these factors could influence our judgment about the justifiability of an operation. This should make us hesitate to draw categorical conclusions like those that occur so often in discussions of the ethics of covert action (for example, that it is always wrong), and it should induce caution about single-factor views regarding its acceptability (for example, that any operation is legitimate if it advances the national interest). Instead, we should expect different operations to be morally problematic for different reasons. Some may not be problematic at all. And, of course, some may combine more than one kind of ethical problem.

One way to chart the terrain is to think about some cases that have been controversial and try to identify the main issues of principle that arose for each one. It seems fairly clear that the issues fall into three groups: sometimes we argue about the ends of covert action, sometimes about the means used to pursue these ends, and sometimes about the constitutional process through which the operations in question were (or were not) authorized and overseen. (Sometimes we argue about all three.) The first of these is basically the problem of justifying intervention: What, if anything, could warrant U.S. interference in the internal affairs of another state? In particular, what role should the national interest play in justifying covert interference? The second category contains a diverse array of problems corresponding to the variety of techniques that covert operations have employed. Not all of these problems are as familiar as one might think; for example, covert action sometimes involves the use of techniques of noncoercive political manipulation that have no analog in other areas of foreign policy (for example, secret financial support of friendly political parties). Both of these areas of dispute focus on the external impact of covert action. In contrast, the third points toward the potential for abuse of the democratic process at home when the executive branch is permitted to conceal its activities from public scrutiny.

In the rest of this essay, I will take up a central issue in each of these categories. But these are not simply three independent discussions. The third topic is the most important for U.S. citizens today, since it raises the question, as a matter of democratic theory, of whether the nation should maintain a standing peacetime capacity to carry out covert operations at all. As I hope will be clear, any persuasive answer to the last question will depend on answers to the earlier two.

JUSTIFYING INTERVENTION

Covert action is interventionist in a broad sense: in almost every case, it aims at influencing the course of political life in the target state by inducing or preventing a change in government or policy. Interference typically risks several kinds of harm, which are reflected in the three most prominent general arguments against intervention: that it offends the political sovereignty of the state being interfered in; that it disrupts a people's common life; and that it upsets international order.

Some people think that its interventionist character is enough to show why all covert action must be illegitimate.[6] But this is too quick. For one thing, the grounds for objecting to foreign interference in domestic life are strongest when there is some meaningful sense in which the interference is coercive.[7] But some forms of covert action—manipulation, for example—are not coercive in the required sense and so might fall through the net of some of the conventional objections to intervention. (There may, however, be other objections to manipulatory techniques. I will come back to them later.)

The anti-interventionist critique of covert action also faces a more fundamental difficulty. All of the prevailing views about ethics in international affairs recognize exceptions to the general prohibition of intervention, such as self-defense, counterintervention, and intervention to prevent gross violations of fundamental human rights.[8] This fact creates an entering wedge for attempts to justify covert interference morally. Moreover, because the exceptions to the general prohibition are theoretically well-founded, we cannot simply dismiss these attempts as obviously wrong or misguided. Instead, we must confront the question whether (and how) the exceptions might apply to covert action. A CIA official suggested one answer when he described "covert auctioneers" as "the 'do-gooders' of the clandestine business" because their aim is usually to lend help to "people and institutions legitimately in need of such assistance."[9] Covert action, this official was claiming, has a paternalistic, other-regarding rationale: its goal is to serve the interests of the residents of the state in which it takes place.

Although not many cases of covert action appear to have been motivated by this kind of rationale, we should not dismiss it altogether. It reflects a long tradition in American foreign policy of justifying intervention on the ground that it is good for those whose societies we intervene in. The Reagan Doctrine is only the most recent formulation of this idea. Moreover, even when other considerations (for example, national security concerns) are appealed to in defense of covert action, paternalistic notions are often in the background. Henry Kissinger illustrated this vividly when he reportedly complained that he did not "see why the United States should stand by and let Chile go communist merely due to the stupidity of its own people."[10]

So it is worth observing that paternalistic considerations could justify intervention, if at all, only if there were good reasons to believe that its consequences really would be in the interests of the target population. This is no small matter. One needs to know enough about the culture and values of the target society to make informed judgments about its welfare, and enough about its politics and history to calculate the likely consequences of the kind of intervention contemplated. Any review of the history of intervention in U.S. foreign policy would quickly conclude that there were few cases in which the principal decision makers could honestly have claimed sufficient knowledge to make these judgments responsibly. Covert interference encompasses additional difficulties arising from the constraints of secrecy. For example, a special problem of operational control occurs when intermediaries are employed to carry out the interference—partly because their aims may differ from ours and partly because the chain of command is more ambiguous and less reliable. This leads to greater uncertainty in predicting the costs of the operation and increased chances of unintended results.[11] These difficulties appear to grow more severe as the degree of force committed to the operation increases and as its paternalistic ambitions become more complex. In all but the most exceptional of cases, there is little room for confident prediction—certainly less than the planners of covert operation in the past have usually believed. Whether paternalistic considerations could justify intervention at all is a controverted question. Even if we answer it affirmatively, these reflections suggest that there are likely to be few actual cases in which a paternalistic justification of covert intervention would be persuasive.

The more common justification for covert intervention, of course, is that it advances the security interests of the nation.[12] But the ambiguities of the idea of the national interest are well-known,[13] and the bare invocation of this idea, and nothing more, can hardly justify any potentially costly venture. For one thing, it may refer to values that are of varying degrees of urgency or moral significance. While protecting a population against unprovoked attack and protecting access to raw materials or markets for goods could both be said to be in the national interest, for example, they represent concerns of dramatically different levels of importance. In addition, the national interest may be invoked in response to threats of differing degrees of immediacy: compare the imminent threat of a military invasion with the long-term threat that a nonaligned but left-leaning and strategically located regime might come to be a Soviet ally.

From a moral point of view, these differences matter. We can see an indication of this in the traditional theory of the just war. The theory does not justify a nation going to war simply because its interests are threatened. More must be said to explain why these interests are sufficiently weighty and why the threat is sufficiently serious that resort to war should be seen as an acceptable remedy. Thus, in the traditional view, war may be justifiable when it is necessary as a means of defending the nation against imminent threats to its territorial integrity and political sovereignty but not (or not normally) when it would secure a less urgent or less immediate, but still desirable, end. In this respect, traditional just-war theory reflects the important fact that the national interest of a state does not operate in a moral vacuum. It is not all there is. There are other interests in the world, and anyone who wants to argue that the nation has a right to inflict harm on others must take these interests into account. If we wish the national interest to play a role in justifying policy—if we want to guard against it becoming a way of evading moral constraints entirely—then we must place it in a larger perspective where we can weigh its importance relative to the values that compete with it.

What this means is that those who would justify a policy of covert intervention on the grounds that it could help avert threats to U.S. interests must explain what values would be advanced by the policy in question, how these are threatened under the status quo, and why these threats are important enough to justify the harms that interference would impose on its victims. For example, consider the case of covert U.S. support of the coup against Iranian prime minister Mossadeq in 1953.[14] This was covert action on a very small scale—it took only a few American and British agents to organize the uprising that swept Mossadeq from power—but it can still serve to illustrate the questions about the nature and significance of the national interests that covert operations are supposed to serve.

First, what was this interest? Since there was no prospective military threat to the United States, intervention was hardly necessary to save American lives or to protect the territorial integrity or political sovereignty of the United States. In this core sense, the national interest was not threatened at all. In view of Mossadeq's nationalization of the Anglo-Iranian Oil Company (AIOC) and the refusal to pay the compensation demanded by the British, it could be argued that there was a threat to U.S. economic interests, or at least to those of U.S. allies. It is debatable whether Mossadeq was warranted in expropriating AIOC, but given the unwillingness of the British to reach a reasonable compromise with the Mossadeq government, there is no plausible argument that covert intervention to help overthrow Mossadeq could be justified on these grounds. And, in fact, the threat that really worried U.S. leaders was both different and less direct: it flowed from fear of the long-term geopolitical and economic consequences of a growth of Soviet influence in Iran.[15]

How significant was this interest? As with any invocation of national security interests, there are two subsidiary questions. First, what values were threatened? Clearly, security of the oil supply from Iran was one of them. Another was control of shipping in the Persian Gulf (which would be threatened under the worst-case prospect of Soviet access to Iranian port facilities). These threats were plainly important matters, not only from the U.S. point of view but even more so from that of our European allies. There is also a second question: How immediate were the threats? Here one must say that at best they were distant and speculative. The Iranian opening to the Soviets was more feared than consummated at the time of the coup, and, in any case, it is a long step from better diplomatic and economic relations to the degree of Soviet control over Iranian affairs that would have been necessary to real-ize the threat to the West. Moreover, an alternative U.S. policy was plainly available—cooperation with the nationalist government (which Mossadeq himself had solicited only a few months earlier)—that would have alleviated the prospective threat altogether.[16]

Of course, these are controversial claims, and in any discussion on the merits of the Iranian case they would need to be argued, rather than merely stated. Still, they are enough for our purposes, for they illustrate how the idea of the national interest can cloud, rather than clarify, thought about the responsible conduct of foreign policy. Invoking the national interest as a rationale for intervention tends to obscure all of the important questions—about the urgency of the values at stake for the United States, the weight of the harms that would be done to others by intervening, the immediacy of the threat to U.S. interests, and the availability of other means to defend them. Yet it is only by answering these questions specifically that we can see whether the national interest provides a persuasive justification for covert interference.

Advocates of covert action often point to its desirability as an instrument of foreign policy, in comparison to the alternative of regular military force, which does more damage and intrudes more deeply on the rights of other states and peoples. Covert action provides a "third way," between diplo-matic pressure and overt economic or military aid, on the one hand, and direct military intervention, on the other.[17] But the familiar tendency to rationalize adventuristic foreign policies by invoking vague and overblown conceptions of national interest suggests that the relatively less damaging character of covert action might be more a liability than an asset. For the low-risk, quick-fix aspect of covert action almost certainly encourages deci-sion makers to commit national power more widely than they would other-wise find it advisable to do. It also reduces the incentives to reach diplomatic solutions. For example, imagine that for some reason, covert action had sim-ply not been available in the Iranian case and that the Eisenhower adminis-tration had had to choose between diplomacy and military intervention. No one could suppose that under those circumstances the administration would have chosen the military option; instead, it would certainly have pursued a more vigorous diplomatic strategy, including a more resolute approach to the British. And there is a high probability that some accommodation with Mossadeq could have been reached.

It will be objected that this is speculation, made plausible only with the benefit of hindsight. Eisenhower and his lieutenants had to make decisions in the face of great uncertainty, and from their point of view covert action was the perfect compromise: a low-cost means of meeting a threat whose probability was unknown but whose long-range potential for damage to the national interest was great. In response, there is little doubt that this is how covert action appeared to them; that is exactly the problem. With the covert option available, there was no apparent need for creative diplomacy, no pressure to seek compromise, and no visible cost for ignoring or devaluing the interests of the Iranian people, in whose eyes Mossadeq was perhaps the most popular nationalist leader of the twentieth century. The familiar irony of the Iranian case is that the easy availability of covert action not only discouraged a more serious effort to understand the point of view of the Mossadeq government and its standing with its own people, it also made possible a U.S. policy that is at least as likely to have set back as to have advanced the long-term interests of the nation.

THE MEANS EMPLOYED

Covert operations can employ a wide variety of means, each of which raises different ethical questions. These include the acceptability of techniques of noncoercive interference such as propaganda and corruption of the integrity of domestic political procedures, the justifiability of political assassinations, and the legitimacy of supporting forces that use indiscriminate military and paramilitary tactics in their efforts to destabilize a government. Some of these questions (particularly those involving the ethics of using violence for political purposes) are relatively well-known, and I will pass by them here. Instead, I would like to concentrate on a different kind of question that is discussed less often but that may arise more frequently in connection with covert operations.

Covert action is often manipulative. The meaning of this, and of the evil connected with it, is not as obvious as it may seem, especially in the context of international relations. One way to clarify these issues is to begin by considering manipulation at the level of relations among individuals and then try to generalize.

Manipulation is a form of power that employs deception of those over whom power is exercised. It is a way of getting what you want despite the possible resistance of others. Manipulation occurs when someone exercises power over other people, inducing them to behave as the exerciser of power wishes, without their awareness that power has been exercised.[18] For example, you might induce people to do one thing rather than another by providing them with skewed or incomplete information, by placing them in unreasonable fear of the consequences of making the other choice, or by altering their preferences in ways they are unlikely to detect (as in subliminal advertising).

Manipulation is different from coercion. To coerce someone involves inducing him to act against his will. Manipulation differs in that it is an attempt to co-opt the will of the person being manipulated. A person who makes one choice rather than another as a result of having been successfully manipulated identifies with the choice in a way that a person who had been coerced into making that choice would not. Unlike coercion, manipulation is sneaky: its aim is to accomplish its goal without being detected. Successful manipulation, therefore, is invisible to the one manipulated. (At least, this is the ideal. It may not quite occur in practice, because deception succeeds by degrees: people may have some vague idea that power is being exercised over them—they may suspect that they are being manipulated—without knowing who is doing the manipulating or what techniques are being used to keep them in ignorance.)

Robert Goodin has written that manipulation is "the nastiest face of power."[19] This is hyperbole, but Goodin is surely correct that manipulation is, prima facie, an evil. Why is this so? It cannot be that manipulation is necessarily bad for those being manipulated. Manipulation can aim at the good of the person being manipulated yet still be objectionable. Its distinctive evil derives instead from the fact that by attempting to hide the exercise of power, manipulation seeks to enlist a person's capacity for self-determination in the service of goals that are not, or not necessarily, the person's own.[20] The evil of manipulation, then, has two related components. First, because manipulation interferes with the normal process of selecting goals and deciding how to pursue them, it is an invasion of a person's autonomy. Second, because it operates invisibly, manipulation leaves a person peculiarly defenseless against this invasion. We see both aspects in the example of subliminal advertising: it subverts our ordinary processes of forming preferences, and it deprives us of the chance to adjust our preferences in light of our understanding of the way they were formed.

This evil is only prima facie: other considerations can affect our judgment about whether manipulation under any particular circumstance is something to be condemned. A great deal depends on whether the capacity for self-determination of the person being manipulated is sufficiently developed and would function normally if not for the manipulation. Whereas manipulation of adults in normal possession of their capacities usually seems wrong even when it is thought to be in their interests, manipulation of a child, or of a drunkard, or of someone whose mental functioning is otherwise impaired does not seem similarly objectionable (provided that it is done for a defensible purpose).

Now consider the international level. Covert action is often characterized as clandestine activity in which the involvement of the U.S. government is not apparent.[21] Does this mean that all covert action is manipulative? The answer is no: covert action always seeks to conceal the involvement of the United States, but it does not (because it cannot) always seek to conceal the fact that power is being exercised. For example, in the Iranian case, even if Mossadeq had had no knowledge of the U.S. role in the coup, he was under no illusions that a coup was being attempted. He was not being manipulated; he was being overthrown. Contrast this with the CIA's plan to bribe members of the Chilean parliament to vote against Allende. In that case, it was not only the involvement of the U.S. government that was to be concealed; the very fact that a deliberate exercise of power was taking place was to be hidden from public view as well.

Many forms of covert action are manipulative in this way—"black" propaganda, covert financial support for cultural and labor organizations, rigging of elections, and corruption of legislatures. I would like to focus on the provision of financial and logistical aid to noncommunist political parties to help improve their electoral performance. This kind of manipulation was pioneered by the CIA in Western Europe in the late 1940s and 1950s and has occurred subsequently in such countries as Chile and Portugal. For many people, it represents covert action at its best—it is nonviolent, noncoercive, relatively cheap, and does not necessarily require breaking local laws or violating democratic principles. Nevertheless, covert support of friendly political parties is clearly manipulative. Is this kind of manipulation evil?

In the individual case, the distinctive evil of manipulation is found in the way it subverts the autonomy of its targets and renders them defenseless against it. There is a clear analogy at the international level. Consider, for example, the CIA's attempts to manipulate the Chilean elections of 1964 and 1970 by funneling funds to conservative forces in order to prevent victories by parties of the left.[22] These activities were not coercive in any strict sense; individuals were not forced to act against their will. Nor were constitutional procedures crudely set aside (as they were in the coup of 1973, for example). Rather, constitutional procedures were used, in the pejorative sense of that term. The United States acted in ways calculated to cause the normal processes of social decision making to produce outcomes that might not otherwise have taken place. Because the U.S. role was kept secret, the Chilean people were defenseless against it; for example, in deciding how to vote, they were unable to compensate for the influence on their attitudes and beliefs of U.S. interference in their domestic political life. This is just as much an assault on the autonomy of those affected as is manipulation in the individual case. Indeed, it is worse. The offense to individual autonomy is compounded at the social level by an offense to democracy, whose integrity depends on the capacity of its people to participate knowledgeably and rationally in political deliberation. This, of course, is precisely what manipulation subverts.

As at the interpersonal level, the evil of manipulation in international affairs is only prima facie. It is hard to think of any good excuse for it in the Chilean case. But other cases are more difficult. For example, in postwar Italy and France, the CIA's efforts to stem the growth of the left by subsidizing middle-of-the-road parties were defended as ways to restore a domestic equilibrium that had already been disrupted because of the financial and logistical support provided to the Italian Communist Party by the Soviet Union and other Eastern-bloc nations.[23] The charge that the CIA's manipulatory intervention constituted an invasion of an otherwise autonomous domestic process therefore seems much less compelling than in the Latin American cases of later years. On the other hand, there is room for dispute about whether the Communists would have succeeded in any event.[24] And there is also a question about whether deception was required to offset the effects of Eastern-bloc interference: Was there really no way to provide the funds openly—say, through something like the National Endowment for Democracy—that would not have been counterproductive? Still, given the circumstances of the postwar years, these interventions seem justifiable—more clearly, perhaps, than any others in the history of U.S. covert action.

COVERT INTERVENTION AND DEMOCRACY

Covert operations have to be kept secret to be effective, but this means that they cannot be subjected to the usual processes of public consideration and review. Treverton refers to this as "the paradox of secret operations in a democracy."[25] "Paradox" may be too strong. There is no paradox in the philosophical sense of a valid argument proceeding from accepted premises to self-contradictory conclusions. What there might be is a conflict of values. On the one hand, Treverton is ready to agree that there may be occasions when covert action would be justifiable on grounds of national security. On the other, he does not see how covert action, even if justifiable on these grounds, can be reconciled with democratic principles. This approach suggests that anyone who seeks a coherent position about covert action must make a choice (covert action or democracy), whereas someone who wants both must abandon the quest for coherence and settle for an uneasy compromise.

The difficulty in this way of seeing things can be explained in two connected points. First, as a philosophical matter, the approach reflects an understanding of democracy that is much too brittle. Democracy is not some sort of mechanical device designed to harness individual political decisions to the popular will, so that any decision not approved by the people must be suspect. The democratic idea is more complicated. Democratic institutions are means for ensuring the responsiveness of policy to the interests of the people and for deterring the unauthorized use of power by those who hold public office. There is no reason to deny that democratic citizens could have good reasons for removing certain categories of decisions from popular control or even popular review. Indeed, a wide range of existing practices in such disparate areas as the administration of justice, macroeconomic policy, and national-security policy suggests exactly this. All of these practices limit opportunities for public review of executive decisions, yet we do not usually regard them as contrary to democratic ideals.

But this does not mean (and this is the second point) that there is nothing more to be said about how the democratic idea constrains the role of secrecy in government. There is a story to tell in connection with each of the practices listed above that explains why it would be reasonable for democratic citizens to permit certain kinds of decisions to be made and carried out in secret. The story tries to connect the provisions for secrecy with the underlying aims of democratic institutions, showing why those aims are likely to be achieved more successfully with secrecy than without it. It also suggests the limits of secrecy—where to draw the line between decisions that may be made secretly and those that must be publicly acknowledged, how extensively and in what ways the legislature should be involved during or after decisions have been made, and what procedural safeguards would be desirable to deter negligence and malfeasance among those officials who operate behind the shield of secrecy.

Taking these points together, the real issue is not whether we make a logical or conceptual mistake in thinking that covert action is compatible with democracy. The serious question is practical, not conceptual: it is whether there are ways to organize the planning and execution of covert operations so that they serve, rather than subvert, the aims of democratic government. Any practice authorizing official secrecy risks depriving us as citizens of information we need to monitor the faithfulness of policy to our interests and values and to ensure against abuses of official power. Are there conditions under which we should be willing to accept this risk?

Without exploring all of the possibilities, let me conclude with a comment about the main answer we have given to this question since the mid-1970s. It revolves around the idea of accountability. To be accountable (to the people or to a legislature) is to be under an obligation to respond to requests for explanation and information about one's official actions. Accountability is one of a family of procedural devices (also including notification requirements, advise and consent rules, the ex post facto legislative veto, and so forth) whose purpose is to operate as safeguards against predictable, unauthorized uses of executive power. The rationale for these devices is instrumental; it holds that this or that procedure is needed to deter public officials from using the powers of their office outside the bounds of their authority. Otherwise, the kind and degree of power granted to the officials involved might simply be too great—the grant of power itself might be too dangerous—to be acceptable.

The new covert-action regime instituted in the mid-1970s employs a form of limited accountability whereby the executive branch is required to inform certain members of Congress about the planning and execution of covert operations.²⁶ The proponents of the new regime were moved by the hope it would help deter several kinds of abuse of executive authority. Chief among these was the danger that covert action would fail to be the servant of official policy—for example, by presupposing an extravagantly permissive conception of the national interest or by underestimating and undervaluing the harms that covert interference does to others. They also hoped to deter transgressions of domestic law and the Constitution and to guard against violations of international law and human rights.

As we can now see, the new emphasis on accountability has ethical as well as political significance. It reflects a judgment about how it could be reasonable for citizens to risk depriving themselves of information that is important to the conduct of democratic political life—in other words, about the practical conditions under which democracy and covert action can coexist. The question before us today is whether that judgment was sound. Events of the Reagan years suggest that the formula worked out in the mid-1970s was a step in the right direction but that it contained loopholes that enabled zealots in the CIA and the National Security Council to repeat the same kinds of abuse of authority that the formula was devised to deter. Certainly efforts should be made to close these loopholes. But as a matter of political ethics, our emphasis should be on a deeper question. This is whether any form of accountability is likely to be sufficient to bring the unauthorized use of executive power under control. If the answer to that question is no, then our democratic principles compel us to consider whether the capacity to conduct covert operations in peacetime should properly belong to the executive branch.

NOTES

1. An earlier version of this paper was presented at a faculty workshop on "Ethics and Covert Action" at Cornell University, sponsored by the Carnegie Council on Ethics and International Affairs. I am grateful to the participants for their comments and suggestions.

2. On the background, legality, and efficacy of covert action, see U.S. Congress, Senate Select Committee to Study Intelligence Activities [the Church committee], *Foreign and Military Intelligence,* book I, 94th Cong., 2d sess., Senate Report 94–755 (Washington, DC: Government Printing Office, April 26, 1976), chap. 8. The best study is Gregory F. Treverton, *Covert Action* (New York: Basic Books, 1987).

3. I have excluded from this list the covert activities carried out by the CIA during the Korean and Indochinese wars because these were operations in direct support of military activities rather than free-standing, peacetime initiatives like the others.

4. For the details of these cases, see Treverton, *Covert Action*; and John Prados, *Presidents' Secret Wars* (New York: William Morrow, 1986).

5. See John M. Oseth, *Regulating U.S. Intelligence Operations: A Study in Defi-*

nition of the National Interest (Lexington: University Press of Kentucky, 1985), 25–27.

6. For example, Tom Wicker, "Not Covert, Not Smart, Not Right," *New York Times,* August 2, 1988, A19.

7. In fact, intervention is best defined simply as "coercive external interference in the affairs of a population organized in the form of a state." The best recent discussion is Jefferson McMahan, "The Ethics of International Intervention," in Kenneth Kipnis and Diana T. Meyers, eds., *Political Realism and International Morality* (Boulder: Westview Press, 1987), 78.

8. For example, Michael Walzer's view in *Just and Unjust Wars* (New York: Basic Books, 1977), chap. 6.

9. Hugh Tovar, "Covert Action," in Roy Godson, *Intelligence Requirements for the 1980s: Elements of Intelligence* (Washington, DC: National Strategy Information Center, 1979).

10. Quoted in Treverton, *Covert Action,* 11.

11. There is a good discussion ibid., chaps. 5–6.

12. William Colby advances one form of this argument in "Public Policy, Secret Action," *Ethics & International Affairs* 3 (1989). He says that covert action should meet the test of "self-defense." His extremely elastic interpretation of this idea illustrates that the cautions set forth above about the ambiguities of the national interest also apply to self-defense.

13. The locus classicus is Arnold Wolfers, "National Security As an Ambiguous Symbol," in *Discord and Colloboration* (Baltimore: Johns Hopkins Press, 1962), 147–66.

14. Barry Rubin, *Paved with Good Intentions* (New York: Oxford University Press, 1980), 54–90; Prados, *Presidents' Secret Wars,* 92–98.

15. Dwight D. Eisenhower, *The White House Years: Mandate for Change, 1953–1956* (Garden City, NY: Doubleday, 1963), 162–64.

16. See the discussion in Richard W. Cottam, *Nationalism in Iran* (Pittsburgh: University of Pittsburgh Press, 1964), 230.

17. In addition to Colby's remarks in "Public Policy, Secret Action," see Richard Nixon, *1999: Victory Without War* (New York: Simon and Schuster, 1988), 109; and Michael J. Barrett, "Honorable Espionage II," *Journal of Defense and Diplomacy* 2 (March 1984), 14 (Barrett was assistant general counsel of the CIA at the time this article was written).

18. Robert Goodin defines manipulation as "power exercised (1) deceptively and (2) against the putative will of its objects." Goodin, *Manipulatory Politics* (New Haven: Yale University Press, 1980).

19. Ibid., 7.

20. Joel Rudinow makes a similar point in "Manipulation," *Ethics* 88 (1978), 347.

21. For example, by the Church committee, *Foreign and Military Intelligence.*

22. Prados, *Presidents' Secret Wars,* 315–21.

23. William Colby with Peter Forbath, *Honorable Men: My Life in the CIA* (New York: Simon and Schuster, 1978), 113–14.

24. See, for example, the generally cautious assessment in Trevor Barnes, "The Secret Cold War: The CIA and American Foreign Policy in Europe, 1946–1956," parts 1 and 2, *Historical Journal* 24 (1981), 412–13; (1982), 25, 660–64.

25. Treverton, *Covert Action*, 222. Similarly, the Church committee reported itself "struck by the basic tension—if not incompatibility—of covert operations and the demands of a constitutional system." *Foreign and Military Intelligence*, 156.

26. For a discussion of the new intelligence regime in the context of the broader adjustment of executive-congressional relations of which it was a part, see Kenneth E. Sharpe, "The Post-Vietnam Formula under Siege: The Imperial Presidency and Central America," *Political Science Quarterly* 102 (1987), 549–69.

15

"Repugnant Philosophy"
Ethics, Espionage, and Covert Action

David L. Perry

Author's note: This article was first published in Journal of Conflict Studies, *Spring 1995. An earlier version was presented on 30 March 1994 at a meeting in Washington, DC, of the Intelligence Study Section of the International Studies Association. Thanks to Jefferson Adams and Abe Miller for encouraging me to submit that paper. I have drawn upon portions of "Covert Action: An Exploration of the Ethical Issues," my 1993 Ph.D. dissertation for the University of Chicago Divinity School. My dissertation research in Washington, DC, was enabled by a fellowship from the University of Chicago's Program in Arms Control and International Security (PACIS), funded by the MacArthur Foundation. I benefited from the impressive range of intelligence literature in the Library of Congress and the Russell Bowen special collection at Georgetown University. Finally, I'm grateful to the following individuals for their insightful comments during various stages of my writing: Jim Barry, William Colby, William Hood, Robin Lovin, James McCargar, Peter Savage, B. Hugh Tovar, David Whipple, David Charters, and two anonymous reviewers for* The Journal of Conflict Studies, *and some former CIA officers who spoke to me in confidence. I was not privy to any classified information prior to 2003, and was therefore not required in 1995 to submit this essay to the U.S. Government for review. Nor have I modified it substantially for this anthology.*

> There are great occasions in which some men are called to great services, in the doing of which they are excused from the common rule of morality.
>
> —Oliver Cromwell

A real diplomat is one who can cut his neighbor's throat without having
his neighbor notice it.

—Trygve Lie

The sources and methods of espionage, the goals and tactics of covert action,
and the professional conduct of intelligence officers are matters typically
hidden from public scrutiny, yet clearly worthy of public debate and philosophical attention. Recent academic studies of intelligence that have had any
intentional bearing on ethics or political philosophy have largely focused on
procedural questions surrounding the proper degree of oversight of intelligence agencies. But what is often missed in such examinations is substantive
ethical analysis of intelligence operations themselves.

This gap in the literature may be due in part to the lingering influence of
the idea that ethical principles are not appropriate to apply to "statecraft" or
international politics, as if in doing so one makes a kind of "category mistake." But an amoralist view of international relations clearly cannot be sustained. Whatever interests or rights that states can legitimately be said to have
must derive from the interests and rights of their individual citizens. War
waged in defense of the nation can be morally justified in ways analogous to
and derivative of individuals' rights to resist an assault on their family. And
because individuals have no right to murder and steal from their neighbors,
there can be no morally sound *raison d'état* for waging aggressive war. The
proper question, then, is not whether ethical principles apply to statecraft
but rather how they should be validly applied to statecraft.

Most of us recognize certain basic moral rules to be binding in most cases:
tell the truth, keep your promises, care for your family, avoid harming others, respect the rights of others, and so on. Rules like these cannot be ignored
even when they prove to be personally inconvenient. But most of us would
also agree that there can be legitimate exceptions to otherwise valid moral
rules. Sometimes, for example, we may be forced to choose *between* two or
more important moral principles when they can't all be fulfilled at the same
time. Occasionally we even face truly tragic decisions, where each of the
available options will result in serious harm and we must therefore choose
the lesser of evils. Morally right actions don't always produce outcomes that
are good without qualification.[1]

Moral conflict can arise in professional life as well as in private life. Professional roles sometimes involve special obligations which can outweigh other
important ethical considerations. Investigative journalists may be permitted
to misrepresent their identity in order to gain the confidence of a government official they suspect of corruption. Or defense lawyers may be
expected to try to undermine the credibility of a prosecution witness in
cross-examination even if they know the witness is telling the truth about
the defendant.

Some of the virtues required for intelligence work, such as discretion, loyalty, and tenacity, are also instrumental to professions like diplomacy, the military, law, business, and journalism.[2] But many of the skills and character traits drawn upon and reinforced by the profession of intelligence are very different from those expected of the average citizen or other professionals. The CIA was created by an act of Congress in 1947, and authorized by the National Security Council the following year to undertake "special projects" (i.e., covert action).[3] An impassioned report to President Eisenhower in 1954 argued that the U.S. faced "an implacable enemy [i.e., international communism] whose avowed objective is world domination by whatever means and at whatever cost," and urged the U.S. to "learn to subvert, sabotage and destroy [its] enemies by more clever" and "more ruthless" methods than those of its opponents. The report conceded that this entailed a "fundamentally *repugnant philosophy*" and contradicted "long-standing American concepts of 'fair play,'" but it insisted that such an approach was necessary given the grave international situation that existed.[4] More recent advocates of strong U.S. espionage and covert action programs have typically focused on the strategies and methods they deem essential to meeting various foreign threats,[5] from the KGB[6] to contemporary drug lords and terrorist organizations.[7]

I do not question the "just cause" underlying the creation of the CIA in the late 1940s, nor do I think that its legitimacy is up for grabs in the wake of the collapse of the Soviet Union. If the CIA did not already exist, it would be necessary to invent it. Furthermore, the fact that CIA is a lawfully authorized arm of a liberal democracy lends it a legitimacy—a "social contract," if you will—which could never be ascribed to the KGB, for example. Dismantling the CIA, as some in Congress have recently proposed, would endanger U.S. national security. Even as persistent a critic of government secrecy as Sissela Bok nonetheless grants that deception can occasionally be justified in national defense: "Honesty ought not to allow the creation of an emergency by the enemy, when deception can forestall or avert it. . . . Whenever it is right to resist an assault or a threat by force, it must then be allowable to do so by guile."[8]

In some essays written by former CIA officers, it has been suggested that the peculiar nature of the knowledge and expertise of intelligence professionals relative to grave external threats requires an extraordinary or specialized morality.[9] In other words, like politicians who "get their hands dirty" in the public interest, the role of intelligence officers is thought by some to warrant excusing them in that capacity from certain ordinary moral constraints. As Arthur Hulnick and Daniel Mattausch wrote:

> Professional standards require intelligence professionals to lie, hide information, or use covert tactics to protect their "cover," access, sources, and responsi-

bilities. The Central Intelligence Agency expects, teaches, encourages, and controls these tactics so that the lies are consistent and supported ("backstopped"). The CIA expects intelligence officers to teach others to lie, deceive, steal, launder money, and perform a variety of other activities that would certainly be illegal if practiced in the United States. They call these tactics "tradecraft," and intelligence officers practice them in all the world's intelligence services.[10]

But can the goals of intelligence truly justify *ruthless* methods? No doubt Machiavelli, Cromwell, Lenin, and others would concur. But it would be highly problematic to grant the profession of intelligence a kind of "strong moral role-differentiation."[11] Of course, we do allow professionals to make certain ethical trade-offs. But professionals are mistaken if they consider their roles to render them immune to moral scrutiny. Physicians may not deceive patients into serving as unwitting subjects of medical experiments even though the knowledge derived from doing so will almost certainly benefit future patients. Soldiers may not maim or slaughter civilians in order to deter their compatriots from harboring guerrillas. Exceptions to *prima facie* ethical principles must be shown to fulfill more important principles, not simply be assumed to be acceptable due to their being professionally "expedient." An affirmation of the legitimacy of the CIA as an institution does not entail moral approval of every end it might pursue nor every method it might employ.

What follows is an exploration of selected ethical problems arising in the work of intelligence officers. I cannot claim to possess the level of knowledge and wisdom requisite to resolving all of these issues satisfactorily, but perhaps my "spadework" will at least serve to stimulate further debate and reflection.

VOLUNTARY AGENTS

When U.S. intelligence officers recruit agents in foreign countries, they may have very specific offensive or defensive goals, or they may wish simply to build "assets"—human sources of information and influence—for future use. Richard Bissell, CIA's Deputy Director for Plans from 1958 to 1962, testified before Congress in 1975: "It was the normal practice in the Agency and an important part of its mission to create various kinds of capability long before there was any reason to be certain whether those would be used or where or how *or for what purpose*. The whole ongoing job of . . . a secret intelligence service of recruiting agents is of that character."[12] Bissell did not estimate what proportion of CIA agents take on that role freely. But that is a matter of significant ethical import.

Foreign citizens apparently become agents of the U.S. Government for a

wide variety of personal reasons: ethical concerns about their own governments; the lure of adventure, excitement, and secrecy; desire for money; sexual and other blackmail; agents' resentment and frustration regarding their
overt careers; or some combination of these factors.[13]

Some agents require little or no persuasion on the part of intelligence
officers to engage in espionage on behalf of the U.S.[14] Many agents are motivated by the sheer excitement of spying and the promise of steady extra
income. But many others decide to engage in espionage out of deep-seated
antagonism toward their native regimes.[15] This was true, for example, of a
number of high-ranking Soviet military and KGB officials who either passed
sensitive documents to the CIA or who defected when they no longer in
good conscience could remain loyal to the Soviet government.

One such agent, a Soviet military intelligence officer named Pyotr Popov,
supplied valuable information to CIA during the 1950s apparently out of
repugnance toward the KGB's treatment of Russian peasants.[16] Another
Soviet defector-in-place, Oleg Penkovskiy, fearing that Khrushchev
intended to launch a preemptive nuclear strike, provided U.S. intelligence
with thousands of pages of Soviet military documents, including information on Soviet nuclear weapon capabilities that proved vital to President
Kennedy's actions during the 1962 Cuban missile crisis.[17] It is perhaps not
too far-fetched to believe that in a state characterized by an oppressive political system, espionage intended to undermine that system's power and pres-
tige can actually provide authentic hope to agents and dissident groups.
Former CIA officer Harry Rositzke argued that although agents sent on
missions against the Soviet Union in the late 1940s and early 1950s "knew
from the beginning that the cards were stacked against them," they were
nonetheless "highly motivated," having witnessed the effects of Soviet
power in Eastern Europe, the Ukraine, and the Baltic States.[18]

However, espionage against one's government is considered treason in
every part of the world and, if exposed, frequently entails severe punishment
for the agent. Both Popov and Penkovskiy (like the many agents betrayed
by CIA officer Aldrich Ames)[19] were reportedly executed after their capture
and interrogation by the KGB. Thus the fact that an agent is a volunteer
does not thereby purge his or her CIA case officer of moral responsibility
or liability.

Although witting agents usually have no illusions about the consequences
of capture, their covert sponsors may ask them to accomplish tasks entailing
greater risk than those of which they are aware or would agree to accept.
Rositzke described how a nervous double agent was emboldened to meet
with his KGB handler: CIA polygraphed the agent, but then showed him a
different graph than his own to convince him that he could successfully
withstand a KGB debriefing.[20] Another agent was asked by U.S. officials to
organize "a small, tightly knit resistance group" of his military colleagues,

but he refused out of fear of the KGB's wholesale infiltration of society. In fact, he wouldn't even provide CIA with the names of anyone who might be a Soviet dissident, fearing that a failed attempt by CIA to recruit any of them could easily "blow back" on him.[21] A more recent case (1990) also illustrates the ominous consequences of agent exposure:

> Two or three undercover agents believed to be working for Israel in a Syrian-based terrorist group were unmasked and killed last fall, not long after the United States gave the Damascus Government information about terrorist activities in the country. . . .
> Officials said the Administration argued that [Syrian President] Assad should be given an unusually detailed briefing about the actions of Syrian-based terrorists to impress upon him the weight of the evidence against his Government. Intelligence officials are said to have warned that such a briefing would put undercover agents and methods of gathering information at risk.
> "It was quite an argument," said one official who has been informed of the debate. "The intelligence guys finally told them, 'O.K., but the blood will be on your hands if something happens.'"[22]

Agents working against tyrannical regimes or terrorist cells have a compelling ethical claim to have information about their clandestine activities very closely guarded by their CIA handlers.

But some voluntary agents have apparently been regarded as "expendable."[23] James McCargar, a former operations officer, wrote that many American agents have been gratuitously slandered by the CIA upon their termination or "disposal" as agents, presumably to render them less credible should they attempt to publicize their former espionage work.[24] Alternatively, an agent who had stopped producing useful intelligence might be intentionally exposed in order to humiliate the target country's counterintelligence personnel. This is especially tempting when the agent is a mole, since such a revelation would cause agents employed by the target country to worry that their own safety was endangered by leaks. The aftermath of the arrest of CIA officer Aldrich Ames as a Soviet/Russian mole is instructive in this regard.[25]

British journalist Tom Mangold learned through extensive research into the long tenure of James Angleton as CIA's head of counterintelligence that a number of *bona fide* Soviet defectors and other CIA agents were grossly mistreated—some even betrayed to the KGB—due to Angleton's unfortunate reliance on the bizarre, self-serving opinions of one particular Soviet defector, Anatoliy Golitsyn. To the Agency's credit, though, following Angleton's forced retirement it made efforts to compensate some of the agents (and CIA officers) who had unjustly suffered as a result of Angleton's and Golitsyn's suspicions.[26]

The CIA has also been criticized for building up the hopes of agents beyond what the U.S. Government really intended to support. According to McCargar, U.S. intelligence developed a cooperative relationship with an unnamed Eastern European monarchist group, deceiving them into believing that the restoration of the monarchy was intended by the U.S. (it was not) in order to benefit from the "considerable intelligence" the group provided.[27] In addition, historian John Ranelagh has accused the U.S. of a "cold ruthlessness" in supporting partisans in postwar Ukraine and elsewhere when it had no intention to commit its military forces to save them from being annihilated.[28]

The culpability of U.S. officials has been mitigated, however, in regard to certain covert operations in Poland, Albania, and Cuba, where U.S. long-term objectives were defeated by the compromise of its operations and communications by enemy intelligence. U.S. officials were unaware, for example, that British intelligence officers Kim Philby and George Blake were actually Soviet agents who would succeed in betraying numerous espionage and covert action projects and cause the deaths of hundreds of Western agents.[29] The temptation to exploit voluntary agents for purposes of Realpolitik must be considered as a plausible moral risk, though. One is reminded of the ways in which various governments have repeatedly inflated Kurdish nationalist hopes solely in order to place temporary pressure on Iran, Iraq, or Syria, only later to abandon the Kurds out of expediency.[30]

DECEPTION AND COERCION

When the CIA is unable to obtain voluntary agents, it sometimes "recruits" them, so to speak, through deception. In some cases, people who wouldn't willingly work for the CIA are made unwittingly to do exactly that by passing information to a trusted friend or associate who happens to be in CIA employ but who presents himself as one with loyalties more congenial to the person being duped.[31] This method is sometimes called "false-flag" recruitment,[32] since the recruiter misrepresents the country that he or she is representing. It's essentially a con game, wherein one first ascertains the potential agent's basic loyalties and core values in order to concoct a scheme to persuade him to provide sensitive information without upsetting his conscience or arousing his suspicions.

Miles Copeland said that "[i]f the prospective agent hates Americans," for example, the recruiter "can tell him he is acting in behalf of the French—or the British . . . or some Senator or crusading newspaperman," whatever his conscience is assessed as most likely to tolerate.[33] David Phillips, another former CIA officer, attested that "there are unsuspecting zealots around the world who are managed and paid as spies; they sell their countries' secrets believing all the while they are helping 'the good guys.'"[34]

"False-flag" cases are odd from a moral perspective, since in one respect the agents willingly provide sensitive information, probably knowing that they would be punished if their activities were exposed. But of course the voluntary nature of such action is only superficial, since if the agents knew to whom the information was actually being passed they would most likely not provide it.

Two general types of coercive recruitment have been cited in the literature.[35] In some cases, knowledge of an agent's potentially embarrassing or patently illegal activities is used to extort espionage service. Prospective agents may be confronted with proof of their past crimes and blackmailed into working as spies in exchange for their covert employer keeping such evidence from their own country's police. As a former CIA officer indicated, in many instances the local police would already be aware of such crimes but would cooperate with CIA in not referring them for prosecution.[36] Since this method closely resembles that of the FBI in coercing criminals into becoming informers, it may be seen to be less objectionable than some other methods of agent recruitment. In cases where prospective agents' perpetration of crimes mitigates their right to be free from *retributive* coercion, the issue of their consent to becoming spies loses some of its force. But this cannot be said to provide a "blank check" to a secret recruiter to coerce a criminal to engage in espionage. (In addition, as I shall argue, there are ethical concerns regarding the agent's society which should not be ignored.)

In other cases, though, embarrassing situations can be created for previously innocent potential agents, and the threat of exposure used to extort their compliance. One technique involves first establishing a seemingly natural friendship with a prospective agent, and gradually "stretching" the person's conscience to the point of accepting tasks that he or she would previously have found unacceptable. Casual requests by the recruiter for seemingly innocuous data evolve subtly to more obviously illegal assignments, until the agent either makes a conscious decision to remain an informant, or continues out of fear of exposure.[37]

> Those cultivating the spy will press favors upon him, without, in the initial stages, asking for anything in return. This is clearly a matter in which sensibilities must be catered to in order to avoid giving offense or having one's motives suspect. Reciprocity obliges most people to respond in kind; the trick is to escalate the exchange to the point where a more compromising engagement can be undertaken.[38]

Espionage activity that is initiated in a deceptive manner can thus at some point take on more obviously coercive characteristics. James Angleton reportedly described this method as "incremental entrapment in a subtle web of irresistible compromises."[39]

The degree to which CIA employs blatantly coercive methods in its agent recruitment and handling has actually been a topic of contention among former CIA officers. James McCargar said that since the case officer is dependent upon the actions of the agent, this naturally inhibits the degree to which an agent can be dominated: "To this extent every agent is a free agent." He also claimed that "compulsion is a very limited technique," since the agent thus "is in no frame of mind to exploit his own skills or possibilities to the fullest."[40] Arthur Jacobs similarly argued that "there is rarely to be found any effective means of exercising absolute control [over an agent], even by such lurid devices as blackmail, exposure of offensive relationships or personal habits of the source."[41] Note that neither Jacobs nor McCargar implied that coercive methods would be morally objectionable *if* they were *effective*.

If CIA officials indeed concluded that absolute control over an agent was impossible, this was not for lack of trying. For at least two decades the Agency funded experiments using mind-altering drugs, electroshock, hypnosis, sensory deprivation, and other techniques in an elusive quest to find foolproof ways to manipulate agents. Some of the motivation behind these efforts lay in fears that the Soviet Union and China had developed technical "brainwashing" methods that needed to be understood and countered by U.S. intelligence. But, sadly, little consideration was given to the rights of the largely unwitting human subjects of CIA mind-control experiments.[42]

Even if agents cannot be completely "controlled" by their covert supervisors, we may infer that espionage agents are regarded by their sponsors primarily as means to the end of collecting intelligence. The full range of habits, beliefs, virtues, and vices making up the character of an individual agent are to prudent espionage officers merely helps or hindrances to the production of useful intelligence for their superiors.[43] Of course, instrumentalist relationships are common to a wide variety of human endeavors, such as business negotiations and contracts. But the element of crude manipulation that can apparently be present in espionage is what ought to elicit our heightened ethical scrutiny.

E. Drexel Godfrey, Jr., former Director of Current Intelligence at CIA, strongly criticized CIA methods of recruiting agents, stating that CIA officers are "painstakingly trained in techniques that will convert an acquaintance into a submissive tool . . . shred away his resistance and deflate his sense of self-worth."[44] Miles Copeland, expressing a more sanguine view, claimed that CIA uses coercion in agent recruitment "only when there is a good chance of converting it into positive motivation":

> As quickly as possible, the principal [an intermediary between officer and agent] must enable the agent to deceive himself into believing that he would have become an agent even had he not been caught with his pants down, and that what he is doing is justifiable on its own merits.[45]

Moreover, Copeland said, the agent must be persuaded that the government employing him in espionage regards his safety as more important than any particular piece of information he might forward.

> Maintaining such an attitude might occasionally mean passing up some item of tremendous importance, but in the long run it pays off because it keeps the agent feeling safe and happy and maintains his productivity over a long period of years.[46]

William Hood has written that an element of control is not simply desirable but imperative in agent recruitment:

> No espionage service can tolerate the merest whiff of independence or reserve on the part of an agent. . . . With a new agent, the case officer's first task is to maneuver him into a position where there is nothing that he can hold back—not the slightest scrap of information nor the most intimate detail of his personal life. Until this level of control has been achieved, the spy cannot be said to have been fully recruited.[47]

James Angleton, Hood's former boss in counterintelligence, apparently held a similar view, according to Edward Epstein:

> Whereas money, sex, ideology, and ambition provide the means for compromising targets, the lever used to convert a man into a mole tends to be blackmail. . . . Whatever lure is used, the point of the sting is to make it impossible for the recruit to explain his activities to his superiors. He is compromised, not so much by his original indiscretion, but for failing to report it.[48]

Note that Angleton here was referring to a special type of agent, the "mole" or penetration agent within an enemy's intelligence service. Not all espionage agents would be necessarily compromised by failing to report certain activities to their employer, but an intelligence officer would.

Another former CIA official, Howard Stone, admitted that CIA often recruits agents by bribery or blackmail. But believing that such methods often produce unreliable agents who only pretend to have access to important information, he urged CIA instead "to win over prominent foreign officials of sound moral character."[49] One former CIA officer who served many years in Latin America told me that none of his agent relations were based on blackmail or other coercion. He believed like Howard Stone that such methods invariably produced "servile" and unreliable agents who "don't exercise good judgment." But this officer went on to say, "[My agents] produced for me because they knew I was reliable and they could count on me in a pinch. They would and did risk their lives for me." He added, though, that different methods might be necessary in other countries where the stakes and pressures were greater, such as the Soviet Union or Cuba.[50] It seems likely that a CIA officer having qualms about deceptive or coercive recruiting methods would simply not be assigned to such countries or would not remain there very long (at least in an agent-recruiting capacity).

MANIPULATION

Perhaps most troubling of the professional skills of an intelligence officer is the ability to manipulate persons. The degree of manipulation can vary from the subtle blackmail threat latent in a financial relationship with an espionage agent to more obviously coercive and even violent measures. The element of control in intelligence operations is directly related to suspicion of the loyalty of the agent. Suspicion is a professional virtue for intelligence officers, especially for those who work in security and counterintelligence, since in theory anyone thought to be trustworthy may in fact be secretly serving the enemy.

The practice of interrogation is a significant component of intelligence work, but also illustrates manipulation in its rawest form. William Johnson, a former CIA counterintelligence officer, has offered a glimpse of the ethical risks involved: "Interrogation is such a dirty business that it should be done only by people of the cleanest character. Anyone with sadistic tendencies should not be in the business."[51]

We are reminded, though, of the ease with which ordinary people can come to rationalize callousness and cruelty in dealing with perceived enemies. Given the natural human capacity for aggression, combined with the right set of biases, incentives, and peer pressures, many ordinarily decent people can succumb to sadism.[52] The line between interrogation and torture is perilously thin.

What is it about interrogation that is "dirty"? To Johnson, it is not the presence of inflicted physical pain, which he regards to be not only morally dubious but counterproductive.

> Physical pain is not relevant in interrogation. Anxiety, humiliation, loneliness, and pride are another story. . . . The person who enjoys hurting is a lousy interrogator in even the most human [humane?] situation. But the humane person who shrinks from *manipulating* his subject is also a lousy interrogator. . . . The interrogator, like a priest or doctor [!], must have a talent for empathy, a personal need to communicate with other people, a concern for what makes other people tick even when he is putting maximum emotional pressure on them.[53]

In everyday moral parlance, empathy is related to compassion. But in intelligence work, the other is considered to be a potential threat to persons and interests that the intelligence officer is sworn to protect. "Knowing one's enemy" in this role means understanding the other, but not in the interest of enhancing his or her freedom or well-being: on the contrary, empathy becomes a manipulative tool.[54] This altered meaning of empathy holds true beyond the practice of interrogation. It also characterizes a significant part of the professional skill involved in recruiting and handling agents, whose trust is often essential to gaining their control. Empathy is also useful in the creation of propaganda, since the power of propaganda to influence its intended audience is largely dependent upon how well it is crafted to address that audience's peculiar cultural milieu.

COVERT ACTION

Harry Rositzke argued that the kind of agent-manipulation that frequently occurs in espionage and counterespionage operations may not apply to some types of covert action. Covert financial support for a political leader or dissident, for example, need not entail his or her coercion since it serves his or her interests.[55] James McCargar expressed a similar opinion:

> In a political operation the case officer must have arrived at a clear and workable accommodation of interests with the agent. Control by the case officer there must be, but not duplicity. The purposes of case officer and agent must have been presented with the maximum permissible clarity, and then a reconciliation of conflicts and limitations negotiated. In brief, the outstanding characteristic of the political case officer-agent relationship is that it must be an alliance, not a utilization of the agent by the case officer, as often occurs in intelligence.[56]

But the fact that this state of affairs applied for a time to CIA relations with Panamanian dictator Manuel Noriega,[57] among others, indicates that these arguments do not dispel moral concern for the wider context of covert action. Knowing that a covert action coincides with the interests of particular foreign nationals is not sufficient to justify it ethically, since covert action may involve the violation of rights that ought to override those interests.

It is also likely that an intelligence officer would seek to "vet" (or test the authenticity of) an agent of covert influence against the evidence supplied by informers or espionage agents, hence the need to use some method of agent recruitment and handling having one or more of the attendant moral concerns previously identified.

Now since the "product" of a covert action agent is in some respects "public" (unlike the product of an espionage agent), it is perhaps more difficult to *deceive* a covert action agent than an espionage agent as to the real intentions of his or her secret employers. One can more easily conceive, though, of a covert action agent (such as a newspaper reporter or editorialist) being *coerced* through blackmail or other threats into engaging in covert action. Such considerations provide further qualification, then, to Rositzke's and McCargar's assertions of the voluntary participation of covert action agents.

Secret financial support for foreign political or labor leaders is morally complex. In some cases it can plausibly be considered a form of humanitarian intervention. For example, CIA aid to centrist political parties in postwar France, Italy, and Japan helped to counter covert Soviet aid to communist parties there, while CIA assistance to Christian Democrats in El Salvador was intended to prevent an election victory by right-wing candidates tied to death squads. Almost certainly the political consequences in those countries would have been grave had no aid been provided by CIA. But often the efforts made by U.S. officials to provide such aid openly have been insufficient.[58] Covert political action has been employed despite the fact that foreign citizens would rightly suspect the objective judgment owed to them by their leaders to have been clouded by their acceptance of secret payments.

Former CIA Director William Colby, who oversaw covert aid to anticommunist politicians in Italy during the 1950s, claimed in his memoirs, "The program in Italy gave aid to the democratic forces to obtain *their* goals. It did not 'bribe' them to follow American direction. . . ."[59] But Colby exhibited a very different view when asked by journalist Oriana Fallaci, ". . . if I came [to the U.S.], as a foreigner, and financed an American party, and 21 of your politicians, and some of your journalists, what would you do?" Colby responded that he would report her to the FBI.[60]

We rightly condemn corporate purchasing agents who accept or extort lavish gifts from would-be suppliers, doctors who receive kickbacks from pharmaceutical companies for prescribing certain drugs, and legislators who seek political contributions from industries they are supposed to regulate. Secret payments to foreign government leaders, even when made with good intentions, create at a minimum the appearance of a conflict of interest on the part of the recipient. They undermine government accountability and the public trust, and should be avoided.

USE OF UNDERWORLD FIGURES

Another significant area of ethical concern has to do with the obstruction of justice in sheltering criminals used as agents, as in, for example, the postwar recruitment by U.S. intelligence of a number of Nazi war criminals to engage in espionage and covert operations against the Soviet Union.[61] Christopher Simpson, a reporter who extensively researched this subject, quoted Harry Rositzke as explaining:

It was a visceral business of using any bastard as long as he was anti-Communist . . . [and] the eagerness or desire to enlist collaborators meant that sure, you didn't look at their credentials too closely.[62]

Simpson claimed, however, that U.S. intelligence did indeed know about the war-crimes "credentials" of many of its postwar recruits, as did the British, French, and Soviets, who also employed suspected and proven war criminals in intelligence roles.[63] He also showed that this practice became risky to U.S. intelligence as well, when ex-Nazis threatened to publicize U.S. covert operations in which they had participated unless the U.S. helped them to escape abroad to avoid prosecution for their wartime atrocities.[64]

The CIA later involved similarly shady characters in plots to assassinate various foreign leaders. Underworld figures like Sam Giancana and Santos Trafficante were approached to kill Fidel Castro.[65] Another individual recruited to kill an African politician was described in an internal CIA memo in the following fashion:

He is indeed aware of the precepts of right and wrong, but if he is given an assignment which may be morally wrong in the eyes of the world, but necessary because his case officer ordered him to carry it out, then it is right, and he will dutifully undertake appropriate action for its execution without pangs of conscience. In a word, he can rationalize all actions.[66]

The Senate committee that investigated the assassination plots appropriately judged this type of rationalization to be "not in keeping with the ideals of our nation." The committee also observed that employing underworld characters "gives them the power to blackmail the government and to avoid prosecution, for past or future crimes."[67]

In hindsight at least, it seems obvious that espionage and covert actions relying upon criminals as intelligence "assets" bear a strong burden of moral justification, chiefly since the victims of their crimes cannot be assumed to give tacit consent to their shelter from prosecution, but also because they can pose a threat to the societies in which they are secretly sheltered. Furthermore, in cases where perpetrators of mass murder (or even "ordinary" murder!) have sought refuge in intelligence work, it is difficult to see how the practice could be justified at all, even under the pressures that CIA officers felt in the early postwar years to quickly develop an underground network in the event of war with the Soviet Union.[68]

ECONOMIC INTELLIGENCE

Recognition of the sometimes grave consequences of espionage and covert action at least ought to have a sobering effect on the consideration of the ends they are intended to serve. If national security can possibly justify deceptive and coercive intelligence methods, it is far from clear that lesser ends can.

To illustrate, no American corporation today could or should hope to achieve the influence that the United Fruit Company had on U.S. policy toward Guatemala in the early 1950s. Before Allen Dulles became CIA Director under Eisenhower, he worked for a powerful law firm that arranged profitable deals for United Fruit in Guatemala, where it owned extensive plantations and rail lines and regularly crushed incipient labor unions. Thus, when the company asked the CIA to overthrow the country's first elected president, its request fell on eager and familiar ears. Allen Dulles even promised the company that whoever CIA selected to be the next Guatemalan leader would not be allowed to nationalize or in any way disrupt the company's operations.[69] The interests and objectives of particular corporations are not necessarily identical to those of the United States, yet this perspective was lost on many U.S. officials during the Cold War. The same people whose prescience enabled the U.S. to meet the many real challenges posed by the Soviet Union and its allies were nonetheless capable of rationalizing the corruption of national ends to serve a scandalously small elite.

The breakup of the Soviet Union has not only resulted in large cuts in U.S. defense spending, but has also caused the CIA's overall mission and budget to be carefully scrutinized. Many people are asking whether CIA resources should now be focused in ways that more directly enhance American economic competitiveness. Some members of Congress and business leaders have called upon the CIA to spy on behalf of American corporations, much as the governments of France and Japan are doing for their native companies. Unless U.S. firms are able to "fight fire with fire," the argument goes, they will be at a decided disadvantage in the global market.[70]

Fortunately, many large U.S. corporations have said that they neither want nor need this sort of help from the Agency, and CIA officials have lobbied against it as well. Former CIA Director Robert Gates said in an oft-quoted April 1992 speech:

> [U.S. intelligence] does not, should not, and will not engage in industrial espionage. . . . Plainly put, it is the role of U.S. business to size up their foreign competitors' trade secrets, marketing strategies, and bid proposals. Some years ago, one of our clandestine service officers said to me: "You know, I'm prepared to give my life for my country, but not for a company." That case officer was absolutely right.[71]

The moral justification of espionage (let alone covert action) is highly dubious in the service of preserving or enhancing the global competitiveness of U.S. corporations. Apart from the defense industry, which is uniquely tied to U.S. national security, the reasons that American companies might offer to persuade the CIA to spy for them almost certainly could not be weighty enough to override the rights of foreign citizens duped or coerced into committing espionage. Nor would voluntary agents incurring great risks to deliver secret intelligence to the CIA be amused to learn that their reports were being forwarded to U.S. corporations to enable them to tap previously untouched consumer markets or to gain an edge over their foreign competitors. Even if it were possible to "sanitize" this data in ways that did not jeopardize intelligence sources and methods, questions of fairness would still arise. For example, which American companies would be given that information? Should it be free (i.e., subsidized by taxpayers), or should companies pay for it?

On the other hand, the current practice of the U.S. Government of providing *counterintelligence* advice to American companies overseas (e.g., how to prevent company phones from being tapped) is in most cases morally acceptable. Such assistance has in fact been provided for many years through the State Department's Overseas Security Advisory Council.

ASSASSINATION

That the CIA developed the capability to disable and assassinate foreign leaders is not in dispute, though precisely when that capability was conceived is unclear. The record indicates that an internal CIA "Health Alteration Committee" existed as early as 1960, and that a CIA "executive action" capability, which included assassination, was authorized by the White House as early as 1961.[72] However, since OSS had developed drugs during WWII for the purpose of assassinating and incapacitating Nazi leaders,[73] it is entirely possible that CIA inherited this capability and maintained it from its inception. Some evidence exists to suggest that CIA was authorized to create a special squad in 1949 whose duties included kidnapping and assassination, though primarily of suspected double agents.[74]

As John Marks has detailed, CIA technicians developed drugs and stockpiled bacteriological toxins that could immobilize an individual for hours, days, or months, or kill him in a manner that could not be ascertained by autopsy or that appeared to be the result of a deadly disease that the individual might plausibly have contracted naturally.[75]

Assassination has been prohibited by U.S. executive orders since the mid-1970s, but there are indications that it may have been authorized since that time at high levels within the U.S. Government. A manual developed for the Nicaraguan *contras* by one or more of their CIA advisers, for example, urged that Sandinista officials be "neutralized" as part of a "selective use of violence for propaganda purposes."[76] In addition, former CIA general counsel

Stanley Sporkin reportedly concluded in the early 1980s that violent actions taken against terrorists would not constitute assassination under U.S. law,[77] and this opinion may have served as the justification for "sensitive retaliation operations" launched against those believed responsible for the 1983 bombings of the U.S. Embassy and Marine compound in Beirut.[78]

Neil Livingstone, an expert on terrorism and low-intensity conflict, argues that "state-sanctioned terminations" can be justified against terrorists:

> Just as it is not a crime to kill the enemy during wartime, so too should it not be regarded as a crime or a morally reprehensible act when a nation, acting in concert with its obligation to protect its own citizens from harm, seeks out and destroys terrorists outside its borders who have committed, or are planning to commit atrocities on its territory or against its citizens.[79]

Livingstone adds, however, that assassination should be considered "only when the potential target cannot be brought to justice in a more conventional manner."[80] His caveat is an important one, in part because assassination by definition excludes due process of law in ascertaining the guilt or innocence of the "accused" as well as in applying an appropriate punishment if and when guilt is established. The assassin in effect acts as prosecutor, judge, jury, and executioner combined; the target is precluded from being represented by counsel before an impartial court. These concerns suggest that assassination ought only to be used as a last resort.[81]

Other writers have favored the assassination of foreign government leaders in particular circumstances. Angelo Codevilla questions the sensibility of the U.S. legal prohibition of assassination, suggesting that the practice is morally preferable to accepting the consequences of aggressive war:

> The military art, the very opposite of indiscriminate killing, consists of striking those people and things most likely to stop the enemy from continuing the war. Today, the specialization of weapons and tactics of war make it easier than ever to go after those whose death is most likely to stop the killing. Often, as in the Gulf War [1990–1991], there is no quarrel with the enemy country, only with its chief. In such cases, it is both futile and immoral to demolish a country in the hope that this will persuade the tyrant to give way. Why not kill the tyrant?[82]

Codevilla's assertion that it is unwise to prohibit assassination *tout court* is supported by numerous arguments in the Western philosophical tradition justifying tyrannicide as a permissible (if last-resort) means to a just end. But missing from Codevilla's argument are other considerations present in the tradition that weigh against employing assassination as an isolated act. One important concern is that unless tyrannicide is coupled with a wider effort to replace the entire regime, it will likely result in greater repression of the populace rather than less.[83] Many of the CIA assassination plots investigated by the U.S. Congress in 1975 seem to belie any real consideration for the well-being of their intended victim's fellow citizens. Too often the death of a foreign leader was an end in itself rather than simply a possible outcome of a comprehensive effort to replace a bad government with one that respected human rights. Removing Fidel Castro, for example, would not by itself have diminished the Cuban regime's oppression of its citizens, yet numerous CIA plots were devised against Castro (with vigorous White House support, to be sure) apart from any coordinated plan to replace him with a viable and more liberal government.[84]

Assassination is often thought to be capable of ending and preventing war and terrorist crimes. No doubt this is true in many cases. But like other forms of covert action, assassination has too often been proposed as an option well before other less morally objectionable measures have been tried. For example, among the covert operations considered by CIA in 1954 against President Arbenz of Guatemala was his assassination by means of a "silent bullet." It is a disturbing commentary on the quality of moral reasoning employed by CIA and other senior U.S. officials at that time that the only apparent reason why the assassination option was discarded was a desire not to make Arbenz a martyr.[85]

PROFESSIONAL STANDARDS

The late Paul Seabury once said: "The exercise of power does not necessarily corrupt. The craft of intelligence can have as its practitioners those who were able to maintain their integrity while being liars and obfuscators."[86] I do not doubt the essential truth of that provocative thought. The United States must be able to depend upon its intelligence officers to be persons of high ethical standards.

But personal integrity can easily be undermined by the wrong kinds of incentives and pressures, and must therefore be cultivated, monitored, and reinforced institutionally. Those who have the authority to establish objectives for intelligence operations must not only weigh the ethical justification of those ends but must also raise ethical questions about the various means being considered to achieve them. Intelligence officers in the field, in turn, must be trained to recognize ethical issues as such, and must be allowed to communicate their concerns to their supervisors without fear for their careers.

To some extent, the CIA already addresses ethical concerns in its internal training and communications. Hulnick and Mattausch claimed that honesty must apply to internal CIA communications and practices. Intelligence judgments must never be altered "to fit the desires of policymakers who might prefer different conclusions,"[87] and intelligence officers "must be scrupulous in managing funds or equipment with which they are entrusted," given the fact that many funds are not subject to outside audit and that certain equipment is designed to prevent its being identified with CIA.[88] They also noted an interesting implication of the oath of secrecy which intelligence officers must swear. Like military personnel, they cannot appeal to a "Nuremberg defense" in the face of a clearly improper order from a superior. But unlike other public servants, they do not have the option of "going public" with an issue or order they consider to be illegal or immoral if the internal "whistle-blowing" procedure proves to be unsatisfactory to them: "public discussion is not possible without a gross violation of classification rules and the professional ethics of the intelligence officer."[89]

In January 1992, James Barry, then Director of the CIA's Center for the Study of Intelligence, responded to a series of questions I had submitted with an interesting letter cleared by higher officials for release. Arguing that "[p]rofessional ethics is a central component of [CIA's] training and career development process," Barry described in general terms the kinds of training provided for new CIA employees, mid-career employees, new supervisors and middle managers, and senior officials. He stated that high ethical standards play an important role in the evaluation and certification of case officers, and that those individuals receive specialized, tutorial training in ethical issues related to foreign intelligence, counterintelligence, and covert action. Barry further noted CIA's standing policy that any employees having ethical concerns "may report them in confidence to the [CIA] Inspector General."[90]

There is further indication that CIA has maintained a form of "conscientious objector" status for its personnel relative to certain morally problematic assignments. Testimony of former CIA officers before the Senate committee investigating assassination plots in 1975 suggests that CIA employees were allowed to decline to participate in those plots without experiencing threats to their career. "Michael Mulroney" (pseud.), a former CIA officer, testified that in 1960 he refused on moral grounds to carry out a political assassination requested by the head of CIA's clandestine division, Richard Bissell, and that his decision was supported by Bissell's deputy, Richard Helms.[91] In addition, during the Vietnam War, American personnel involved with the Phoenix program were apparently granted a similar "conscientious objector" option.[92]

CONCLUSIONS

Although space does not permit review of all of the issues examined in this essay, some concluding reflections on selected categories of intelligence operations are warranted. The use of secret agents—voluntary and non-voluntary—is intended to provide valuable information believed to be unobtainable through methods overt or technical. The risks inherent in all espionage activities suggest, though, that for the sake of the agent alone, efforts should be made to determine before the agent is recruited that the information needed cannot in fact be ascertained by less problematic methods. In addition, since after an agent is recruited the agent-officer relationship takes on a life and momentum of its own, care must be taken to avoid situations where innocent third parties would be harmed or justice obstructed in the interest of preserving the agent's identity and continued service.

Recruiting voluntary agents has the advantage of involving no deception about the identity and general motives of the recruiter. Furthermore, a just cause can be served by intelligence officers and voluntary agents working together to undermine an unjust regime. But such agents deserve not to be deceived about the risks involved in the operations they are asked to carry out. Nor should the fact that their work is secret tempt their handlers to treat them as expendable, to allow them callously to be sacrificed to Realpolitik or the shifting winds of diplomacy.

The chief advantage of employing a false-flag approach or blackmail in certain situations is that a just cause can be pursued even where foreign citizens are highly unlikely to serve voluntarily as CIA agents. But such methods raise very difficult questions. False-flag methods deceive the agent as to the identity of the recruiter, and thus hide from the agent the full risks inherent in his or her tasks as well as their true purposes. Blackmail is blatant coercion. It is difficult enough to justify its use against known criminals; all the more so when it arises out of the calculated entrapment of a previously innocent person who merely happens to have probable access to sensitive information desired by the CIA. Finally, to the extent that recruitment tactics seek to "stretch" the agent's conscience, they can result in the corruption of the agent in addition to his or her victimization. Deception and coercion in agent recruitment should certainly not be used as routine methods of obtaining "assets" whose future value as sources of vital intelligence is dubious. (Recall Richard Bissell's 1975 testimony about agents being recruited "long before there [is] any reason to be certain whether those would be used or where or how or for what purpose.")[93]

These concerns about espionage are challenged, though, by the claim that if one rules out an espionage source or method one may thereby eliminate the possibility of knowing certain kinds of vital information. It's not difficult to construct hypothetical cases in which knowing the intentions of a tyrannical regime or a terrorist cell could mean the difference between life and death for many people, cases which would therefore question the validity of strict prohibitions on deceptive and coercive intelligence methods or the use of criminals as agents.

In addition, if we imagine a prospective agent who works in a sensitive capacity for the government of a manifestly tyrannical state, there is a sense in which, since that government itself is not and cannot be rationally willed by its oppressed citizens, neither can service to that government in ways that maintain its tyrannical nature be justified. Some regimes simply do not deserve the loyalty of their citizens. But given the fact that opportunities to persuade citizens and government officials in tyrannical states that they ought to commit treason are sometimes quite limited, the justification of coerced recruitment of agents to achieve this becomes more plausible, in spite of the fact that unless the tyranny poses a dire threat to other countries, coercive recruitment would appear to be a form of paternalistic intervention. Coercive recruitment of agents within a tyrannical state may become even more acceptable as that state's threat to other countries becomes more grave or imminent. Remembering Sissela Bok's assertion that "whenever it is right to resist an assault by force, it must then be allowable to do so by guile,"[94] espionage and covert action can serve as effective ways to prevent a tyranny from launching an aggressive war or intimidating its neighbors.

Of course, to say that a decision or action is morally right does not necessarily mean that the outcome is unequivocally good. It may be, for example, that coercive recruitment of an agent can be morally justified in a particular situation, given the dire consequences of not having the information he or she can provide, say, plus a lack of morally acceptable alternatives. But since coercion involves an infringement of the agent's freedom (and conceivably other basic rights), the external good that may result from the recruitment cannot do away with the fact that the agent—a human being with emotions, hopes, and dreams, not merely an abstract "source," "asset," or "penetration"—suffers real harm in the process.

Tragic choices are inevitable to some degree in intelligence work. The challenge, then, is to specify intelligence goals and manage operations in ways that recognize the myriad ethical issues at stake, in order to minimize the occurrence of avoidable tragedy.

NOTES

1. Cf. W. D. Ross, *The Right and the Good* (New York: Oxford Univ. Press, 1930). Ross thought it impossible to derive all valid moral duties from one fundamental principle, let alone to construct an absolute code encompassing every possible moral dilemma. He argued that human beings have numerous *prima facie* ethical obligations, i.e., duties that are strong enough to override less important preferences, but which are nevertheless not absolute, since they can be overridden by one another in particular situations. In some cases one's paramount moral duty will be to promote happiness; in others, to prevent or alleviate harm; in others, to protect rights; etc. The need for moral deliberation and wisdom is simply part of the human condition, in Ross's view. But it's important to note that his theory does not entail ethical relativ-

ism, i.e., the (illogical) view that two contradictory ethical principles can both be true at the same time. Nor is one permitted to treat similar cases in dissimilar ways.

2. Affinities between intelligence and the practice of law (e.g., in the importance of secrecy and aggressive tactics against opponents) were suggested in John Ranelagh, *The Agency: The Rise and Decline of the CIA*, revised and updated edition (New York: Simon & Schuster, 1987), pp. 27–31.

3. NSC Directive 10/2 (18 June 1948), in William M. Leary, ed., *The Central Intelligence Agency: History and Documents* (Univ. of Alabama Press, 1984), p. 131.

4. James Doolittle et al., "Report on the Covert Activities of the Central Intelligence Agency," ibid., pp. 143–145, emphasis added.

5. See, e.g., Peer de Silva, *Sub Rosa: The CIA and the Uses of Intelligence* (New York: Times Books, 1978); B. Hugh Tovar, "Covert Action," in Roy Godson, ed., *Intelligence Requirements for the 1980's: Elements of Intelligence* (Washington, DC: National Strategy Information Center, 1979), pp. 67–79; and Donald Jameson, "The Clandestine Battlefield: Trenches and Trends," *Strategic Review*, Winter 1983: pp. 19–28.

6. Three excellent histories of Russian/Soviet intelligence are Ronald Hingley, *The Russian Secret Police: Muscovite, Imperial Russian, and Soviet Political Security Operations, 1565–1970* (London: Hutchinson, 1970); George Leggett, *The Cheka: Lenin's Political Police* (New York: Oxford Univ. Press, 1981); and Amy W. Knight, *The KGB: Police and Politics in the Soviet Union* (Boston: Allen & Unwin, 1988). Another impressive assessment is J. Michael Waller, *Secret Empire: The KGB in Russia Today* (Boulder, CO: Westview, 1994).

7. Some recommendations on future U.S. uses of covert action were made by Roy Godson et al. in *Covert Action in the 1990s* (Washington, DC: Consortium for the Study of Intelligence, 1992).

8. Sissela Bok, *Lying: Moral Choice in Public and Private Life* (New York: Pantheon, 1978; Random House, 1979), pp. 149 and 151.

9. See Arthur Jacobs, letter to the Editor, *Foreign Affairs* 56/5 (July 1978): pp. 867–875, Miles Copeland; *The Real Spy World* (London: Sphere, 1978), pp. 282–283; and Arthur S. Hulnick and Daniel W. Mattausch, "Ethics and Morality in United States Secret Intelligence," *Harvard Journal of Law & Public Policy* 12/2 (Spring 1989): pp. 520–522.

10. Hulnick and Mattausch, "Ethics and Morality in United States Secret Intelligence," pp. 520–521.

11. Alan Goldman discusses that concept in relation to business, medicine, and the legal profession in *The Moral Foundations of Professional Ethics* (Totowa, NJ: Rowman & Littlefield, 1980). Compare Alan Gewirth, "Professional Ethics: The Separatist Thesis," *Ethics* 96/2 (January 1986): pp. 282–300. The literature on political "dirty hands" is extensive. Two important essays are Michael Walzer, "Political Action: The Problem of Dirty Hands," *Philosophy and Public Affairs* 2/2 (Winter 1973): pp. 160–180; and Leslie Griffin, "The Problem of Dirty Hands," *Journal of Religious Ethics* 17/1 (Spring 1989): pp. 31–61.

12. Cited in Congress, Senate Select Committee to Study Governmental Operations with Respect to Intelligence Activities, *Alleged Assassination Plots Involving Foreign Leaders*, Interim Report #94–465, 94th Congress, 1st session, 1975, p. 186, ellipsis in the original, emphasis added.

13. See Christopher Felix [James McCargar], *A Short Course in the Secret War* (New York: Dutton, 1963; Dell, 1988), pp. 54ff.; H. H. A. Cooper and Lawrence J. Redlinger, *Making Spies: A Talent Spotter's Handbook* (Boulder, CO: Paladin, 1986), ch. 2; and Chapman Pincher, *Traitors* (New York: St. Martin's, 1987; Penguin, 1988).

14. In the interest of "compartmentation" (the restriction of information to only those who can justify their "need to know" it), even voluntary agents are rarely told how the information they provide is actually used.

15. Jacobs, letter to *Foreign Affairs*, p. 870; Joseph Burkholder Smith, *Portrait of a Cold Warrior* (New York: Ballantine, 1981), pp. 114–115.

16. William Hood, *Mole* (New York: Random House, 1982; Ballantine, 1983); Harry Rositzke, *CIA's Secret Operations* (Boulder, CO: Westview, 1988), pp. 67–69.

17. Oleg Penkovskiy, *The Penkovskiy Papers*, trans. Peter Deriabin (New York: Doubleday, 1965). See also Rositzke, *CIA's Secret Operations*, pp. 69–71; and Ranelagh, *Agency*, pp. 400–402.

18. Rositzke, *CIA's Secret Operations*, pp. 26–28.

19. I'm aware that those agents were not all "voluntary": some KGB officers were entrapped into working for the CIA and FBI. Cf. Tim Weiner, "Spy Suspect Betrayed 10 U.S. Agents, F.B.I. Says," *New York Times*, 24 February 1994, pp. A1 and A13.

20. Rositzke, *CIA's Secret Operations*, pp. 123–124.

21. Hood, *Mole*, pp. 96–97.

22. Michael Wines, "2 or 3 Agents Are Believed Killed After Rare U.S.-Syrian Contacts," *New York Times*, 7 February 1991, pp. A1 and A18.

23. Orrin DeForest and David Chanoff, *Slow Burn: The Rise and Bitter Fall of American Intelligence in Vietnam* (New York: Simon & Schuster, 1990); Felix, *Secret War*, p. 107.

24. Felix, *Secret War*, pp. 62–63.

25. Tim Weiner, "Mole's Damage to C.I.A. Could Take Years to Fix," *New York Times*, 23 February 1994, p. A12; Oleg Gordievsky, "Aldrich Ames, My Would-be Killer," *The Spectator*, 5 March 1994, pp. 15–16.

26. Tom Mangold, *Cold Warrior: James Jesus Angleton: The CIA's Master Spy Hunter* (New York: Simon & Schuster, 1991).

27. Felix, *Secret War*, pp. 112–113.

28. Ranelagh, *Agency*, pp. 137, 226–228, 287, 302–309. See also John Prados, *Presidents' Secret Wars: CIA and Pentagon Covert Operations Since World War II* (New York: William Morrow, 1986), chs. 2–3.

29. Pincher, *Traitors*, p. 24. On Albania, see Nicholas Bethell, *The Great Betrayal: The Untold Story of Kim Philby's Biggest Coup* (London: Hodder and Stoughton, 1984).

30. Michael Gunter, "Mulla Mustafa Barzani and the Kurdish Rebellion in Iraq: The Intelligence Factor," *International Journal of Intelligence and Counterintelligence* 7/4 (Winter 1994): pp. 466–469.

31. Copeland, *Real Spy World*, pp. 125–129; Felix, *Secret War*, p. 112.

32. David Atlee Phillips, *The Night Watch* (New York: Ballantine, 1982), pp. 263–264; Edward J. Epstein, *Deception: The Invisible War Between the KGB and the CIA* (New York: Simon & Schuster, 1989), pp. 89, 182–183. Phillips preceded his descrip-

tion of "false-flag" recruitment with this interesting comment (p. 263): "Most intelligence officers who set out to persuade someone to become a traitor have to reach an accommodation of some sort with the code of ethics and morality they have inherited or adopted. Sometimes dirty tricks are involved in the recruiting of spies."

33. Copeland, *Real Spy World*, pp. 128–129. Copeland also asserted (p. 129) that *"most* spies really don't know which espionage service they are working for"! But that hypothesis was deemed nonsensical by three former CIA officers in separate confidential interviews with me in 1992.

34. Phillips, *Night Watch*, p. 264.

35. I have seen no evidence to suggest that CIA has ever imitated the tactic of the Mafia, KGB, or Viet Cong of threatening to kill persons or their families if they do not agree to cooperate. In fact, a former CIA officer told me emphatically that any CIA officer who made such a threat "would have been fired outright." B. Hugh Tovar, letter to David Perry, 25 February 1992, pp. 5–6.

36. Smith, *Portrait of a Cold Warrior*, p. 115.

37. Copeland, *Real Spy World*, pp. 127–128.

38. Cooper and Redlinger, *Making Spies*, p. 108.

39. Epstein, *Deception*, p. 180. It is not actually clear whether these were Angleton's words or Epstein's only. Epstein conducted numerous interviews with Angleton before the latter's death in 1987.

40. Felix, *Secret War*, pp. 51 and 56.

41. Jacobs, letter to *Foreign Affairs*, p. 871. The ineffectiveness of blackmail in agent recruiting was also suggested by former CIA Director William Colby in an interview with me on 14 September 1991.

42. John Marks, *The Search for the "Manchurian Candidate": The CIA and Mind Control* (New York: W. W. Norton, 1979, 1991).

43. Cooper and Redlinger, *Making Spies*, pp. 10 and 19.

44. E. Drexel Godfrey, Jr., "Ethics and Intelligence," *Foreign Affairs* 56/4 (April 1978): p. 631.

45. Copeland, *Real Spy World*, pp. 150–151.

46. Ibid., p. 130.

47. Hood, *Mole*, p. 29.

48. Epstein, *Deception*, p. 183.

49. David Ignatius, "In from the Cold: A Former Master Spy Spins Intriguing Yarns of His Past Intrigues," *Wall Street Journal*, 19 October 1979, pp. 1 and 41. Ignatius added his own opinion that agents recruited by the CIA "can be a rather scurvy lot."

50. Confidential interview, 1991.

51. William R. Johnson, "Tricks of the Trade: Counterintelligence Interrogation," *International Journal of Intelligence and Counterintelligence* 1/2 (1986): p. 104.

52. One of the most compelling studies of this phenomenon is Christopher R. Browning, *Ordinary Men: Reserve Police Battalion 101 and the Final Solution in Poland* (New York: HarperCollins, 1992). See also Ari Shavit, "On Gaza Beach," *New York Review of Books*, 18 July 1991, pp. 3–6.

53. William R. Johnson, *Thwarting Enemies at Home and Abroad: How to Be a Counterintelligence Officer* (Bethesda: Stone Trail Press, 1987), pp. 33 and 32, emphasis in the original.

54. Ralph K. White, "Empathy as an Intelligence Tool," *International Journal of Intelligence and Counterintelligence* 1/1 (Spring 1986): pp. 57–75.

55. Rositzke, *CIA's Secret Operations*, pp. 185–186.

56. Felix, *Secret War*, pp. 144–145.

57. Frederick Kempe, "Ties That Blind: U.S. Taught Noriega to Spy, but the Pupil Had His Own Agenda," *Wall Street Journal*, 18 October 1989, pp. A1 and A20.

58. This was one of the findings of a panel appointed by President Johnson and headed by Nicholas Katzenbach in 1967 to investigate CIA political action. "Texts of Statement and Report on Covert C.I.A. Aid," *New York Times*, 30 March 1967, p. 30.

59. William E. Colby and Peter Forbath, *Honorable Men: My Life in the CIA* (New York: Simon & Schuster, 1978), p. 115, emphasis in the original.

60. Oriana Fallaci, "The CIA's Mr. Colby," *New Republic* 174/11 (13 March 1976), pp. 12–21.

61. See Christopher Simpson, *Blowback: America's Recruitment of Nazis and Its Effects on the Cold War* (New York: Weidenfeld & Nicolson, 1988), chs. 8–12, on "Operation Bloodstone." A major drawback of this book, though, is its sanguine view of postwar Soviet capabilities and intentions.

62. Ibid., p. 159, ellipsis and brackets in the original.

63. Ibid., p. 73. Rositzke mentions in *CIA's Secret Operations*, pp. 27–28, 166–173, that ethnic Russians, Balts, Ukrainians, Armenians, and Georgians were recruited as agents for missions against the Soviet Union. He stresses their justified resentment against Soviet oppression, but does not discuss how any Nazi collaborators who may have been identified among them were handled.

64. Simpson, *Blowback*, p. 175.

65. U.S. Senate, *Alleged Assassination Plots*, pp. 43–48, 74–77.

66. Ibid., p. 46.

67. Ibid., p. 259.

68. Simpson, *Blowback*, pp. 159–160, quotes Franklin Lindsay, who apparently in the early 1950s oversaw CIA paramilitary operations in Eastern Europe that involved some former Nazi collaborators: "You have to remember that in those days even men such as George Kennan believed that there was a fifty-fifty chance of war with the Soviets within six months. . . . We were under tremendous pressure to do something, do anything to prepare for war."

69. See Stephen Schlesinger and Stephen Kinzer, *Bitter Fruit: The Untold Story of the American Coup in Guatemala* (Garden City, NY: Doubleday, 1982); and Richard H. Immerman, *The CIA in Guatemala* (Austin: Univ. of Texas Press, 1982). I discuss that coup as well as covert operations in Iran and Italy in chapter four of Perry, "Covert Action."

70. "Should the CIA Start Spying for Corporate America?" *Business Week*, 14 October 1991, pp. 96–100; Thomas McCarroll, "Next for the CIA: Business Spying?" *Time*, 22 February 1993, pp. 60–61; Peter Schweizer, *Friendly Spies: How America's Allies Are Using Economic Espionage to Steal Our Secrets* (New York: Atlantic Monthly Press, 1993).

71. George Lardner, Jr., "U.S. Demands for Economic Intelligence Up Sharply, Gates Says," *Washington Post*, 14 April 1992, p. A5. A view similar to Gates' was expressed by Randall M. Fort in *Economic Espionage: Problems and Prospects* (Washington, DC: Consortium for the Study of Intelligence, 1993).

72. U.S. Senate, *Alleged Assassination Plots*, pp. 181–187.

73. Marks, "*Manchurian Candidate,*" pp. 16–18, 119.

74. Simpson, *Blowback*, p. 153.

75. Marks, "*Manchurian Candidate,*" pp. 80–81.

76. "Tayacán," *Psychological Operations in Guerrilla Warfare*, with essays by Joanne Omang and Aryeh Neier (New York: Random House, 1985), pp. 57–59. B. Hugh Tovar, in a 25 February 1992 letter to me, wrote (p. 9), "'Neutralization' was not authorized at high levels [within CIA], and the individuals responsible for the [Nicaragua] manual were censured severely."

77. Bob Woodward, *Veil: The Secret Wars of the CIA 1981–1987* (New York: Simon & Schuster, 1987), p. 362.

78. See Russell Watson, Nicholas M. Horrock, and Abdul Hajjaj, "Fighting Terror with Terror: An Abortive CIA Operation in Lebanon Is Uncovered," *Newsweek*, 27 May 1985, pp. 32–33; and William Cowan, "How to Kill Saddam," *Washington Post*, 10 February 1991, p. C2.

79. Neil C. Livingstone, *The War Against Terrorism* (Lexington, MA: Lexington Books, 1982), pp. 174–175.

80. Ibid., p. 175.

81. One alternative is to kidnap unsavory individuals and bring them to the U.S. for trial, a tactic which has been allowed by the U.S. Supreme Court. Ruth Marcus, "Kidnapping outside the U.S. Is Upheld," *Washington Post*, 16 June 1992, pp. A1 and A4.

82. Angelo Codevilla, "Get Rid of Saddam Hussein Now: The Moral Justification," *Wall Street Journal*, 25 February 1991, p. A8.

83. The theologian Dietrich Bonhoeffer, who participated in an unsuccessful attempt on Hitler's life in 1944, reportedly believed that "the act of assassination must be coordinated with the plans of a group capable of quickly occupying, or remaining in, the key organs of the totalitarian dictatorship," a principle which resembles the *jus ad bellum* criterion of probable success. Larry L. Rasmussen, *Dietrich Bonhoeffer: Reality and Resistance* (Nashville: Abingdon, 1972), p. 145.

84. On the various plots against Castro, see U.S. Senate, *Alleged Assassination Plots*, pp. 71–90; and Thomas Powers, *The Man Who Kept the Secrets: Richard Helms and the CIA* (New York: Knopf, 1979; Simon & Schuster, 1981), ch. 9.

85. Schlesinger and Kinzer, *Bitter Fruit*, p. 112.

86. Paul Seabury, quoted in Roy Godson, ed., *Intelligence Requirements for the 1980's: Covert Action* (Washington, DC: National Strategy Information Center, 1981), p. 107.

87. This is an issue that was hotly debated during the 1991 Senate confirmation hearings of Robert Gates as Director of Central Intelligence. Some CIA analysts testified that Gates had slanted intelligence to fit the biases of former director William Casey, and that this violated a fundamental CIA ethical principle. See George Lardner, Jr., and Benjamin Weiser, "Spy vs. Spy: 4 CIA Veterans Criticize, Defend Gates," *Washington Post*, 2 October 1991, pp. A1 and A14.

88. Hulnick and Mattausch, "Ethics and Morality in U.S. Secret Intelligence," p. 521.

89. Ibid., p. 522.

90. Since most of CIA's training methods and materials are classified, it is virtually impossible for an outsider to come to any sound conclusion about their adequacy relative to the issues and concerns explored in this article.

91. U.S. Senate, *Alleged Assassination Plots*, pp. 37–42.

92. See William Colby with James McCargar, *Lost Victory* (Chicago: Contemporary Books, 1989), pp. 247–248.

93. U.S. Senate, *Alleged Assassination Plots*, p. 186.

94. Bok, *Lying*, p. 151.

16

Managing Covert Political Action
Guideposts from Just War Theory

James A. Barry

In 1954, at the height of U.S. concern about the threat from international Communism, President Eisenhower appointed a panel to make recommendations regarding covert political action as an instrument of foreign policy. The panel, named after its chairman, Gen. Jimmy Doolittle, included the following statement in its report:

> It is now clear that we are facing an implacable enemy whose avowed objective is world domination by whatever means and at whatever costs. There are no rules in such a game. Hitherto acceptable norms of human conduct do not apply. If the U.S. is to survive, longstanding American concepts of "fair play" must be reconsidered. We must develop effective espionage and counterespionage services and must learn to subvert, sabotage and destroy our enemies by more clever, more sophisticated means than those used against us. It may become necessary that the American people be made acquainted with, understand and support this fundamentally repugnant philosophy.[1]

In counseling such a radical departure from American norms, the authors of the Doolittle report adopted an argument that appears in hindsight to be extreme. But in the context of the times, it was consistent with several overlapping schools of thought in international affairs that formed the basis for many Cold War policies. The first was the "realist" tradition in international affairs, which traces its origins from the Greek historian Thucydides through the philosophies of Machiavelli, Hobbes, Spinoza, and Rousseau to modern theorists such as Hans Morgenthau and Reinhold Neibuhr. Although realists differ significantly in their views, they tend to emphasize the primacy of power in international affairs, and to exclude morality from considerations of making foreign policy.[2] Modern realism encompasses views ranging from George Kennan's proposals to combat Communism through a patient policy of containment and a low-profile approach to moral issues to Henry Kissinger's opportunistic use of moral language coupled with a belief that moral norms could not govern the conduct of states. Reinforcing the views of the early Cold War realists were the arguments of ideological crusaders who conceived of the struggle with Communism as a kind of holy war, as well as those of American nationalists who, like General Sherman, believed that "war is hell" and that the merciful thing is in fact to wage it ruthlessly. Members of these several groups supported the need for covert action against Communism either because they believed that the exceptional circumstances of the times required it or because they judged that it was simply one of the methods that states used to struggle with each other.[3]

But it is clear that even the authors of the Doolittle report were uncomfortable with the "repugnant philosophy" that they deemed necessary. Indeed, although covert political action became an important tool of U.S. policy, America never completely abandoned its moral traditions. The threat of international Communism, however, became a compelling rationale for covert action, to the extent that many operations needed no more specific justification. Thus the Cold War, and the perceived severity of the Soviet threat, made it possible for policymakers to ignore competing ethical considerations when they endorsed covert actions.

This Cold War rationale began to crumble in the late 1960s with popular opposition to the Vietnam War and the subsequent revelation in congressional inquiries of abuses by the CIA. The result was that greater attention has been paid to the process of managing covert actions. Until recently, however, despite changes in decisionmaking and oversight mechanisms, the Soviet threat was a dominant consideration in most covert action decisions.

COVERT ACTION AND THE
NEW WORLD ORDER

Since the dismantling of the Berlin Wall, the abortive coup in the Soviet Union, and the dissolution of the Soviet empire, the confluence of ideological, nationalist, and realist thought that formed a compelling rationale for covert action in the early Cold War period has lost more validity. In a dangerous world, however, presidents probably will not eschew this particular element of foreign policy, even in a "new world order." The Persian Gulf war shows that aggression by hostile states remains a threat to U.S. interests, and other challenges such as terrorism, narcotics trafficking, and the potential for proliferation of weapons of mass destruction are likely to motivate the U.S. to consider covert responses. What frame of reference, then, should replace the Cold War philosophy that has shaped covert action policy since the founding of the CIA?

Although the ideological crusade, American nationalism, and political realism dominated U.S. thinking about international affairs in the immediate post-World War era, there are other enduring philosophical traditions. Some emphasize the ends of policy (utilitarianism and Marxism); others are "rule-based" (international law and Kant's rationalism are in this category).[4]

One of the "rule-based" traditions has received greater attention in recent years. This is the natural law tradition, and in particular its rules regarding the use of force by states, which fall under the rubric of "Just War Theory." Just War Theory was used extensively by the Bush Administration in explaining its decision to go to war, under UN auspices, against Iraq.[5] More recently, a symposium of jurists, philosophers, theologians, government officials and military officers affirmed that Just War Theory is useful in deliberations regarding low-intensity conflict.[6]

JUST WAR THEORY

The origins of the Just War Theory can be traced to Saint Augustine in the 4th century A.D., and especially to Saint Thomas Aquinas, who extended and codified it in the 13th century. Just War Theory is in essence a set of guide-lines for going to war (the so-called *jus ad bellum*), and for the conduct of hostilities (*jus in bello*).[7] Though largely associated with Catholic scholars, Just War Theory is not a religious teaching per se, but rather part of a tradition of theological and philosophical thought, dating from Aristotle, which emphasized the importance of ethical processes in decisionmaking.

Aquinas specified three conditions for the decision to go to war: the action must be ordered by proper authority, the cause must be just, and the authority must have a right intention of promoting good or avoiding evil.[8] Other authorities subsequently added three further criteria: the action must be a last resort and all peaceful alternatives must have been exhausted, there must be a reasonable probability of success, and the evil and damage which the war entails must be proportionate to the injury it is designed to avert or the injustice which occasions it.[9]

Once these conditions are met, the belligerent is subject to two further constraints in seeking his military objectives: his actions must be directed against the opponent, not against innocent people; and the means of combat must "be proportionate to the just ends envisioned and must be under the control of a competent authority."[10]

The first of these constraints has been further refined, under the "principle of double effect," to encompass situations in which injury to innocent parties is unavoidable. Aquinas formulated the principle as follows: "There is nothing to hinder one act having two effects, of which one only is the intention of the agent, while the other is beside his intention. But moral acts receive their species from what is intended, not from what is beside the intention, as that is accidental."[11]

Under this principle, then, a belligerent may, if there is good reason, be justified in permitting incidental evil effects. The conditions governing this, however, are held by most commentators to be exceedingly strict. For example, the action taken must not be evil in itself; the good effect, and not the evil effect, must be intended; and the good effect must not arise out of the evil effect, but both must arise simultaneously from the action taken.[12]

Modern political theorists have continued the Just War tradition and focused primarily on the criterion of just cause. Currently, the majority school of thought appears to favor the view that the only justifiable cause for armed conflict is to repel aggression. Traditionally, however, there were two other acceptable causes: to retake something wrongfully taken and to punish wrongdoing.[13] Another area of debate has been whether forcible intervention in another state could be justified in order to reform that state's political system, for example, in the case of flagrant human rights abuses.[14]

THE THEORY AND COVERT ACTION

But what can an arcane theological and philosophical doctrine that is more than 1,600 years old and which was codified to regulate war during the Middle Ages have to do with covert action following the collapse of Communism? At least one former practitioner, William Colby, has argued that "a standard for selection of covert actions that are just can be developed by analogy with the longstanding efforts to differentiate just from unjust wars."[15] Perhaps more to the point, former Director of Central Intelligence (DCI) William Webster has noted that in its deliberations, the CIA's Covert Action Review Group explores three key questions regarding a proposed covert action: "Is it entirely consistent with our laws? Is it consistent with American values as we understand them? And will it make sense to the American people?"[16] With respect to the last two considerations, a reformulation of the Just War criteria in commonsense terms would probably appeal to the American people. It seems fair to conclude that the people would want the government to undertake covert actions only if:

- The action is approved by the President, after due deliberation within the Executive Branch and with the full knowledge and concurrence of appropriate members of the Congress.

• The intentions and objectives are clearly spelled out, reasonable, and just.
• There is a reasonable probability of success.
• The methods envisioned are commensurate with the objectives.

Moreover, in conducting covert action, it is reasonable to presume that the American people would approve of methods that minimize physical, economic, or psychological injury to innocent people and that are appropriate to the threat and under firm U.S. control.[17]

Formulated this way, the Just War guidelines seem to be directly applicable to covert paramilitary operations or other actions involving the use of violence or coercion. Those who advocate or approve such covert actions, however, bear the additional burden of demonstrating why they must be conducted covertly. As ethicist Sissela Bok has pointed out, every state requires a measure of secrecy to defend itself, but when secrecy is invoked citizens lose the ordinary democratic checks on those matters that can affect them most strongly.[18] In addition, a special problem of operational control can arise when intermediaries (agents) are employed—because their aims may differ from ours, and because the chain of command may be ambiguous or unreliable.[19] Finally, most covert actions will necessarily lack the public legitimacy and legal status under international law of a declared, justifiable war. This makes it incumbent on those advocating such actions to take into account the consequences of possible public misunderstanding and international opprobrium.

THE CHILE CASE

It would appear that a framework similar to the Just War Theory could be useful in evaluating covert actions that result in economic dislocation, distortion of political processes, or manipulation of information, because these cause suffering or moral damage, as war causes physical destruction.[20] To explore this, consider how the guidelines would have applied to two instances of covert U.S. intervention in Chile, in 1964 and 1970.[21]

The 1964 Election Operation

As part of its worldwide buildup of covert action capabilities in the early 1950s, the CIA established a capacity to conduct covert propaganda and political influence operations in Chile. In 1961, President Kennedy established a hemispheric policy to promote the growth of democratic institutions, the Alliance for Progress. That same year, the President became convinced that the Chilean Christian Democratic Party shared his belief in democratic social reform and seemed to have the organizational competence to achieve their common goals. It lacked the resources, however, to compete with the extremist parties of the left and right.

During 1961, the CIA established relationships with key political parties in Chile, as well as propaganda and organizational mechanisms. In 1962, the Special Group (the interagency body charged with reviewing covert actions) approved two CIA proposals to provide support to the Christian Democrats. The program was modeled on that conducted in Italy in the late 1940s and 1950s, and it was intended to strengthen center-democratic forces against the leftist challenge from Salvador Allende, who was supported by the Soviet Union and Cuba. When President Johnson succeeded Kennedy, he continued the covert subsidies, with the objective of making Chile a model of democracy, as well as preventing the nationalization by a leftist government of the Chilean components of American multinational corporations.

The Chilean presidential election of 1964 came down to a battle between Allende and Eduardo Frei Montalva, a liberal Christian Democrat. The election was viewed with great alarm in Washington. *The New York Times* compared it to the Italian election of 1948, when the Communists had threatened to take over the country through the ballot box, and the U.S. had intervened covertly to support democratic parties. Similarly, in 1964 the Johnson administration intervened in Chile, according to the Church Committee report, to prevent or minimize the influence of Chilean Communists or Marxists in the government that would emerge from the election. Cord Meyer, a former CIA covert action manager, argues that the intervention was for the purpose of preserving the Chilean constitutional order.

In considering the 1964 election operations, the Johnson administration used the established mechanism, the interagency Special Group. By 1963, according to Professor Gregory Treverton, the Special Group had developed criteria for evaluating covert action proposals. All expenditures of covert funds for the 1964 operation (some $3 million in all) were approved by the Group. (There is no indication that the Congress approved these expenditures or was even informed in detail of the operation.) In addition, an interagency committee was set up in Washington to manage the operation, and it was paralleled by a group in the U.S. Embassy in Santiago. Meyer contends that covert intervention on behalf of Christian Democratic candidates had wide support in the administration, and the Church Committee confirms that the covert action was decided upon at the highest levels of government.

During the early 1960s, the U.S. pursued a dual-track policy in Chile, conducting covert action in support of broader, overt objectives. Overtly, the U.S. undertook a variety of development programs, and Chile was chosen to become a showcase of such programs under the Alliance for Progress. Between 1964 and 1969, Chile received well over $1 billion in direct, overt

U.S. aid—more per capita than any other country in the hemisphere. Moreover, funding to support the Frei candidacy was funneled overtly through the Agency for International Development, as well as secretly through the CIA. Frei also received covert aid from a group of American corporations known as the Business Group for Latin America. Thus, the U.S. used a variety of mechanisms to assist Frei. Covert support apparently was justified by the U.S. Government on the grounds that Frei would be discredited if it were known that even more substantial support was flowing from the U.S.

That the 1964 covert action had a reasonable probability of success is evident from the outcome—Frei won a clear majority (56 percent) of the vote. According to Church Committee records, a CIA postmortem concluded that the covert campaign had a decisive impact. It is not clear from the available records whether a calculation of the likelihood of success was a specific part of the decisionmaking process. According to Treverton, the CIA was required under Special Group procedures to make such an estimate, and it is likely that its view would have been optimistic, because by the mid-1960s the Agency had managed to penetrate all significant elements of the Chilean Government and political parties. In the 1964 operation, the CIA used virtually its entire arsenal of nonlethal methods:

- Funds were passed through intermediaries to the Christian Democrats for their own use.
- The CIA provided a consultant to assist the Christian Democrats in running an American-style campaign, which included polling, voter registration, and get-out-the-vote drives.
- Political action operations, including polls and grassroots organizing, were conducted among slum dwellers, peasants, organized labor, and dissident Socialists.
- CIA-controlled assets placed propaganda in major Chilean newspapers and on radio, erected wall posters, passed out political leaflets, and organized demonstrations. According to the Church Committee, some of this propaganda used "scare tactics" to link Allende to Soviet and Cuban atrocities.
- Other assets manufactured "black propaganda," material falsely purporting to be from Allende and his supporters, and intended to discredit them.[22]

Significant constraints were imposed, however. Paramilitary and other lethal methods were not used. The CIA explicitly rejected a proposal from the Chilean Defense Council to carry out a coup if Allende won. The Department of State turned down a similar proposal from a Chilean Air Force officer. Moreover, the Special Group turned down an offer from a group of American businessmen to provide funds for covert disbursement by the

CIA. According to the Church Committee, the Group considered this "neither a secure nor an honorable way of doing business."

The 1970 Elections and "Track II"

Under Chilean law, Frei could not serve two consecutive terms as president. As the 1970 elections approached, the U.S. faced a dilemma. The Christian Democrats had drifted to the left, and they were out of step with the Nixon administration's policy views. (The principal architect of those views was Henry Kissinger, who as an academic had been a prominent member of the realist school.) The conservative candidate, Jorge Allesandri, was not particularly attractive to the U.S., but there was even greater concern about an Allende victory.

The CIA began to warn policymakers early in 1969 that an Allende victory was likely. In March 1970, the 303 Committee (successor to the Special Group) decided that the U.S. would not support any particular candidate. Instead, it authorized the CIA to conduct a "spoiling operation," aimed at discrediting Allende through propaganda. The effort failed when Allende won a slim plurality in the 4 September election. Because no candidate won a clear majority, the election was referred to a joint session of Congress, which in the past had always endorsed the candidate who had received the highest popular vote. The joint session was set for 24 October 1970. Senior U.S. officials maintained that their preoccupation with Allende was defensive and aimed at allaying fears of a Communist victory both abroad and at home. As Nixon noted in a *New York Times* interview:

> There was a great deal of concern expressed in 1964 and again in 1970 by neighboring South American countries that if Mr. Allende were elected president, Chile would quickly become a haven for Communist operatives who could infiltrate and undermine independent governments throughout South America.[23]

Kissinger noted that what worried the U.S. was Allende's proclaimed hostility and his perceived intention to create "another Cuba." He maintained that nationalization of American-owned property was not the issue, though he did emphasize U.S. interest in adequate compensation.

The Intelligence Community, however, held a more nuanced view. According to an assessment by the CIA's Directorate of Intelligence:

> Regarding threats to U.S. interests, we conclude that:
>
> 1. The U.S. has no vital national interests in Chile. There would, however, be tangible economic losses.
> 2. The world balance of power would not be significantly altered by an Allende government.

3. An Allende victory would, however, create considerable political and psychological costs:

- Hemispheric cohesion would be threatened by the challenge that an Allende government would pose to the OAS, and by the reactions that it would create in other countries. We do not see, however, any likely threat to the peace of the region.

- An Allende victory would represent a definite psychological setback to the U.S. and a definite psychological advance for the Marxist idea.[24]

Kissinger tacitly acknowledged the lack of vital U.S. interests in Chile when he called it "a dagger pointed at the heart of Antarctica."

When Allende won a plurality of the popular vote, the thrust of U.S. covert action shifted to preventing his accession to the presidency. The objective had now become to stop Allende by manipulation of the congressional vote. The committee asked Edward Korry, the U.S. Ambassador in Santiago, for a "cold-blooded assessment" of the likelihood of mounting a coup and organizing an effective opposition to Allende. With negative evaluations from both Korry and the CIA, the committee met on 14 September and explored a "Rube Goldberg" gambit, in which Alessandri would be elected by the Congress and then resign, thus allowing Frei to run in a second election. The ploy was turned down.

By this time, Nixon had taken a personal role. He met on 15 September with Donald Kendall, chief executive officer of Pepsi Cola, and Augustine Edwards, an influential Chilean publisher who had supported Frei during the 1964 election. According to Kissinger, Nixon was incensed by what he heard, and decided that more direct action was necessary. As a result, he called in DCI Richard Helms and ordered a major effort to prevent Allende's accession. The CIA was instructed to play a direct role in organizing a military coup. Further, Helms was directed not to coordinate the CIA's activities with the Departments of State and Defense and not to inform Ambassador Korry. The 40 Committee was not informed, nor was the Congress. This activity became known as "Track II," to distinguish it from the 40 Committee program, "Track I."[25]

Track II was a carefully guarded secret, but U.S. displeasure with the prospect of an Allende victory was not. According to Kissinger, all agencies were working to prevent the election. The Chilean Government was threatened with economic reprisals, and steps were taken to inform the Chilean armed forces that military aid would be cut off. Separately from the CIA's effort, several large American companies had financed Alessandri's campaign. One company, ITT, offered the CIA $1 million, but Helms turned it down.

When Helms left the Oval Office on 15 September, he had a page of handwritten notes. The first entry read, "less than one in ten chance of success." His pessimistic assessment was echoed by Ambassador Korry. According to his correspondence with the Church Committee, Korry consistently warned the Nixon administration that the Chilean military was no policy alternative. From Santiago, according to the Church Committee documents, the CIA reported: "Military action is impossible; the military is incapable and unwilling to seize power. We have no capability to motivate or instigate a coup."

This view was shared by the managers of Track II. According to David Phillips, chief of the CIA's Chile Task Force, both he and his immediate supervisor were convinced that Track II was unworkable. The CIA's Deputy Director for Plans, Thomas Karamessines, was adamant that the Agency should not refuse the assignment, but he personally briefed Nixon several times on the progress of the operation, always pessimistically.[26]

Track I included funding to bribe Chilean congressmen, propaganda and economic activities, and contacts with Frei and elements of the military to foster opposition to Allende. Track II was more direct, stressing active CIA involvement in and support for a coup without Frei's knowledge. The CIA specifically offered encouragement to dissident Chilean military officers who opposed Allende, but who recognized that Gen. Rene Schneider, the Chilean Chief of Staff, would not support a coup. These dissidents developed a plan to kidnap Schneider and take over the government, and this became known to CIA officials. Two unsuccessful kidnap attempts were made, and on the third attempt, on 22 October 1970, General Schneider was shot and subsequently died. Both the Church Committee and the Chilean inquiry concluded that the weapons used were not supplied by the U.S. and that American officials did not desire or encourage Schneider's death. Neither, however, did they prevent it.

Unlike 1964, the 1970 covert operation did not involve extensive public-opinion polling, grassroots organizing, or direct funding of any candidate. Moreover, Helms made it clear that assassination of Allende was not an option. And when a right-wing Chilean fanatic, Gen. Arturo Marshall, offered to help prevent Allende's confirmation, the CIA declined because of his earlier involvement in bombings in Santiago.

Evaluating the Two Operations

A Just War theorist reviewing the two covert operation would likely reach two conclusions: first, the 1964 operation was more justifiable than the 1970 activity, which would not have been approved if the officials concerned were natural law advocates rather than realists or ideological crusaders; and, second, both operations would have benefited from a more rigorous application of the *jus ad bellum* and *jus in bello* criteria.

U.S. authorities probably would have considered that their covert intervention in the 1964 election was generally consistent with the *jus ad bellum*.

It had clear objectives: preservation of an important democratic force in Chile and defense against the establishment of another Communist stronghold in the Western hemisphere. These were set by President Kennedy, based on his assessment of the commonality of U.S. and Chilean interests. While not strictly speaking a last resort, it was conducted in the context of, and consistently with, an overall overt policy (the Alliance for Progress); was likely to be successful; and the overall effort was limited in scope and generally proportionate to the perceived threat It was approved in accordance with the established procedures, though in retrospect the process would have been strengthened if the Congress had been consulted.

Some doubts can be raised regarding consistency with the *jus in bello*. The need for "scare tactics" and "black propaganda" is not obvious. (If indeed Allende's affinities for the USSR and Cuba were on the public record, promulgation of this truthful information should have been adequate.) Such activities inherently carry the possibility of distortion and deception. As Sissela Bok notes, lying and deception carry a "negative weight." They require explanation and justification, while the truth, including presumably the "truth" promulgated through propaganda mechanisms, does not.[27] If not clearly justifiable in terms of necessity or to respond to Cuban or Soviet activities, such deceptive actions would not meet the test of proportionality of the *jus in bello*.

The 1970 Track II operation, in contrast, violated virtually all the Just War guidelines, though this might not have been of great consequence to those who directed it. Its objective was to prevent Allende's confirmation, but little thought apparently was given to the consequences for the Chilean people or the political system. The normal consultative process was bypassed, and Nixon made the fateful Track II decision in a state of high emotion.[28] No expert believed that success was likely. The methods chosen were initially inadequate and subsequently, when support for coup plotting took center stage, the intermediaries could not be controlled. What began as a nonlethal action quickly turned lethal. Despite the fact that injury to innocent parties was a foreseeable outcome of the envisioned coup, no advance provision was made to prevent or minimize it. In light of the intelligence assessment that the U.S. lacked vital interests in Chile, it is hard to rationalize support for a potentially violent military coup as a proportionate response.

In sum, the Chile case shows that Just War Theory can provide a useful framework for evaluating covert political action by asking certain penetrating questions: Is the operation directed at a just cause, properly authorized, necessary, and proportionate? Is it likely to succeed, and how will it be controlled? Is it a last resort, a convenience, or merely an action taken in frustration? In the case of the 1964 operation, the answers to most of these questions were satisfactory; in 1970, they were not.

REFORMS SINCE THE 1970s

In the more than two decades since Track II, significant improvements have been made in controlling covert action. The old doctrine of "plausible denial," which allowed senior officials to disclaim responsibility for their actions, has been replaced by one intended to secure direct presidential accountability. Beginning with the Hughes-Ryan Amendment of 1974, a series of laws has been enacted requiring the president personally to "find" that proposed covert actions are important to the national security, and to report such operations to Congress in a timely manner. (Debate has continued over what constitutes a timely notification.) In the wake of the Iran-Contra scandal, it became obvious that the system of presidential "Findings" needed to be strengthened, and even more stringent procedures were implemented, first by the Executive Branch and then by the Congress.

Under the current system, established by the Reagan administration in 1987 and refined by legislation in 1991, a written Finding must be signed before a covert action operation commences, except that in extreme circumstances an oral Finding may be made and then immediately documented in writing. A Memorandum of Notification (MON), also approved by the president, is required for a significant change in the means of implementation, level of resources, assets, operational conditions, cooperating foreign countries, or risks associated with a covert action. Each Finding or MON includes a statement of policy objectives and goals; a description of the actions authorized, resources required, and participating organizations; a statement that indicates whether private individuals or organizations of foreign governments will be involved; and an assessment of risk. Each proposed Finding or MON is reviewed by a senior committee of the National Security Council (NSC), and coordinated with the NSC Legal Adviser and with the Counsel to the President. Copies of Findings and MONs are provided to the Congress at the time of notification, except in rare cases of extreme sensitivity.[29]

TAKING A NEW APPROACH

These reforms are positive, especially with regard to the criterion of proper authority, because they provide for broader consultation, a legal review, presidential accountability, and congressional involvement in covert action decisions. However, the content of Findings and MONs, as described above, leaves much to be desired from the perspective of Just War Theory. If, as the Chile case suggests, explicit use of Just War guidelines can strengthen the ethical content of covert action, more emphasis should be placed on the substance of discussions, not just the mechanics of the process. Further, the now widely accepted view that Just War Theory can be used to justify and explain resort to armed force strongly suggest that a similar approach would be useful in framing substantive debate on covert political action. In short, the current system addresses the legality, feasibility, and political sensitivity of proposed covert actions.[30] It does not, however, ensure that they are right, according to a widely accepted ethical standard.

To come closer to this ideal, it is important that, at each stage in the covert action approval process, difficult questions be asked about the objectives, intentions, methods, and management of a proposed operation. It is equally important that they be answered in detail, with rigor, and in writing—even (perhaps especially) when time is of the essence. Covert operators are understandably reluctant to commit sensitive details to paper, but this seems essential if the U.S. is to meet high standards of morality and accountability in an era in which the easy rationalization of fighting Communism is no longer available.

A decisionmaking process structured explicitly around Just War guidelines is, in many ways, simply a restatement of Judge Webster's criteria of consistency with law, American values, and public mores. In that sense, Just War criteria merely reiterate the obvious and make explicit the goals that the U.S. has striven toward in its reforms of the covert action process since the mid-1970s. But there is value to building a more systematic framework for substantive debate, constructed from specific questions derived from Just War Theory, even if many of these questions are already considered in the CIA's Covert Action Review Group, the senior NSC groups, or the oversight committees. The questions of concern include:

Just cause. Exactly what are the objectives of the operation? Is it defensive—to repel an identifiable threat—or is it intended to redress a wrong, to punish wrongdoing, or to reform a foreign country? Who or what are we conducting the operation against? Who are we for? What specific changes in the behavior or policy of the target country, group, or individual do we seek?

Just intention. What will be the likely result in the target country and in other foreign countries? How will we or the international community be better off? How will we know if we have succeeded? What will we do if we win? If we lose?

Proper authority. Who has reviewed the proposal? Are there dissents? What is the view of intelligence analysts on the problem being considered? Have senior government officials discussed the proposal in detail? Has the Congress been advised of all significant aspects of the covert activity? If notification has been restricted, what is the justification?

Last resort. What other policies have been tried? Why have they not been effective? What overt policy options are being considered? What are their strengths and weaknesses? Why is covert action necessary? Why must the proposed activity be secret?

Probability of success. What is the likelihood that the action will succeed? Are there differing views of the probability of success? Is the view of disinterested observers different from that of advocates or opponents? Why? What is the evidence?

Proportionality. What specific methods are being considered? Does the proposal envision the use of lethal force, sabotage, economic disruption, or false information? Why are these methods necessary? Are they the same as those being used by the adversary, or are they potentially more damaging or disruptive? If so, what is the justification?

Discrimination and control. What steps will be taken to safeguard the innocent against death, injury, economic hardship, or psychological damage? What will be done to protect political institutions and processes against disproportionate damage? If some damage is inevitable, what steps are being taken to minimize it? What controls does the U.S. exercise over the agents to be employed? What steps will be taken if they disregard our directions? What steps will be taken to protect the agents, and what are our obligations to them? How will the operation be terminated if its objectives are achieved? How will it be terminated if it fails?

Each of these questions should be investigated at some step of the initial approval process, though some clearly exceed the competence of the CIA. Perhaps the NSC Staff and the congressional oversight committees are the most appropriate bodies to probe these issues. Not all may be answerable at the outset, though this fact alone should signal caution. In addition, they should be posed again whenever there is a significant change in objectives, methods, or circumstances. The current management process calls for an annual review of all covert actions by the NSC, as well as periodic examinations by the oversight committees. These questions can guide such reviews as well.

THE CASUISTRY OF COVERT ACTION

Rigorous examination of the questions enumerated above would emulate the technique of moral reasoning recommended by the natural law tradition. This method, known as casuistry, is acknowledged by scholars to be complex and difficult, especially in cases involving politics and international affairs.[31] Moreover, in the hands of advocates, Just War criteria can deteriorate into mere rationalizations of intended actions. Just War Theory, then, can be exceedingly useful as an organizing principle, but in itself does not necessarily provide clear answers.[32] How can the inherent uncertainty of this casuistry, and its potential misuse, be minimized?

William Colby has suggested that our process of moral reasoning concentrate primarily on the criteria of just cause and proportionality.[33] These fundamental points do indeed appear to be the keys to an effective process of policy formulation. With respect to just cause, a recent report by a panel of distinguished scholars has recommended that covert action should be undertaken only in support of a publicly articulated policy.[34] Such an approach would ensure that the objectives of the policy could be debated publicly, even though some of the exact methods to be employed might be known to only a small group of elected and appointed officials. Open, public debate would go a long way toward determining whether a proposed course of action could be construed as a just cause. The need for such debate is so fundamental to the casuistry of covert action that, if it cannot be conducted, this in itself would seem to be grounds for rejection of any suggested operation.

Assessments of proportionality are not susceptible to the same kind of open scrutiny, because they involve specific descriptions of secret methods. Nevertheless, it is important to ensure that proposed activities meet strict tests of consistency with American values and mores. Just War Theory does not offer specific guidance for such choices, despite its stress on necessity and minimal damage to innocent parties. Loch Johnson, a longtime commentator on intelligence activities, has suggested that, in addition to having a sound ethical framework, decisions on covert action must take into account other factors, such as the type of target regime and the severity and immenence of the threat that is to be countered.[35] These would seem to be useful guides to evaluating proportionality, to which could be added the types of actions, overt or covert, being undertaken by the target regime against U.S. interests.

Johnson has also tried to rank-order various types of covert operations into a 38-rung "ladder of escalation," and he introduces a useful concept of "thresholds" that involve different degrees of risk and interference in foreign countries.[36] Following Johnson's concept, proposed covert activities could be arrayed for debate under thresholds of increasing ethical concern as follows:

Limited concern. Benign provision of truthful information or support to existing political forces; intervention to keep election processes honest.

Significant concern. Manipulative use of information; rigging of elections or other distortion of political processes; creating new opposition forces or increasing the strength of existing ones out of proportion to their indigenous support.

Serious concern. Deceptive use of information, nonlethal sabotage, and economic disruption.

Grave concern. Use of lethal force; forcible changes in government.

Such actions are often taken in combination, rather than step by step in a scenario of escalation. Moreover, the amount or degree of covert support provided will vary in significance and moral weight depending on the nature of the foreign countries involved. And, as noted above, it is necessary to justify the actions proposed and the need to carry them out secretly. But clarity about what is being done, and whether or not it is proportional to the threat and proposed objectives, is a key element in sound policymaking.

CONCLUSION

Such an application of the Just War framework would not end controversy regarding covert action, nor would it guarantee that inappropriate or unethical actions will not be taken in the future. Debate over just cause and proportionality are likely to be particularly difficult—especially when, as was the case in U.S. policy in Central America, there is no political consensus—but these are precisely the elements that most require informed scrutiny. Those who oppose covert action in all forms will not be reassured by a process based on the Just War framework; realists or crusaders will see it as unnecessary and unduly restrictive; Executive Branch officials and members of Congress may perceive that they already probe these questions in one way or another; and bureaucrats will regard it as just another "paper exercise." The claim for a conscious application of Just War guidelines is a modest one: it will help to make more rigorous Judge Webster's commonsense criteria, and to improve the quality of decisions regarding one of the most controversial aspects of U.S. national security policy.

More generally, in light of recurring problems in the use of covert action as an instrument of policy, and the fact that it is likely to remain in the arsenal of states for the foreseeable future, greater rigor and structure in debates over specific proposals are essential. Reforming the process along the lines suggested would signal that the U.S. is concerned—even in secret activities—with issues of right and wrong and not merely with power. It would promote openness and accountability and underscore that we firmly reject the "repugnant philosophy" of the Doolittle report.

NOTES

1. "Report of the Special Study Group (Doolittle Committee) on the Covert Activities of the Central Intelligence Agency, 30 September 1954 (excerpts)," in William M. Leary, ed., *The Central Intelligence Agency, History and Documents* (The University of Alabama Press, 1984), p. 144.

2. Jack Donnelly, "Twentieth-Century Realism," in Nardin and Mapel, eds., *Traditions of International Ethics* (Cambridge University Press, 1992), p. 93.

3. The author is indebted to the Rev. John P. Langan for this typology of Cold War political thought. Letter to the author, 28 May 1992.

4. A penetrating assessment of covert action from the perspective of international

law can be found in W. Michael Riesman and James E. Baker, *Regulating Covert Action* (New Haven: Yale University Press, 1992).

5. See James Turner Johnson and George Weigel, *Just War and the Gulf War* (Washington, DC: Ethics and Public Policy Center, 1991).

6. *Symposium on Moral and Legal Constraints on Low-Intensity Conflict,* sponsored by the Office of the Assistant Secretary of Defense for Special Operations and Low-Intensity Conflict, U.S. Naval War College; Newport, RI, April 1992.

7. National Conference of Catholic Bishops, *The Challenge of Peace* (Washington, DC: U.S. Catholic Conference, 1983), pp. 25–29.

8. Thomas Aquinas, *Summa Theologica,* Joseph Rickaby, SJ., trans. (London: Bums and Gates, 1892), Question XL, Article 1.

9. National Conference of Catholic Bishops, *op. cit.,* pp. 29–32.

10. Aquinas, Q. XLI, Art. I.

11. Aquinas, Q. XLIV, Art. VII.

12. Paul Ramsey, *War and the Christian Conscience* (Duke University Press, 1969), pp. 47–8.

13. The classic modern work on Just War Theory is Michael Walzer, *Just and Unjust Wars* (New York: Basic Books, 1977).

14. Charles R. Beitz, "Recent International Thought," *Ethics and International Affairs,* 1989, Vol. 3, p. 190.

15. William E. Colby, "Public Policy, Secret Action," *Ethics and International Affairs,* 1989, Vol. 3, p. 63.

16. Address to the Eighth Circuit Judicial Conference, 12 July 1991.

17. There is some empirical research that suggests a correlation between these classic Just War criteria and American attitudes regarding war and peace. See Donald Secrest, Gregory G. Brunk, and Howard Tamashiro, "Moral Justification for Resort to War With Nicaragua: The Attitudes of Three American Elite Groups," *Western Political Quarterly,* September 1991, pp. 541–559.

18. Sissela Bok, *Secrets: On the Ethics of Concealment and Revelation* (New York: Pantheon Books, 1982), p. 191.

19. Charles R. Beitz, "Covert Intervention as a Moral Problem," *Ethics and International Affairs,* 1989, Vol. 3, pp. 49–50.

20. Langan notes that Just War Theory has both material and formal aspects, and that the formal aspects, such as just intention and proportionality, are applicable to a broad range of situations where one has to do harm to another, including punishment, surgery, and—by extension—political or economic intervention. (Langan, *op. cit.*)

21. The following discussion is drawn primarily from documents of the Church Committee, which investigated CIA covert actions in the mid-1970s, as well as memoirs of some of the participants and other government officials and commentators. (These include William Colby, Henry Kissinger, Cord Meyer, David Atlee Phillips, and Arthur Schlesinger.) A summary of the Church Committee's findings, and recommendations for reform, can be found in Gregory Treverton, *Covert Action: The Limits of Intervention in the Postwar World* (New York: Basic Books, 1987). A case study based on Treverton's research has been published by the Carnegie Council on Ethics and International Affairs; an abridged version appeared in *Studies In Intelligence,* Winter 1992.

22. United States Senate, *Staff Report of the Select Committee to Study Government Operations with Respect to Intelligence Activities: Covert Actions in Chile, 1963–73.* (Washington, DC: U.S. Government Printing Office, 1975) pp. 15–17.

23. 12 March 1976.

24. Assessment dated 7 September 1970, declassified and quoted in the Church Committee report.

25. The U.S. decision process is described in detail in the Church Committee report, *Alleged Assassination Attempts Involving Foreign Leaders,* as well as in Kissinger's memoirs and John Ranelagh, *The Agency: The Rise and Decline of the CIA* (New York: Simon and Schuster, 1986), pp. 514–520.

26. David Atlee Philips, *The Night Watch* (New York: Ballantine Books, 1977), pp. 283–287.

27. Sissela Bok, *Lying: Moral Choice in Public and Private Life* (New York: Random House, 1978), p. 30.

28. Another tenet of the natural law tradition, the notion of *prudentia* or prudence in statecraft, cautions against such hasty and passionate decisions. See Alberto R. Coll, "Normative Prudence as a Tradition of Statecraft," *Ethics and International Affairs,* 1991, Vol. 5, pp. 36–7.

29. *National Security Decision Directive (NSDD)* 286, partially declassified on 15 December 1987; *Intelligence Authorization Act, Fiscal Year 1991,* Title VI.

30. "Political sensitivity" can sometimes become a euphemism for morally questionable activities. This semantic twist means that such activities are then discussed as though they were merely political rather than ethical issues.

31. Joseph Boyle, "Natural Law and International Ethics," in Nardin and Mapel, *op. cit.,* p. 115.

32. The author is indebted to Joel Rosenthal of the Carnegie Council on Ethics and International Affairs for this point (Letter to the author dated 12 May 1992).

33. Colby, *op. cit.* Colby concentrates on the self-defense aspect of just cause.

34. *Report of the Twentieth Century Fund Task Force on Covert Action and American Democracy* (New York: Twentieth Century Press, 1992), p. 8.

35. Loch K. Johnson, "On Drawing a Bright Line for Covert Operations," *American Journal of International Law,* Vol. 86, No. 2, April 1992, pp. 296–7.

36. *Ibid.,* p. 286. Johnson's analysis is complicated by his mixing of traditional intelligence collection activities with covert actions, and his attempt to rank-order both categories hierarchically. At the lowest level of escalation ladder, Johnson enumerates routine, passive activities to collect information. Above his first threshold of risk and interference he lists the placement of truthful, benign information in the foreign press, and low-level funding of friendly political groups. His second threshold involves the placement of "contentious information" in the media, large-scale funding of foreign groups, economic disruption without loss of life, limited supplies of arms, small-scale hostage-rescue attempts, and disinformation. Above his highest threshold are large-scale and potentially violent acts, including major secret wars, assassination plots, and hostage taking. Johnson argues that actions in this category should never be undertaken by the U.S. He also includes in this list of proscribed actions the supply of sophisticated weapons. This, however, would appear to be an option that might be considered in response to specific, serious threats.

17

Ethics of Covert Operations

Loch K. Johnson

"We must learn to subvert, sabotage and destroy our enemies by more clear, more sophisticated and more effective methods than those used against us," advised a secret annex to a presidential commission (the Doolittle report to the Hoover Commission) in the 1950s. The United States would have to "fight in the back alleys of the world," concluded Secretary of State Dean Rusk a decade later. "Must the United States respond like a man in a bar-room brawl who will fight only according to Marquis of Queensberry rules?" a retired senior intelligence officer rhetorically asked in the 1980s. Even when the Cold War had come to an end, a former intelligence official continued to emphasize the "ruthlessness that international espionage requires."[1]

Should one conclude from these perspectives that intelligence activities must be set apart from moral considerations? The first section of this chapter presents a "ladder of escalation" for covert operations, based on a rising level of intrusion abroad as policy officers climb upward from low-risk to high-risk activities. The second briefly surveys leading ethical, philosophical, and practical issues involved in trying to evaluate the effects of secret intelligence activities. The final section offers a set of guidelines for evaluating the propriety of proposed covert operations, from clandestine collection to counterintelligence and covert action. Despite a tendency for commentators on national security to overlook the subject of covert intervention abroad, the topic is important. For in contemporary global relations, secret acts of hostility between nations occur frequently.[2]

266

A LADDER OF ESCALATION
FOR COVERT OPERATIONS

In 1965, the strategist Herman Kahn of the Hudson Institute published an influential volume in which he offered an "escalation-ladder metaphor" for understanding the coercive features of international affairs. Kahn described the ladder as a "convenient list of the many options facing the strategist in a two sided confrontation."[3] It addressed primarily the overt manifestations of hostile acts carried out by one state against another, building from low-level expressions of enmity ("subcrisis maneuvering," which included political, economic, and diplomatic gestures, as well as—a step up—solemn and formal declarations of displeasure) and continuing ultimately to "spasm or insensate war": Rung 44, a full-scale nuclear exchange.

Similarly, covert operations can be arrayed for heuristic purposes according to their degree of intrusiveness abroad, from non-forcible to forcible intervention (with all the accompanying caveats Kahn advanced regarding the limitations of a ladder metaphor).[4] In a ladder of escalation for covert operations, the underlying analytical dimension traveling upward is the extent to which most observers would view the options as increasingly serious violations of international law and national sovereignty, and, therefore, as intensified assaults on the international order.

THRESHOLD ONE: ROUTINE
INTELLIGENCE OPERATIONS

At the lower end of the ladder for covert operations—Threshold One—are arrayed such relatively benign activities as routine sweeps of a nation's own embassy facilities overseas to detect possible electronic implantations and the giving of instruction and security equipment to enhance the personal safety of friendly foreign leaders against threats to their lives (Rung 1 counterintelligence/security measures). Also at this threshold is the assignment of intelligence officers to gather information from foreign officials in their normal daily rounds, say, at an embassy reception (a Rung 2 collection operation). At this threshold, too, low-level information is exchanged between friendly intelligence services by intelligence "liaison" officers (Rung 3)—a common arrangement among Western democracies. The following is a partial ladder of escalation for intelligence options:

C = collection of intelligence
S = security
CE = counterespionage
P = covert propaganda

POL = political covert action
E = economic covert action
PM = paramilitary covert action

Threshold Four: Extreme Options

38. Use of chemical-biological and other deadly agents (PM)
37. Major secret wars (PM)
36. Assassination plots (PM)
35. Small-scale coups d'etat (PM)
34. Major economic dislocations; crop, livestock destruction (E)
33. Environmental alterations (PM/E)
32. Pinpointed retaliation against noncombatants (PM)
31. Torture (POL/C)
30. Hostage taking (POL/C)
29. Major hostage-rescue attempts (PM)
28. Theft of sophisticated weapons or arms-making materials (PM)
27. Sophisticated arms supplies (PM)

Threshold Three: High-Risk Options

26. Massive increases of funding in democracies (POL)
25. Small-scale hostage-rescue attempt (PM)
24. Training of foreign military forces for war (PM)
23. Limited arms supplies for offensive purposes (PM)
22. Limited arms supplies for balancing purposes (PM)
21. Economic disruption without loss of life (E)
20. Large increases of funding in democracies (POL)
19. Massive increases of funding in autocracies (POL)
18. Large increases of funding in autocracies (POL)
17. Sharing of sensitive intelligence (C)
16. Embassy break-ins (CICE)
15. High-level, intrusive political surveillance (C)
14. High-level recruitment and penetrations (CICE)
13. Disinformation against democratic regimes (P)
12. Disinformation against autocratic regimes (P)
11. Truthful but contentious information in democracies (P)
10. Truthful but contentious information in autocracies (P)

Threshold Two: Modest Intrusions

9. Low-level funding of friendly groups (POL)
8. Truthful, benign information in democracies (P)

7. Truthful, benign information in autocracies (P)
6. Stand-off TECHINT against target nation (C)
5. "Away" targeting of foreign intelligence officer (C/CE)
4. "Away" targeting of other personnel (C)

Threshold One: Routine Operations

3. Sharing of low-level intelligence (C)
2. Ordinary embassy-based observing and conversing (C)
1. Passive security measures; protection of allied leaders (S)

These activities represent little or no serious infringement of a nation's sovereignty and the widely held view that nations should not intervene blatantly in one another's internal affairs (the "noninterventionist norm"). They are widely practiced, with minimal international repercussions.[5] The first rung (counterintelligence/security measures) represents the least controversial of all the intelligence activities carried out between states, since every nation maintains some form of passive defense—most put in place within the defending nation's own territories with no intrusion against another nation, a basic shield against attack.

THRESHOLD TWO: MODEST INTRUSIONS

With Threshold Two, the degree of intrusiveness begins to escalate, and with it the risks involved in using the intelligence option. This category could include attempts to recruit, say, a foreign ministry clerk somewhere outside his or her homeland—in this sense "away" (Rung 4, collection); recruitment attempts against a low-level intelligence officer, still *outside* the target nation but more risky than the previous rung because an intelligence officer— someone with access to the target nation's deepest secrets—becomes the specific object of recruitment (Rung 5, counterespionage); and the use of distant (or "stand-off") technical intelligence (TECHINT) surveillance against the target nation—high-altitude reconnaissance satellites, for instance (Rung 6, collection).

This category would also include the insertion of truthful covert propaganda material on relatively noncontroversial themes (say, on the importance of preserving NATO) into the foreign media outlets of nondemocratic regimes as a means of reinforcing overt policy pronouncements (Rung 7, covert action); again propaganda, but this time targeted against democratic regimes with a free press (Rung 8, covert action); and the payment of modest sums to political, labor, intellectual, and other organizations and individuals abroad favorably disposed toward one's foreign policy objectives (Rung 9, covert action). All of these examples represent common and widely, if begrudgingly, accepted practices, even though they obviously infringe on a nation's sovereign rights. Even violations of a nation's airspace by satellites and reconnaissance airplanes—TECHINT collection methods once considered highly provocative—are now largely accepted (with existential resignation) as part and parcel of international affairs in the modern age of surveillance.

Still, the lines of demarcation between acceptable and unacceptable intervention can be fuzzy and controversial. Texts on the subject published by the United Nations General Assembly have elicited divided views from members. One illustration comes from the Special Committee on Friendly Relations, established by the General Assembly. In 1967 it reported the opinion of some committee members that covert propaganda and the secret financing of political parties represented "acts of lesser gravity than those directed towards the violent overthrow of the host government."[6] Other Assembly representatives, however, rejected this perspective—especially those who wished to avoid legitimizing covert operations that (in their view) had harmed their nations in the past. As a result of this divided opinion, the special committee equivocated, neither supporting nor prohibiting covert propaganda and secret political funding. A perspicacious student of the committee's work has concluded: "The texts that the General Assembly approved represent compromise formulations that are open to multiple interpretations."[7]

THRESHOLD THREE: HIGH-RISK OPERATIONS

Threshold Three marks a series of steps toward dangerous covert activity that could trigger within the target nation a response damaging to international comity. Key features of this escalation zone include close-up, on-the-ground, direct operations against more sensitive targets, including activities within the target nation's own territory, as well as the use of methods and material that can lead to violence.

This third category consists of more intense covert actions. At Rungs 10 and 11, propaganda operations remain truthful and in accord with the overt policy statements of the sponsoring nation; but now they pump into the media of nondemocratic and democratic regimes more contentious themes—say, in the days before the end of the Cold War, attributing the prowess of the West European peace movement to financial and propaganda support from Soviet intelligence agencies.

At Rungs 12 and 13 (maintaining the distinction between nondemocratic and democratic regimes), propaganda activities take a nastier turn, employing deception and disinformation that run contrary to the aggressor nation's avowed public policies—say, falsely blaming an adversary for an assassination attempt or falsifying documents to stain an adversary's reputation.[8] Even propaganda operations against nations without free media are of concern here (albeit less so than against democracies), because of the "blowback" or "replay" phenomenon by which information directed toward adversaries abroad can find its way home to decide citizens in democratic regimes with free media.[9]

At Rung 14, an intelligence service "pitches" (that is, tries to recruit) a high-level potential agent or defector inside the target nation or attempts a high-level penetration into the opposition service—again on the adversary's own turf (counterespionage). The recruitment carries higher risks still if the potential agent is in the employment of a foreign intelligence service with a controversial record of real (or suspected) human rights abuse; or if the potential agent has been implicated in wrongdoing within his or her own country.

In 1995 it became public that Julio Roberto Alpirez, a colonel in the Guatemalan army charged with complicity in the murder of a leftist guerrilla and an American innkeeper in Guatemala, had served as a CIA agent. For months media stories in the United States pilloried the Agency for its unsavory ties in Guatemala and elsewhere, while "senior CIA officials" defended themselves as best they could by paraphrasing Henry Kissinger's famous remark that espionage should not be confused with missionary work.

If policymakers wanted to know what was going on in the world, argued defenders of the Alpirez relationship, the CIA and the American people would have to hold their noses and pay those foreign agents best able to provide the necessary information about their government's intentions, the whereabouts of narcotics dealers, and the entry of suspected terrorists into their country. "In cases of counterterrorism and counternarcotics," said John M. Deutch, DCI to President Clinton, "we are, of necessity, drawn into relationships with people of questionable character." The director made it clear, however, that there would be limits and ordered his general counsel to determine what the intelligence community should do about agents who "may have violated human rights or U.S. law."[10]

The Agency's inspector general, Frederick P. Hitz, offered this remedy in his still-classified seven-hundred-page report on the Alpirez case: fire any agent involved in narcotics, terrorism, human rights violations, or transgressions against any American law.[11] The Hitz report underlined another disturbing feature of the case: once again the CIA had failed to report an impropriety to its congressional oversight committees, as the law required.

At Rung 15, the aggressor undertakes intrusive surveillance operations (wiretaps, for instance) against prominent political leaders within their own native country. Or the aggressor may employ TECHINT or HUMINT "tradecraft"—the techniques or modus operandi of intelligence officers and their agents—against the target nation's highest decision councils (a collection operation); if discovered, a serious diplomatic rift could likely result.

At Rung 16, the covert aggressor attempts a break-in (a "second-story" or "black-bag" job) against a target nation's embassy, either in a foreign capital or in the aggressor's own capital (collection and counterespionage)—operations considered extremely risky and requiring high-level approval when resorted to by the government of the United States.[12] Rung 17 involves the sharing of intelligence with other secret services; but unlike Rung 3, in this case the information is highly sensitive—say, related to U.S. nuclear targeting plans, offered in an effort to gain greater attack coordination among NATO nations should war break out against the West. (A U.S.-French example is presented in table 17.1.)

Rungs 18 and 19 reflect first a large and then a massive increase in funding for covert political purposes in an autocratic regime—in a poor country a rise in secret expenditures of $1 million, then $5 million, or $10 million and then $20 million in a more affluent one. These large amounts of money can have a significant effect on elections, particularly within a small developing country. It is these sizable sums that no doubt most concerned those members of the General Assembly special committee who opposed permissive language that would condone non-forcible covert influence in the domestic politics of other nations.[13]

Again, as with propaganda, a distinction is made between nondemocratic target nations, at Rungs 18 and 19, and those which are democratic, at Rung 20. Interference in the internal affairs of democracies is considered a more serious step—all the more so if the operation is designed to rig a free election, in contrast, say, to building up a political party between elections (though the distinctions here can be fine). In a similar fashion, Damrosch argues that "a political system that denies basic political rights is in my view no longer a strictly internal affair," but rather one properly subject to international interventions.[14]

At Rung 21, the aggressor undertakes limited covert attacks against economic entities within the target nation. A power line is destroyed here, an oil storage depot contaminated there; perhaps labor strikes are encouraged inside the adversary's major cities—all carefully planned to remain within the limits of harassment operations, with a low probability that lives will be lost.

At Rung 22, a nation resorts to paramilitary operations (arms supplies) to counter weapons already introduced into a territory by an adversary. The United States might provide a modest supply of unsophisticated but still deadly arms to a favored rebel faction (or factions) as a means of balancing the correlation of forces in a civil war. At Rung 23, the weapons are supplied to a friendly faction without prior intervention by an outside adversary; and Rung 24 involves the secret training of foreign armies or factions for combat

Table 17.1 Examples of Western Intelligence Operations since 1945 Arrayed on the Ladder of Escalation.

Threshold	Nation	Operation
Four	United States	Paramilitary action in Laos (1960s); assassination plots in Cuba and the Congo (1960s)
	United Kingdom	Paramilitary operations in Albania (1949), Iran (1953), and Oman (1960s)
	Chile	Assassination *of* Ambassador Orlando Letelier (1976)
	South Africa	Assassination plots in Zimbabwe (1980s)
	Israel	Assassination of PLO leader (1980) and other assassination plots, bombing *of* nuclear reactor storage sites in France (1979), paramilitary actions in Egypt (1950s), theft of uranium oxide (1968)
	France	Sinking *of* the *Rainbow Warrior* (1985), sabotage and various assassination plots against leaders in Algeria and Egypt (1950s) and Libya (1980)
Three	Israel/U.S. Israel	Covert weapons sales to Iran (1986)
	Israel	Training Sri Lanka security forces (1984)
	West Germany	Economic disruption in Guinea (1958)
	U.S./France	Sharing of sensitive nuclear intelligence (1970s–)
	United Kingdom	Propaganda in the Middle East (1950–1960s)
Two	United States	TECHINT surveillance worldwide
	France	Spying on U.S. officials in Paris (1964)
	United Kingdom	Worldwide intelligence collection
One	U.S./U.K.	Sharing of low-level intelligence
	United States	Assisting security of Egyptian leaders (1978), worldwide U.S. embassy security

Sources: Threshold Four: Colby and Forbath, *Honorable Men* (on Laos); S. Rept. No. 465, 1975 (on assassination plots); Andrew, *Her Majesty's Secret Service,* 492–93 (on U.K. in Albania); Richelson, *Foreign Intelligence Organizations,* 26; Roosevelt, *Countercoup* (on U.K. in Iran); David Charters, "The Role of Intelligence Services in the Direction of Covert Paramilitary Operations" in Maurer, Tunstall, and Keagle, eds., *Intelligence: Policy and Process,* 339 (on U.K. in Oman); G. Lardner, "Pinochet Linked to Murder Cover-Up," *Washington Post* (Feb. 5, 1987), AI (on Chile); S. Rule, "Trial in Zimbabwe Leads to Pretoria," *New York Times* (June 18, 1988), A3 (on South Africa); Raviv and Melman, *Every Spy a Prince,* and Richelson, 203, 205–10 (on Israel); B. and M.-T. Danielson, *Poisoned Reign* (1986) (on the *Rainbow Warrior*); and Richelson, 163, 167 (on France). Threshold Three: S. Rep. No. 216 and H. Rep. No. 433 (1987); Cohen and Mitchell, *Men of Zeal,* 235, and Richelson, 204–5 (on Israeli arms sales to Iran); Raviv and Melman, "Killing of Wazir Ruthless and Inefficient," *Los Angeles Times* (Apr. 22, 1988), AI, and Richelson, 204 (on Israel) and 167 (on W. Germany); R. H. Ulmann, "The Covert French Connection," *Foreign Policy* 75 (Summer 1989), 3 (on U.S.-French intelligence sharing); and Richelson, 26 (U.K.). Threshold Two: Bamford, *The Puzzle Palace,* and D. Kahn, "Big Ear or Big Brother?" *New York Times* (May 16, 1976), 13 (on U.S. TECHINT operations); Richelson, 160 (on France); and Richelson and Ball, *Ties That Bind* (on U.K. espionage). Threshold One: Richelson and Ball, *Ties That Bind* (on U.S.-U.K. intelligence sharing); S. M. Hersh, "Congress Is Accused of Laxity," *New York Times* (June 1, 1978), AI (on security equipment for Egypt) and Johnson, *America's Secret Power,* 31–35.

(for an Israeli-Sri Lankan example, see table 17.1). Rung 25 envisages a hostage rescue attempt that could involve loss of life, but one carefully designed to be small in scale so as to limit the potential for losses—the Son Tay village raid in Vietnam in contrast to the more ambitious Iranian rescue attempt during the Carter administration.[15]

At Rung 26, massive expenditures are dedicated to improving the political fortunes of friendly factions within a democratic regime (around $20 million in a small democracy and $50 million or more in a larger one), in hopes of bringing them to power—tampering with electoral outcomes in free societies (political covert action). Attempts at covertly influencing truly democratic elections—those in which the rights of political dissent and opposition are honored—represent violations of the noninterventionist norm (and related rules of international law) and have no claim to legitimacy, in contrast to operations directed against self-interested autocratic regimes.

THRESHOLD FOUR: EXTREME OPTIONS

With Threshold Four, a nation enters an especially dangerous and controversial realm of intelligence activities—a covert "hot zone." Here is where the lives of innocent people may be placed in extreme jeopardy. At Rung 27, the types of weapons provided to a friendly faction are more potent than at earlier rungs. Rebellious factions inside the target nation (or within its theater of war) are secretly supplied with highly sophisticated weapons—say, Stinger and Blowpipe antiaircraft missiles—that enable them to take the offensive, causing a drastic escalation in the fighting. The 1988–89 Afghanistan scenario, in which the CIA provided anti-Communist rebels with such weapons, is a good example. Rung 28 represents access to sophisticated weapons through theft, the most extreme case being the stealing of nuclear bombs—or the material for making them, as Israeli intelligence has been accused of doing (see table 17.1).

At Rung 29, hostage rescue operations present a nation with the prospect of extensive casualties—what President Bush referred to in 1989 as "collateral damage" (civilian deaths) in a public explanation of his rejection of this approach, for the time being, to freeing U.S. hostages held by terrorist groups in Lebanon.[16] At Rung 30, the taking of hostages, force is intended, carefully planned, and directed against specific individuals. Opposition intelligence personnel or foreign leaders are kidnapped ("arrested") for information (a collection operation), for instance, or as pawns in secret negotiations (political and paramilitary covert action). An illustration is the 1989 abduction by Israeli commandos of Sheik Abdul Karim Obeid, a leader of the Party of God, a pro-Iranian faction in Lebanon believed to have been holding three Israeli soldiers.

At Rung 31, hostages are tortured in a cruel attempt to coerce compliance in a hostage swap or some other deal (political covert action) or to obtain information (collection). At Rung 32, acts of brutality are directed against lower-level noncombatants in retaliation for hostile intelligence operations (counterespionage).

Beginning with Rung 33, intelligence activities escalate to include violence-laden economic covert actions as well as paramilitary operations against targets of wider scope—often affecting sizable numbers of noncombatants in the civilian population. The aggressor intelligence agency tries to bring about major environmental alterations, from the defoliation or burning of forests to the contamination of lakes and rivers, the creation of floods through the destruction of dams, and even operations (tried by the United States during the war in Vietnam) to control weather conditions through cloud seeding in hopes of ruining crops and bringing about mass starvation. At Rung 34, the aggressor attempts to wreak major economic dislocations within the target nation by counterfeiting currencies to fuel inflation and economic chaos (as the CIA has been reported to have done against Saddam Hussein in 1990–91), sabotaging industrial facilities, or perhaps destroying crops by introducing agricultural parasites into the fields or spreading hoof-and-mouth disease among livestock.

Rung 35 intimately involves the aggressor intelligence service in the overthrow of a foreign adversary—though at this rung with minimal intended bloodshed (such as in Guatemala in 1954). Rung 36 designates the assassination of specific foreign officials—murder of the highest order. Finally, at the top of the escalation ladder are two forms of secret warfare that inevitably affect large numbers of combatants and noncombatants: the launching of protracted, full-blown covert warfare against an inimical regime, with the sponsoring, combat-ready intelligence officers guiding indigenous rebel armies comparable in scope to the CIA's lengthy "secret" war in Laos during the 1960s (Rung 37); and the possibility of spreading biological, chemical, or other toxic substances to bring about widespread death in the target nation (Rung 38).[17]

The examples of intelligence operations presented in this section have been drawn largely from the American experience. The various official investigations into the U.S. intelligence community conducted in 1975–76 and in 1987 provided a rich source of data on the activities of the American secret services since 1947. Further, the scholarly research on American intelligence stimulated by the new data is much more extensive than anything available about the secret agencies of other nations. Yet it must be emphasized that most developed nations in the West (and certainly the former USSR in the East) have vigorously engaged in most of the operations found on the ladder of escalation presented earlier in the chapter.[18] The public record on intelligence operations carried out by Western nations other than the United States is sparse because these nations have been more successful in concealing their "dark arts" from public scrutiny; nevertheless, table 17.1 presents some illustrations from other countries (as well as from the United States) to underscore the point that covert intelligence operations are a global phenomenon.

The primary usefulness of the ladder metaphor resides in the opportunity it affords for a visual inspection of covert options, roughly organized according to the growing risk and degree of violence involved in their implementation (and the rising moral qualms and legal controversies that attend them). Ladder construction is an opening exercise toward accomplishing the more difficult task of drawing a "bright line" separating acceptable intelligence operations from those that may be rejected as unacceptable.

INFLUENCES ON THE USE
OF COVERT OPERATIONS

What, if anything, is beyond the pale of acceptability in the spectrum of strategic intelligence operations? Can—and should—a "bright line" be drawn, proscribing certain repugnant covert practices? A considerable amount of printer's ink has been devoted to these important questions.[19] The issues are complex, and good people part company in response.[20] As with most complicated social topics, where one stands regarding the usefulness and legitimacy of intelligence options depends on one's education, socialization, evolving political and international perspectives ("operational codes")[21] and peer group influences, not to mention global circumstances and media reporting, among other influences on the formation of foreign policy belief. Before attempting to answer the difficult bright-line question, it may be useful to consider at least briefly some key influences that shape a person's attitudes toward covert operations.

ETHICAL PERSPECTIVES

How one views the place of ethics in the conduct of international affairs provides an indication of how one will assess intelligence options. "Do no evil, though the world shall perish," admonished the eighteenth-century German philosopher Immanuel Kant. Taken to the extreme for intelligence operations, the Kantian school would reject every rung on the ladder of escalation beyond the first. This was the spirit in which Secretary of State James Stimson initially decided to close down his department's cryptographic division in 1929, politely explaining that "gentlemen do not read each other's mail."[22] One undersecretary of state suggested that the United States "ought to discourage the idea of fighting secret wars or even initiating most covert operations [because] when . . . we mine harbors in Nicaragua . . . we fuss the difference between ourselves and the Soviet Union. We act out of character . . . When we yield to what is, in my judgment, a childish temptation to fight the Russians on their own terms and in their own gutter, we make a major mistake and throw away one of our great assets."[23]

At the opposite ethical extreme is a point of view so nationalistic that virtually any use of secret intelligence agencies in defense of the nation-state becomes acceptable. The consequences of one's acts are more important, from this vantage point, than the intrinsic worthiness (or unworthiness) of the acts themselves. If the consequence is to help preserve the citizenry of a nation against a foreign threat, the act is justifiable. In light of the present anarchic and hostile world environment, a nation must defend itself in every possible way, including the use of all the dark arts available through the auspices of secret services—thus the Doolittle report, Rusk's war in the back alleys, and the rejection of Marquis of Queensberry rules. G. Gordon Liddy, a former CIA operative and Watergate conspirator, stated this point of view more colloquially on the campus lecture circuit: "The world isn't Beverly Hills; it's a bad neighborhood at two o'clock in the morning."[24] The CIA would have to act accordingly.

In between the poles of Kantian and consequentialist morality lies a vast expanse of intelligence options less pure in form than the two extremes of "Do no evil" and "Do anything." Even consequentialists like Gen. James Doolittle, Rusk, and Liddy would no doubt disagree on how far a nation ought to march down the road of "anything goes." Certainly Secretary Rusk had a more refined sense of moral limits than G. Gordon Liddy. In making moral judgments about covert options in this middle ground, most analysts would not blanch at the measures listed for Thresholds One and Two on the ladder of escalation. Ethical debate can grow quite heated, however, over the more intrusive interventions against national sovereignty envisaged at Thresholds Three and Four.

Yet even those ethicists who generally prefer nonintervention are prepared to acknowledge the existence of certain conditions in which the aggressive use of secret intelligence agencies abroad may be in order. Foremost among these conditions, for some analysts, is simple self-defense—a central stanchion in the traditional theory of the just war (though the term "self-defense" can be notoriously slippery).[25] High on the list too is the moral imperative to help people who face enslavement, wholesale brutality, or genocide—covert intervention on humanitarian grounds.[26] (See table 17.1.)

Others would add to this list the need to assist oppressed friends of Western democratic values who ask for help (or, during the Cold War, at least those who were anti-Communists)—a considerable opening of the interventionist door.[27] Going a step further, some ethicists would defend the sovereign independence of any state, regardless of regime type; they prefer to honor above all the inviolability of national boundaries as a central postulate of contemporary international law. This was the main public defense of the U.S. insistence, supported by the United Nations in 1990, that Iraq remove its invasion force from neighboring Kuwait.[28] Some would use only the degree of force that was proportional to the perceived threat—another central postulate of the just-war theory.[29]

Still others would eschew most unilateral actions, seeking greater moral legitimacy in multilateral intervention.[30] Practical considerations are also essential to some analysts. They argue that to be acceptable, covert intervention must have a good chance of succeeding and should be in harmony with the overt policy positions of the sponsoring nation.[31]

Although these propositions (as with the wider literature they briefly summarize) are clouded in ambiguities, the spires of four fundamental conclusions poke through the mist. The first, expressed by two intelligence officials, posits that "given the depravity of the world around us . . . free societies have no choice but to engage in intelligence activities if they are to remain free."[32] The underlying assumption here—one accepted by most contemporary scholars, government officials, and citizens—is an acceptance of the preeminence of the nation-state and the correctness of its defense. World order theorists have a different vision, perhaps ultimately a better one, in which global human needs gain ascendancy over state interests; but, for the present at least, their arguments remain quixotic.[33]

If one accepts the need for some intelligence activities, the next question becomes: Which ones are acceptable? At this point the second major ethical conclusion emerges, namely, that this determination depends morally on the extent to which one is willing to accept loss of life and the physical destruction of property as a part of a covert intervention.[34] Here are the considerations that give pause to Threshold Four and lend it the name "Extreme Options."

A third major conclusion follows from the second: agreement on the moral acceptability of low-threshold intelligence activities is widespread, but the appropriateness of higher-threshold activities is a topic riven by dissension. As a former DCI properly notes, "There are few absolutes in the ethics of covert action."[35] Experts and laypersons alike are frequently of two minds on when or even whether covert violence ought to be part of a nation's foreign policy.

In light of this disagreement, the fourth conclusion—a procedural one that lies at the heart of this book and of my earlier studies on intelligence—is that no single authority ought to make this important decision. Rather, in a free society it is appropriate that decisions on contentious issues be made by a group of elected officials (though, for sensitive intelligence matters, one small in size and whose deliberations are conducted in secrecy). In a democracy the great moral issues of covert intervention warrant debate, even if it is confined to a more limited number of elected officers than normally participate in policy deliberations. These often far-reaching choices stand to benefit significantly from the advantages of a candid dialogue between the branches, from the airing of different points of view, and the sharing of experience and insight—in a word, from democracy.

Difficult ethical issues may not be resolved in any definitive fashion by a group decision process, but pooling the moral judgments of leading officials gives a better chance at arriving at a worthy outcome than entrusting the results to one or two individuals deciding alone. This, at any rate, is the gamble that underpins the theory of constitutional government.

VIEW OF THE ENEMY

Just as ethical perspectives are important in determining the proper level of intrusiveness abroad, so too is one's perception of the adversary. For some, the adversary is so venal, so intractable, so dangerous—the devil incarnate— that the us-them relationship can only be thought of as a zero-sum game in which any gain for one side must mean a defeat for the other. Mixing realpolitik with Bible-thumping morality, a chairman of the U.S. House Committee on Armed Services once referred to the Cold War as "a battle between Jesus Christ and the hammer-and-sickle."[36] Extreme intelligence options designed to subdue the Soviet Satan became acceptable, even attractive.

Others hold a more hopeful outlook, viewing the adversary as someone with whom one might deal—cautiously, to be sure—in order to achieve positive gains for both sides. Attitudes toward an enemy can change—witness Ronald Reagan's transition from denouncing the Soviet Union as an "evil empire" to rejecting this bleak characterization a few years later—and as they do, harsh intelligence options directed against the foe may become unacceptable.[37]

TARGET REGIME

The nature of the target regime can be another factor in assessing the ethics of covert operations. Some analysts believe that in selecting intelligence options, it makes a difference whether one has targeted free and open societies or closed totalitarian and authoritarian regimes. In targeting the former, they argue, one ought to be more circumspect and less intrusive. As regards the latter, restraints can be fewer—especially against the totalitarian regimes, which (the argument goes) represent a greater threat to Western civilization than authoritarian ones.[38]

Take covert propaganda. To interfere with the free press in a democracy say, the *Times* of London or New York—is abhorrent to some, striking at the root of Western values. But since during the Cold War *Pravda* and *Isvestia* were widely considered mere organs of the Soviet Communist party, their content was fair game.[39]

LEADERSHIP PERSONALITY

The personal characteristics of the DCI can move policy officers toward particular views on the efficacy and appropriateness of the various intelligence options. The Reagan administration's first DCI, William J. Casey—by reputation a hard-core, zero-sum, anti-Communist tough guy—seemed more prepared to climb rapidly up the ladder of escalation than some of his predecessors. For example, William E. Colby, a Nixon appointee, was more of a pragmatist who acknowledged some moral restraints on covert operations and harbored some sense of the possibilities for detente with the Soviet Union.[40]

Funding for covert action declined precipitously under Colby and rose sharply under Casey. Although the causes of covert-action budget trends extend far beyond the personalities of the DCIs, the directors' individual perspectives on the world certainly have played a role.

IMMINENT THREAT

If information is the sine qua non of good decisionmaking, time keeps it close company.[41] An assessment of intelligence options depends on one's sense of imminent threat to the national security. If (to use an extreme scenario) a nation's leaders believed that a major city was about to be vaporized by a nuclear device stolen by terrorists, they would no doubt use every means available to avoid this calamity. Constitutional safeguards would be thrown out the window. Even the assassination of the suspected terrorists would be an option if the nation's leaders were persuaded that murder would prevent the nuclear annihilation of millions—a consequentialist's imperative. Given the luxury of more time (the normal circumstance), the ladder of escalation can be climbed more prudently and with greater deliberation.

SEVERITY OF THE THREAT

As the nuclear scenario implies, the perceived severity of the threat is also relevant. Terrorists armed with nuclear weapons demand a quick and highly intrusive response. In contrast, Greenpeace environmentalists in creaky old sailing ships protesting nuclear testing in the Pacific Ocean represent a much more modest threat to a nation's sovereignty, warranting at best a low-rung covert response (if any at all).

Clearly, the 1983 bombing of Greenpeace's *Rainbow Warrior* in Auckland harbor by two French intelligence officers, in which a Greenpeace photographer was killed, represents a response far out of proportion to the threat. The bombing was a provocative slap at New Zealand's sovereignty, not to mention an infringement of the civil liberties of the ship's owners and passengers. If the French had felt that their interests were so threatened by the *Rainbow Warrior* (a "bucket of bolts," according to a high-ranking New Zealand national security official), disabling the ship at sea with a low-charge explosion on the propeller shaft—or even with tangled wire—would have been enough covert action to deter its further passage.[42]

Prevailing conditions of war or peace are necessary considerations as well. If one nation is involved in an overt military conflict with another nation, whether or not war has been formally declared, its leaders have decided that the threat to their national interests is sufficiently grave to warrant a major foreign policy response. In these conditions—and especially in circumstances of a formally declared war—covert operations are likely to be stepped up. Indeed, assassination plots against the adversary's leaders, along with other extreme measures, become standard—although even the rules of open warfare proscribe some activities, such as the use of chemical and biological agents against noncombatants. In times of overt warfare, *almost* anything goes when it comes to supportive intelligence options.

SHORT-TERM AND LONG-TERM EFFECTS

Ideally, one would also like to know before judging the appropriateness of a covert operation what its effects will be on the future of the target nation, its people, and their relationship with the perpetrator of the covert operation. Such prognosticating is the most difficult task of all.

To what extent does the United States (or other nations using covert operations) have a confident sense of the historical forces their secret activities may unleash? Very little, especially over the long term. Certainly the United States was unable to anticipate how despised the shah of Iran would become within his own nation after the CIA (and British intelligence) helped him into power in 1953.[43]

The inherent difficulty of predicting long-range historical results has been exacerbated by the lack of knowledge the United States has sometimes exhibited concerning the circumstances within target nations. Ignorance of Fidel Castro's wide popularity in Cuba—a phenomenon well appreciated by

CIA analysts in the Directorate of Information but not by paramilitary covert-action specialists in the Directorate of Operations, who had closer ties to the Kennedy administration—led White House officials to endorse the ill-fated Bay of Pigs operation. Can-do covert-action bureaucrats displaced the more scholarly intelligence analysts from the decision process, leaving policymakers with a one-sided view that Castro could easily be toppled.[44]

Though mistakes and misjudgments are inevitable, governments contemplating covert intervention ought at a minimum, as Charles Beitz has stressed, "to know enough about the culture and values of the target society to make informed judgments about its welfare, and enough about its politics and history to calculate the likely consequences of the kinds of intervention contemplated."[45] This level of understanding requires greater attention by decisionmakers to the recommendations of intelligence analysts and outside academic experts. It is worth remembering, however, that covert-action specialists themselves can be insightful, and their views ought to be weighed. Operations Directorate case officers often have more direct knowledge and experience from having lived in the target country than anyone else in the American government.

A BRIGHT LINE ON THE
LADDER OF ESCALATION

Where should the line be drawn against excessive covert operations? No single policy officer, not even a president, can settle the answer. Each covert operation requires inspection. A decision must draw on the substantive knowledge and ethical wisdom of a small number of well-informed individuals: elected officials in the executive and legislative branches (assisted by their top aides), who understand the theory and practice of intelligence, have studied the conditions in the target nation and its region, and, most significant in a democracy, are sensitive to the likely attitudes of the American people toward the proposed secret intervention.

THE IMPORTANCE OF PROCESS

Making ethical decisions about covert operations requires a thorough decisionmaking process. The process should involve elected officials with national security experience, assisted by well-trained intelligence and foreign policy specialists who understand the possibilities—as well as the dangers and limitations—of using clandestine agencies in support of democratic values.

Who should stand within this "witting circle" of intelligence decisionmakers? The model in use in the United States approaches a good balance between secrecy and accountability. Important initiatives are first scrutinized by intelligence professionals, then by top policy aides in the executive branch, followed by their principals (including, since 1975, formal presidential approval for covert actions); finally, operations are vetted by the House and Senate Intelligence Committees. In times of emergency, the number of legislative participants is limited to just the top eight leaders of Congress.[46]

Ambiguity and controversy have surrounded these procedures, especially over whether the congressional Intelligence Committees (or at least the Gang of Eight) should be notified prior to all important intelligence operations. Following passage of the 1980 Intelligence Oversight Act, which seemed to require prior notice (though the language contained ambiguities), the White House failed to honor this understanding in only a single known instance: the Iran-contra affair.[47]

The 1991 Intelligence Oversight Act clarified congressional expectations and at the same time yielded to the White House somewhat on the question of prior notice. The clarification came in the form of the first explicit statutory definition and authority for covert action, coupled with a reemphasis that prior notice was expected in most instances. But in times of emergency the president could delay his "finding" report to Congress for a few days. This proviso, inserted at the insistence of President Bush, overrode the understanding since the Hughes-Ryan Act in 1974 that reporting would occur within twenty-four hours.[48]

Most officials in the intelligence community, the White House, and the Congress have come to accept the "New Oversight" as an appropriate means for deciding on intelligence options while at the same time trying to keep the secret agencies within the bounds of American law and the prevailing sense of ethical propriety. The great tragedy of the Iran-contra episode was the disdainful attitude of high officials toward this delicate balance. Although according to one report "the intelligence scandals and institutional reforms of the 1970s remain living lessons in the secret world,"[49] obviously some individuals in the Reagan administration failed to get the message. Or, more likely perhaps, they understood but rejected the idea of legislative supervision of intelligence policy.[50] Gregory F. Treverton pinpoints the unfortunate implication: "Excluding Congress also excluded one more 'political scrub,' one more source of advice about what the range of American people would find acceptable."[51]

Why was Congress excluded? The administration's national security adviser, Vice Admiral John M. Poindexter, said he wished to avoid "any interference."[52] Nor did William J. Casey want legislators peering over his shoulder. According to testimony from Poindexter's assistant, Lieutenant Colonel Oliver L. North, the DCI sought nothing less than a secret entity (nicknamed "the Enterprise") "that was self-financing, independent of appropriated monies, and capable of conducting activities similar to the ones that we had conducted [during the Iran-contra operations]."[53] Investigators learned, moreover, that the Iran-contra conspirators had even excluded the president from their machinations, as a way of allowing the White House "plausible deniability"—a slippery doctrine bitingly criticized by the Church Committee a decade earlier.[54] In short, they excluded democracy.

The rejection of democratic procedures by NSC staffers during the Iran-contra affair points to another critical element of intelligence: the personal integrity of those holding positions of public responsibility. As the ancient Greeks well understood, the *forms* of government are but empty shells in themselves; they must be made to work by honest individuals who possess more than love for country. Leaders must also have a deep appreciation for the principles of democracy—a system of governing that, as a guard against the abuse of power, depends vitally on the kind of "interference" so disdainfully dismissed by Admiral Poindexter.[55] Military personnel are generally imbued with a strong sense of ethics and the importance of democratic procedure—above all, the idea of civilian supremacy in decisionmaking. The Iran-contra case, however, showed that this socialization sometimes fails to take.

Admiral Poindexter professes to have been the victim of a liberal attack aimed at the Reagan revolution.[56] How widely this view is shared is unknown, although some Republicans on the congressional Iran-contra investigating committees seemed prepared in their Minority Report to fully exonerate the admiral and his staff.[57] To many critics, however, the affair went much deeper than partisan politics, striking at the foundations of constitutional government by undermining the appropriations process, not to mention the sanctity of laws (the Boland Amendments limiting covert action in Nicaragua, among other statutes) and the established covert-action reporting requirements (the Hughes-Ryan Act and the 1980 Intelligence Oversight Act). During hearings and investigations into the affair, leading Republicans and Democrats—conservatives and liberals alike—spoke against the controversial operations of the NSC staff.[58]

Consequently, in speaking of process as vital to the selection of intelligence options, one must in the same breath add a caveat: in a democracy officeholders are expected to honor the laws and respect the rights and opinions of those to whom they owe their office—the people. In turn, the people in modern society are forced to rely chiefly on their elected surrogates in both Congress and the White House to monitor and assess the wisdom of secret foreign policy initiatives. When the surrogates are shut out, so are the people.

GUIDELINES FOR APPRAISING PROPOSED COVERT INTERVENTIONS

In a society where ethical standards can change, a case-by-case examination relying on a small bipartisan group of executive-legislative overseers is the most sensible approach to evaluating the acceptability of covert operations. This review process, however, need not begin anew each time; some widely accepted standards can provide at least general guidance to the deliberations.

Threshold Four

On the ladder of escalation (see earlier in this chapter), most observers would probably agree that the democracies can shun altogether the highest rung—the use of chemical-biological agents and other toxic substances. The other extreme options at this threshold (Rungs 27–37) should garner support in only the most extraordinary circumstances: when the survival of one's society is at stake (self-defense) or for humanitarian purposes when passivity might lead to enslavement, wholesale brutality, or genocide within a heinous regime.

One perplexing scenario at Threshold Four arises when an indigenous, democratically inclined faction asks for covert assistance to overthrow an autocratic regime or to repel foreign intruders. In such instances sophisticated arms supplies (Rung 27), small-scale coups (Rung 35), and even major "secret" wars—the classic oxymoron of an "overt-covert" intervention (Rung 37) may be worth considering. First, however, the prudent policy officer will want to see whether the pro-democracy faction displays signs of legitimacy among the indigenous populace, whether it has a viable leadership and a credible organization—that is, some reasonable chance of succeeding—and whether less extreme responses might work instead. Among the latter is massive funding to the pro-democracy faction (Rung 17) or, better still, open activity, including economic inducements and punishments, diplomatic negotiations, moral suasion, and organizational support.[59]

Above all, those who propose secret intervention must remember the risks of being drawn into a swamp of protracted and costly warfare, with no victory in sight—indeed, with the possible decimation of the supported faction. The fate of the Kurds in Iraq and the Meos in Laos, abandoned by the CIA to sure defeat after they had been encouraged and armed to fight for their freedom, is a painful reminder of this unfortunate outcome.

The temptation can be strong to move quickly forward toward Threshold Four in an effort to rid the world of an evil dictator. After a few failed attempts at mounting a coup against Panama's General Manuel Antonio Noriega,[60] the United States finally chose to depose him in 1989 through an overt military operation. In retrospect, though, even some analysts who normally reject clandestine intervention have wondered whether more persistent covert efforts to topple Noriega might not have been the lesser of two evils. The appeal of a coup or assassination in this and similar cases lies partially in the more limited loss of life that may accompany a stealthier approach to foreign policy than open warfare. Several hundred Panamanian civilians died in the U.S. attack against Noriega; thousands of Iraqi civilians perished in 1991 during the attack against Saddam Hussein's armies in the Persian Gulf. The avoidance of deaths among innocent noncombatants, a central tenet of the just-war tradition, is a principle that enjoys widespread support. Yet the promise of a quick coup or assassination—even though such tactics have the attraction of safeguarding innocent civilians—can draw a nation all too readily into unsavory remedies for its international grievances. Is it not better to renounce these dark and slippery options in favor of open military action (if all the other overt options have failed)—even if the cost in human lives may be higher than in a more narrowly focused paramilitary operation? If intervention had to be open and highly visible, with the possibility of considerable loss of life—civilian and military—policymakers might be inclined to think twice about the necessity for using force to influence affairs in other nations, and about the extent to which the American people would be likely to support the use of force.

More broadly, America's leaders might well consider whether it is really the responsibility of the United States to rid the world of its dictators and other assorted scoundrels. Does the United States have the resources—the blood, the treasure, the will—for this responsibility? Was Noriega—as revolting an individual as he was—a more heinous threat to U.S. interests than, say, the Colombian drug lords? Was his forced extradition to the United States as a drug dealer worth the lives of those people killed, American and Panamanian, during the invasion?

If force is to be used against a foreign dictator, a multilateral overt operation would be preferable to a U.S. paramilitary activity in all but a few extreme situations. Overt intervention itself, however, ought to be a matter of last resort, turned to only when American interests are directly and obviously assailed. For the most part, the sad problem of autocratic regimes must be combatted with diplomatic initiatives, trade sanctions (directed toward the adversary's rich, not the poor), and moral suasion by means of such tools as the increasingly strong force of worldwide media condemnation to make tyrants international pariahs. Above all, the United States must rely on the indigenous population itself to rise up against a cruel master, just as the American colonists did in 1776 and the courageous citizens of Eastern European nations and the Soviet republics did at the end of the Cold War. These democratic rebellions may warrant measured support, overt and covert, from the outside world—especially in places where political and other human rights have been suffocated.

There are two important exceptions where covert may be preferred to overt action: in self-defense against possible attack with weapons of mass destruction and for humanitarian purposes against autocrats with genocidal designs. If a dictator (or a renegade faction) is reliably believed to be on the verge of obtaining a capacity to use nuclear, biological, or chemical (NBC) weapons against other nations or groups, this threat must be dealt with before it is too late. In 1981 Israel chose an overt military air strike to destroy an Iraqi nuclear reactor near Baghdad thought to be used for making nuclear bombs; in 1991 the United States and its allies took advantage of the opportunity to seek the destruction of Saddam Hussein's NBC weapons capacities at the same time that they drove his troops out of Kuwait. In lieu of unilateral or multilateral actions of these kinds, a limited paramilitary strike (multinational, if possible) may be necessary in the future against an outlaw regime that threatens a chemical-biological or nuclear surprise attack.

Ideally, the covert action would involve a small force acting under the United Nations Security Council or other international authority, with the right of a U.S. veto and *with the most exacting supervision.* When diplomatic initiatives fail to curb the appetite of heinous regimes for weapons of mass destruction, this approach may serve as a better alternative—in the extreme instance of chemical-biological or nuclear threats—than a full-scale military invasion costing thousands of civilian lives.

The second exception is in response to a genocidal regime. Leaders who have engineered and encouraged mass murder invite arrest by a multinational paramilitary arm—again, ideally under the authority and supervision of the Security Council—followed by a fair trial before a respected international tribunal of jurists. The precedent for this exception was established after World War Two when Nazi leaders were put on trial at Nuremberg for crimes against humanity.

Threshold Three

The options of Threshold Three are similarly clouded by broad patches of gray. The best approach is to incline against their use, unless the reasons for accepting them are highly compelling. In the American system, during normal times, the president and the members of the congressional Intelligence Committees should be consulted; in times of emergency, the president and the "Gang of Eight." Moreover, policy officers should never turn to an option that would violate the laws of the United States, unless they believe—as did Lincoln in 1861—that the very survival of the nation is at stake if the law is honored. In such cases they must explain themselves thoroughly and be held accountable (through impeachment proceedings, if necessary) as soon as the danger subsides. For Thresholds Three and Four, those in power would do well to recall the prudent prescription tendered by John Quincy Adams in his inaugural address. America should be "the friend of all the liberties in the world, [but] the guardian of only her own."

Thoughtful critics have long emphasized the wisdom of reserving the more extreme covert options for only the most pressing circumstances. At congressional hearings in 1975 Cyrus Vance, soon to be named secretary of state by Jimmy Carter, thought they should be used only when "absolutely essential"; and Clark Clifford, a drafter of the National Security Act of 1947, testified that they should be undertaken only in circumstances that "truly affect our national security." In 1976 the Church Committee admonished that such measures should be contemplated only in response to "a grave, unforeseen threat"; more than ten years later the Majority Report of the Iran-contra Congressional Investigating Committees declared that they had to be "conducted in an accountable manner and in accordance with law."[61]

Thresholds One and Two

At the bottom of the escalation ladder, Thresholds One and Two will probably continue to be acceptable behavior in the eyes of most practitioners and observers. Perhaps even these options will be scaled back one day, if more nations embrace democracy and conduct their affairs in a more open fashion.

SPELLING OUT THE GUIDELINES

The preceding discussion suggests eleven guidelines by which the merits of proposed covert operations may be judged by policymakers and their overseers.[62]

1. Whenever possible, policymakers should shun covert operations in favor of a diplomatic resolution of international disputes.
2. Covert operations should be kept in harmony with publicly stated policy objectives, except in the rarest of occasions when deception is deemed vital to the safety of the United States.
3. Only those covert operations should be conducted which, if exposed, would not unduly embarrass the United States.
4. Before proceeding, policymakers should consult extensively with intelligence analysts and other experts on a target nation, not just covert-action specialists.
5. Policymakers should never bypass established decision procedures, including congressional reporting requirements (which ought to honor the concept of prior notice—except in times of the most acute emergency).
6. In support of covert operations, policymakers should never violate the laws of the United States, short of the rare need to save the nation in a time of desperation.
7. Against fellow democracies policymakers should eschew all but the most routine, low-level covert operations—unless a democracy is

engaged in activities inimical to the well-being of other democracies (such as abetting the illicit spread of weapons of mass destruction).

8. Even against non-democratic regimes, policymakers should strive to remain at the lower, less-intrusive end of the escalation ladder, applying the just-war rule of proportionality, and climb higher up the ladder only when all else fails.

9. Case officers should repeatedly warn foreign agents that their relationship with U.S. intelligence agencies will be terminated if they engage in acts of murder, terrorism, narcotics trafficking, human rights abuses, or violation of American law.

10. In almost all cases, policymakers should reject secret wars, coups d'etat, and other extreme measures, for if American interests are so jeopardized as to require major forceful intervention, then properly authorized overt warfare ideally multinational in nature and at the invitation of a legitimate government or faction is a more appropriate and honorable option.

11. In considering covert operations, America's long-standing and widely admired tradition of fair play should not be forgotten.

The first guideline may seem obvious enough. All too often, though, policy officers are tempted to try a silent "quick fix" through the use of covert action rather than to employ trained diplomatic negotiators—who themselves may have to engage in secret discussion with adversaries, a more acceptable process than clandestine intelligence operations. An overly hasty dismissal of the diplomatic approach in favor of a paramilitary hostage-rescue attempt in Iran led Secretary of State Cyrus Vance to resign in protest from the Carter administration.[63]

The second guideline, if followed, would have stopped the Reagan administration's secret sale of arms to Iran (another paramilitary operation)—a policy in sharp contradiction to the overt U.S. stance against the sale of weapons to terrorist groups *or* their allies. Some thoughtful observers maintain that a two-track foreign policy may be necessary at times, with the open track going in one direction to fool adversaries and the secret track heading toward a nation's true objectives. In time of war, deceptive operations are *obviously* useful and will always be employed in combat situations; but, short of open warfare *or* acute emergencies, the existence of two diverging tracks leads only to a disjointed foreign policy and ought to be avoided. Seeking detente with the Soviet Union, for example, while carrying out aggressive covert actions against it rarely made sense.

The third guideline would make policy officers think twice about secret alliances with particularly unsavory people. The recruitment of Panama's General Noriega for intelligence collection, former Nazis like Klaus Barbie for counterintelligence, Saddam Hussein for covert action against Iran, and organized crime figures for assassination plots backfired.[64] This is not to suggest that the United States should deal only with angels (they are in short supply) but that even in the pursuit of national objectives, some limits ought to be recognized.

The fourth guideline seeks to avoid the trap of groupthink. Study after study of U.S. intelligence has revealed a tendency to drive analysts and other lower- and middle-level officials—precisely the people with a rich experience in foreign countries—out of decision forums in favor of covert-action specialists who may understand less about the history and culture of the target nation.[65] This does not mean that policymakers should go to the other extreme and discount the views of covert-action experts; the best of those in the Operations Directorate have genuine country expertise and a level-headed sense of what will work. A key objective of these consultations with specialists (including outside academicians) should be to calculate, to the extent possible, the likely side effects (short-term and long-term) of a proposed covert intervention.

Guidelines 5 and 6 stress the importance of honoring the established decision processes for covert operations—blatantly disregarded during the Iran-Contra affair. Here the purpose, so vital in a democracy, is to maintain both dialogue and accountability, drawing on the collective judgment of Congress and the president. In circumstances of acute emergency the president retains the right to take those steps he or she considers necessary to save the nation—steps for which the president will be held accountable. Of the various prescriptions presented here, none is more cardinal than this emphasis on process: *never bypass established decision procedures.*

The remaining guidelines, 7 through 11, underscore the special place of democratic values in the world's political evolution.[66] The seventh, for example, acknowledges the value that Americans place in the global fellowship of democracies. The nurturing of free societies—perhaps never more promising than now in the nations of Eastern Europe and the former Soviet republics—is done great harm when America's leaders order harsh covert operations against fellow democracies.

The ninth guideline means rejecting some potentially useful intelligence sources, like Guatemala's Colonel Alpirez. Admittedly, though, if Alpirez were a colonel in the Russian intelligence service providing the United States with a direct espionage channel to military planning in the Kremlin unavailable through any other source, severing ties would be more problematic. But even in this hypothetical instance, if the Russian colonel were involved in the murder of an American citizen (as has been alleged in the Guatemalan case), that would go beyond the pale of acceptability.

This final set of guidelines recognizes that the higher rungs on the ladder of escalation are fraught with risk and clouded with ethical doubt. Indeed, in circumstances serious enough to warrant considering covert options above

Rung 23, the use of overt force backed by a formal declaration of war (or at least given legitimacy through the provisions of the War Powers Resolution of 1973) would be in order. As for the exceptions—when a renegade regime with avowed hostile intentions approaches chemical-biological or nuclear weapons sufficiency, or when a mass murderer begins a campaign of genocide within his society—a paramilitary operation (as described earlier) can be justified.

Among the more controversial, and questionable, options on the escalation ladder is the assassination plot. Almost always, it remains an unworthy, illegal, and for that matter impractical approach to America's international problems.[67] Even if one places ethical considerations aside, assassination plots invite retaliation against U.S. leaders, who are highly vulnerable in an open society. Further, the execution of a foreign leader offers no assurance that the successor will be any more favorably disposed toward the United States. Such plots are also difficult to implement; Fidel Castro was able to elude the many CIA attempts against his life.[68]

The counterargument in favor of assassination in extraordinary circumstances usually raises the example of Adolf Hitler. What if the United States, France, or Britain had murdered Adolf Hitler before Germany invaded Poland? Is it not possible that his successor might have forgone exterminating millions of Jews and overrunning Europe? And even if Hitler's assassination had brought about a retaliation against President Franklin D. Roosevelt, would it not still have been worth trading two lives for the six million lost in the Holocaust?

The trouble with these and similar questions is that they are too speculative: Hitler's monstrous intentions were less clear before the war than they became later. Further, his underlings seem to have been as mad as he—perhaps even more insane in some instances. Should it be U.S. policy to assassinate all who are, or might become, venal tyrants—and their immediate staff and relatives, too, just to be on the safe side? And is the matter of retaliation unimportant?

In times of war, properly authorized by Congress, assassination takes on a different coloration. As former DCI Admiral Stansfield Turner has observed:

[Assassination] is tempting to me only in wartime. I would have approved assassinating Saddam Hussein after the 16th of January [1991, the date when Congress gave its authority to use military force against Iraq]. And that's exactly the reason: there's a big difference between a President—and, heaven help us, somebody below him—taking on him- or herself to say, "Noriega ought to die," and the Congress of the United States and the public of the United States saying, "We're going to war with Panama, and Noriega is just as much a target as Joe Jones, Private First Class." And if you happen to target Noriega specifically—and surely we targeted Saddam Hussein, [but] it didn't work—I think that's all right.[69]

The eleventh guideline stands as a reminder that Americans take pride in the difference between their country and autocratic regimes. America's reputation for fair play—often stained by CIA excesses—has distinguished U.S. foreign policy from the approach of more brutal governments and has won respect and friendship for the United States in many parts of the world. In the interests of maintaining this vital difference between dictatorships and democracies, Roger Fisher (among others) has argued against using the coercive instruments of covert action. He urges, instead, greater reliance on "the most powerful weapons we have: idealism, morality, due process of law, and belief in the freedom to disagree, including the right of other countries to disagree with ours."[70] In table 17.2, instances of failed U.S. covert operations are presented to suggest how they might have been avoided (or at any rate modified) by adherence to these eleven guidelines.

CONCLUSION

Can the United States and other democracies truly compete in the present international arena without resorting to extreme covert operations, when their adversaries have often seemed prepared to carry out the most ruthless measures against the open societies? I am persuaded that the democracies will win their ideological battle with the nondemocratic regimes mainly by virtue of their higher principles and more humane behavior, along with their more appealing economic systems. The people of the world care most about food and shelter, clean air and pure water, the education of their children, and their rights to political dissent, liberty, justice, and happiness. The democracies have much to offer here.

Table 17.2   Failed U.S. Intelligence Operations That Might Have Been Rejected or Modified If Filtered through the Recommended Guidelines

Guidelines	Operations
1	Iran hostage rescue attempt (1980)
2	Iran arms sale (1984)
3	Funding of Christian Democratic Party in Italy (1979)
4	Bay of Pigs invasion (1961)
5	Diversion of arms to Nicaraguan contras (1985)
6	Operation CHAOS (1967–74)
7	Anti-Allende operations in Chile (1963–73)
8	Escalation of covert actions in Nicaragua (1982–87)
9	Ties with Panamanian dictator Noriega (1975–89)
10	Anti-Diem activities in Vietnam (1963)
11	Assassination plots in Cuba and the Congo (1960–65)

As a leading member of the U.S. House Committee on Foreign Affairs once said, "The best way to promote our interests is to promote our ideals."[71] In contrast, brutality, coercion, and violence—too often the specialties of nondemocratic regimes—are poor alternatives. Those who ply these wares have attracted no admiration, only fear.

The excessive use of highly intrusive intelligence options has done much to discredit the United States and other democracies, making their secret services seem at times little different from their erstwhile enemy during the Cold War, the Soviet KGB and GRU. By employing its secret agencies mainly for relatively nonintrusive collection operations, and by resorting to more aggressive operations—particularly covert actions—only with an abiding regard for the principles presented here, the United States can lay claim again to the high esteem it enjoyed throughout the world in the aftermath of World War Two.

NOTES

1. See the Doolittle report, cited in the Senate Select Committee to Study Governmental Operations with Respect to Intelligence Activities (the Church Committee), *Final Report,* Book I, 94th Cong., 2d Sess., S. Rept. No. 94–755, 1976, p. 9; author's conversations with Dean Rusk, when he resorted to this phrase frequently in explaining the use of covert operations during the Cold War (Athens, Ga., 1980–85), and also in the Church Committee, *Final Report,* Book I, p. 9; Ray S. Cline, a retired CIA officer, in "Should the CIA Fight Secret Wars?" *Harper's,* September 1984, p. 39; and Stewart A. Baker, "Should Spies Be Cops?" *Foreign Policy* 97 (Winter 1994–95), 37.

2. On the frequency of U.S. covert operations since 1947, see Loch K. Johnson, *America's Secret Power: The CIA in a Democratic Society* (New York: Oxford University Press, 1989).

3. Herman Kahn, *On Escalation: Metaphors and Scenarios* (New York: Praeger, 1965), 37.

4. Ibid., 38.

5. On the nonintervention norm, see Lori Fisler Damrosch, "Politics across Borders: Nonintervention and Nonforcible Influence over Domestic Affairs," *American Journal of International Law* 83 (January 1989), 6–13.

6. See *Report of the Special Committee on Principles of International Law concerning Friendly Relations and Co-operation among States,* U.N. Doc. N6799 (1967), 161, quoted in Damrosch, "Politics across Borders," 10–11.

7. Damrosch, "Politics across Borders," 11.

8. The Reagan administration evidently believed, and wanted to spread the word, that the assassination plot in 1984 against Pope John Paul II had been an operation by the Soviet secret service, the KGB, even though the U.S. intelligence community had no compelling evidence to this effect. See remarks by Donald Gregg, a former CIA officer on the NSC staff, in Loch K. Johnson, "Making the Intelligence 'Cycle'

Work," *International Journal of Intelligence and Counterintelligence* 2 (Winter 1986–87), 17. On a CIA counterintelligence scheme to falsify and distribute copies of Soviet premier Nikita Khrushchev's "secret speech" denouncing the Stalin era, see Seymour M. Hersh, "The Angleton Story," *New York Times Sunday Magazine,* June 25, 1978, 13.

9. See "The CIA and the Media," *Hearings,* Subcommittee on Oversight, House Permanent Select Committee on Intelligence, 96th Cong., 1st Sess. (1979).

10. Walter Pincus, "CIA Steps Up 'Scrub Down' of Agents," *Washington Post,* July 28, 1995, A25. For a criticism of the CIA's "moral checklist," see Jonathan Clarke, "The CIA Drifts between Fear and Loathing," *Los Angeles Times* (September 3, 1995), M5, who wonders: "If human rights abusers are out, what about pedophiles? Embezzlers? Wife beaters? Delinquent dads?" For Clarke, "the CIA [should] operate according to one ironclad rule: A relationship [with a foreign asset] will continue as long as there is a net benefit to U.S. interests; when it is not, it will be cut loose."

11. Discussed in "The CIA and Guatemala," *Washington Post,* August 4, 1995, A22.

12. On the advantages and risks of embassy break-ins, see the testimony of former Attorney General John Mitchell, *Huston Plan Hearings,* vol. 2, Church Committee, 94th Cong., 1st Sess. (1975), 123; Richard M. Nixon, response to Interrogatory No. 17, Church Committee, *Final Report,* Book IV; *Supplementary Detailed Staff Reports on Foreign and Military Intelligence,* Church Committee, Book III, 157–58; Church Committee, *Final Report,* Book I, 123; and author's interview with James J. Angleton, former CIA Chief of Counterintelligence, cited in Johnson, *America's Secret Power,* 297–98n5.

13. Damrosch, "Politics across Borders," 10–11.

14. Ibid., 36.

15. On the Son Tay prison raid, designed to free U.S. prisoners of war in Vietnam (unsuccessfully, since the prisoners had been evacuated by the North Vietnamese three weeks earlier—an unfortunate intelligence failure), see Henry Kissinger, *White House Years* (Boston: Little, Brown, 1979), 282; and Benjamin F. Schemmer, *The Raid* (New York: Harper & Row, 1976). On the Iran rescue attempt, see Morton H. Halperin and David Halperin, "The Key West Key," *Foreign Policy* (Winter 1983–84), 114.

16. President George Bush, White House press release, Washington, D.C. (August 15, 1989).

17. On the CIA's paramilitary operations in Laos, see William E. Colby and Peter Forbath, *Honorable Men: My Life in the CIA* (New York: Simon and Schuster, 1978), 191–202; and Victor Marchetti and John D. Marks, *The CIA and the Cult of Intelligence* (New York: Knopf, 1974).

18. See, for example, Jeffrey T. Richelson, *Sword and Shield: The Soviet Intelligence and Security Apparatus* (Cambridge, Mass.: Ballinger, 1986); Roy Godson, ed., *Comparing Foreign Intelligence: The US, the USSR, and the Third World* (New York: Pergamon-Brassey, 1988); and Richard H. Shultz and Roy Godson, *Dezinformatsia: Active Measures in Soviet Strategy* (New York: Pergamon-Brassey, 1984).

19. See, for example, the series of lead articles in *Ethics and International Affairs* 3 (1989); Arthur S. Hulnick and Daniel W. Mattausch, "Ethics and Morality in

United States Secret Intelligence," *Harvard Journal of Law and Public Policy* 12 (Spring 1989), 509; Joseph S. Nye, Jr., *Ethics and Foreign Policy: An Occasional Paper,* Aspen Institute Human Studies, no. 1 (1985); E. Drexel Godfrey, Jr., "Ethics and Intelligence," *Foreign Affairs* 56 (1978), 624; and Richard Falk, "CIA Covert Action and International Law," *Society* 12 (1975), 39.

20. See the useful summary of these issues in Michael J. Smith, "Ethics and Intervention," *Ethics and International Affairs* 3 (1989), 1–26.

21. On operational codes, see Loch K. Johnson, "Operational Codes and the Prediction of Leadership Behavior," in Margaret Herman, ed., A *Psychological Examination of Political Man* (New York: Free Press, 1977), 80; for an analytic framework outlining these interrelationships, see Loch K. Johnson, *America as a World Power: Foreign Policy in a Constitutional Framework,* 2d ed. (New York: McGraw-Hill, 1995), chap. 2.

22. Henry L. Stimson and McGeorge Bundy, *On Active Service in Peace and War* (New York: Octagon Books, 1947), 188. Stimson subsequently disavowed this position, perhaps realizing that America's adversaries were seldom gentlemen.

23. George W. Ball, "Should the CIA Fight Secret Wars?"

24. G. Gordon Liddy, public lecture, University of Georgia, Athens, May 4, 1986, based on author's notes.

25. See Charles R. Beitz, "Covert Intervention as a Moral Problem," and William E. Colby, "Public Policy, Secret Action," *Ethics and International Affairs* 3 (1989), 48 and 63, 69, respectively.

26. See Michael Walzer, *Just and Unjust Wars: A Moral Argument with Historical Illustrations* (New York: Basic Books, 1977).

27. See, for example, Colby, "Public Policy," 69. Damrosch writes: "[T]he nonintervention norm must not become a vehicle for exalting the abstract entity of the state over the protection of individual rights and fundamental freedoms" ("Politics across Borders," 37).

28. See Smith, "Ethics and Intervention," 21.

29. On proportionality, see Colby, "Public Policy," 65–66.

30. See Gregory F. Treverton, "Imposing a Standard: Covert Action and American Democracy," 27 and 32, and Ralph Buultjens, "The Ethics of Excess and Indian Intervention in South Asia," 82, both in *Ethics and International Affairs* 3 (1989).

31. See Treverton, "Imposing a Standard," and Colby, "Public Policy."

32. Hulnick and Mattausch, "Ethics and Morality."

33. See, for example, Robert C. Johansen, *The National Interest and the Human Interest: An Analysis of U.S. Foreign Policy* (Princeton: Princeton University Press, 1980), 386.

34. See Buultjens, "The Ethics of Excess."

35. Colby, "Public Policy," 69.

36. South Carolina representative L. Mendel Rivers, quoted in Charles McCarry, "Ol' Man Rivers," *Esquire* (October 1970), 171.

37. This transformation can also operate in the reverse direction, as shown by President Carter's switch to a harder line—and a sudden attraction to covert action—against the Soviets following their surprise invasion of Afghanistan in 1979. On Reagan's move away from "evil empire" rhetoric toward more cordial relations with

his Soviet counterpart, see the two-part series by John Newhouse, "Annals of Diplomacy: The Abolitionist," *New Yorker* 64 (January 2 and 9, 1989), 37 and 51, respectively. Reagan's first public rejection of the "evil empire" label occurred on May 31, 1988. On Carter's reaction to the Soviet invasion of Afghanistan, see his own account in Jimmy Carter, *Keeping Faith: Memoirs of a President* (New York: Bantam Books, 1982), 471–89.

38. See Jeane Kirkpatrick, "Dictatorships and Double Standards," *Commentary* (November 1979), 34; and, with a far different conclusion, Damrosch, "Politics across Borders."

39. See Loch K. Johnson, "The CIA and the Media," *Intelligence and National Security* 1 (1986), 143. These distinctions between regimes lose much of their force, however, at Threshold Four, where the dangers to innocents are greatly magnified.

40. For Colby, on the decline of the Soviet ideological threat (several years before the *glasnost* era), see "Interview with William E. Colby," *U.S. News & World Report* (July 3, 1978), at 37, 39. On Casey's aggressive approach to the use of intelligence operations, see David M. Alpern, "America's Secret Warriors," *Newsweek* (October 10,1983), 38; and Roger Morris, "William Casey's Past," *Atlanta Constitution* (August 31, 1987), A11. See also DCI Director Stansfield Turner's higher tolerance for the Marxist regime in Nicaragua than that expressed by his successor, DCI Casey: "From an Ex-CIA Chief: Stop the 'Covert' Operation in Nicaragua," *Washington Post* (April 21, 1983), C1.

41. See Theodore C. Sorensen, *Decision-Making in the White House: The Olive Branch or the Arrows* (New York: Columbia University Press, 1963).

42. Author's conversations with Air Marshal Sir Ewan Jamieson (in charge of New Zealand's counterintelligence at the time of the investigation into the *Rainbow Warrior* bombing), Conference on Military Strategy, Georgia Institute of Technology, Atlanta, August 24–26, 1989.

43. For this story, see Kermit Roosevelt, *Countercoup: The Struggle for the Control of Iran* (New York: McGraw-Hill, 1979).

44. Peter Wyden, *Bay of Pigs: The Untold Story* (New York: Simon and Schuster, 1979).

45. Beitz, "Covert Intervention."

46. On this "Gang of Eight" leading legislators, see Johnson, *America's Secret Power,* 222–29. The 1991 Intelligence Oversight amendments, Title VI of the Intelligence Authorization Act, Fiscal Year 1991, Pub. L. No. 102–88, 105 Stat. 429, 441 (adopted August 14, 1991), continue this procedure; see page 443, 503(c)(2). David L. Boren, president of the University of Oklahoma and a former chairman of the Senate Select Committee on Intelligence, has suggested that in extraordinary times the executive branch should be allowed to report to just the Speaker and Minority Leader of the House and their Senate counterparts—a "Gang of Four," removing the chairman and ranking minority members of the two Intelligence Committees (who were part of the wider Gang of Eight). See Boren's remarks, Association of Former Intelligence Officers (March 28, 1988), quoted in the association's newsletter, *Periscope* (Spring 1988), 8. This same recommendation was advanced in the Minority Report of the Inouye-Hamilton Committees, *Report,* 585. (I am grateful to Donald Milner, a Toronto attorney, for his thoughts on the importance of process.)

47. On the strict adherence to this law before the Iran-contra violation, see H.R. Rept. No. 705, 100th Cong., 2d Sess. (1988), 54. On the debate over prior notice, see Johnson, *America's Secret Power*, 225–28; *The Need to Know*, Report of the Twentieth Century Fund Task Force on Covert Action and American Democracy, New York, 1992; and W. Michael Reisman and James E. Baker, *Regulating Covert Action: Practices, Contests, and Policies of Covert Coercion Abroad in International and American Law* (New Haven: Yale University Press, 1992).

48. The law states that the report should be forthcoming "in a timely fashion" (the same hazy prescription found in the Hughes-Ryan Act of 1974), but the accompanying legislative history stresses the expectation of a "few days" maximum delay.

49. Baker, "Should Spies Be Cops?" 40.

50. See, for example, "Elliott Abrams Is Guilty," *New York Times* (October 11, 1991), A14, an unsigned editorial that cites the State Department official Elliott Abrams's disdain for congressional involvement in intelligence supervision. Abrams was convicted of lying to Congress about the illegal supply of weapons to the Contras during the Iran-contra affair. For a more scholarly argument against any serious legislative oversight of intelligence, see Paul Seabury, "A Massacre Revisited," *Foreign Intelligence Literary Scene* 1 (1988), 2.

51. Treverton, "Imposing a Standard," 43.

52. For Poindexter's statement, see *Hearings,* Senate Select Committee on Secret Military Assistance to Iran and the Nicaraguan Opposition and House Select Committee to Investigate Covert Arms Transactions with Iran, 100th Cong., 1st Sess. (1987), 159, chaired by Sen. Daniel K. Inouye and Rep. Lee H. Hamilton, respectively (hereinafter Inouye-Hamilton Committees, *Hearings).*

53. Ibid., 24–31. See also *Report of the Congressional Committees Investigating the Iran-contra Affair,* S. Rept. No. 216 and H. Rept. No. 433, 100 Cong., 1st Sess. (1987), 333 (hereinafter Inouye-Hamilton Committees, *Report).* For an overview of the Iran-contra affair, see Theodore Draper, *A Very Thin Line: The Iran-Contra Affair* (New York: Hill and Wang, 1991); Lawrence E. Walsh, *Final Report of the Independent Counsel for Iran/Contra Matters* (Washington, D.C.: U.S. Court of Appeals, District of Columbia Circuit, 1994).

54. See, for example, Vice Admiral Poindexter's testimony, Inouye-Hamilton Committees, *Hearings*; Inouye-Hamilton Committees, *Report,* 16, 339; the Tower Commission Report (1987); and Church Committee, *Final Report,* Book I.

55. As Justice Louis Brandeis put it in 1926, "The doctrine of the separation of powers was adopted by the [Constitutional] Convention of 1787, not to promote efficiency but to preclude the exercise of arbitrary power. The purpose was, not to avoid friction, but, by means of the inevitable friction incident to the distribution of the governmental powers among three departments, to save the people from autocracy." *Myers* v. *United States,* 272 U.S. 52, 293.

56. Fund-raising letter to "Fellow American," signed by John M. Poindexter, Rear Admiral, USN (Ret.), and reading in part: "I must now face the liberals' accusations surrounding the 'Iran-Contra affair.' And as I stand, one man, alone against the massive onslaught of liberal special interests who want to imprison me for serving my country, I must turn to you for help" (undated, but received by the author in August 1989).

57. Inouye-Hamilton Committees, *Report,* 431–585 (Minority Report).

58. See William S. Cohen and George J. Mitchell, *Men of Zeal: A Candid Inside Story of the Iran-Contra Hearings* (New York: Viking, 1988); and Elizabeth Drew, "Letter from Washington," *New Yorker* (March 30, 1987), 111. The case against North was dismissed by a U.S. district court in 1991 after the Iran-contra independent prosecutor announced that he would abandon the prosecution because the immunity granted to North by Congress in 1987 (to gain his testimony in hearings) had created too great an obstacle. See David Johnston, "Judge in Iran-Contra Trial Drops Case against North after Prosecutor Gives Up," *New York Times* (September 17, 1991), A1, A12.

59. See the Bush Administration's $9 million request to Congress (September 21, 1989) for open support of the anti-Sandinista candidate in Nicaragua's approaching presidential election, reported in "Bush Seeks $9 Million for Nicaraguan Opposing Ortega in Presidential Bid," *Atlanta Journal and Constitution* (September 22, 1989), A4.

60. See Margaret Scranton, *The Noriega Years: U.S.-Panamian Relations, 1981– 1990* (Boulder, Colo.: Lynne Rienner, 1991).

61. The Vance and Clifford testimonies are in Church Committee, *Hearings: Covert Action,* 94th Cong., 2d Sess., 1976, 7:50–55. For the Church Committee's conclusion, see Church Committee, *Final Report,* Book I, 159; for the Inouye-Hamilton Committees' conclusion, see Inouye-Hamilton Committees, *Report,* 383. See also the discussion in *The Need to Know;* and Reisman and Baker, *Regulating Covert Action.*

62. In offering these guidelines, I am not unmindful of Clemenceau's wry comment on President Woodrow Wilson's Fourteen Points: "God gave us his Ten Commandments and we broke them; Wilson gave us his Fourteen Points—we shall see." Quoted in W. A. White, *Woodrow Wilson* (Boston: Houghton Mifflin, 1929), 384.

63. See the former secretary's account in his memoirs, *Hard Choices: Critical Years in America's Foreign Policy* (New York: Simon and Schuster, 1983), 398–413.

64. On U.S. intelligence ties with Noriega, see *Drugs, Law Enforcement and Foreign Policy: Hearings before the Senate Subcommittee on Terrorism, Narcotics, and International Operations,* 100th Cong., 2d Sess. (1989), 234–43; on Barbie, see "Klaus Barbie, Lyons Nazi Leader, Dies," *New York Times* (September 26, 1991), C19; and on CIA ties with organized crime in the 1960s, see Church Committee, *Alleged Assassination Plots Involving Foreign Leaders: Interim Report,* S. Rep. No. 465, 94th Cong., 1st Sess. (1975). On refusing intelligence cooperation with regimes engaged in human rights violations, see Thomas Farer, "Low-Intensity Conflict and International Order: The Prospect for Consensus," paper, U.S. Institute of Peace Project on Strengthening World Order and the United Nations Charter System against Secret Warfare and Low-Intensity Conflict, 1990, p. 63. Professor Farer has emphasized the importance of the second guideline, too, in a U.S. Institute of Peace discussion group of which I was a member in 1990. Professor James Berry of James Mason University has graciously corresponded with me on the proper sequencing of rungs on the escalation ladder and has stimulated helpful revisions.

65. On the phenomenon of banishing intelligence and other experts from high councils when key decisions are being made (and related policymaking pathologies), see Irving L. Janis, *Groupthink: Psychological Studies of Policy Decisions and Fiascoes,*

2d ed. (Boston: Houghton-Mifflin, 1982); Robert Jervis, "Intelligence and Foreign Policy," *International Security Studies* 11 (1986–87); and Betts, "Analysis, War, and Decision: Why Intelligence Failures Are Inevitable," World Politics (October 1978), 31:61–89.

66. On this theme, see Damrosch, "Politics across Borders," esp. 37–50; and Farer, "Low-Intensity Conflict."

67. However, in the two exceptional cases mentioned here, if the regime leader is killed during the destruction of the chemical-biological and nuclear facilities (in the first instance), or during his or her arrest (in the second instance), this unintended result is defensible in light of the need to protect large civilian and innocent populations—a consequentialist verdict that in these situations seems compelling. On the illegality of assassinations, see Executive Order No. 12,333, signed by President Ronald Reagan on December 4, 1981; *Public Papers (Ronald Reagan)*, 1981, p. 1128. The order continued a prohibition against assassination initiated by President Gerald R. Ford, Executive Order No. 11,905 (February 18, 1976), *Public Papers (Gerald R. Ford)*, 1976–77, p. 349. Since Presidents Bush and Clinton never revoked the order, it remains in force. See W. Hays Parks, "Memorandum of Law: Executive Order 12333 and Assassination," *Army Law* (December 1989), 4. Pointing to Article 2(4) of the U.N. Charter, Parks, chief of the Army's International Law Branch, maintains: "Assassination is unlawful killing, and would be prohibited by international law even if there were no executive order proscribing it" ("Memorandum of Law," 4).

68. Church Committee, *Alleged Assassination Plots.*

69. Author's interview with Stansfield Turner, May 1, 1991, McLean, Va.

70. Roger Fisher, "The Fatal Flaw in Our Spy System," *Boston Globe* (February 1, 1976), A9.

71. Remarks, Rep. Steven J. Solarz, C-Span television broadcast, May 22, 1988.

18

Military and Civilian Perspectives on the Ethics of Intelligence

Report on a Workshop at the Department of Philosophy

Jean Maria Arrigo

Author's note: Philosopher Charles Young contributed to the conceptualization of this paper. For review of the manuscript I thank Charles Young and John Crigler. Cynthia Ford negotiated with workshop presenters for permission to reveal their case histories to varying degrees. Robert Roetzel introduced me to Michael Walzer's concept of "supreme emergency." Audio-recordings and transcripts from the workshop are deposited in the Intelligence Ethics Collection at Hoover Institution Archives, Stanford University, Stanford, CA.

The study of military ethics is incomplete, even evasive, unless coordinated with ethics of military and political intelligence, for military and intelligence operations are interdependent and share personnel and resources. A doctrine of just war should coordinate with a doctrine of just intelligence, especially for human source intelligence, counterintelligence, and covert operations. This was the premise of The Pilot Workshop on Ethics of Political and Military Intelligence for Insiders and Outsiders, held at the Department of Philosophy, Claremont Graduate University, September 29, 2000. Here I offer (1) a rationale for the essential involvement of outsiders in intelligence ethics, (2) an overview of the workshop, (3) a framework for interpretation of case presentations, (4) highlights from the plenary session, and (5) a summary of workshop follow-up activities. The appendix argues for the specific importance of intelligence ethics to the Joint Services Conference on Professional Ethics.

RATIONALE FOR THE ESSENTIAL INVOLVEMENT OF OUTSIDERS IN INTELLIGENCE ETHICS

A previous paper that I wrote, "Ethics of Weapons Research for Insiders and Outsiders" argued that insiders—members of the military and political intelligence community—and outsiders—nonmembers and even nonsympathizers—must jointly negotiate practicable ethical standards for intelligence operations. In short: Outsiders cannot ultimately impose moral constraints on intelligence operations because they cannot monitor operations. Outsiders would have to breach barriers designed to thwart enemy intelligence agencies and to override the decisions of people who are willing to sacrifice their lives for national security goals. Insiders cannot ultimately impose moral constraints on operations because, under duress, their moral commitments to national security goals may override their moral commitments to military and civilian codes . . .

But how can outsiders contribute to a practical understanding of intelligence ethics? Here the difference between military ethics and intelligence ethics comes into play. Apart from law enforcement officers and prison guards, few civilians employ physical force against enemies of the public good, so few civilians can bring practical experience to military ethics. Almost all citizens, though, have practical experience as intelligence agents. Some familiar civilian intelligence contests are: Internal Revenue Service versus taxpayers, insurance underwriters and claims adjusters versus policy owners, lenders and credit agencies versus borrowers, plaintiffs versus defendants in the judicial system, corporations versus competitors, marketers versus consumers, educational testing services versus students, and job recruiters versus job candidates. To the extent that these enterprises involve transcendent goals, such as fair taxation, equal access to education, and equal employment opportunities, they generate difficult moral problems like those confronted by intelligence on behalf of national security. This is to say that outsiders to political and military intelligence can indeed bring practical experience to intelligence ethics.

OVERVIEW OF THE PILOT WORKSHOP

At the Claremont Workshop, six insiders and six outsiders presented case histories of intelligence operations to several ethicists and a few artists. We construed intelligence operations in the broad sense of strategic collection, analysis, and deployment of information for advantage over adversaries or protection from adversaries.

Our goals were to search out the moral parameters for intelligence operations and to seek a common framework for military and civilian operations, not to establish moral principles or methods at this early stage of inquiry.

In most of the case histories, presenters had played morally significant roles, and operations had involved substantial moral trade-offs. One insider had served as an Office of Strategic Services (OSS) agent behind enemy lines in World War II and another insider had served as a military counternarcotics agent in Latin America. One outsider, a principal at a private school, had blown the whistle on an unethical academic intelligence operation, and another outsider, a civil litigation attorney, had revealed corporate fraud using a standard judicial intelligence operation. The workshop ethicists, drawn from the Claremont Colleges, were philosophers from various specialties, such as epistemology and naturalistic ethics, but all were broadly competent in traditional ethics. The task of the philosophers-as-ethicists was to inquire into a moral theory for intelligence operations—if possible, a moral theory encompassing both civilian and military perspectives. The artists consisted of a poet, a printmaker, and a composer-guitarist. The task of the artists was to keep an eye on the limitations of case analysis and to expand the scope of inquiry with later art works. The ethicists were recruited by CGU Professor Charles Young, whose field is ancient Greek moral philosophy, especially Aristotelian ethics. As a social psychologist studying intelligence ethics and as a daughter of an undercover intelligence officer, I recruited the insiders, outsiders, and artists for the workshop. Because of participants' concerns about confidentiality, attendance was by invitation only.

The pilot workshop was built around three work groups, each consisting of two insiders and two outsiders, an artist, and one to three ethicists, with one ethicist serving as moderator. Inasmuch as some military, legal, and personal matters of confidentiality are still unsettled, at this point I will discuss the presentations in generalities and omit names of a few presenters.

AN INTERPRETATION OF
CASE PRESENTATIONS

In the plenary session, speaking for the philosophers, Charles Young identified what might be called a moderate consequentialist moral dynamic for intelligence operations. Loosely paraphrasing the transcript:

> A lot of moral theories nowadays are consequentialist, in holding that morality requires you to do in any circumstance whatever makes for the best outcome—

however it is you measure good outcomes. . . . But most of us believe there are constraints, cases or situations in which it's positively wrong for me to do what makes for the best outcome. It's immoral. Most of us, for example, probably think it's wrong for me to take your kid's book and give it to the library, even though—let's agree for the sake of the point—that would result in the greater public good . . .

One thing that seemed to come out in our sessions is that the constraints on intelligence practitioners turn out in many cases to be very small. The reason is that the good outcome that intelligence workers are aiming at—the continued existence of the United States with its military and industrial capacity and its political systems intact—is so important a goal that the usual constraints against harming other people are overridden. The result is that lots of things happened that just look on their face to be immoral. The higher the stakes, the easier it is to override the constraints.

Points on the graph represent operations. The height on the vertical axis indicates the degree of harm resulting from an operation. The width on the horizontal axis indicates the severity of the stakes. The curve—*the moral divide*—indicates the severity of stakes that entitle operators to override moral constraints on harms of a certain degree. Points below the moral divide represent morally tolerable operations, from the perspective of the political constituency of the intelligence unit (e.g., a congressional oversight committee). Similarly, points above the moral divide represent morally intolerable operations. (Of course, harms and stakes both have many aspects and can only be ranked approximately, at a particular point in history.)

The case history presented by a high school principal is illustrative. She reported on an academic intelligence operation at a private school. As a new principal, she had discovered an administrator's scheme for ensuring straight As for a child of affluent parents. The administrator was a charismatic personality and a successful fund-raiser for the school. The parents were influential and capable of making large donations to the school. The administrator's grade scheme might be construed as a (barely) morally tolerable academic intelligence operation (point A on Figure 18.1), considering the high stakes: possible financial failure of the most successful school in the area to offer children a Christian education. The principal attempted to correct the situation by backing a teacher who gave the student an honest B grade. The administrator responsible for the grading scheme fired the teacher, sidelined the principal, and surreptitiously changed the student's transcript. The principal believed that it was illegal to change grades without the teacher's consent (although the state statute may not have applied to private schools). The principal notified the assistant pastor of the church associated with the school, who passed on the information to the head pastor, who passed it on to the school board. Preoccupied with large financial losses due to a fraudulent building contractor, the school board did not respond. Even-

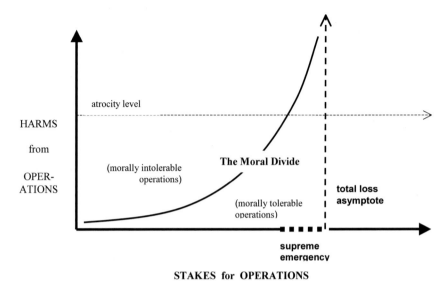

Figure 18.1   The realistic moderate-consequentialist model of moral dynamics for intelligence operations with a supreme emergency.

tually the head pastor confronted the administrator. Through months of apparent espionage and sabotage (e.g., taping telephone and private conversations secretly and sending tapes around), the administrator had allegedly laid the groundwork to discredit the head pastor, rally the school parents against him, and stage a successful coup in the congregation. This was surely a morally intolerable academic intelligence operation (point B), as the school board came to agree, and finally dismissed her—with the assistance of the police because the administrator would not vacate the school premises.

In a strictly consequentialist model, the moral tolerability of operations would be tied only to their utility (to be discussed later), not to constraints based on the relationship between harms and stakes, as delineated by the moral divide in Figure 18.1. In this optimistic version of the moderate consequentialist model for intelligence operations, as the stakes increase, the tolerable harms never reach the point of atrocity but only rise asymptotically. I will elaborate this moral-dynamics graph as an interpretive framework for the workshop case histories. Then I will return to sample the comments in the workshop plenary session by insiders and outsiders, ethicists, and artists.

THE MORAL DYNAMICS GRAPH AS AN
INTERPRETIVE FRAMEWORK

Severe harms on the part of intelligence operations may be tolerated under threat of total loss. The prototypical example is the OSS response to Japanese and Nazi aggression in World War II. The former OSS agent, Tom Moon, said of operations in North Burma behind Japanese lines: "We had absolutely no compunction about what we were doing against the Japanese. We were losing the war at this time, and when somebody's got you up a dark alley and they're about to cut your throat, . . . you'll do anything it takes to survive—immediately." He described paying 8,000 guerilla troops with opium because money was worthless in the jungle and turning over probable spies, after interrogation, to the Burmese natives for "release"—then hearing the reliable gunshots of execution. "Two of our men were buried alive by the Japanese. One of their men then got burned at the stake in retaliation. It got that brutal. But word had to get back that we weren't going to take it." Yet Moon and his fellow agents embraced certain moral constraints. For instance, they refused to place in Japanese hospitals the cyanide-laced aspirins supplied to them for this purpose, because Burmese doctors and nurses or their children, that is, noncombatants, might consume the aspirins. But the severity of morally tolerable operations did increase beyond the atrocity level. In the realistic moderate-consequentialist model, Figure 18.2, the degree of morally tolerable harms rises without bound as the stakes increase toward total loss, in the perception of the constituency of the intelligence unit. For the OSS, the total loss point was Nazi or Japanese defeat of the United States. Under conditions evocative of total loss, or "supreme emergency," operations that result in atrocities may even be morally tolerable.[1] In Figure 18.2 the moral divide rises above the atrocity level in conditions of supreme emergency when the stakes are close to total loss.

Different stakeholders, such as militarists and environmentalists, may dis-

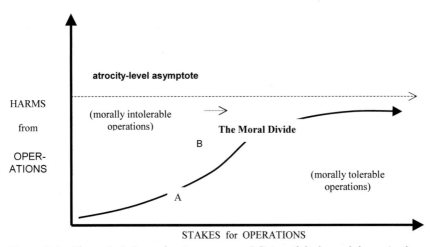

Figure 18.2   The optimistic moderate-consequentialist model of moral dynamics for intelligence operations.

agree as to what constitutes total loss. For militarists, total loss may mean military defeat of their own nation. For environmentalists, total loss may mean destruction of all human life or of ecological systems. John Lindsay-Poland, a specialist on U.S.-Panama relations for the Fellowship of Reconciliation, described his research into secret chemical weapons dumps in the Canal Zone. The chemical weapons could create uncontrollable environmental and human disasters. The departing U.S. military cannot clean up the weapons without acknowledging the problem, which militarists would believe jeopardizes security interests. For the Fellowship of Reconciliation, whose primary sphere of moral concern includes Third World peoples and local environments, the point of total loss is far beyond military defeat of the United States, as shown in Figure 18.3. (The harms and stakes axes for militarists and environmentalists are superimposed on a single graph for a very crude comparison.) In their view, jeopardy to U.S. military supremacy does not justify overriding major moral constraints, such as the "provision in the Canal treaties for the U.S. to 'remove hazards to human health and safety, insofar as may be practicable' by the time the U.S. withdraws." Severe threats to the habitability of the planet, however, would warrant overriding constraints.

Moon stated a moral principle for intelligence operations that his OSS unit had employed in evaluating "the whole catalogue of 'James Bond gadgetry'" the government had supplied to them. According to his utility principle, no

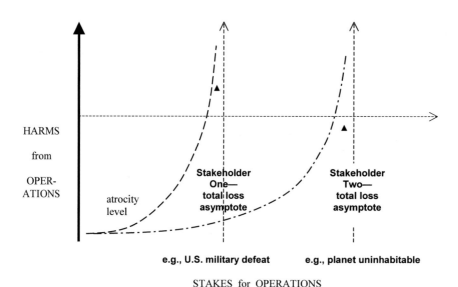

Figure 18.3   The realistic moderate-consequentialist model of moral dynamics for intelligence operations with two stakeholders with supreme emergencies.

harm can be justified unless it is actually believed to be useful in reducing the threat to security. Harms that are morally intolerable, however, such as burning enemy spies at the stake, may be useful if concealed from the constituency of the intelligence unit.

The likelihood of exposure and, further, censure of secret operations depends very much on the political power of the intelligence unit. For a poorly positioned intelligence unit, even operations that are morally tolerable to its constituency may not be useful, because of the likelihood of exposure and censure by more powerful factions. Tashi Namgyal, a former security official of the Tibetan Government-in-Exile, presented this example. In most countries, punishments for treason and sabotage are very severe—long imprisonment or execution. The Tibetan Security Department currently functions within other countries and must obey the laws of their hosts in prosecuting Tibetan agents who betray their compatriots. This results in near immunity for traitors and saboteurs, in spite of the great risk to the Dalai Lama from collaborators with the Chinese government. On the moral dynamics graph in Figure 18.4, the utility line for a very poorly positioned ("weak") intelligence unit rises no higher than the maximum level of harms legally permitted in host countries, which is well below the moral divide when the stakes are high.

For a very well positioned ("powerful") intelligence unit, operations may be useful that are not morally tolerable because exposure, or at least censure, can be suppressed. Jose Quiroga, the personal physician of President Salva-

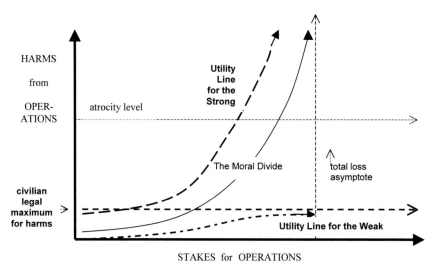

Figure 18.4 The realistic utility model of moral dynamics for weak and powerful intelligence units.

dor Allende, presented the case of the CIA-engineered military coup in Chile in 1973, which was instigated by President Richard Nixon and his national security adviser, Henry Kissinger. In this case, as documented by Quiroga, neither U.S. congressional investigation nor presidential orders have forced revelation of all relevant CIA documents. Even the eventual exposure of morally intolerable aspects of the operation did not result in significant censure. As shown in Figure 18.4, the utility line for such a well-positioned intelligence unit as the CIA may run above the moral divide.

A civil litigation attorney, Rafael Chodos, contrasted this variable vulnerability to disclosure and censure, on the international political scene, to fairness in judicial intelligence operations under California's discovery process. By law, both plaintiff and defendant must fully disclose all evidence that is likely to be admitted into trial proceedings. When one party petitions the other for relevant information, the other party must supply it, if the court agrees to the relevance. Of course, there are flaws in the process. In the particular case presented, after a two-year delay and various deceptions by the defendant, Chodos was permitted to examine 37,000 of the defendant's documents, for only two hours, at a cost of $10,000—which he nevertheless accomplished to his satisfaction with a handheld scanner. In California, he legal penalty for completely refusing to produce relevant information requested by the other party is a court decision in favor of that party. That is, in order to avoid disclosure the party must default. In military and political intelligence operations, only the defeated can be forced to show their hand.

INDIVIDUAL ROLE PLAYERS IN INTELLIGENCE OPERATIONS

From a consequentialist perspective, the points on the moral-dynamics graph must represent operations, not decisions or actions by individual agents, because operations coordinate the actions of individuals to produce the consequence. In intelligence operations, individuals are frequently uninformed or deceived as to the full meaning of their actions, or they are goaded by hard circumstance to act contrary to their intentions. The poor correspondence among knowledge, intention, and action on the part of individuals is not remediable because it is essential to the success of secretive and deceptive operations.

A medical engineer, Eldon Byrd, reported a case that illustrates this point. After working on the Polaris submarine, which carried long-range nuclear weapons, Byrd developed nonlethal weapons with reversible effects. He regarded this as a humanitarian alternative to "punching holes in people and having their blood leak out" in battle. His inventions used magnetic fields at biologically active wave frequencies to affect brain function. Byrd could put animals to sleep at a distance and influence their movements. When the success of his research became evident, suddenly he was pulled off the project and it went "black." His believes the electromagnetic resonance weapons he developed have been used for psychological control of civilians rather than for exigencies in battle. That is, to ensure his participation, he was uninformed about the true nature of the project. Byrd's case also illustrates how morally tolerable operations may transition to morally intolerable operations, or at least rise above the atrocity line.

Moon, the OSS agent, spoke more favorably of the moral choices accorded him: "One thing I liked about our government was we were told if ever we were given an assignment and you don't want to do it, you just say, 'choose not to do that,' and you walk away and you will not be questioned. It will be given to someone else. If someone else accepts the assignment, though, the operation itself may proceed in the same way with different role players, with no change of location on the moral dynamics graph.

Another presenter, who can only be identified as a military commissary man, related a worse moral experience in the "war against drugs." He was repeatedly drawn into irregular procedures, such as the burial at sea of a boat pilot shot by narcotics traffickers. When the counternarcotics unit he supported met armed resistance, he was pressed into hostilities against noncombatants, including children. Serious violations of the military rules of engagement led to very bad morale in his unit: "We wouldn't even talk to each other for days. . . . Most of us felt so dirty, like the filth we thought we were stopping." One of his fellow agents responded by committing suicide on military premises. But crew members who had remained aboard ship to provide regular logistical support "were almost euphoric" with the success of the drug interdiction and praise from superiors. Closely coordinated participants in an operation can have very different moral experiences because of their different roles and the tight compartmentalization of knowledge.

As a further complication, individuals can play sincere roles in conflicting operations. In researching abandoned U.S. weapons and contaminants in the Canal Zone, Lindsay-Poland depended on covert assistance from both U.S. and Panamanian officials. A U.S. military intelligence officer passed him critical information—once—and encouraged him to continue his environmentalist efforts for the good of the whole system.

BREAKDOWN OF THE
MORAL-DYNAMICS GRAPH

As an interpretative framework for the cases, the moral-dynamics graph breaks down at extremes. The two axes are not truly independent (in spite of their perpendicularity on the graph): the stakes are not independent of the harms committed in intelligence operations. Large, powerful systems may be able to absorb the harms, such as citizens' diminished trust of government, without much overall change, but small systems may collapse, as did the Christian school described by the principal. In the fracas with the charismatic administrator, the head pastor, and the school board, the enrollment dropped from 750 to 250 students in one month, which brought financial collapse.

A physician at the workshop, Sue Arrigo (my sister), discussed medical intelligence operations in hospital intensive care units (ICUs). Especially in regard to terminal patients, hospital administration, residents and nurses, and patients' families have competing intelligence goals. Her case of an ICU patient with Adult Respiratory Distress Syndrome, among other ailments, offers a striking metaphor for small-system interdependence of operational harms and security risks. The patient "lost his ability to speak when put on a ventilator [to help him breathe], lost his clarity of mind when sedated to prevent his gagging on the ventilator tube in his mouth, lost his ability to move when tied down so as not to pull out his tubes, and finally lost his sanity as he developed ICU psychosis."

A second cause of breakdown of the moral-dynamics graph derives from the confound in some intelligence operations between *responding* to reality and *creating* reality. A targeting intelligence officer illustrated how—in this era of high-speed communications and technologies—intelligence operations can create the image of risk and damage in which the war is conceptualized and fought. But on the moral-dynamics graph, the stakes falsely appear to underlie such formative intelligence operations.

HIGHLIGHTS OF THE PLENARY SESSION

Returning now to the workshop plenary session, here are sample agreements and disagreements cited by insiders and outsiders. As a point of agreement, the legal separation of church and state in American society tends to separate professional conduct from individual moral beliefs in all professions. We need to conceptualize intelligence activities in a way that unites them with fundamental belief systems so practitioners can make moral decisions in the grip of "supreme emergency." Outsiders felt that insiders, because of the secrecy, compartmentalization, and urgency of their work, fail to seek guidance about the broader and long-term consequences of operations, as in the CIA overthrow of Allende's government. Insiders regarded secrecy as a positive device for societal security. Outsiders tended to hold intelligence personnel morally responsible for the unintended consequences of their actions, whereas insiders tended to take moral responsibility only for intended consequences. But it was noted that this discrepancy is found between insiders and outsiders in law enforcement, medicine, science, and other specialties.

At the plenary session, the participating philosophers-as-ethicists were Charles Young (chair), Ann Davis, Grant Marler, and Kurt Norlin. (Paul Hurley, Brian Keeley, Dion Scott-Kakures, and John Vickers participated in earlier sessions.) In critiquing the moderate consequentialist position for intelligence operations, philosophers called attention to the slippery-slope phenomenon in overriding constraints: morally tolerable operations easily gain momentum and slide into morally intolerable operations. Philosophers pursued the related problems of insufficient time for moral deliberation and of limited rationality by decision makers. They proposed that intelligence practitioners, like everyone else, need strong moral principles that can be used under pressure, even though this method is imperfect. Marler, who had a prior career in intelligence, emphasized the special moral injury of depriving personnel, such as the counternarcotics agent and the medical engineer, of agency by not involving them in the decision-making process. Their sense of moral violation contrasted with the moral well-being of Moon in OSS operations, whose unit in North Burma, beyond the range of military supervision, had exercised thoughtful moral autonomy.

As for a moral theory that could encompass both civic and intelligence ethics, the philosophers were cautious. A unified field theory? I don't know. One needs to know a lot more about the kinds of problems that come up to see whether there's a common structure or not. What might strike one as a remote analogy is the drug use controversy in Olympic athletes. There are things you're prepared to do that you probably ought not to do to win an Olympic medal—taking certain kinds of drugs—and then various sorts of secrecies that attach to that. There are many similarities and probably many differences between those cases and military intelligence cases. I think the idea of a casebook, in which lots and lots of cases are compiled, is a great idea (C. Young, paraphrased).

When you look at different applications [of moral theory], whether it's primarily in bioethics, or in so-called business ethics, or in environmental ethics, or in ethics of intelligence operations, certain features are more salient and your principles are going to be more responsible, or your sensibility more responsive, to those features. . . . What we want to do is get enough credibility for a theory of application that people who are concerned with moral theory are paying attention to it (A. Davis, paraphrased).

On the one hand, I don't see how a piecemeal approach can carry much weight with people. Right and wrong are not discipline-specific concepts, and people intuitively understand that. Any bag of discipline-specific theories will therefore always be recognized as a mere patchwork of ideas that betrays our lack of deep understanding of the concepts involved. On the other hand, I'm pessimistic about getting widespread acceptance for a unified moral theory, because accepting a moral theory involves accepting the worldview in which the theory naturally fits. Our moral theory is bound to look very different depending on whether we view human beings as God's greatest creation, or as biologically evolved organisms, or as souls traveling an eternal cycle of death and rebirth, or what have you. . . . So the Unified Theory is unforeseeably far down the road (K. Norlin, paraphrased from later comments).

Finally, the artists reflected on the workshop. John Crigler, a guitarist-composer, asserted that the ethical good is distinct from the aesthetic good, and it damages human beings to limit either one. We should stop struggling, as we had earlier in the workshop, with the image of a Nazi death camp commander enjoying Mozart. James Groleau, a printmaker, questioned whether we had missed a nonpolitical motive for secrecy, related to personal identity and work process. He prefers to keep his preparatory sketches private, but gave participants a glimpse of one workshop sketch, just as they had offered glimpses of their secrets. Cynthia Ford, a poet, remarked on the marvel of workshop participants just being there together: people we believe to be monsters or absurd are sitting next to us at dinner eating lettuce with us.

THE RELEVANCE OF INTELLIGENCE
ETHICS TO THE MILITARY

The full moral dignity of the armed services in American society requires coordination among intelligence ethics, military ethics, and civilian ethics. In the public mind, the military is morally bound to its affiliates: the CIA, the Atomic Energy Commission, the weapons industry, and so on. The military is also inseparable institutionally. Col. L. Fletcher Prouty, "the Focal Point officer for contacts between the CIA and the Department of Defense on matters pertaining to the military support of the Special Operations of that Agency" from 1955 to 1963, has detailed the penetration of the military by the CIA and the usurpation of military resources for CIA operations.[2] Military virtue notwithstanding, for moral legitimization with the "liberal elite," I believe the military will have to answer for CIA covert operations.

Contemporary multinational military interventions for humanitarian purposes further create a demand for conspicuously "clean hands" intelligence. "Dirty hands" intelligence may be tolerated for the sake of national interests, but only "clean hands" intelligence supports the moral rationales for peacekeeping operations, disaster relief, care of refugees, arms inspection and control, war crimes prosecution, and monitoring of environmental conventions.[3] Explicit ethical standards would also assist intelligence services in collaboration with idealistic disciplines, such as anthropology and medicine, and with altruistic nongovernmental organizations, such as the Red Cross.

Further, intelligence services themselves need recognized ethical standards for recruitment, morale, and retention of personnel, as emphasized by former Inspector General of the Central Intelligence Agency Frederick P. Hitz.[4]

NOTES

1. Michael Walzer, *Just and Unjust Wars* (New York: Basic Books, 1977), p. 247.

2. Col. L. Fletcher Prouty, *The Secret Team*, 173, Englewood Cliffs, N.J.: p. vii.

3. Par Eriksson, "Intelligence In Peacekeeping Operations," *International Journal of Intelligence and Counterintelligence* 10(1), 1–18.

4. Frederick P. Hitz, "The Future of American Espionage," *International Journal of Intelligence and Counterintelligence*, 13(1), 1–20.

19

Sociology: The Ethics of Covert Methods

Roger Homan

Author's note: The appearance of this paper will make clear to Bob Skelton, Senior Lecturer in Sociology at Brighton Polytechnic, how great is the debt I owe him for advice and guidance: this I gratefully acknowledge. In referring to previous covert researches I have drawn heavily upon Erikson (1967).

ABSTRACT

This paper concerns ethical issues raised by a covert research enquiry conducted in a community of primitive sectarians described as "old-time pentecostals." Covert methods—interviewing and fully participant observation—were chosen on pragmatic grounds and in view of the subjects' marked rejection of "the world" in general and of sociology in particular.

Two types of ethical problem are considered: matters of individual morality and those of professional ethics. Covert research is a pragmatic expedient, ideally nonreactive and giving access to secret transactions; but it is also justifiable in view of the right of subjects to be free from disturbance and inhibition. It is argued that covert methods are in certain cases favorable to and in the interests of subjects but potentially detrimental to the personality of the fieldworker, in whom certain traits may persist even after he has left the field.

INTRODUCTION

This paper is a confession: it is a critical reflection on the use by its writer of the method of covert participant observation, of which covert interviewing is regarded to be a part. I used such a method with commitment over a period of about eighteen months but now wish to express serious reservations on its adoption.

The purpose of my work in the field was to describe and analyze the language-behavior prevailing in a range of sectarian groupings which I identified as "old-time pentecostal." To this end, field research was conducted by a number of methods, the major of which were observation and interviewing; each of these two methods took overt and covert forms.[1]

The pentecostal churches trace their present-day history back to supposed manifestations of the Holy Spirit which first appeared in the United States in 1900 in the forms of outbreaks of "the speaking in tongues" and other ecstasies. It was not until 1907 that pentecost arrived in Great Britain, and there are now pentecostal churches throughout the world; they are theologically fundamentalist and evangelical and operationally revivalist. While pentecostals rightly claim to represent all social classes, the emphatic appeal is to the socially and physically disadvantaged, and old-time pentecostals characteristically reject "the world" of the present day and offer the hope of a more glorious existence "when He comes."[2]

The category "old-time" distinguishes the subjects of my research from believers in "new pentecost" and the similar but better-known "charismatic movement." The pentecostal historian Donald Gee regarded old-time pentecost to have had its swan song in the great conventions at Preston in 1945 and 1946.[3] However, I use "old-time" to distinguish the extant culture of old-time pentecost, which persists in groups of dominantly first-generation pentecostals. The "old-time" and the "new" were seldom observed to co-exist within a single assembly. To a significant degree, the two types are peculiar to separate generations, and the "new" form has been seen as a means of solving "the problem of the second generation."[4]

Old-time pentecost has characteristics of language and behavior that clearly distinguish it from contemporary revivalist traditions. It is enthusiastic, and its performers are even aggressive; rhythmic clapping is the normative congregational support of hymns and choruses while preaching and announcements are interrupted with the "praise phrases" "Alleluya," "Amen," "Glory to God," and "Praise God." Women's heads are covered and the world is systematically rejected: old-timers resist and condemn social change; are conservative in ethos; and derive great comfort from the assurance that "Jesus Christ is the same yesterday, today, and forever." The normal form of address in interpersonal greetings is "brother" or "sister" while the addressee of prayer is "God" or "Lord." Testimonies are given with great frequency and old-timers in each other's company lose no opportunities of attributing sacred significance to a secular report or occasion: thus the greeting "happy new year" occurs as "I wish you a happy new year—in the Lord." In "seasons of prayer," one voice prevails from a person who stands for the purpose while those sitting murmur in support.

New pentecost lacks the esoteric language and references that characterize the old-time. Greetings are more often wholly secular, and the forms of address "brother" and "sister" have given way to the use of names. Performers offer prayers simultaneously, and a prayer time may be prolonged before any single voice emerges or dominates. New pentecost is in many respects less hierarchical, and its social relations are less competitive than in the old-time. Guitar music is popular, and new pentecost favors a distinctive repertoire of quieter and more meditative choruses including "He is Lord," "Hallelujah hallelujah," and "Amazing Grace." The pastor exercises a less-obtrusive role, and many assemblies practice "body ministry" as a means of using many or all the talents of members in worship. Prayer is most frequently addressed to "Father."

Old-time pentecost was judged to be highly disfavorable to the conduct of overt sociological research: such a judgment was made during the course of non-participant observation which was conducted in an overt way in some sixty assemblies in England and Wales, Canada and the United States and had the function of a period of "watchful waiting."[5] Notes and recordings were made during the meetings, but at the same time it was possible to test and rehearse a variety of roles and stances and—in the absence of a comprehensive literature of appropriate strategies for a researcher among pentecostals—to choose and design procedures for participant observation.

In observed situations in old-time pentecost, there was a consistent denigration by preachers of education in schools and universities. Old-timers are chiefly suspicious of schools for their teaching of the theory of evolution in contradiction of a fundamentalist interpretation of the Genesis narrative: assaults on universities were a feature of a more general iconoclasm, the intention of which was to "bring down the mighty from their seat." Pentecostals are great levelers: they like to see the proud sinner break down in tears and to hear again that "it is easier for a camel to go through the eye of a needle than for a rich man to enter the kingdom of heaven." The medical profession, it was noted, was not so much respected for its achievements as cited for its limitations. The consistent disposition of pentecostals was to deprive institutions respected in "the world" of the esteem they were accorded. Pentecostals receive the solace offered by preachers to the disadvantaged with "Amen," "Praise God," and other interpolations of approval:

What does it profit a man, dear ones tonight, if he gain the whole world and lose his soul? (preacher).

The greatest scholars and the greatest intellectuals think they know it all.

They don't know anything at all. They know so very, very little (crusade speaker).

While there are conspicuous exceptions, such as the billing of "Professor John Robertson D.D." by George Jeffreys' old-time Revival Party in 1932, old-time pentecost has in general expressed indifference or even hostility to worldly honors. This is not at all the case in new pentecost, which is well populated by students and members of other ascending classes.

Of all the people in universities, the sociologist is for old-time pentecostals the real bogeyman. In the period of watchful waiting it transpired that old-timers hold a generalized view of sociology as "communist inspired" or "atheistic." The likelihood of the prevalence of such a view adversely affecting field relations between old-timers and the overt researcher was attested in pilot interviews. One pastor, for example, felt he could not communicate his understanding of recruitment to the young people's fellowship as the interviewer did not accept his idea of "redemption" and therefore would not appreciate in his heart what the informant was saying. A number of informants gave short or inadequate answers and explained that pentecost was something in the heart, in implicit contradistinction to sociological research which belonged to the head. While new pentecostals did not register such an antipathy to sociological research, their language and behavior lacked the peculiarities and sectarian qualities which it was the intention to investigate. Clearly, the presentation of a researcher in that explicit role would have involved the purposeful education of subjects in research interests, methods, and objectives, and, even then, the method would have been likely to be highly reactive in affecting language-behavior available for observation.

The selection of covert methods was thus based on pragmatic considerations: it was judged that going underground would afford the greater opportunity of observing the normal language-behavior of old-time pentecostals.

The stance adopted in observation was that described by Buford Junker, Raymond Gold, and others as "complete" and by Fink as "genuine participation."[6] That is to say, the field observer conformed his outward behavior in all possible respects with the norm existing in the assembly. He adopted the appropriate postures for prayer, singing, and listening; in singing he allowed his voice to be audible, in listening to addresses and announcements he interpolated the "praise phrases" as appropriate. He carried a black leather bible with him to the assembly. He shook hands with other members of the assembly and exchanged sacred greetings, thereby presenting himself as "saint" rather than "sinner" and preempting the special attention (evangelism) given to outsiders. He took standard initiatives like interrupting a hymn and reciting the forthcoming verse; he occasionally requested choruses. When, after some months of membership, he was called upon to open a meeting in prayer, he did as he was asked. He accepted and reciprocated invitations to tea with other members of the assembly. He contributed to the "tithes and offerings," brought forward prayer needs, took the weekly magazine of the sect, *Redemption Tidings*. Having heard that some ministers can discern a spurious "tongue" from a real one, he did not jeopardize his studiously achieved credibility by testing their skill; but as the gift of tongues was in any case operant in only six members of the assembly, the lack of such a performance did not distinguish him. He dressed tidily but soberly, refrained from the wearing of denim and from using pubs in the neighborhood of the assembly. After the fashion of other members of the assembly, he chose a place in the meeting that could be called his own; this was near the back to facilitate observation and to render his own behavior as nonreactive as possible. He kept a low profile, aiming at a balance between being so marginal a member that his commitment would be questioned and being so central as to impede the observer role and to become himself a nonnative factor in assembly behavior. The use of a tape recorder in pentecostal meetings is often allowed to "carry the blessing to dear ones": this pretext was occasionally used to obtain recordings for transcription. Written notes were never made during the meetings except in cases where a preacher had suggested "you might like to write this down"; such an invitation afforded the use of pen and used envelope carried for the contingency on which the field worker recorded whatever data he was having to remember. Accommodation was taken within a two-minute walk of the chosen assembly, and field notes were recorded there after each observation.

Honesty, while not necessarily being the most effective policy, was in some aspects of the researcher's self-presentation judged as the simplest to maintain. Occupation, name, age, address, and spiritual history were readily given in response to inquiry, though conveniently inquirers were often satisfied with incomplete answers and ecclesiastical allegiance, and the reason for joining the assembly were never thoroughly investigated by subjects. The policy was carefully to conceal the research interest, and the researcher attempted to play down his knowledge of pentecostal organizations and his unnatural curiosity in some aspects of pentecostal behavior; to that end, all religious volumes were removed from the shelves in his home so as not to be observed by visiting members of the assembly, should any have occasion to call.

PRECEDENTS

The use of methods even more clandestine and dishonest than these is long and well-established in sociological and related research. The anthropologist Caudill posed as a mental patient by complaining of symptoms he did not feel.[7] Mortimer Sullivan reenlisted in the air force with a spurious name, birth date, and personal history and developed a new set of mannerisms and personal appearance in order to investigate enlisting procedures.[8] John A. Lofland's graduate students posed as alcoholics and attended meetings of Alcoholics Anonymous in that guise.[9] Perhaps the most remarkable and controversial of participant observation studies in disguise, however, is that of Laud Humphreys who adopted the role of lookout-voyeur to observe homosexual encounters in men's toilets and took the registration numbers of his subjects' cars in order to trace and interview them under the pretext of a social health survey.[10] Humphreys' method earned an arrest for loitering.[11]

It appears that William F. Whyte misled his subjects by professing that he was studying the history of an urban area when his real interest was the sociology of the slum.[12] His strategy was not to deny a research interest altogether but to explain his conspicuous presence and notebook in terms of a false interest; he developed a special role (social historian) rather than one that already existed among his subjects, but his purpose remained covert.

Less use has been made of a complete and covert participant strategy in the study of religious behavior. The best known of such work is probably that of Festinger and his colleagues[13] who joined a gathering of mystics by professing religious beliefs they did not hold. Von Hoffman and Cassidy attempted to operate a covert participant strategy in a black pentecostal church in Chicago but found it "unbearable" to pose in a dishonest role in such a situation; they complained that their feelings of invading privacy became too acute for them to continue.[14] In their study, however, being white and middle class[15] may in any case have threatened the guise and precipitated anxiety. In a rather more short-term observation in British pentecost, Walker and Atherton adopted independent and complementary roles, one posing as "a committed believer, and the other as an evangelical, interested but sceptical about Pentecostalism itself."[16]

Surreptitious methods have been particularly favored by investigators of speech behavior, the first effective—and arguably normative—use of covert methods being made by Moore, who slowly walked up and down Broadway at 7:30 each evening noting fragments of conversation.[17] Later Carlson, Cook, and Stromberg monitored foyer conversations during the intervals of symphony concerts[18] and Henle and Hubble pursued unwitting subjects in the streets and department stores and even the home, "concealed themselves under beds in students[']" rooms where tea parties were being held, eavesdropped in dormitory smoking rooms and washrooms, and listened to telephone conversations.[19] Webb and his associates even recommend rigging a microphone in a mock hearing aid for the purpose of recording; "it works extremely well in inducing the subject to lean over and shout directly into the recording apparatus."[20]

THE PROBLEM

In many respects my methods were more straightforward and less invasive of privacy than those adopted in some of these studies, but there remains a substantial body of opinion within the profession which would disapprove the manner of my field work. For example, the British Sociological Association has designed principles of practice that I did not adopt:

> The sociologist should subscribe to the doctrine of "informed consent" on the part of subjects and accordingly take pains to explain fully the objects and implications of his research to individual subjects. The sociologist has a duty to explain as fully as possible and in terms meaningful to the subjects what his research is about, who is undertaking and financing it and why it is being undertaken.[21]

Again, Edward Shils, whose treatment of the ethical issues of participant observation I respect as the most considered and scholarly analysis to date, is clearly critical of such methods as that which I adopted:

> It is wrong for an inquirer ostensibly to take up membership in a community with the intention of conducting a sociological inquiry there without making it plain that that is what he is doing. His self-disclosure might occasionally hamper research he is conducting but the degree of injury suffered does not justify the deviation from straightforwardness implied by withholding his true intentions.[22]

In view of these strong objections, a covert researcher owes to the profession a defense of his methods. In my case, a concern on ethical grounds with the use of surreptitious methods only developed after I had become committed to and established within them; this concern was in some ways substantiated and in some ways resolved by a subsequent finding in the literature of perennial objections to disguises, whether based on ethical or pragmatic grounds.[23]

My own reservations and the objections of commentators have operated at two levels. First, questions have been raised regarding issues of *individual morality*: for example, clandestine research acts may involve students or research workers in a crisis of conscience, not least when lying or "acting a lie" and when exposing themselves to the potentially harmful influences and experiences to be encountered by participants in some communities.[24] Second, the use of disguises raises questions of *professional ethics*, and the argument is made that covert methods are not appropriate to the conduct of bona fide sociological enquiry. I propose now to deal with these distinct categories of problem in turn.

INDIVIDUAL MORALITY

Concern here is with the ethical code the fieldworker adopts in his personal life which may render unacceptable or uncongenial some of the expectations made of him either directly by supervisors or indirectly as a consequence of a tradition or fashion for particular methodologies in his discipline. Erikson has been concerned that the division of labor within (American) sociology is such that research studies are set up by academics and executed by their graduate students.[25] In such a system, students may find themselves developing skills and procedures known to them formerly as the practice of espionage.

In the case of my research, for which I chose my own methods, there emerged two kinds of ethical problem at the individual level:

Problems peculiar to participation in religious communities. There is something about religious behavior that is rather private, and when a group of believers is praying, it might be supposed, anyone present ought to be doing likewise or at least to grant them immunity from observation. To make notes or recordings during prayer would be tantamount to talking or laughing throughout a funeral service. Even to regard prayer as a "performance" may seem to some to be rather insensitive. In the event, I did not find this a problem for myself though sociologists who on occasion joined me in the field found observation as "unbearable" as had von Hoffman and Cassidy.[26] I have been engaged in the sociological or phenomenological study of religion since my introduction to it as an undergraduate in 1967 and by now—for better or worse—have "hardened" to it in the way that professionals in other places—operating theaters, consulting rooms, abattoirs—also develop strategies that distance them from their subjects. In fact, it might be argued in favor of covert methods in the study of religious behavior that they constitute a more considerate and sensitive strategy to those in which conspicuous recording devices and modes of behavior or the self-disclosure of the researcher cause the performers to know that their activities are being monitored. Such a self-consciousness as a disclosure of the researcher may engender would adversely affect the character and quality of the performance for the subjects themselves: for example, it may become less sincere.

Participation in the "breaking of bread" was the occasion for a crisis of conscience. To have declined the offer of bread would have been a conspicuous dissociation from the worship of the assembly, yet my own religious convictions inclined me against receiving. I participated on the grounds that it was expedient for the research, that it was both in the pentecostal definition and in my own no more a "mystery" than a friend's coffee, and that the invitation was in any case open to "all who love the Lord," in which category I could include myself. Again, whenever I was asked to pray or testify, I did so within the beliefs and values that I could accept and share: I could happily pray for the deliverance of Christians serving prison sentences in the Soviet Union but could not take sides with Ian Smith of Rhodesia, whom the assembly favoured as a "born-again believer."

However, there were even more sensitive behavior patterns in pentecost, and these I eschewed. Although I practiced the speaking of tongues at home, I could not persuade myself either that it was fair to test it out among those whom I had befriended or that it was expedient for my research, and in any case I feared that it might be "discerned" as the tongue of a demon. Similarly, I could not offer myself for baptism. Somehow these measures seemed inordinately fraudulent.

It was fortunate that those activities in which misgivings prevented me from taking part were not ones that were critical for my enquiry or credibility whereas those which were necessary happened to be ones in which I could conscientiously participate. But another fieldworker with a different set of beliefs and sensitivities might not as happily assume such a role or strategy as those which I adopted.

Problems of personal ethics not involving specifically religious principles or the location of the fieldwork in a religious institution. The chief of these were those which involved the communication either by behavior or by verbal declaration of understandings that were not in fact true; for example, both in answer to questions and by the use of a "password" greeting, the fieldworker allowed it to be thought that his allegiance was already to a pentecostal institution and that he subscribed to its beliefs. It happened that problems in this category were those most easily resolved in terms of the personal conscience of the researcher. The line taken was that the truth often hurts, causes discomfort, or disturbs behavior; nonreactivity, as explained above, was desirable not only methodologically for the researcher but spiritually for his subjects. A guest offered a burnt cake by an old lady may more kindly give a favorable assessment than an honest one; Similarly, clandestine strategies and occasionally dishonest professions of identity and belief were potentially less disruptive of the stable worship behavior of an assembly to which its members were arguably entitled than open declarations and disagreements.

In retrospect, however, two ethical problems persist at the individual level. The researcher in the field forms relations that he knows—as his subjects do not—to be predicated upon a dishonest representation of his interests and developed through the simulation of "warmth" which Shils finds so contemptible.[27] The fieldworker has an ulterior motive of which his subjects are not aware when they kindly invite him to tea or shower him with Christmas cards. At the end of my time in the field this endures as a problem, and the contemplation of it engenders feelings of guilt. Within the institutional context of the assembly I observed, the sense of exploiting relationships was alleviated by participating as a giver as well as a receiver,[28] but, in the inevitable and profitable less formal encounters, I could not escape the feeling that Abraham might have had as he went up the mountain to sacrifice Isaac: though guided by a higher purpose, the rationale of the activity was such that he could not share it and was scarcely in the perceived interests of the cooperating party.

Only after withdrawal from the field at the conclusion of the enquiry, did it become possible to begin to assess the seriousness of the second enduring reservation held at the individual level: this has to do with the effects that covert methods have upon the researcher as a person. I have already found (in shops and lifts, on trains and at coffee with colleagues) that I am continually sifting and noting potentially significant social data: my fear is that the "phatic communion" type of interaction that has always featured in my behavior repertoire now has the further function of "covert interview." Formerly close friends remark that I have become "very analytical." What I am saying may be more than a statement of the familiar problem of involvement in, say, higher education alienating the student from the folk from whence he came; for I am supposing that the use of covert methods, especially if sustained, has serious implications for the subsequent development of open and honest relationships. I am suggesting that the habit of masquerading in a disguised role is not easily discontinued outside the field and that the treatment of subjects as friends readily transforms into the treatment of friends as subjects. To some extent this reservation consists with a major objection expressed by Shils, who is concerned with the development of techniques to perceive the deeper and subtler aspects of human life, such as motives for behavior.[29] But, whereas Shils is disturbed by the very development and practice of such techniques in view of the threat they constitute to individual privacy, my concern is that they may endure and be detrimental in the personal life of those who adopt them in the field. This being my suspicion, however, it somewhat consoles me to think that more overt and traditional methods might also have had lasting and adverse effects upon the personality; for example, it is supposed that a skilled interviewer will have learnt to control and suppress his feelings on sensitive issues, and so training and sustained practice may bring about a less responsive behavior pattern in him. These possibilities and fears await empirical verification.

PROFESSIONAL ETHICS

Von Hoffman and Cassidy[30] and Erikson[31] have expressed the view that while masquerading may be an acceptable and appropriate strategy in some professions—such as espionage and journalism—the professional ethics of sociologists are developed on a different basis. The sociologist operates with a different kind of warrant and has a different set of professional and scientific interests; while the detective is fortified by social sanctions in many of his activities, the sociologist does not draw the same support from the values he espouses.

The argument that declarations that are dishonest or incompletely honest may damage the reputation of sociology applies with particular force in relation to research among pentecostals, for whom sociology is in any case the prince of devils. I was aware always of a need to conserve the countryside for the enjoyment of future visitors. This problem has two aspects:

1. Discomfort may be caused among subjects by the very act of research. I have indicated above what measures I took to minimize this discomfort and have suggested the appropriateness of covert methods in view of this.
2. The reporting and possible publication of findings raises separate ethical problems. Many transactions observed might not have taken place at all had it been supposed that the press was present.

Fichter and Kolb have observed that the obligations of the modern scientist are to search for truth, be objective, discern the relevant, check data meticulously, and, in some cases, accept responsibility for the effects of publication.[32] Such a view may be based upon the conceptualization of phenomena as *objects*. The ethical issues specific to the conduct of the social sciences, however, arise from the conceptualization of phenomena as *subjects*; and subjects—that is, people and their behavior—have rights which must be respected. For practical as well as moral reasons, the sociologist must consider the rights of those persons who have, even unwittingly, allowed, facilitated, and cooperated with his fieldwork. I reckoned that members of the communities I studied had rights to secrecy, privacy, freedom from disturbance, reputation, and respect, both individually and collectively. However, the reputation of a community was not regarded to be sacrosanct. If I observed that techniques used in divine healing appeared to precipitate heart attacks—as I did not—I would have wanted to be free to report it, even though such effects were not widely known outside pentecost; that is to say that I would not allow a perception of the perceived rights of a community to develop into a "false sentimentality" or to overprotect my subjects from a candid interpretation of their behavior and its consequences. Nor did I acknowledge a right among my subjects not to be observed.

THE END AND THE MEANS

Julius Roth has argued that there is no clear line to be drawn between those methods which are covert and those which are overt. "Is it moral," he asks, "if one gets a job in a factory to earn tuition and then takes advantage of the opportunity to carry out a sociological study, but immoral to deliberately plant oneself in the factory for the express purpose of observing one's fellow workers?" By what criteria, we are being asked, would we establish material gain to be a more laudable motive than the opportunity for research enquiry? Such a question might be asked, for instance, of Joan Emerson's observations of gynaecological consultations conducted by her in the profession of a nurse.[33] Or again, I and many sociologists spend available Saturday afternoons observing professional football. As far as we are aware we hope for skilled and creative performances, an enjoyable match, and possibly a victory for the favored side; and are much less motivated to attend matches by the opportunity to observe crowd behavior or interaction between professionals. Inevitably, however, there are moments when one's observation is guided by sociological principles, and I have even recorded notes after a match. It would be absurd to announce that there was a sociologist on the terraces making casual observations and to explain his purpose and methods. For those who pay their money at the turnstile, sociological observation is, unlike throwing beer bottles or running on to the pitch, an acceptable and unobtrusive activity. Similarly, pentecostals proclaim unconditionally that "all are welcome." My covert research was my reason for being among the pentecostals, and worship was the form which my behavior took; while for others worship was the reason for attendance, but no doubt there were moments, human nature being what it is, when observation was the form of their behavior. I find that I cannot attend any religious service without also behaving at least for some of the time as an observer, and I am inclined to Roth's view that the distinction between casual and purposeful observation is both arbitrary and difficult to establish for the purpose of ethics.

There remains the possibility that the end justifies the means, and the British Sociological Association allows covert methods "where it is not possible to use other methods to obtain essential data."[34] In one interpretation, this argument amounts to an arrogant claim about the significance of research findings. Another approach might begin to defend this concession with the supposition that no situation which in principle is open to observation[35] ought not also to be observable in practice. This view takes various forms in the literature: for example, there are contentions that there is an inherent right to know, that knowledge is superior to ignorance, and that sociological knowledge is a value of such an order that anything which impedes its achievement is undesirable.[36] At this point the espousal of sociological knowledge amounts to a denial of the right of subjects to privacy. However, the community which declares "all are welcome" thereby forgoes its privacy. In formal—almost legal—terms, it has no grounds for excluding the social researcher and few for withholding its normal behavior from him. Yet I have contended that normal behavior cannot be available in pentecost for the overt researcher to observe, and this is why I was obliged to go underground. My subjects and I could not have been honest with each other at the same time; if I disclosed my researcher identity, they would have withheld certain data, and their behavior would have been inhibited. My experience in the field confirmed that the concealment of my identity facilitated communication by subjects.

I remain, therefore, relatively satisfied that the covert methods I have described need not significantly affect or damage either one's subjects or the standing of sociology: my abiding concern is rather with the effects of such methods upon those who practice them.

NOTES

1. The full account is Roger Homan, *A Sociological Analysis of the Language-behaviour of Old-time Pentecostals,* unpublished Ph.D. thesis, University of Lancaster, 1978; a fragment appears as Roger Homan, "Interpersonal Communication in Pentecostal Meetings," *Sociological Review,* vol. XXVI, no. 3 (August 1978), pp. 499–518.

2. Bryan Wilson, *Sects and Society: A Sociological Study of Three Religious Groups in Britain.* London: Heinemann, 1961, pp. 89–91.

3. Donald Gee, *Wind and Flame.* Nottingham: Assemblies of God Publishing House, 1967, pp. 2–3.

4. Interview with national executive member of one of the major pentecostal organizations in Great Britain.

5. This term is owed to Florence R. Kluckhohn, "The Participant Observer Technique in Small Communities," *American Journal of Sociology,* vol. XLVI, 1940, p. 334.

6. Buford H. Junker, *Field Work: an Introduction to the Social Sciences.* Chicago: University of Chicago Press, 1960; Raymond L. Gold, "Roles in Sociological Field Observations" in McCall and Simmons, *Issues in Participant Observation: a Text and Reader.* Reading, Massachusetts: Addison-Wesley, 1969, p. 33; and R. Fink, "Techniques of Observation and their Social and Cultural Limitations," *Mankind,* vol. V, 1955, pp. 60–8.

7. William C. Caudill et al., "Social Structure and Interaction Processes on a Psychiatric Ward," *American Journal of Orthopsychiatry,* vol. XXII, 1952, pp. 314–34.

8. Mortimer A. Sullivan, Stuart A. Queen, and Ralph C. Patrick, "Participant Observation as Employed in the Study of a Military Training Program," *American Sociological Review,* vol. XXIII, 1958, pp. 660–7.

9. John A. Lofland and Robert A. Lejeune, "Initial Interaction of Newcomers in Alcoholics Anonymous: a Field Experiment in Class Symbols and Socialization," *Social Problems,* vol. VIII, 1960, pp. 102–11.

10. Laud Humphreys, *Tearoom Trade: a Study of Homosexual Encounters in Public Places.* London: Duckworth, 1970, pp. 41–4.

11. Laud Humphreys, op. cit., pp. 95–6.

12. William F. Whyte, "Observational Field-work Methods," in Jahoda, Deutsch

and Cook, *Research Methods in Social Relations: Part Two, Selected Techniques.* New York: Dryden Press, 1951, pp. 493–513. Whyte comments, p. 494; "I did later publish an article in a historical journal."

13. Leon Festinger, Henry W. Riecken, and Stanley Schachter, *When Prophecy Fails.* Minneapolis: University of Minnesota Press, 1956.

14. Nicholas von Hoffman and Sally W. Cassidy, "Interviewing Negro Pentecostals," *American Journal of Sociology,* vol. LII, 1956, p. 195.

15. Ibid., p. 196.

16. Andrew G. Walker and James S. Atherton, "An Easter Pentecostal Convention: the Successful Management of a 'Time of Blessing,'" *Sociological Review,* vol. XIX, 1971, p. 368.

17. H. T. Moore, "Further Data Concerning Sex Differences," *Journal of Abnormal and Social Psychology,* vol. XVII, 1922, pp. 210–14.

18. J. Carlson, S. W. Cook, and E. L. Stromberg, "Sex Differences in Conversation," *Journal of Applied Psychology,* vol. XX, pp. 727–35.

19. M. Henle and M. B. Hubble, "'Egocentricity' in Adult Conversation," *Journal of Social Psychology,* vol. IX, 1938, p. 230.

20. Eugene J. Webb, Donald T. Campbell, Richard D. Schwartz, and Lee Sechrest, *Unobtrusive Measures: Nonreactive Research in the Social Sciences.* Chicago: Rand McNally, 1966, p. 150.

21. British Sociological Association, "Statement of Ethical Principles and their Application to Sociological Practice," 1973, p. 3.

22. Edward A. Shils, "Social Inquiry and the Autonomy of the Individual" in Daniel Lerner, *The Human Meaning of Social Sciences.* Cleveland, Ohio: Meridian Books, 1959, p. 128.

23. For examples, Whyte, op. cit.; Shils, op. cit.; Joseph H. Fichter and William L. Kolb, "Ethical Limitations on Sociological Reporting," *American Sociological Review,* vol. XVIII, 1953, pp. 544–50; Julius Roth, "Comments on 'secret observation,'" *Social Problems,* vol. IX, 1962, pp. 283–4; Jurgen Friedrichs and Harmut Ludtke, *Participant Observation: Theory and Practice.* Lexington, Mass.: Lexington Books, 1975; and Kai T. Erikson, "A Comment on Disguised Observation in Sociology," *Social Problems,* vol. XIV, 1967, pp. 366–73.

24. Perhaps the most extreme case here is the participant method of Timothy Leary in investigating the effects of hallucinogenic drugs. See Timothy Leary, Ralph Metzner, and Richard Alpert, *The Psychedelic Experience.* New York: University Books, 1965.

25. Erikson, op. cit., p. 568.

26. Von Hoffman and Cassidy, op. cit., p. 195.

27. Shils, op. cit., p. 123.

28. Rosalie H. Wax, *Doing Fieldwork: Warnings and Advice.* Chicago: University of Chicago Press, 1971, reckons to feel happier in the field when reciprocating helpfulness.

29. Shils, op. cit., p. 123.

30. Von Hoffman and Cassidy, op. cit., p. 195.

31. Erikson, op. cit., p. 368.

32. Fichter and Kolb, op. cit., p. 544. Roth, op. cit., p. 284.

33. Joan Emerson, "Behaviour in private places: sustaining definitions of reality in gynaecological examinations" in Salaman and Thompson, *People and Organizations*, London: Longman, 1973, pp. 358–71.

34. British Sociological Association, op. cit., p. 2.

35. I here mean to exclude some of the more intimate of adult relationships.

36. See Gideon Sjoberg, *Ethics, Politics and Social Research.* Cambridge, Mass.: Schenkman, 1967, p. 72.

20

Comment on "The Ethics of Covert Methods"

Martin Bulmer

> It hadn't occurred to me yet that the whole thing was a particularly ironic version of the means-justify-ends argument: with the excuse that we were seeking Truth, we were proposing to lie ourselves blind to the Truth Seekers.
>
> —Alison Lurie, *Imaginary Friends!* (London: Heinemann, 1967, p. 11): The novel contains a fine account of the stresses and strains of covert sociological research, and bears a curious resemblance in some respects to L. Festinger et al., *When Prophecy Fails*, Minneapolis, University of Minnesota Press, 1956.

Roger Homan's thoughtful reflections on the ethics of covert participant observation are an important contribution to a debate that has gone on for at least a quarter of a century.[1] They are also an effective reply to criticisms of Homan's earlier report on his research[2] on the grounds that it failed to analyze the ethical issues at stake.[3] Homan's conclusions, however, that "covert methods . . . need not significantly affect or damage either one's subjects or the standing of sociology" are of doubtful validity.

Misinformation, dissimulation, deception, and lying are features of a range of social relationships to a greater or lesser extent. Indeed, in "open" participant observation where the researcher's role is known to those whom he or she is studying, it is not unknown to play down, gloss over, or be evasive about the ultimate purpose of the research and its outcome. The issue raised by covert participant observation is not whether lying is ever justified; for in some specified circumstances it may be.[4] It is rather whether out-and-out

329

deception, disregard for the informed consent of the subjects of research, and gross invasion of privacy are justified in the cause of furthering social science. Is it legitimate to adopt the methods of undercover intelligence and espionage to further social knowledge? Is "complete" or secret observation desirable, and is it necessary?

The distinction between individual morality and professional ethics which Homan proposes is too sharply drawn. Behavior in the research situation is professional behavior as well as individual behavior, and the two are not neatly divisible. Moreover, the researcher is seen by those he is studying as occupying a special role (in this case, potential convert) as well as other more general roles. The pretense of role playing and the individual moral consequences of doing so are bound up together. If the researcher employs "a dishonest representation of his interests" and indeed of his identity, he does so as a sociologist in a professional role as well as an individual in his role as citizen.

Some of the main objections to Homan's position are as follows: Observational studies such as that described disregard the principle of informed consent. This states that "the voluntary consent of the human subject (of research) is absolutely essential." According to this principle, the subject must be competent, informed about the purposes of the research, understanding what he or she is told, and giving consent voluntarily and not under any form of duress. This principle is fully established in biomedical research practice and in the United States is increasingly being extended to all social research through federal regulations.[5] There are some difficulties in extending this principle from medical to social research—what, for example, constitutes informed consent on the part of a survey respondent[6]—but nevertheless it is a clear ethical principle framed for the defense of individual freedom against the depredations of professional researchers. Secret participant observation clearly violates this principle almost totally. Is it justifiable to depart from it on the grounds that the ends justify the means?

A different objection to the use of deception in research is that it constitutes a betrayal of trust. If the personal relationships are based upon falsehood, this may harm the subjects of the research. In his recent study of West Indian churches in Bristol, for example, Pryce describes finding himself in such a situation—being a member of two churches at the same time, concealing this fact from the other, and then finding himself with members of both churches simultaneously and being introduced as a recent convert to one. Pryce found himself unable to maintain the deception and withdrew from the second church. He then, however, found himself in a difficult ethical situation with the pastor of the church in which he remained active. He told the pastor of his research interests. This information the pastor concealed from the congregation, but put very strong pressure on Pryce to convert and be baptized in his adopted church. Despite strong personal reservations this

Pryce eventually did, apparently as part of some sort of tacit bargain with the pastor in a semi-covert research situation. Baptism did facilitate subsequent research, for rank-and-file members of the congregation showed much greater openness to the researcher after it. But they remained in ignorance of his research role.[7]

Pryce's research was only semi-covert. In entirely covert research, the potential betrayal of trust is greater. It is not a satisfactory defense to argue that in published research the identities and location of those studied is concealed. Even if this is done successfully,[8] the preservation of anonymity and confidentiality does not preserve them from harm. If those studied subsequently read or learn of the publication of the research, they must come to terms with the fact that they have been cheated and misled by someone in whom they reposed trust and confidence. Valued behavior on the part of the (secret) observer in the past—for example professions of faith, or conversion—must painfully be reinterpreted as merely instrumental and deceitful "front work." Moreover, in some cases the most cherished values and beliefs of the group may be threatened by publication, a fact recognized by anthropologists in the case of some ritual practices, where publication has been managed to avoid, for example, revelations destructive to the traditions of Australian aboriginal society.[9] And regardless of whether individuals may be identified, the publication of a study may cause harm to a group as a *group*. A world too full of pseudo-converts, pseudo-patients, pseudo-students, pseudo party-members, and others playing pseudo-roles will not promote a healthy climate for social science.

Covert participant observation looked at from the point of view of the individual subject may clearly also be a gross invasion of personal privacy. Homan quotes with sympathy the strictures of Edward Shils, who elsewhere has argued that intrusions on privacy are baneful because they interfere with an individual in his disposition of what belongs to him. The "social space" around an individual, the recollection of his past, his conversation, his body and his image, all *belong* to him. He does not acquire them through purchase or inheritance. He possesses them and is entitled to possess them by virtue of the charisma which is inherent in his existence as an individual soul—as we say nowadays, in his individuality—and which is inherent in his membership in the civil community. They belong to him by virtue of his humanity and civility.[10]

It may be argued that the benefits of research outweigh the damage which may be done by invading people's privacy. Homan also argues that in the study of certain types of demonstrative public behavior such as prayer, the privacy of the research subjects was better protected by their being unaware that he was doing research, the discomfort of having to interact with him *as a researcher* being removed. But would the same argument commend itself to members of political groups which had been infiltrated by undercover

agents or even agents provocateur?[11] Though the actions of the secret participant observer may be mild by comparison, the same objections can be made
to using such methods in both cases.

One of the most refreshing features of Homan's article is his recognition
of the effects which covert participant observation may have on the observer:
"The use of covert methods, especially if sustained, has serious implications
for the subsequent development of open and honest relationships." The
same point was made by Margaret Mead:

> Encouraging styles of research and intervention that involve lying to other
> human beings . . . tends to establish a corps of professionally calloused individu-
> als, insulated from self-criticism and increasingly available for clients who can
> become outspokenly cynical in their manipulation of other human beings, indi-
> vidually and in the mass.[12]

Homan's own self-awareness is a good defense against cynicism, but it is not
a rebuttal of the criticism. Those whose mode of operation depends on
deception may tend to develop behavior patterns of dissimulation and deceit.

The objections stated so far all rest ultimately upon moral judgments.
Some would reject such considerations as the ruminations of "ignorant and
absolutist moralists who can only see black and white."[13] Others might
argue, more legitimately, that the position is complicated by the fact that
sociologists investigate society as both researchers *and* citizens, and may well
have legitimate interests as citizens in participating and, for example, may
genuinely wish to undergo conversion to a particular set of beliefs. Nevertheless, there is powerful evidence from research in a wide variety of different styles that trust rather than distrust, openness rather than concealment,
provides a more satisfactory basis for starting on research and explaining
what one is about. Whatever one's personal involvement as a citizen, this
does not provide a justification for concealing entirely one's research purposes.

One rejoinder to this argument is to maintain that the methods used by
social scientists reflect the nature of the world they are dealing with. If they
use covert methods, it is because social order rests on deceitfulness, evasive-
ness, secrecy, front work, and basic social conflicts. Secrecy and deceit are
particularly characteristic of the centers of power in society; in order to penetrate these, secrecy to outsiders must be matched by deception to get in.
The Woodward-Bernstein exposé of Watergate provides one model.[14] There
are, however, some weaknesses in such an essentially political justification.

First, it is not clear that an argument for the use of such methods in the
study of political and business power is necessarily applicable to pentecostal
groups, juvenile gangs, professional criminals, or geographic communities.
Trust rather than distrust may still be a better strategy to adopt in the case

of the latter. Secondly, what are the unintended consequences of using covert methods? It is surely naive to claim in their support that "we know of no single instance in which our research has injured anyone, but we know of scores of individuals we have helped. . . ."[15] The investigator may make such a statement in good faith, but he has no control over the effects of publishing his research. Research on the powerful, as indeed Watergate shows, may damage public confidence in democratic processes. And it is not a reply to that to say that such *exposés* are desirable, though they may be in particular cases from particular points of view. For the third and most powerful objection is, whose causes are the right causes in social research? Why is it justifiable to use covert methods in one context and not in another? Those who advocate the use of covert methods would be the first to complain if they were used by others in other contexts—for example, to invade their own privacy or to study their own place of work or to spy on their own political activities. The problem is like that of the sociologist of knowledge. Who is to say what is the correct standpoint from which to observe objectively or to decide that the use of covert methods is legitimate?

Homan states that his initial adoption of a covert strategy was based on pragmatic grounds. In conclusion, two pragmatic arguments against the use of covert methods will be stated. The first is not wholly pragmatic, but largely so. It is that the use of covert methods in any particular study is likely to make future research in that locale or in that area either impossible or very difficult, since those studied will react adversely when they learn of the deception that has been practiced on them. Whether or not the beliefs of old-time pentecostals about sociology stemmed from previous research experiences is not stated, but the prospects for future sociologists who identify themselves as such will not be improved if news of Homan's research is widely known among those studied. But the general objection is more compelling. If sociologists adopt covert methods on a large scale, *all* research will become more difficult. Covert studies reinforce "an image already prevalent in some circles that sociologists are sly tricksters who are not to be trusted. The more widespread this image becomes, the more difficult it will be for any social scientist to carry out studies involving active participants."[16]

The second pragmatic argument is simply that covert methods are often not necessary, and that the same objectives can be achieved by overt or "open" observational studies. Many accounts of observational research stress that the success of such research depends more on the acceptance of the individual by those he is studying as someone they can trust, than on elaborate fronts and role pretense. Polsky, for example, is emphatic that in studying professional criminals, the sociologist should not "spy" or become "one of them." His task is rather to become accepted while making clear the distinction between himself and those he is studying.[17] Klockars's study of the professional "fence" encountered few problems despite the fact that the author was open about his research intentions.[18] Apparently closed and impenetrable institutions have opened themselves up to researchers who did not conceal their research interests, and yet were able to persuade those whom they studied that to allow them research access would not be threatening to them. They include the higher civil service in Britain, of whom Heclo and Wildavsky have produced a fascinating anthropological account based mainly on observation and informal interviewing.[19] Ianni's study of the Mafia was carried out openly, as he describes in the methodological appendix.[20]

Homan's account is a welcome discussion of the difficulties of the covert mode of observational research. Its conclusions about that mode of research are, however, of doubtful general ability for the moral and pragmatic reasons which are stated here. It is not argued that covert observation should *never* be used as a method of research, but that its use should be highly exceptional, and that the decision to use complete deception requires the most careful justification, if indeed it is used at all.[21]

NOTES

1. For a representative selection see W. J. Filstead (ed.), *Qualitative Methodology*, Chicago: Markham, 1970, containing papers by J. A. Barnes (1963, first published in this journal), Erikson (1967), Fichter and Kolb (1953), Sullivan et al. (1958), Lofland and Lejeune (1960), Davis (1961), and Roth (1962). For a recent discussion see J. A. Barnes, *Who Should Know What: Social Science, Privacy and Ethics*, Harmondsworth: Penguin, 1979, esp. pp. 103–28.

2. R. Homan, "Interpersonal Communication at Pentecostal Meetings," *The Sociological Review* 26, 1978, pp. 499–518.

3. "Covert Observation: a Question of Ethics," correspondence between R. Dingwall and R. Frankenberg (editor of *The Sociological Review*) in *Network: the newsletter of the British Sociological Association*, no. 11, May 1979, p. 7.

4. Cf. S. Bok, *Lying: Moral Choice in Public and Private Life*, Hassocks, Sussex: Harvester, 1978.

5. Cf. *The American Sociologist* 13, August 1978, pp. 134–72; M. L. Wax and J. Cassell (eds.), *Federal Regulations: Ethical Issues and Social Research*, Boulder, Colorado: Westview Press for the American Association for the Advancement of Science, 1979.

6. Cf. E. Singer, "Informed Consent," *American Sociological Review* 43, 1978, pp. 144–62; M. Bulmer (ed.), *Censuses, Surveys and Privacy*, London: Macmillan, 1979, esp. ch. 5.

7. K. Pryce, *Endless Pressure: a Study of West Indian Life-styles in Bristol*, Harmondsworth: Penguin, 1979, esp. pp. 282–7.

8. Cf. D. C. Gibbons, "Unidentified Research Sites and Fictitious Names," *The American Sociologist* 10, 1975, pp. 32–6.

9. Cf. Barnes, *Who Should Know What?* pp. 156–7.

10. E. Shils, "Privacy and Power," in *Center and Periphery: Essays in Macrosociology*, University of Chicago Press, 1975, p. 344.

11. G. T. Marx, "Thoughts on a Neglected Category of Social Movement Participant: the Agent Provocateur and Informant," *American Journal of Sociology* 80, 1974, pp. 402–42.

12. M. Mead, "Research with Human Beings: A Model Derived from Anthropological Field Practice," *Daedalus*, 1969, p. 376.

13. J. D. Douglas, *Investigative Social Research*, London: Sage, 1976, p. xiv.

14. C. Bernstein and B. Woodward, *All the President's Men*, London: Seeker and Warburg, 1974. The argument outlined in favor of the use of covert methods is most clearly stated in Douglas, op. cit.

15. Douglas, op. cit., p. xiv.

16. D. P. Warwick, "Tearoom Trade: Means and Ends in Social Research," in L. Humphreys, *Tearoom Trade*, Chicago: Aldine, 1975, 2nd edition with new appendixes, p. 211. See also D. P. Warwick, "Social Scientists ought to Stop Lying," *Psychology Today* 8, February 1975, pp. 38–40 and 105–6.

17. N. Polsky, *Hustlers, Beats and Others*, Harmondsworth: Penguin, 1971, esp. pp. 126–34.

18. C. Klockars, *The Professional Fence*, London: Tavistock, 1975; and C. Klockars, "Field Ethics for the Life History" in R. S. Weppner (ed.), *Street Ethnography*, London: Sage, 1977, pp. 201–26.

19. H. Heclo and A. Wildavsky, *The Private Government of Public Money*, London: Macmillan, 1974, esp. ch. 3, "Village Life in Civil Service Society."

20. F. A. J. and E. R. Ianni, *A Family Business: Kinship and Social Control in Organised Crime*, London: Routledge, 1972, esp. pp. 175–89.

21. For comments on an earlier draft, from different standpoints to my own, I am grateful to Roger Homan and Jennifer Platt. Some of the issues raised here will be further explored in M. Bulmer (ed.), *Social Research Ethics*, London: Macmillan, forthcoming.

21

Science: Anthropologists as Spies

David Price

On December 20, 1919, under the heading "Scientists as Spies," *The Nation* published a letter by Franz Boas, the father of academic anthropology in America. Boas charged that four American anthropologists, whom he did not name, had abused their professional research positions by conducting espionage in Central America during the First World War. Boas strongly condemned their actions, writing that they had "prostituted science by using it as a cover for their activities as spies." Anthropologists spying for their country severely betrayed their science and damaged the credibility of all anthropological research, Boas wrote; a scientist who uses his research as a cover for political spying forfeits the right to be classified as a scientist.

The most significant reaction to this letter occurred ten days later at the annual meeting of the American Anthropological Association (AAA), when the association's governing council voted to censure Boas, effectively removing him from the council and pressuring him to resign from the national research council. Three out of four of the accused spies (their names, we now know, were Samuel Lothrop, Sylvanus Morley, and Herbert Spinden) voted for censure; the fourth (John Mason) did not. Later Mason wrote Boas an apologetic letter explaining that he'd spied out of a sense of patriotic duty.

A variety of extraneous factors contributed to Boas's censure (chief among these being institutional rivalries, personal differences, and possibly anti-Semitism). The AAA's governing council was concerned less about the accuracy of his charges than about the possibility that publicizing them might endanger the ability of others to undertake fieldwork. It accused him of "abuse" of his professional position for political ends.

In 1919 American anthropology avoided facing the ethical questions Boas raised about anthropologists' using their work as a cover for spying. And it has refused to face them ever since. The AAA's current code of ethics contains no specific prohibitions concerning espionage or secretive research. Some of the same anthropologists who spied during World War I did so in the next war. During the early cold war Ruth Benedict and lesser-known colleagues worked for the RAND corporation and the Office of Naval Research. In the Vietnam War, anthropologists worked on projects with strategic military applications.

Until recently there was little investigation of either the veracity of Boas's accusation in 1919 or the ethical strength of his complaint. But FBI documents released to me under the Freedom of Information Act shed new light on both of these issues.

The FBI produced 280 pages of documents pertaining to one of the individuals Boas accused—the Harvard archeologist Samuel Lothrop. Lothrop's FBI file establishes that during World War I he indeed spied for Naval Intelligence, performing "highly commendable" work in the Caribbean until "his identity as an Agent of Naval Intelligence became known." What is more, World War II saw him back in harness, serving in the Special Intelligence Service (SIS), which J. Edgar Hoover created within the FBI to undertake and coordinate all intelligence activity in Central and South America. During the war the SIS stationed approximately 350 agents throughout South America, where they collected intelligence, subverted Axis networks, and at times assisted in the interruption of the flow of raw materials from Axis sources. Lothrop was stationed in Lima, Peru, where he monitored imports, exports, and political developments. To maintain his cover he pretended to undertake archeological investigations.

From his arrival in Lima in mid-December 1940, Lothrop was dogged by constant worries that his communications with Washington were being intercepted by British, Peruvian, Japanese, or German intelligence operatives. By August 1941 he became concerned that his lack of significant archeological progress might lead to the discovery of his true work in Peru. Lothrop reported his fears of being detected to FBI headquarters: "As regards the archaeological cover for my work in Peru, it was based on the understanding that I was to be in the country six months or less. It is wearing thin and some day somebody is going to start asking why an archaeologist spends most of his time in towns asking questions. This won't happen as soon as it might because the Rockefeller grant for research in Peru makes me a contact man between the field workers and the government."

Lothrop was referring to the Rockefeller Foundation, which financed twenty archeologists who were excavating in Peru, Chile, Colombia, Mexico, Venezuela, and Central America. He also used his ties to a variety of academic and research institutions—including Harvard, the Peabody Museum, the Institute of Andean Research, and the Carnegie Institute—as cover in

Peru. Archeologist Gordon Willey, who worked on an Institute of Andean Research Project in Peru and had some contact with Lothrop at this time, recalled that "it was sort of widely known on the loose grapevine that Sam was carrying on some kind of espionage work, much of which seemed to be keeping his eye on German patrons of the Hotel Bolivar Bar."

In fact, Lothrop was considered a valuable agent who collected important information on Peruvian politics and leading public figures of a nature usually difficult to secure. An FBI evaluation reported that headquarters "occasionally receive[s] information of sufficient importance from Mr. Lothrop to transmit to the President." Lothrop's principal source was an assistant to the Peruvian minister of government and police. In the spring of 1944 this informant resigned his governmental position and began "working exclusively under the direction of Dr. Lothrop." In May 1944 the U.S. Embassy reported that Lothrop's principal informant was fully aware of Lothrop's connection to the SIS and FBI. Lothrop's cover was compromised by four Peruvian investigators in the employ of his top informant. His informant had been heard bragging to the Peruvian police that he made more by working for the U.S. Embassy than the police made working for the Peruvian government.

The FBI decided to test the reliability of Lothrop's key informant by assigning him to collect information on nonexistent events and individuals. The informant was given background information about a nonexistent upcoming anti-Jewish rally that he was to attend, including a list of specific individuals who would be present. Though the rally did not occur, the informant provided a full report on it. He also filed detailed reports on a nonexistent commemorative celebration of the bombing of Pearl Harbor held in a distant town, and on a fictitious German spy who supposedly had jumped ship in Peru.

Lothrop was instructed not to tell the informant that his duplicity had been detected; instead, he was to say he was out of funds to pay for informants. Lothrop refused to believe his informant was lying and sent a letter of resignation to J. Edgar Hoover. His resignation was accepted, and he returned to the United States to resume his academic duties at Harvard's Peabody Museum and the Carnegie Institute.

What is now known about Lothrop's long career of espionage suggests that the censure of Boas by the AAA in 1919 sent a clear message to him and others that espionage under cover of science in the service of the state is acceptable. In each of the wars and military actions that followed the First World War, anthropologists confronted, or more often repressed, the very issues raised by Boas in his 1919 letter to *The Nation*.

While almost every prominent living U.S. anthropologist (including Ruth Benedict, Gregory Bateson, Clyde Kluckhohn, and Margaret Mead) contributed to the World War II war effort, they seldom did so under the false pretext of fieldwork, as Lothrop did. Without endorsing the wide variety of activities to which anthropological skills were applied in the service of the military, a fundamental ethical distinction can be made between those who (as Boas put it) "prostituted science by using it as a cover for their activities as spies" and those who did not. World War II did, however, stimulate frank, though muted, discussions of the propriety of anthropologists using their knowledge of those they studied in times of war, creating conditions in which, as anthropologist Laura Thompson put it, they became "technicians for hire to the highest bidder." Although the racist tenets of Nazism were an affront to the anthropological view of the inherent equality of humankind, Boas (who died in 1942) would probably have condemned anthropologists who used science as a cover for espionage during World War II. Approximately half of America's anthropologists contributed to the war effort, with dozens of prominent members of the profession working for the Office of Strategic Services (OSS), Army and Navy intelligence, and the Office of War Information.

In the following decades there were numerous private and public interactions between anthropologists and the intelligence community. Some anthropologists applied their skills at the CIA after its inception in 1947 and may still be doing so today. For some of them this was a logical transition from their wartime espionage work with the OSS and other organizations; others regarded the CIA as an agency concerned with gathering information to assist policy-makers rather than a secret branch of government that subverted foreign governments and waged clandestine war on the Soviet Union and its allies. Still other anthropologists unwittingly received research funding from CIA fronts like the Human Ecology Fund.

The American Anthropological Association also secretly collaborated with the CIA. In the early 1950s the AAA's executive board negotiated a secret agreement with the CIA under which agency personnel and computers were used to produce a cross-listed directory of AAA members, showing their geographical and linguistic areas of expertise along with summaries of research interests. Under this agreement the CIA kept copies of the database for its own purposes with no questions asked. And none were, if for no other reason than that the executive board had agreed to keep the arrangement a secret. What use the CIA made of this database is not known, but the relationship with the AAA was part of an established agency policy of making use of America's academic brain trust. Anthropologists' knowledge of the languages and cultures of the people inhabiting the regions of the Third World where the agency was waging its declared and undeclared wars would have been invaluable to the CIA. The extent to which this occurred is the focus of ongoing archival and FOIA research. When the CIA overthrew Jacobo Arbenz in Guatemala in 1954, an anthropologist reported, under a pseudonym, to the State Department's intelligence and research division on the political affiliations of the prisoners taken by the military in the coup.

During the Korean War linguists and ethnographers assisted America's involvement with little vocal conflict of conscience. Norwegian sociologist Johan Galtung's revelations in 1965 of Project Camelot, in which anthropologists were reported to be working on unclassified counterinsurgency programs in Latin America, ignited controversy in the AAA. During America's wars in Southeast Asia the AAA was thrown into a state of upheaval after documents purloined from the private office of UCLA anthropologist Michael Moerman revealed that several anthropologists had secretly used their ethnographic knowledge to assist the war effort.

As a result of inquiries made into these revelations, the 1971 annual meeting of the AAA became the scene of a tumultuous showdown after a fact-finding committee chaired by Margaret Mead maneuvered to create a report finding no wrongdoing on the part of the accused anthropologists. An acrimonious debate resulted in the rejection of the Mead report by the voting members of the association. As historian Eric Wakin noted in his book *Anthropology Goes to War*, this "represented an organized body of younger anthropologists rejecting the values of its elders." But the unresolved ethical issue of anthropologists spying during the First and Second World Wars provided a backdrop to the 1971 showdown. Almost two decades later, during the Gulf War, proposals by conservatives in the AAA that its members assist allied efforts against Iraq provoked only minor opposition.

Today most anthropologists are still loath to acknowledge, much less study, known connections between anthropology and the intelligence community. As with any controversial topic, it is not thought to be a good "career builder." But more significant, there is a general perception that to rake over anthropology's past links, witting and unwitting, with the intelligence community could reduce opportunities for U.S. anthropologists to conduct fieldwork in foreign nations.

In the course of research in this area I have been told by other anthropologists in no uncertain terms that to raise such questions could endanger the lives of fieldworkers around the globe. This is not a point to be taken lightly, as many anthropologists work in remote settings controlled by hostile governmental or guerrilla forces. Suspicions that one is a U.S. intelligence agent, whether valid or not, could have fatal consequences. As Boas prophetically wrote in his original complaint against Lothrop and his cohorts, "In consequence of their acts every nation will look with distrust upon the visiting foreign investigator who wants to do honest work, suspecting sinister designs. Such action has raised a new barrier against the development of international friendly cooperation." But until U.S. anthropology examines its past and sets rules forbidding both secret research and collaboration with intelligence agencies, these dangers will continue.

Over the past several decades the explicit condemnations of secretive research have been removed from the AAA's code of ethics—the principles of professional responsibility (PPR). In 1971 the PPR specifically declared that "no secret research, no secret reports or debriefings of any kind should be agreed to or given" by members of the AAA. By 1990 the attenuation of anthropological ethics had reached a point where anthropologists were merely "under no professional obligation to provide reports or debriefing of any kind to government officials or employees, unless they have individually and explicitly agreed to do so in the terms of employment." These changes were largely accomplished in the 1984 revision of the PPR that Gerald Berreman characterized as reflecting the new "Reaganethics" of the association: In the prevailing climate of deregulation the responsibility for ethical review was shifted from the association to individual judgments. As anthropologist Laura Nader noted, these Reagan-era changes were primarily "moves to protect academic careers . . . downplaying anthropologists' paramount responsibility to those they study." The current PPR may be interpreted to mean that anthropologists don't have to be spies unless they want to or have agreed to do so in a contract. A 1995 Commission to Review the AAA Statements on Ethics declared that the committee on ethics had neither the authority nor the resources to investigate or arbitrate complaints of ethical violations and would "no longer adjudicate claims of unethical behavior and focus its efforts and resources on an ethics education program."

Members of the current ethics committee believe that even though the AAA explicitly removed language forbidding secretive research or spying, there are clauses in the current code that imply (rather than state) that such conduct should not be allowed—though without sanctions, this stricture is essentially meaningless. Archaeologist Joe Watkins, chairman of the ethics committee, believes that if an anthropologist were caught spying today, "the AAA would not do anything to investigate the activity or to reprimand the individual, even if the individual had not been candid [about the true purpose of the research]. I'm not sure that there is anything the association would do as an association, but perhaps public awareness would work to keep such practitioners in line, like the Pueblo clowns' work to control the societal miscreants." Watkins is referring to Pueblo cultures' use of clowns to ridicule miscreants. Although it is debatable whether anthropologist intelligence operatives would fear sanctions imposed by the AAA, it is incongruous to argue that they would fear public ridicule more. Enforcing a ban on covert research would be difficult, but to give up on even the possibility of investigating such wrongdoing sends the wrong message to the world and to the intelligence agencies bent on recruiting anthropologists.

Many factors have contributed to the AAA's retreat from statements condemning espionage and covert research. Key among these are the century-old difficulties inherent in keeping an intrinsically diverse group of scholars aligned under the framework of a single association. A combination of atavistic and market forces has driven apart members of a field once mythically united around the holistic integration of the findings of archaeology and physical, cultural, and linguistic anthropology. As some "applied anthropologists" move from classroom employment to working in governmental and industrial settings, statements condemning spying have made increasing numbers of practitioners uncomfortable—and this discomfort suggests much about the nature of some applied anthropological work. The activities encompassed under the heading of applied anthropology are extremely diverse, ranging from heartfelt and underpaid activist-based research for NGOs around the world to production of secret ethnographies and time-allocation studies of industrial and blue-collar workplaces for the private consumption of management.

As increasing numbers of anthropologists find employment in corporations, anthropological research becomes not a quest for scientific truth, as in the days of Boas, but a quest for secret or proprietary data for governmental or corporate sponsors. The AAA's current stance of inaction sends the dangerous message to the underdeveloped world that the world's largest anthropological organization will take no action against anthropologists whose fieldwork is a front for espionage. As the training of anthropology graduate students becomes increasingly dependent on programs like the 1991 National Security Education Program—with its required governmental-service payback stipulations—the issue takes on increased (though seldom discussed) importance.

It is unknown whether any members of the AAA are currently engaged in espionage, but unless the scientific community takes steps to denounce such activities using the clearest possible language and providing sanctions against those who do so, we can anticipate that such actions will continue with impunity during some future crisis or war.

Many in the American Anthropological Association are frustrated with its decision neither to explicitly prohibit nor to penalize secretive government research. It is time for U.S. anthropologists to examine the political consequences of their history and take a hard, thoughtful look at Boas's complaint and the implications implicit in the association's refusal to condemn secret research and to reenact sanctions against anthropologists engaging in espionage.

22

Business: Ethical Issues in Competitive Intelligence Practice
Consensus, Conflicts, and Challenges

Linda K. Trevino and Gary R. Weaver

Editor's note: This overview of the state of ethics in competitive intelligence practice is based on interviews the authors conducted with a diverse group of CI professionals. They found that while some organizations are addressing CI ethics quite seriously, most CI practitioners feel left on their own, relying on personal background and intuition to make tough ethical decisions. Current ethical guidance is too vague to be truly helpful. Moreover, support from employers, industry groups, and the CI profession is needed to counteract pressures and incentives to overstep ethical boundaries. The author's analysis identifies a number of ambiguous issues and conflicting expectations for which there is currently no consensus within the profession, such as misrepresentation that occurs by omission (rather than commission). Another area of concern involves consultants and the potential for conflicts of interest in their work. Finally, the authors offer a number of recommendations for supporting ethical CI practice.

In 1994, the Society for Competitive Intelligence Professionals (SCIP) asked us to study ethics in competitive intelligence practice. During 1994 and 1995, we interviewed CI practitioners asking them about the tough, ethical issues they face in their work, how they think about these issues, and how they deal with them. The results provide new insights into the current state of ethics in the CI (competitive intelligence) profession—the ambiguities practitioners face and the challenges the profession must address in the future.

Why should SCIP and its members care about ethics? One important reason is the profession's public image. Ethical concerns in CI periodically receive attention from the business press, particularly when unethical practices overlap with clearly illegal behavior. For example, *Business Ethics Magazine* (Western, 1995) reported these examples:

- An employee steals blueprint designs and sells them to a competing firm.
- A firm removes 10,000 pages of documents from a dumpster on its competitors' property.

When the general media discuss competitive intelligence work, they frequently use terms like "snoop," "corporate spooks," "James Bond tactics," and "spies/spying," implying illegality or at least questions about the legitimacy of the field (Dumaine, 1988). Therefore, those who care about the profession and its reputation should be concerned about ethics. Even if most CI practices and practitioners are ethical, a few incidents of real or even perceived ethical failure can damage the profession's credibility.

It would be easy to say that CI should simply clean up its act so that the scandal-hungry media would be motivated to look elsewhere. However, some of the ethical issues facing CI practitioners are sufficiently ambiguous or debatable that they are not likely to go away unless CI practitioners can agree about what is and is not appropriate. For example, a 1988 *Fortune* magazine article outlined Marriott's practice of using headhunters to interview regional managers from each of five competitors' economy hotel chains when it was investigating that market. Marriott was able to obtain information regarding salaries, training, and managerial expectations. Some people may view such tactics as unethical. Marriott maintained that they were ethically acceptable because job candidates were told no jobs were currently available, but might be available in the future, and because several of the interviewees were later hired (Dumaine, 1988).

Given the potential for disagreement about what is ethical in this and other real-world situations, it is in the profession's interest to surface the important ethical issues and attempt to arrive at consensus about what is and is not appropriate. At the least, CI professionals should be prepared to explain or justify their practices in cases like Marriott's to observers of CI from the press, business, or government.

PROFESSIONAL STANDARDS

One of the requirements of the designation "professional" is that the professional community develops agreed-upon standards and guidelines. These standards and guidelines contribute to the legitimacy of the profession's work in the eyes of external stakeholders, and provide a common set of assumptions and standards that are taught to new members and expected of current practitioners. Competitive intelligence practice is relatively young and ethical guidelines are not yet well specified, as was noted in a recent review of CI literature (Collins and Schultz, 1986). In contrast, ethical guidance has been formalized in more established areas of business practice (e.g., accounting, with its highly detailed standards) and other professions (e.g., medicine, with its Hippocratic oath). Even legal issues are not always clearcut in CI. Yet, ethical issues clearly exist concerning the kind of information sought and the methods used to gather it.

Why care about ethics? 1) Ethical failures diminish reputation, 2) articulating ethical standards now makes it easier to respond to criticism later, and 3) adoption of ethical standards is a hallmark of a profession.

CI practitioners are beginning to develop more explicit standards. For example, the Society of Competitive Intelligence Professionals Code of Ethics (printed at the front of every issue of its publication) exhorts members to maintain the highest degree of professionalism and to avoid unethical practices; to comply with all applicable laws; to adhere to their own companies' practices, objectives, and guidelines; to identify themselves and their organization prior to interviews; and to respect requests for confidentiality. However, these guidelines are somewhat general and don't provide a beginning practitioner with the specific guidance needed to make decisions in ethically ambiguous situations. For example, what should an SCIP member do when the law provides insufficient guidance or when his or her company seems to encourage unethical conduct? As the profession continues to grow, its challenge will be to develop consensus about acceptable and unacceptable CI practice.

Some CI practitioners have made progress along these lines. For example, Leonard Fuld, a consultant and author of books on CI, offers "ten commandments of legal and ethical intelligence gathering" including (a) thou shalt not lie when representing thyself, (b) thou shalt not bribe, (c) thou shalt not plant eavesdropping devices, (d) thou shalt not deliberately mislead anyone in an interview (e) thou shalt not steal a trade secret (or steal employees away in hopes of learning a trade secret), and (f) thou shalt not knowingly press someone for information if it may jeopardize that person's job or reputation (Fuld, 1995).

Similarly, in its materials, the Futures Group (a large consultancy) states that its intelligence collection is "always legal and ethical." They specify that they will not use illegal methods, misrepresent themselves, misuse consultants or agents, compromise customer proprietary information, conduct false job interviews, or exploit new employees for proprietary information. These statements, similar to Fuld's commandments and more specific than the SCIP code, raise further questions. For example, exactly what is misrepresentation? What constitutes misuse of a consultant? Exactly how is proprietary information defined? What constitutes exploitation of a new employee? Is it exploitation only if there is a *quid pro quo*, or is any attempt to extract information from a new employee exploitation? What makes a false job interview false? Would Marriott's practice, described above, qualify?

The Futures Group does provide more explicit detail on each of these areas. For example, their policy on false interviews says, "Company employees may not conduct 'false' job interviews of competitors' employees for the purpose of collecting intelligence information" (Herring, DeGenaro, Harleroad, 1993, p. 124). Would Marriott's practice be acceptable according to this principle? One can presume that if Marriott's primary goal were to collect intelligence information (the *Fortune* article implied it was), then the practice would be considered to be unethical according to the guideline. But, what if the goal were to gather information on competitors and to develop a file for possible future openings? Or, what if the goal were simply to be prepared for future position vacancies, and the interview process just happened to turn up competitively useful information? CI practice is full of situations like this with multiple interpretations. Where does one draw an ethical line?

This SCIP-supported study aimed to contribute to the further development of agreed-upon standards of conduct for CI by asking current practitioners to identify the types of pressures and ethical issues that arise in their work, where they look for guidance, and the standards they use for decision making. We interviewed a diverse set of 25 competitive intelligence practitioners, 20 men and five women representing a variety of backgrounds (degrees in technical areas, information science, business), experience (in libraries, law enforcement, military or government intelligence, business, and consulting) tenure in the field (from a beginner to more than 30 years in a single large firm), types of CI work (primary vs. secondary-source research, intelligence vs. counterintelligence), types of organizations (17 corporations, four small and four large consultancies), and national cultures (primarily North America, plus two from Europe, one from the Mideast, and one from Japan).

Most interviewees were drawn from the Mid-Atlantic region near where the researchers are located (New York, New Jersey, Pennsylvania, Delaware, Maryland). However, the researchers also traveled to SCIP's Annual Conference to interview a number of international members and members from other parts of the U.S. Most of the interviews were audiotaped (with permission); otherwise notes were taken. The tapes were transcribed, and transcripts and notes were analyzed by the researchers. As, a result of our analysis, we learned how practitioners think about the ethical issues they face. In this article, we focus on areas of consensus, as well as the gray areas, ambiguities, and unanswered questions currently facing the profession.

ETHICAL ISSUES FACING CI PRACTITIONERS

A review of the competitive intelligence literature led Paine (1991) to propose that questionable intelligence gathering falls into four categories:

1. Misrepresentation
2. Attempts to influence the judgments of those entrusted with confidential information (e.g., bribery)
3. Covert surveillance
4. Theft

Our interviewees identified these areas as well. In fact, misrepresentation (discussed further below) was the most frequently mentioned category. But most interviewees dismissed the other three categories rather quickly—not because they're not important, but because they were considered to be clearly unethical and often illegal, and our interviews focused more on ethically ambiguous issues.

MISREPRESENTATION OF IDENTITY AND INTENT

Paine (1993) included the following practices under misrepresentation:

- Posing as a student
- Posing as a private research firm
- Phony job interviews
- Posing as a potential joint venturer, supplier, or customer

What all of these examples share is deception—falsely representing one's identity with the intent of gathering information that the other party would not willingly share if one's true identity were known.

OMISSION VERSUS COMMISSION

As suggested above, misrepresentation was the most frequently-discussed category in our study, in part because it is replete with ambiguities about what constitutes misrepresentation. One example of a gray area involves the difference between omission and commission. Most people would agree that lying about one's identity is unethical (e.g., falsely representing oneself as a college student). But what if relevant information is omitted? For example, one interviewee, an independent consultant, believed that acts of omission were appropriate, while acts of commission were not:

> Frankly, a lot of times they assume that my client is a _____ company as opposed to a _____ company. I haven't told them that, and if they assume that, that's fine by me. It's not an act of commission, it's an act of omission.

For another example of omission, suppose you're pursuing an MBA part-time while working in the strategic planning department of a firm? Your professor gives you a competitive analysis problem and expects you to make telephone calls to gather information from one of your firm's competitors. Is it misrepresentation to withhold the information that you're also a strategic planner at ABC Company? There's no act of lying here, but you've omitted relevant information; if the person on the other end of the telephone knew your full identity (strategic planner and graduate student), the information would certainly not be shared. The most clearly ethical solution to such a problem would be to choose an industry different from your own for the assignment or to identify yourself as both a student and an associate of your particular firm when making the telephone calls. Neither of these solutions involves deception of any kind.

Other examples of omission from our interviews involve situations in which individuals overhear the conversations of their competitors' employees and fail to identify themselves. Some interviewees evaluated this as acceptable:

> Certainly if you have a bar room conversation with somebody and somebody divulges something that maybe they shouldn't have, well that's their problem . . . It's up to them to control what they say. . . . We won't drug somebody and then ask him questions. . . . [But] if they provide information that I'm very interested in, I will make sure that it comes back here and it gets appropriately disseminated.

However, commission clearly enters these examples when one goes out of one's way to put oneself in that position, raising questions about the propriety of the action:

> People will visit a site and they'll go into the local bar to see what they can overhear and talk to people. That I think is a gray area. That's misrepresenting yourself. . . . They might be talking about confidential information. You're sitting there taking it all down.

These examples raise the following question. Is it misrepresentation (and therefore inappropriate) to fail to identify yourself in a public place when others around you are talking openly about a competitor's proprietary information? Some interviewees, as suggested above, argued that this was the talker's problem. If the talker wasn't tricked into sharing the information (e.g., plied with drinks, lied to about one's identity), it was their problem if they talked too much. The underlying criterion here seems to be intent. It is considered to be wrong if you intend to deceive the other party in order to obtain information. But, if you just happen to be in the right place at the right time, some would argue that the information is then "out there" in the public domain and you should feel free to use it.

Other interviewees saw this kind of case as misrepresentation by an act of omission. In this view, the individual on the receiving end of the information is obliged to identify him- or herself along with any relevant information about affiliation. However, the issue became grayer if the individual spouting the proprietary information doesn't then stop—perhaps she or he had had a few too many drinks. What then? Some argued that the individual should then leave the area to avoid the ethical issue. An exception might be when you're in an assigned seat on an airplane, and the people behind you are busily talking about your competitor's strategic plan. You turn around and identify yourself, "Excuse me, I work for your competitor. I can hear everything you say," and they continue their conversation despite your warnings. At that point, one interviewee said that your ethical obligation had been fulfilled.

MISREPRESENTING INTENT

Another type of misrepresentation involves misrepresenting one's intent rather than one's identity. If one's intent is to "mislead, disarm, or render [someone] less defensive," that's unethical, according to one interviewee. For example, a consultant hired to gather information about a client's competitor may tell that competitor that the information is being sought for a more general industry analysis. A number of consultants conduct industry analyses, so the statement is plausible, if misleading.

> We never say we're representing Company A. We always identify ourselves . . . accurately as to who we are. . . . Then a second level is, why do you want to know? This is where the industry advantage comes into play because in all honesty, as an industry specialist I want to know more about your industry. . . . I can ask them in all honesty, "I want to know about your service."

Some callers may find this type of data-gathering perfectly acceptable. However, some of our interviewees had been the target of this type of information-gathering technique, and they rejected it as improper and claimed to be able to see through it. Moreover, these experiences left them wary and distrustful of all callers, ethical or not.

> We had a consulting firm come in and all they do is market research. They do it by calling and saying, "We're doing a survey on the industry and we want to get this information." They're not. They're hired by XYZ company to find out something about you. Three-quarters of the way through these surveys they always get to the nuts-and-bolts questions. The ones they really want to know.

Another example might involve collecting small bits of information from a variety of sources, often targeting lower-level firm employees who might be less guarded or who might enjoy talking about their work. The goal is to put the seemingly innocuous pieces together to answer a broader CI question, but those offering the separate pieces are not aware of the broader intent. The question is, if they knew it, would they share the piece of information they are offering? And, if not, is the practice ethical?

CI practitioners seem to agree that misrepresenting one's identity is unethical (e.g., saying that you're a student when you're not, or saying that you're a customer when you're not). Many interviewees felt comfortable with their stance on misrepresentation because they always identified themselves accurately. However, agreement was less clear about misrepresenting one's intent (e.g., saying that you are conducting an industry analysis when your intent is to gather information about a particular company or product, or saying that you need a single piece of information when your intent is to gather multiple pieces of information from different individuals in the same firm). Our interviews suggested that both should raise ethical concerns, and that the most clearly ethical approach is to honestly identify one's identity and intent to the information-gathering target.

OBLIGATIONS AND RESPONSIBILITIES
OF CI PRACTITIONERS

To a large degree, ethics is about obligations and responsibilities and the conflicts between them. Our interviewees suggested that, in some competitive intelligence situations, the obligations and responsibilities are unclear, particularly in the client/consultant relationship, or when a consultant represents multiple clients within the same industry.

CONFLICTING OBLIGATIONS
TO CLIENTS AND SOURCES

Some of the toughest ethical issues are those that involve conflicts between obligations. A number of interviewees raised this type of issue, particularly within the context of the relationship among corporations, external CI consultants, and information sources. For example, consultants consistently cited their obligation to respect their clients' requests for confidentiality, and corporate representatives cited their expectation that consultants would not reveal the company's identity: "Obviously one reason why we hire someone to do it is because they don't reveal who they're doing it for." They have an ethical responsibility to the guy who hired them not to tell who hired them.

But there are various ways of not revealing a client's identity, and company representatives sometimes questioned the ethical propriety of that stance, particularly when they were the target of such inquiries: "We know that they're going to be asking for information on our behalf. But that . . . is a little bit of a gray area. You're using a third party to ask a question because you don't feel you can ask it yourself."

Given the discussion above about misrepresentation, ethical concerns arise if the consultant does not say that he or she is representing a client, but says instead that the information is being collected for an industry analysis or for some other purpose. To many of our interviewees, that is a case of misrepresentation of intent.

By contrast, if the consultant identifies him- or herself and honestly represents the reason for the inquiry, the target has the option of declining to offer any information and the ethical concern disappears. Our interviewees' observations highlight a clear conflict of obligations in this situation. The consultant has an obligation to the client. But, the consultant also has an obligation to accurately represent his or her identity and intent to the target of the inquiry. The CI profession needs to find the right balance between these obligations to clients and sources.

THE CLIENT/CONSULTANT RELATIONSHIP

Our interviews also revealed ambiguity about who is responsible for the consultant's ethics in the client/consultant relationship. A few company representatives, generally from large, visible corporations, were adamant about the care they take in selecting consultants who are viewed as an extension of the firm and its valuable public image. They expressed concern about the possibility that the firm's reputation could be sullied by an overaggressive consultant's behavior. They conduct lengthy interviews with consultants, check references, evaluate written proposals, and require adherence to laws and to the company's own ethical codes.

> We require that they [consultants] adhere to the company's code of business ethics . . . and then we require that the critical paragraph or two be incorporated word for word in any contract we sign with them. We also insist on a hold harm-

less clause . . . which says that if they do anything that is illegal or unethical, that reflects either financially or image-wise on the company, that they will pay all of the costs and penalties involved. They will hold us harmless. . . . There are some that will not sign that contract and they don't get our business, obviously.

When I bring in outside firms, they [management] want to know to the nth degree what the methodology is, how it will be represented, because they seem to have a very deep concern that just by virtue of having engaged that firm, it's their reputation. . . . I think corporations know today that "not knowing" is no excuse at all.

However, consultants suggested that the corporate behavior suggested by the above quotes was the exception rather than the rule. They noted that clients (even large, visible companies) rarely ask about their methods or their ethics, and they acknowledged the potential advantages, at least in the short term, of leaving such parameters unspecified.

By and large most people [clients] are trying to establish some type of ethical or legal working procedures. But a lot of times, it never comes up. . . . It's the exception to the rule when somebody says, here's what we *don't* want you to do. Most of the time it's here's what we want. We're hiring you because you know how to get it. So, they're sort of in denial. . . . You know, I don't think once has anybody ever asked me, "Do you have a code of ethics?"

Never have we been asked to go by a client's ethics statement. . . . I think people assume we follow some code of ethics. . . . I think there's also a little bit of cognitive dissonance. . . . They don't want to prevent something else being done that would cause a successful project. . . . We've also been asked to do things that we won't do . . . wiretapping . . . stealing business plans.

Our analysis of the interviews suggests hesitancy among some consultants and their corporate clients to discuss the ethics issue in much detail. They seemed content to live with some ambiguity in this aspect of the relationship and to take their chances with the outcome. Yet, the only way a corporate client can be sure that a consultant is using ethical collection methods is to make the corporation's expectations and standards explicit, discuss them during negotiations, and make them a part of the contractual relationship. If client firms do not do this, they are putting themselves at risk, and putting consultants in a difficult ethical bind. They are saying, in effect, "be ethical (without specifying what that means), but get the information we've hired you to get." Consultants who are committed to using only ethical means should be pleased to discuss these with their clients and to make high ethical standards a part of the ongoing relationship. Further, consultants shouldn't wait for their clients to raise these issues. Their ethics are their own responsibility and should be made clear to their clients. In the end, our analysis suggests that agreement on explicit ethical standards and expectations should be a part of every client/consultant relationship and the responsibility of both parties.

CONFLICTS OF INTEREST FOR CONSULTANTS

Many consultants develop expertise in a particular industry. That makes sense, but it also increases the likelihood that the consultant will be asked to work for competing companies within the same industry. Some of the consultants referred to this as "working a vertical" and they had developed several ways of dealing with these situations, including building "Chinese walls" within the consulting firm, turning down work, and essentially redoing work that's been done before. Some large corporations require that their consultants agree not to work for their competitors. But, in this case, the corporation must have an ongoing relationship and must enter into a long-term contract (a retainer) with the consultant. More typically, the relationship leads to situations, questions, and solutions such as the following:

> What responsibilities do we have, or don't we have, if we're working for clients in the same industry? . . . Should we tell the first client that we're working for the second? Should we avoid doing work for the second?

> You're not allowed to give [a competitor] documents you've generated. If you did a literature search, for example, it wouldn't be fair game to take that and give it to somebody else. . . . You may run the same database search three times using the same key words and paying for that output. . . . Where it gets gray is, each time you do an assignment, you learn new things, you get smarter. What things can you share and not share?

The ethics burden is on the consultant in these situations because generally the clients have no way of knowing about the conflict. But one consultant suggested that there are currently few disincentives to keep consultants from stepping over the ethical/unethical line in situations like these.

> The only disincentive is that you'll never have that company as a client again. But, I don't know that they'll ever be found out.

Consultants should think carefully about these types of situations and decide, in advance, how they will be handled to avoid conflicts of interest. The obligations and responsibilities inherent in the client/consulting relationship need to be specified. Some large corporations that are particularly concerned about their public image, as well as some consulting firms, have made progress dealing with these issues. Others could learn from what they have done. (See table 22.1.)

Table 22.1   Ethical Issues in CI: Consensus versus Open Questions

Consensus	*Open Questions*
Misrepresentation of identity	Misrepresentation of intent
Sins of commission	Sins of omission
Manipulation to get information (e.g., plying with liquor)	Taking advantage of other's mistakes (e.g., eavesdropping)
Responsibilities to clients	Responsibilities to sources
Conflicts of interest (e.g., giving client A information about client B)	Conflicts of interest (e.g., refusing work done for client A for client B)

WHAT MAKES A DIFFERENCE? THE INDUSTRY AND THE ORGANIZATION

In addition to identifying ethical ambiguities and conflicts, we also wanted to learn about the pressures (to be ethical or unethical) that exist in the current CI environment. Any attempt to more specifically address ethical issues in CI will need to be realistic about the constraints and pressures under which CI professionals work. We learned a great deal about the corporate and industry environments and how those affect CI practitioners' thinking about ethics.

Competitive Environment in Industry

CI practitioners and their organizations exist in qualitatively different environments with regard to CI ethics, whether defined in terms of industry or market, legal or regulatory environments, or national culture. Each of these environments has its own formal structures and informal norms that can influence how people see ethical issues and what people are willing to do to gain a competitive edge. For example, competition is viewed differently in different market segments, ranging from competition as "war" to more cooperative norms within the context of a "game."

The War Metaphor

The war metaphor was reflected in some interviews. When business is viewed as "war," the goal is to harm or defeat one's "enemy." Translated to the CI context, this means putting the competition out of business. If this is the language and the goal, then harm to a competitor, no matter how large, may not be considered an ethical issue at all. In warfare, killing the enemy is not considered to be unethical. As one interviewee claimed, "Business is basically warfare. In warfare, no self-respecting company would think of going to war without a G-2 operation. And how can you engage in warfare where you really don't have a good picture of your competition."

The Game Metaphor

Another view sees competition in business as an exciting game in which each competitor strives to achieve excellence, satisfy customers, and succeed as a result (Paine, 1993). The motive in this type of game is not to drive out the competition, but to work hard, play by the rules of the game, and do one's best in order to succeed.

In our interviews, we found a number of individuals who described a kind of industrywide "gentlemen's agreement" aimed at balancing competition with a concern for not intentionally hurting other firms. In particular, individuals who worked in organizations/industries with a public image to protect were more likely to see harm to competitors as ultimately harming the industry as a whole (including their own firm) and therefore unacceptable. By contrast, interviewees suggested that smaller firms, subject to less public scrutiny, are under less pressure to be careful about their ethics.

> People have tried to sell us information on our competitors (ex-employees, consultants). We're not interested. It doesn't look good for the whole industry. If [one pharmaceutical company] has a problem, it doesn't do us any good. . . . The public's trust in medication is diminished. . . . If someone is selling information they don't come to the big pharmaceutical companies. Small companies may be different.

> If a disgruntled employee goes to a competitor and says, "Gee, you know I have this, this, and this," most American companies will just go, "Nope, we don't want any part of you." And a lot of times within the industry, they'll call you up and say, "Hey, just to let you know, Joe Blow contacted us."

> I've heard of someone stealing a lab notebook and mailing it to another company and the other company just puts it in an envelope and returns it.

Our corporate interviewees generally represented larger firms, many of which were quite concerned about their public image, perhaps because their size makes them more vulnerable to public criticism. A number of them mentioned that smaller firms and firms in less-regulated environments might be willing to take more chances. Our interviews suggest that larger firms in more highly regulated environments are more likely to engage in "ethical best practices" that could be emulated by others. The important lesson here is that particular industries and firms have their own norms which reflect their circumstances. CI practitioners who work within corporations need to be aware of industry norms and metaphors and how these can affect their own judgments and actions.

The Organization's Ethical Culture

A number of our interviewees, especially those in corporate settings, cited the organizational context as an important influence on their decision making regarding ethical issues. The organization can either exert pressure to be unethical, or it can provide guidance toward and support ethical conduct. The pressure to be unethical generally comes from managers within the organization who are themselves under pressure to meet tough goals. Most of our interviewees acknowledged the intense pressure that exists in today's highly competitive business environment.

> I would be lying if I said that people don't want you to be a little underhanded, because they do. They want the information. They don't care how you get it.

> One of the dilemmas I constantly get is when somebody comes and asks for information about a company or a market or whatever. They want perfect information. They want to know it all.

The company's general ethical culture influences how CI practitioners react to these sorts of pressures. In companies with a strong ethical culture that stresses correct behavior, CI practitioners receive clear messages from top management, and training and guidance regarding appropriate and inappropriate practices.

> [ABC Co.] is an aboveboard company. If they have any question whatsoever they put out a bulletin that says, "Don't do this." . . . The image starts at the top and goes all the way [down]. . . . You don't get ahead in this place by being underhanded. The company is very competitive . . . but it is also scrupulously honest.

> The CEO and the senior staff has sort of set the tone, and you know it's drilled into them. . . . In the big companies, completely different people, completely different product lines, but you'll see you're following the same procedure. . . . It's almost as if they have a checklist of what they have to do. I think it's through training and awareness-building within the company.

People in organizations like those described above feel supported by management in saying no to the pressures to be unethical, and they're sure they won't be punished.

> I would say a good bit of it is knowing that people will not be punished in our [CI] group if we don't deliver that. . . . Knowing that we have credibility with

the upper executives . . . that whenever we turn one down and say, "No," everybody feels supported internally. . . . . We really feel like there's an infrastructure of support for making the right decision about what we ought to have and what we can't have.

Because of the intense pressures that can exist, however, it is important to consider the organizational status of people who are assigned CI tasks. For example, one interviewee suggested that novices should not be given responsibility for CI within a firm. At the very least, a more senior, experienced person who will be more able to resist pressure to cross the unethical line should be available to run interference for them.

The young person that gets that kind of pressure ought to have an older, more experienced person to go to, to say, "Hey, so and so is really putting the thumb screws on me. What'll I do?" And then it seems to me that at that point, the supervisor says, "Don't worry, I'll take care of it."

Industry norms and corporate support for ethical CI conduct were important to our interviewees. Those who work for companies that explicitly address ethics issues clearly took pride in their company's approach and were comfortable with the guidance they were receiving. CI ethics, in particular, were more likely to be addressed in companies that had a group devoted primarily to CI work. However, in many corporate settings, CI practitioners received little explicit guidance about ethical issues and felt that they were left to rely upon their own inner compasses (discussed in more detail below). Their companies either didn't have the expertise or the inclination to address CI ethics. These findings suggest that the profession can play an important role in defining the ethical issues and providing decision-making guidance for CI practitioners.

WHAT MAKES A DIFFERENCE?
HANDLING ETHICAL PRESSURES

- Industry and organizational norms, language, and metaphors (is competition viewed as war? as a game?)
- Exposure to public scrutiny, which increases concern with ethics
- Organizational culture, which can encourage or discourage ethics
- Status in the organization, which can help you resist pressure
- A larger CI group, which can provide support and a sounding board

How They Decide

When we asked our interviewees to tell us how they knew they were facing an ethically problematic issue and how they decided what to do about it, they frequently began by identifying ethically unambiguous situations that can be easily dismissed. For example, if one's work relies primarily on gathering public domain information from secondary sources (e.g., databases), few ethical issues arise, with the exception perhaps of copyright concerns. Similarly, anything that is against the law was considered to be relatively straightforward, and one can rely on the firm's legal counsel for advice. However, in ethically ambiguous situations, interviewees reported that they rely on simple methods including the "public disclosure" test and the time-honored "gut check."

The Public Disclosure Test

The most frequently mentioned basis for decision making among both corporate and consultant interviewees was the "disclosure rule" which asks, how would you feel if your action were publicly disclosed to your relevant community (via the *New York Times, Wall Street Journal,* or television news magazines)? Consultants generally considered themselves an extension of the company in these cases. If they did something unethical in the client's interest, it would reflect badly on both of them.

> A pretty good way of determining what's ethical and what's not, if you were to wake up tomorrow morning and not mind seeing what you did on the front page of the newspaper, then do it. This public disclosure rule is particularly useful because it encourages you to step outside yourself, your company, and even your industry, to consider how the community at large would react to a particular action.

The "Gut Check"

Because most companies didn't provide a strong ethical culture that offered the interviewees lots of guidance about ethics, most felt that they were essentially left on their own to figure out what was right and wrong in many ethically ambiguous situations. They relied on their upbringing, education, and their professional background for guidance. Sometimes, their only guide was what one of our interviewees called "the rotten-smell detector," that is, an almost automatic or instinctive revulsion to certain kinds of behavior.

> I think for every person it's different, but . . . you get that gut and you know when something strikes you as being trouble. A little bell goes off and then. . . . That's not very scientific, but that's how it works.

> The rotten-smell detector comes from us. . . . It's really a gut-level thing . . . and it has been things that make you feel as if you want to go and immediately take a shower.

However, because of the wide variety of educational and professional backgrounds individuals bring to their CI work, one individual's rotten-smell detector may pick up something quite different from another's. As one interviewee put it, "I guess that internal gyroscope is different on different people." For example, someone with a journalism background may be more attuned to concerns about the confidentiality of sources while someone with a background in library science may pay more attention to copyright concerns. This provides another reason why members of the profession need to come to consensus about ethical issues in CI practice.

COMMON ETHICS TESTS

- Public Disclosure Test
- Gut Feeling/Rotten-Smell Test

IMPLICATIONS FOR COMPETITIVE INTELLIGENCE PRACTICE

As the CI profession grows, it will become more and more crucial that members can identify the issues of concern and reach consensus about what is and is not appropriate. With growth, concerns about reputation become more important. One individual's or organization's unethical activity can bring negative media attention to an entire profession.

Our interviews with 25 CI professionals suggested that some organizations are addressing CI ethics quite seriously—working hard to draw clear lines between ethical and unethical activities, and backing up CI practitioners who "walk the ethical talk." However, the overwhelming message was that many (if not most) CI practitioners feel very much on their own, relying on personal background and intuition to make tough ethical decisions. Many of the available guidelines are too general to be truly helpful; their existence may even generate a false sense of security, suggesting that ethical issues have been dealt with when in fact many conflicts and ambiguities remain. Also, today's competitive business environment creates many pressures and incentives that can counteract the effect of vague ethics guidelines. Finally, although guidelines are important, our interviews indicate that they alone will not be enough to satisfy CI practitioners' needs. Equally important is support from employing organizations, industries, and the CI profession. Industry-level agreements about ethics may be most useful, given that they create a level playing field for all competitors.

Our analysis identified a number of ambiguous issues and conflicting expectations. For example, practitioners agree that misrepresentation of identity is wrong, but ambiguity remains about misrepresentation that occurs by omission (rather than commission) and about misrepresentation of intent. The profession should address these issues explicitly but, until then, CI groups within organizations should attempt to come to agreement amongst themselves about what is and is not appropriate.

A second area of concern involves consultants and how they balance complex obligations and responsibilities to clients and targets. Consultants should not feel that they have resolved all ethical issues simply because they can say that they identify themselves accurately or that they protect client confidentiality. The ethical issues consultants face are more complex than that. For example, the ethical obligation to protect client confidentiality needs to be balanced with the obligation not to deceive information targets. The consultant, the client, and target of information-gathering should all be working under the same assumptions. Similarly, consultancies should explicitly address the potential for conflicts of interest within their work.

Solutions are likely to be more effective if these potential conflicts are discussed and decisions are made in advance about how they will be handled. Finally, companies and their consultants should explicitly address the ethical guidelines that govern the relationship.

Within corporations, ethical CI practice can be supported in a number of ways. For example, the organization's ethics code should address information-gathering and information-sharing issues; CI practitioners should receive training regarding antitrust and other legal and ethical issues, and they should be encouraged to discuss ethical issues that arise in their work. Further, the organization's ethical culture should reward—not punish—ethical conduct. Novices should not be left to fend for themselves, but should be supported by strong managers who can help them resist pressures to bend the rules.

Obviously, SCIP can and should play an important role in bringing the competitive intelligence community together in forums to address the remaining ambiguous issues and by offering guidelines for effective ethical decision making. As a professional society, SCIP can act to legitimize its members' concerns with ethical issues, concerns which often are left unspoken because of perceived or real pressure from other organizations (e.g., employers, clients). It can also help to provide a level playing field by defining standards for CI practice and holding its members to them. The payoff will be growing public approval for the profession, and trust among practitioners and between practitioners and other stakeholders.

TASKS FOR THE CI PROFESSION

- Hold consensus-building conversations on the open questions.
- Clarify guidelines to create a "level playing field."

- Encourage clients and employers of CI practitioners and practitioners themselves to support good ethics for the good of the profession.

REFERENCES AND RELATED READING

Bayles, M. D., *Professional Ethics,* Wadsworth Publishing. 1989.

Collins, A. and Schultz, N., (Summer 1986). "A Review of Ethics for Competitive Intelligence Activities," *Competitive Intelligence Review,* vol. 7, no. 2, pp. 56–66.

Dumaine, B., "Corporate Spies Snoop to Conquer," *Fortune,* November 7, 1988, pp. 68–76.

Fuld, L. M., *The New Competitor Intelligence,* John Wiley & Sons, Inc., 1995.

Herring, J., DeGenaro, W. E., Harleroad, D., *The Role of Business Intelligence in Formulating Competitive Strategies,* The Futures Group, 1993.

Paine, L. S. (1993). "Corporate Policy and the Ethics of Competitive Intelligence Gathering," *Journal of Business Ethics* 10: 423–436.

Western, K. (September/October 1995). "Ethical Spying," *Business Ethics:* 22–23.

23

Business: The Challenge of Completely Ethical Competitive Intelligence and the "CHIP" Model

Darren Charters

Editor's note: This article examines difficulties that are present for competitive intelligence practitioners endeavoring to conduct ethical CI. It explores the basic schools of ethical thought and combines them to create a model for evaluating the ethics of potential competitive intelligence activities. It concludes by suggesting that using rigorous ethical evaluation in assessing CI activities does not have to sacrifice the competitive position of an organization.

Is competitive intelligence conducted ethically? Most CI practitioners believe other practitioners engage in unethical competitive intelligence activities (Cohen and Czepiec, 1988, p. 202). More recent anecdotes suggest the continued existence of unethical CI activities (Penenberg and Barry, 2000).

Can effective, successful competitive intelligence be conducted ethically? The Society of Competitive Intelligence Professionals (SCIP) takes the position that it can. In SCIP's Code of Ethics it expressly states that competitive intelligence practitioners should avoid all unethical practices. All SCIP members agree to try to conduct CI in a completely ethical manner.

What is completely ethical CI? That is not so clear. Ideally, CI practitioners would consider their personal ethical mores, the general principles expressed in SCIP's Code of Ethics, and a corporate policy to answer the question. Even with these aids it may not be clear whether a contemplated CI action would be completely ethical. Unfortunately, CI practitioners are frequently without a corporate policy, may be unable to extrapolate from the general statement of principles in SCIP's Code of Ethics, and only have a crudely developed personal sense of why certain CI actions "feel" unethical.

If practitioners of CI want to avoid all unethical situations, they should be rigorously assessing potential CI activities against established ethical frameworks. Most commentary intending to provide practical assistance to CI practitioners has focused on examining personal moral codes and, where they exist, corporate ethics policies. Within established ethical frameworks, personal morality plays a role. However, it is only one approach among others.

This paper proposes a model for evaluating CI activities using established ethical frameworks. Further, employing the stringent approach to CI ethics described below does not need to compromise the competitive position of a firm.

The first section will discuss the factors that contribute to unethical CI practices and the current sources of ethical guidance available to CI practitioners. Next, there will be a necessary review of the primary ethical frameworks that are relevant to assess the ethics of contemplated CI activities, followed by the proposal of a simple but comprehensive test for evaluating the ethics of such activities. The final section will discuss why the conduct of completely ethical CI does not automatically leave one at a competitive disadvantage relative to firms using ethically questionable methods.

A central assumption should be specified at the outset. It is assumed that the ethical issues discussed herein will touch on CI activities that are completely legal but ethically questionable. It is assumed that CI activities that are potentially illegal are not undertaken, for exactly that reason. While some practitioners will ignore the requirement of legality, this discussion speaks to practitioners who, as a basic premise, conduct legal CI and who are also striving to conduct totally ethical CI.

Can effective, successful competitive intelligence be conducted in a completely ethical manner?

SOURCES OF ETHICAL PRESSURE
FOR CI PRACTITIONERS

As noted above, many CI practitioners believe that unethical activities pervade the profession. If CI is not being conducted ethically, then one is left to question why. The factors that drive unethical competitive intelligence are both external and internal to the firm and individual practitioner.

External

The external competitive environment is an important factor that influences unethical behavior (Hallaq and Steinhorst, 1994, p. 787). A harsh competitive environment and the struggle to survive and prosper in business can influence CI professionals to engage in behavior that they personally consider unethical. A CI professional may engage in such behavior grudgingly, and with significant moral qualms; however, the potential negative ramifications for failing to act overcome any internal ethical reservations. External forces can be significant enough that it is only the threat of legal sanction that restrains an individual from acting unethically. In cases of extreme external pressure, the threat of legal sanction may not be enough to prevent such behavior.

The variations in ethical norms that exist between countries are also a factor that can contribute to unethical competitive intelligence activities. Klein noted the different methods that CI practitioners from different countries were willing to employ when given the same task (Klein, 1998, p. 22). A CI practitioner operating in a foreign country may engage in activities that he or she would be unwilling to undertake within his or her home country. Alternatively, firms may elect to hire CI practitioners from different countries who are willing to use methods that are, in the CI practitioner's mind, entirely ethical, although such methods would not be considered ethical in the firm's home country. The variations may place CI practitioners who are attempting to conduct CI in a completely ethical manner in a challenging position.

Internal

The internal factors that prompt a CI professional to act unethically are threefold:

1. Personal moral considerations introduce a relativistic element that may allow individuals to ethically justify behavior that others might deem unethical. Take an individual whose "ideal" life focuses on wealth maximization, and another whose "ideal" life is premised on human equity and personal development. These two CI practitioners may develop significantly different virtues and vices against which they evaluate the ethics of their actions. However, within the confines of their respective ethical constructs they might well be able to ethically justify their actions.

2. Many CI practitioners have limited ethics training to assist them in assessing the ethics of their actions. In other professions, individuals receive some ethics instruction (i.e., doctors, lawyers) as part of the requirement of entry into the profession. If individuals are without a reasonably developed understanding of their own ethical framework, when external factors do exert pressure to act unethically, such individuals will be that much less prepared to counter them with solid ethical reasoning.

3. A CI practitioner may face pressure from within the firm to use unethical, or at least questionably ethical, competitive intelligence gath-

ering methods. When the individuals applying the pressure are in a position of authority, with the corresponding power to influence the terms of employment, the pressure to act unethically can be significant—despite the personal moral qualms of a CI practitioner. When combined with a lack of ethics training and/or the lack of a corporate policy, a CI practitioner will have a limited ethical foundation upon which to counteract such pressure.

External business pressures and a lack of ethics training contribute to otherwise well-intentioned practitioners conducting unethical competitive intelligence.

SOURCES OF ETHICAL COMPETITIVE INTELLIGENCE GUIDANCE

SCIP Code of Ethics

The Society of Competitive Intelligence Professionals (SCIP) has taken the position that CI can, and must, be conducted in an ethical manner. As noted by Schultz and Collins, SCIP members voluntarily enter in to a social contract with SCIP, agreeing to abide by SCIP's Code of Ethics in exchange for receiving membership benefits (Collins and Schultz, 1998, p. 65). The Code of Ethics also provides a specific position with respect to disclosure of information and confidentiality requests. All requests for confidentiality are to be respected, and complete disclosure must be provided to interviewees prior to a CI interview. The Code does not address specific CI activities apart from these.

Corporate Codes of Ethics

Ideally, a company will have a sufficiently developed corporate code of ethics that CI practitioners can refer to for guidance. Unfortunately, more than one commentator has lamented the fact that corporate policies addressing CI are sparse and often woefully inadequate (Sharp Paine, 1991, p. 429). There have already been valuable recommendations provided for developing, implementing, and monitoring corporate policies that will encourage ethical CI practices. Businesses would do well to implement them (Fiora, 1998, p. 40; and Tyson, 1996, p. s15). Some key factors to keep in mind in developing a policy is that there should be input from a variety of relevant organizational areas, it should focus on principles as opposed to specific situations, and it should be championed by an appropriate executive manager to ensure its successful development and implementation (Prescott, 1998, p. 8).

If there is another point to add to such commentaries, it is that corporate policies can do more than function as an effective action control. In time, they can also create a powerful personnel/cultural control within the organization. Previous studies have noted the convergence of ethical position of a firm and the personal perspectives of the employees (Cohen and Czepiec, 1988, p. 201). An effective policy is one that promotes the behavior desired by management. A powerful policy is one that imbues the organization with a culture that maintains itself even if the policy is removed. At that point, the policy has translated itself into a personnel/cultural control. This should be the ultimate goal of all ethics policies pertaining to corporate intelligence. The discussion that follows is also relevant to the process of developing a corporate code of ethics for CI activities. Without a reasonable understanding of the primary ethical frameworks, there is an increased risk of developing and implementing codes that are not entirely ethically consistent.

Some commentators have provided specific suggestions that aim to limit the possibility of finding oneself in an ethical dilemma, such as relying on in-house contacts, or using external contractors (Berger, 1998, p. 40). If there is a potential concern with such recommendations, it is that they may not resolve the ethical issue as much as transfer the issue to a third party. Further, willful blindness by the principal party to questionable activities by the third party should not be ethically condoned.

Personal Ethical Considerations

Where firms fail to take an active role in establishing appropriate CI policies, contemplated actions are most frequently evaluated against the personal moral preferences of individual practitioners or key members of the intelligence unit. That is, if CI practitioners are left without ethical guidance from the firm, they will evaluate their conduct based on their own ethical principles. The ability to engage in some form of ethical reasoning becomes paramount since the firm is providing little guidance. Ideally, if a SCIP member, the specific requirements and spirit of the Code of Ethics will also infuse their personal considerations. However, many CI practitioners do not have a systematic understanding of the various ethical principles that should infuse their considerations. Much of the discussion on assessing CI activities has focused on personal ethics.[1] But personal ethics frameworks are reflective of only one type of ethical reasoning, and CI practitioners would benefit from having basic knowledge of all major ethical frameworks.

The following ethical theories each provide a different basis for assessing the ethical justification of an action. Each theory has strengths and weaknesses. However, to date, a survey of each of the major ethical frameworks has been lacking in discussions regarding ethical CI. The next section of the paper provides a brief synopsis of major ethical frameworks and builds them into a tool for evaluating potential CI activities.[2]

Without a corporate policy and only general guidance from SCIP, CI practitioners must rely on their own moral frameworks to assess the ethics of CI activities.

ETHICAL FRAMEWORKS TO ASSIST CI PRACTITIONERS

Utilitarian Ethics

Utilitarianism assesses the ethics of an action solely based on its result. To evaluate whether an action is ethical in utilitarian terms, the overall harm realized is measured against the overall benefit resulting from the activity. If the overall harm exceeds the overall benefit, then the action is unethical (Boatright, 2000, p. 196). There are two key points to note.

1. Individual motivations are irrelevant in determining whether an action is ethical. It is the end result that determines if an action is ethical.
2. The overall harms are measured against the overall benefits.

The basic supposition of utilitarianism is that activities that maximize benefits/utilities for the community are ethical. It is not sufficient to measure harms and benefits accruing solely to the individual (or the firm) contemplating the action. The assessment should account for the harms and benefits accruing to all impacted stakeholders. As a result, it is *more* complex than a simple cost-benefit analysis that many individuals conduct.

As a tool for determining the ethical "rightness" of an action, the strength of utilitarianism is in its focus on harm. The litmus test of whether a situation contains an ethical issue is whether it has potential for harm. Utilitarianism forces one to undertake this consideration. For example, if a certain CI activity yielded information that had minimal benefit to a CI practitioner's organization but had tremendous power to harm another firm, then the ethics of engaging in the activity should be questioned from a utilitarian perspective.

However, assume the same situation with the only change being that the public at large would benefit substantially (i.e., the CI activity yielded information showing the competitor's product actually put the public at risk). Then the activity might well be ethical from a utilitarian perspective, as it can be argued that more people will benefit than will be harmed. Utilitarianism does not prohibit harm as a precondition to determining the ethical "rightness" of an action, but it does require that there be a greater good to justify any harm that will result. Utilitarianism also has limitations:

1. It is difficult to forecast the harms or benefits that might accrue as a consequence of an action taken. Even if all harms and benefits could be accurately forecast, most individuals only weigh the harms and benefits that impact the individual and his or her organization. That is, most individuals are only concerned about the consequences on a limited community.

2. CI, by its nature, is a self-interested activity. If the CI action benefits the practitioner's firm, it is likely at the expense of another firm. In strict utilitarian terms, the CI action could be justified only if the benefit to the practitioner's firm exceeded the harm to another firm and the community benefited overall as a result.

Accepting that it is difficult to engage in a determination of potential harms and benefits, does utilitarianism have practical applicability to the CI practitioner? Yes, specifically because it forces practitioners to consider potential harms. CI practitioners should debate undertaking a potential CI activity that has a strong likelihood of creating significant harm with minimal corresponding personal, firm, or other stakeholder benefits.

Kantian Ethics

From a Kantian perspective, the ethics of an action are not determined by the consequences of an act. An action is ethical if it conforms to certain fundamental imperatives. At the foundation of Kantian ethics is the supposition that human rationality must be respected. A categorical imperative established by Kant is that all humanity should be treated as an end and never as a means only (Boatright, 2000, p. 56).

Kantian ethics is easily applied to potential actions that impact other individuals, but it creates an onerous ethical standard. Any action that fails to respect individual rationality and arguably treats people as a means to an end will be considered unethical. SCIP has forcefully taken the position that any type of misrepresentation in competitive intelligence-gathering is unethical. It is a position that would be ethically favorable from a Kantian perspective.

The practical difficulty with Kantian ethics is that it does not accord with many modern business practices. Intentional or otherwise, people are frequently treated as a means to an end in business relationships. The value of Kantian ethics is that it requires one to consider how other individuals are being treated. It differs from utilitarianism in that even if an action results in substantial harm, as long as the risk of harm has been freely and knowingly assumed, the action is considered to be ethical.

Individual Virtue Ethics

Virtue ethics is the most frequent ethical perspective employed by practitioners in assessing the ethics of an action. John Boatright has noted that virtue ethics does not focus on the question, "what actions are right?" Rather it focuses on the question, "what kind of person should I be?" (Boatright, 2000, p. 62). Two considerations are necessary to establish a complete concept of virtue ethics:

1. It requires a concept of an ideal end.
2. It necessitates the identification of virtues that promote the ideal end and the corresponding vices that detract from it.

By pursuing and maintaining the virtues, while avoiding corresponding vices, individuals develop toward their ideal (Boatright, 2000).

In a business context, this requires one to decide the end to which business activity is directed. Wealth creation is often accepted as the primary ideal to which business activity should aspire. However, others see business as a means to the ideal of personal fulfillment and/or a communal activity in which people work toward a common good (Boatright, 2000, p. 65). While many people consider all of these ideals to be part of business activity, they frequently consider one to be paramount. Such differing ideals may well result in different virtues against which behavior is ethically evaluated. Justice and fairness may by ill placed as a virtue in the former but revered in the latter.

The practical strength of virtue ethics is that it reflects the reasoning that many individuals engage in to evaluate the ethics of an action (Boatright, 2000). That is, individuals often assess potential actions against long-established personal moral virtues. The virtues may not be recognized as part of a larger construct, but the virtues themselves are identifiable.

The weakness of virtue ethics is identified in the example above. That is, the concept of the ideal end may vary significantly between individuals. The result is that people develop different, and even conflicting, virtues and vices that are, however, consistent within each individual's concept of the ideal.

Community Virtue Ethics

The weakness of personal virtue ethics might well have been unintentionally resolved in other discussions of ethical CI. Many commentators suggest using a "rule of thumb" test to assess the ethics of a potential action. While the hypothetical scenarios vary, they quite typically involve placing the individual in the position of having to explain and justify his or her action to a community. For example, one rule of thumb test proposed by a writer is to ask yourself whether you would be comfortable explaining the action on TV to the general public (Laczniak and Murphy, 1991, p. 264).

While the scenarios seem disarmingly simple, they have tremendous value for a specific reason. The community standard introduces a concept frequently employed in legal reasoning—the standard of the "reasonable" person. If the individual knows the community at large would not condone the action, it suggests that the majority of individuals in the community subscribe to substantively different virtues. Such scenarios force a CI practitioner not just to consider their actions in terms of their own virtues and vices but also those of the community at large. But what should be the community of comparison?

It is proposed here that the proper standard to use is not the business community, but the larger social community. In fact, Laczniak and Murphy's "rule of thumb" test pitches the consideration at the level of the larger social community. Collins and Schultz have addressed the notion that the business community should establish the virtues of ethical business behavior. They have noted that dishonesty occurs frequently in many business contexts (i.e., business negotiations) and the business community rarely expects complete disclosure. Absent any expectation of honesty, they argue that there is no ethical requirement or duty (although there may be an SCIP social contract requirement) to provide complete disclosure (Collins and Schultz, 1996, p. 65). It is an interesting argument, and they deserve credit for taking a commonly expressed opinion and arguing that there is, in theory, an ethical justification for it. It is suggested here that there are still two problems with such a justification:

1. The external business forces already discussed can impact business culture to the point that the business community tolerates behavior that would not be morally condoned in general society.
2. The attitudes of the business community might already be reflected in the personal virtue ethic frameworks of individual CI practitioners.

It has been shown that veteran CI practitioners take a more liberal view to questionable CI activities then less-experienced practitioners. This may be the result of the ethically relaxed culture of the business community infusing itself into personal moral codes. If it is already reflected in personal standards, there is little value in replicating it in the community standard.

There is one important caveat pertaining to community virtue ethics. If this framework is to have practical value, than the CI practitioner must respect the standards of the community. CI professionals who hold community standards in low regard will be minimally concerned if an action does not appear ethical from a community perspective. Table 23.1 summarizes the foregoing ethical frameworks providing the major points of each. In addition, it also shows how, where applicable, the principles of each perspective are infused in the SCIP Code of Ethics, and how they can arise in a CI practitioner's professional undertakings.

The CHIP Model

The CHIP model of ethical CI (see figure 23.1) integrates the above ethical frameworks into a simple model for evaluating the ethics of CI activities.

Table 23.1 Comparison of Ethical Theories

Ethical Theory	Basic Features	Basic Question	Ethical Theory & SCIP Code	CI Challenge
Utilitarianism	Maximizing overall utility is the highest end of human experience. Ethics determined solely by action consequences.	Do the total benefits exceed the total harms resulting from the action?		Could another individual or organization be seriously harmed by your CI activity?
Kantian ethics	Individuals' rationality is the highest end of human experience. Action consequences irrelevant so long as rationality respected.	Does the action respect other individuals' rationality and autonomy?	Respect all requests for confidentiality. Disclose all relevant information prior to interviews. Avoid conflict of interests.	A firm or individual you are contacting would not help you if they knew the true intentions of your CI activity.
Virtue ethics	Individuals are free to select their ideal end. Virtues and vices are developed based on the ideal end.	Does the action respect personal virtues? Does the action respect community virtues?	Provide honest and realistic CI. Disclose all relevant information prior to interviews.	You feel guilty when forced to undertake a certain CI activity. You know friends/family would not approve of your CI activity.

CHIP is an acronym that has been developed to prompt CI practitioners to consider the following factors:

- Community virtues
- Harm
- Individual as end
- Personal virtues

The CHIP model directs CI practitioners to consider the ethics of a proposed CI activity from each of the utilitarian, Kantian, and virtue ethics per-

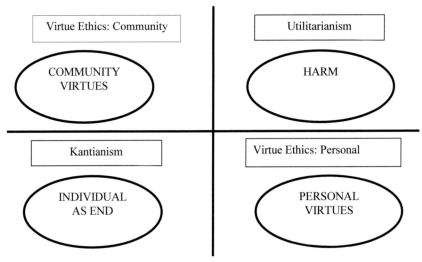

Figure 23.1 CHIP model for ethical competitive intelligence.

spectives. The *harm* quadrant represents the utilitarian consideration. As noted previously, it is not always possible to engage in a calculated weighing of harms and benefits from a utilitarian perspective. However, if it is apparent that a potential CI activity will result in substantial harm with little benefit accruing, it is likely to be unethical from a utilitarian standpoint.

In such a circumstance, the CI practitioner should seriously consider forgoing the proposed CI activity.

The Kantian consideration is represented by the *individual as end* quadrant. This consideration will be most relevant when the CI action involves interaction with another individual. It requires that in all such circumstances the individual be treated as an end and not solely as a means. If the proposed activity does not pass this consideration, then the CI activity should not be undertaken. SCIP's requirement for full and complete disclosure prior to interviews is a reflection of this position in a specific context. In fact, the principles enunciated in SCIP's Code of Ethics probably give voice to the Kantian perspective more than any other ethical framework. Virtue ethics are encapsulated in the *community virtues* and *personal virtues* quadrants.

The personal virtues quadrant requires that CI professionals identify the virtues or moral standards that they adhere to and assess whether a proposed CI activity respects those virtues. This is what many CI practitioners already do as a baseline ethical evaluation. The community virtues quadrant incorporates the community standards test that other commentators have proposed. It is useful in that it serves as a benchmark against personal virtues. Since personal virtues can vary depending on the ideal end to which one subscribes, the community test forces the individual to examine his or her virtues under the community microscope to assess whether it is a commonly held belief.

The CHIP model provides a simple but comprehensive framework for evaluating the ethics of potential CI activities. The various quadrants will not have equal relevance in every circumstance. Nonetheless, by considering each ethical framework explicitly and arriving at a conclusion in relation to it, CI practitioners maximize the likelihood of conducting completely ethical CI. Now that the model has been explained, it may be most beneficial to apply it to a CI situation.

It has been noted that CI practitioners face a variety of potential situations that are ethically questionable. An example of just such an activity is the act of misrepresentation by omission. Many agree that actively misrepresenting oneself is unethical. However, is it unethical when the act is simply failing to provide sufficient information, such that another individual or entity is potentially left with an incorrect perception as to who you are, what you are doing, who you are doing it for, or why you are doing it?

Previous studies suggest that CI practitioners are quite capable of taking advantage of unsuspecting individuals provided that they do not have to actively misrepresent themselves (Schultz, Collins, and McCulloch, 19, p. 310). Applying the CHIP model to the action of misrepresentation by omission, it is difficult to argue that conscious acts of omission are anything but unethical.

Since it would be very difficult to assess the potential harm that would result from an act of omission, it is not certain it would fail the harm consideration. It is not that there is no potential for harm, just that it would be difficult to evaluate. However, using the "individual as end" consideration, an act of omission most certainly appears to be unethical. When engaging in deception of individuals, even if only an act of omission, it is unlikely that individual autonomy and rationality are being respected. In this respect misrepresentation by omission would be rejected as unethical from the Kantian perspective.

A personal ethics consideration would frequently arrive at the same behavior. Honesty, for many, is considered to be a noble virtue. Many people will not misrepresent themselves due to this internal virtue. An example is the practitioner who wrote of her failure to fully disclose her reasons for calling to another individual. Her guilt was such that she rectified the situation by subsequently providing full disclosure. This is a prime example of personal virtue ethics in practice. From the community virtues perspective, it there is consensus the primary end of business is exclusively wealth generation, one might arrive at a point where totally honesty is not accepted as a virtue. Within the business community this might well be the preferred end. However, the community at large tends to view business as a means of not just wealth generation, but also building community and promoting self-development. With such a perspective, honesty will more likely be considered a virtue. Although it is not unequivocal, conscious misrepresentation by omission might well be considered unethical from the community virtues perspective.

CI's competitive advantage rests in its analysis and synthesis—not in the information itself. Competitive advantage is not compromised by conducting CI in an ethical fashion.

Having evaluated misrepresentation by omission using the CHIP model, it is clear that it would be considered unethical conduct from more than one ethical perspective. However, the CHIP model helps identify and refine specific ethical objections. Once identified, a CI practitioner can evaluate whether the proposed activity is ethically salvageable and, if possible, alter the proposed activity to satisfy ethical objections.

THE MYTH OF COMPETITIVE ADVANTAGE AND UNETHICAL ETHICAL CI

The argument has been made that firms that fail to use questionably ethical CI means place themselves at a potential competitive disadvantage relative to those firms that do. Are firms forgoing a potential competitive advantage by employing policies that are too restrictive? It depends on the perspective one takes to competitive intelligence. A practitioner such as Leonard Fuld would argue the vast majority of useful intelligence is available by totally ethical means. The challenge is in accessing it. At least one writer has noted that a CI practitioner who used ethical means was able to achieve measurably similar objectives to a CI practitioner who did not (Klein, 1998, p. 22).

To this a second point can be added. There is a common consensus that CI involves the collection, synthesis, and analysis of data.[3] In fact, the real competitive advantage of CI does not rest in the information collected, but in the creative, insightful synthesis and analysis of the gathered information. It is in the synthesis and analysis that the true challenges are presented, not in its collection. Accepting this premise, a firm's competitive advantage will not be compromised solely using ethical CI activities. It is naive to suggest that unethical behavior does not yield useful information. However, the real value and competitive advantage results from the synthesis and analysis developed from the information. What ethical standards should be employed when operating in jurisdictions that have a very different understanding of what constitutes ethical behavior? To employ a common phrase and turn it into a question, "When in Rome is it ethical to do as the Romans?" Kantian perspectives are unaffected by cultural variations. Basic categorical imperatives will not be impacted by location. Utilitarian considerations might be marginally impacted to the extent that the perception of what is a harm or benefit may be influenced by cultural variations. The greatest impact will be in virtue ethic frameworks. Different cultures may result in people developing very different virtues. However, CI practitioners can still use the CHIP model, taking care to taking precaution to govern themselves by the virtues framework that is the most ethically conservative. This will result in taking the most ethically prudent course of action.

CONCLUSION

This paper has established a tool of analysis to provide assistance in conducting totally ethical CI. At the outset it was noted that CI professionals, ideally, consult corporate policies, SCIP's Code of Ethics, and personal moral standards to evaluate the ethics of an action. The CHIP model proposed for evaluating potential competitive intelligence actions will provide significant guidance where an employer does not have an existing policy, or the policy in place is very general in its scope. Further, the CHIP model offers a challenging but achievable benchmark for totally ethical CI, which is the goal and responsibility of all SCIP members.

The CHIP model is not intended to be a substitute or replacement for appropriate ethics training and corporate codes of ethics. Organizations should consider the possibility of formal ethics training for new CI practitioners. Further, ethics training should be an ongoing activity for all CI practitioners. For example, an internal communications network that continually encourages and allows for the discussion of ethical issues and difficult ethical situations can better equip all CI practitioners within an organization to deal with challenging ethical situations. The CHIP model can be used as a tool for developing ethically consistent codes of ethics and minimizing, or eliminating, the occurrence of such conflicts.

What about the possibility of conflict between an existing corporate policy and the CHIP model? Although it is possible that a corporate policy could prohibit a CI activity ethically condoned by the CHIP model, it is more likely to be a situation of conflict where a corporate policy condones a CI activity that would be considered unethical using the CHIP model. While it would create a difficult situation, in either situation the more stringent standard should prevail, be it a corporate policy or the CHIP model.

Exceeding the behavioral requirements of a corporate code to meet the ethical obligations set out by the CHIP model will not usually place a CI practitioner in a legally or ethically untenable situation. Failing to live up to the requirements of a more stringent corporate code could, while being ethically tenable, present potential legal difficulties.[4]

For those who propose that CI is simply not conducted in this manner, this final comment is offered. If CI activities are evaluated against ethical standards and found wanting, it is a shortcoming of the CI behavior and not the ethical framework. Ethical frameworks should not be altered to fit the preferences of practitioners. CI practitioners are free to use whatever ethical standards they deem appropriate apart from any requirements imposed by an employer or the law. However, for practitioners striving to conduct CI in an entirely ethical manner, the CHIP model provides a framework to assist in achieving that objective.[5]

NOTES

1. Table 3 on p. 63 of A. Collins and N. Schultz, "A Review of Ethics for Competitive Intelligence Activities," provides a useful summary of previously proposed guides to ethical behavior. Many of the considerations are based on personal or community-oriented moral codes.

2. Although the discussion of the frameworks is referenced to J. Boatright, *Ethics and the Conduct of Business,* the first chapter of T. L. Beauchamp and N. Bowie's *Ethical Theory and Business* also provides an effective overview of the respective ethical frameworks.

3. See C. Lackman et al., "Organizing the Competitive Intelligence Function"; B. Gilad, "What Is Intelligence Analysis: Part 2"; and C. Fleisher et al., "A FAROUT Way to Manage CI Analysis" for articles discussing the challenges of effectively analyzing intelligence.

4. It is acknowledged that refusing to undertake an unethical CI activity that has been ordered by a superior, and is expressly authorized by a code of conduct, would likely provide grounds for disciplining, and if serious enough, dismissing an employee. However, failing to meet the basic requirements of a corporate code of conduct would likely provide grounds for disciplining the CI practitioner and potentially expose the entire company to liability for harm to third parties.

5. An original draft of this paper was prepared for a course in competitive intelligence offered through Wilfrid Laurier University's MBA program. I would also like to thank Dr. John Prescott for his comments and editorial suggestions. Any errors are mine alone.

REFERENCES

Berger, A. (1998). "Being Honest in a Dishonest World: Lessons Learned as a Competitive Intelligence Analyst," *Competitive Intelligence Magazine* 1(2), July–September, pp. 38–40.

Boatright, J. (2000). *Ethics and the Conduct of Business* (Prentice Hall), pp. 29–71.

Beauchamp, T. L., and N. Bowie, eds. (1993). *Ethical Theory and Business,* 4th edition (Prentice-Hall), pp. 1–48.

Cohen, W., and H. Czepiec (1988). "The Role of Ethics in Gathering Corporate Intelligence," *Journal of Business Ethics* 7(3), March, pp. 199–203.

Collins, A., and N. Schultz (1998). "A Review of Ethics for Competitive Intelligence Activities," *Competitive Intelligence Review* 7(2), pp. 56–66.

Fiora, B. (1998). "Ethical Business Intelligence is NOT Mission Impossible," *Strategy & Leadership,* January–February, pp. 40–41.

Hallaq, J., and K. Steinhorst (1994). "Business Intelligence Methods: How Ethical," *Journal of Business Ethics* 13(10), October, p. 787.

Klein, C. (1998). "Cultural Differences in Competitive Intelligence Techniques," *Competitive Intelligence Magazine* 1(2), July–September, pp. 21–23.

Laczniak, G., and P. Murphy (1991). "Fostering Ethical Marketing Decisions," *Journal of Business Ethics* 10, October, pp. 259–271.

McGonagle, J. (2000). Ethics and Client Identification," *Competitive Intelligence Magazine* 3(1), January–March, pp. 42–43.

McGonagle, J., and C. Vella (2000). "Ethics and Client Information," *Competitive Intelligence Magazine* 3(2), April–June, pp. 43–44.

Murphy, P., and G. Laczniak (1992). "Emerging Ethical Issues Facing Marketing Researchers," *MarketingResearch* 4(2), June.

Penenberg, A., and M. Barry (2000). *Spooked: Espionage in Corporate America* (Perseus Press).

Prescott, J. (1998). "A Manager's Guide to the Ethics of Competitive Intelligence," *Ethics in Economics,* no. 3 & 4, pp. 4–9.

Sapiaa-Bosch, A., and R. Tancer (1998). "Navigating through the Legal/Ethical Gray Zone: What WouldYou Do?" *Competitive Intelligence Magazine* 1(1), April–June, pp. 22–31.

Sawyer, D. (1998). "Uncompetitive CI Policies: The Noose Around Your Own Neck," *Competitive Intelligence Magazine* 1(3), October–December, pp. 45–46.

Sharp Paine, L. (1991). "Corporate Policy and the Ethics of Competitor Intelligence Gathering," *Journal of Business Ethics* 10(10), pp. 423–436.

Schultz, N., A. Collins, and M. McCulloch (1988). "The Ethics of Business Intelligence," *Journal of Business Ethics* 13(6), pp. 305–314.

Tyson, K. (1996). "The Problem with Ethics: Implementation," *Competitive Intelligence Review* 7 (Supp. 1), pp. s15–s17.

Jones, W., and N. Bryan (1995). "Business Ethics and Business Intelligence: An Empirical Study of Information-Gathering," *International Journal of Management* 12(2), June, p. 204.

Zahra, S. (1994). "Unethical Practices in Competitive Analysis: Patterns, Causes and Effects," *Journal of Business Ethics* 13(1), January, p. 1.

A

Principles, Creeds, Codes, and Values

EXECUTIVE ORDER 12674 OF APRIL 12, 1989 (AS MODIFIED BY E.O. 12731) PRINCIPLES OF ETHICAL CONDUCT FOR GOVERNMENT OFFICERS AND EMPLOYEES

By virtue of the authority vested in me as President by the Constitution and the laws of the United States of America, and in order to establish fair and exacting standards of ethical conduct for all executive branch employees, it is hereby ordered as follows:

Part I: Principles of Ethical Conduct
Sec. 101. Principles of Ethical Conduct

To ensure that every citizen can have complete confidence in the integrity of the Federal Government, each Federal employee shall respect and adhere to the fundamental principles of ethical service as implemented in regulations promulgated under sections 201 and 301 of this order:

(a) Public service is a public trust requiring employees to place loyalty to the Constitution, the laws, and ethical principles above private gain.
(b) Employees shall not hold financial interests that conflict with the conscientious performance of duty.
(c) Employees shall not engage in financial transactions using nonpublic Government information or allow the improper use of such information to further any private interest.
(d) An employee shall not, except pursuant to such reasonable exceptions as are provided by regulation, solicit or accept any gift or other item of monetary value from any person or entity seeking official action

from doing business with, or conducting activities regulated by the employee's agency, or whose interests may be substantially affected by the performance or nonperformance of the employee's duties.

(e) Employees shall put forth honest effort in the performance of their duties.

(f) Employees shall make no unauthorized commitments or promises of any kind purporting to bind the Government.

(g) Employees shall not use public office for private gain.

(h) Employees shall act impartially and not give preferential treatment to any private organization or individual.

(i) Employees shall protect and conserve Federal property and shall not use it for other than authorized activities.

(j) Employees shall not engage in outside employment or activities, including seeking or negotiating for employment that conflict with official Government duties and responsibilities.

(k) Employees shall disclose waste, fraud, abuse, and corruption to appropriate authorities.

(l) Employees shall satisfy in good faith their obligations as citizens, including all just financial obligations, especially those such as Federal, State, or local taxes that are imposed by law.

(m) Employees shall adhere to all laws and regulations that provide equal opportunity for all Americans regardless of race, color, religion, sex, national origin, age, or handicap.

(n) Employees shall endeavor to avoid any actions creating the appearance that they are violating the law or the ethical standards promulgated pursuant to this order.

Sec. 102. Limitations on Outside Earned Income

(a) No employee who is appointed by the President to a full-time noncareer position in the executive branch (including full-time noncareer employees in the White House Office, the Office of Policy Development, and the Office of Cabinet Affairs), shall receive any earned income for any outside employment or activity performed during that Presidential appointment.

(b) The prohibition set forth in subsection (a) shall not apply to any full-time noncareer employees employed pursuant to 3 U.S.C. 105 and 3 U.S.C. 107(a) at salaries below the minimum rate of basic pay then paid for GS-9 of the General Schedule. Any outside employment must comply with relevant agency standards of conduct, including any requirements for approval of outside employment.

Part II: Office of Government Ethics Authority
Sec. 201. The Office of Government Ethics

The Office of Government Ethics shall be responsible for administering this order by:

(a) Promulgating, in consultation with the Attorney General and the Office of Personnel Management, regulations that establish a single, comprehensive, and clear set of executive-branch standards of conduct that shall be objective, reasonable, and enforceable.

(b) Developing, disseminating, and periodically updating an ethics manual for employees of the executive branch describing the applicable statutes, rules, decisions, and policies.

(c) Promulgating, with the concurrence of the Attorney General, regulations interpreting the provisions of the post-employment statute, section 207 of title 18, United States Code; the general conflict-of-interest statute, section 208 of title 18, United States Code; and the statute prohibiting supplementation of salaries, section 209 of title 18, United States Code.

(d) Promulgating, in consultation with the Attorney General and the Office of Personnel Management, regulations establishing a system of non-public (confidential) financial disclosure by executive branch employees to complement the system of public disclosure under the Ethics in Government Act of 1978. Such regulations shall include criteria to guide agencies in determining which employees shall submit these reports.

(e) Ensuring that any implementing regulations issued by agencies under this order are consistent with and promulgated in accordance with this order.

Sec. 202. Executive Office of the President

In that the agencies within the Executive Office of the President (EOP) currently exercise functions that are not distinct and separate from each other within the meaning and for the purposes of section 207(e) of title 18, United States Code, those agencies shall be treated as one agency under section 207(c) of title 18, United States Code.

Part III: Agency Responsibilities
Sec. 301. Agency Responsibilities

Each agency head is directed to:

(a) Supplement, as necessary and appropriate, the comprehensive executive branch-wide regulations of the Office of Government Ethics, with regulations of special applicability to the particular functions and activities of that agency. Any supplementary agency regulations shall be prepared as addenda to the branch-wide regulations and promulgated jointly with the Office of Government Ethics, at the agency's expense, for inclusion in Title 5 of the Code of Federal Regulations.

(b) Ensure the review by all employees of this order and regulations promulgated pursuant to the order.

(c) Coordinate with the Office of Government Ethics in developing annual agency ethics training plans. Such training shall include mandatory annual briefings on ethics and standards of conduct for all employees appointed by the President, all employees in the Executive Office of the President, all officials required to file public or nonpublic financial disclosure reports, all employees who are contracting officers and procurement officials, and any other employees designated by the agency head.

(d) Where practicable, consult formally or informally with the Office of Government Ethics prior to granting any exemption under section 208 of title 18, United States Code, and provide the Director of the Office of Government Ethics a copy of any exemption granted.

(e) Ensure that the rank, responsibilities, authority, staffing, and resources of the Designated Agency Ethics Official are sufficient to ensure the effectiveness of the agency ethics program. Support should include the provision of a separate budget line item for ethics activities, where practicable.

Part IV: Delegations of Authority
Sec. 401. Delegations to Agency Heads

Except in the case of the head of an agency, the authority of the President under sections 203(d), 205(e), and 208(b) of title 18, United States Code, to grant exemptions or approvals to individuals is delegated to the head of the agency in which an individual requiring an exemption or approval is employed or to which the individual (or the committee, commission board, or similar group employing the individual) is attached for purposes of administration.

Sec. 402. Delegations to the Counsel to the President

(a) Except as provided in section 401, the authority of the President under sections 205(d), 205(e), and 208(b) of title 18, United States Code, to grant exemptions or approvals for Presidential appointees to committees, commissions, boards, or similar groups established by the President is delegated to the Counsel to the President.

(b) The authority of the President under sections 208(d), 205(e), and 208(b) of title 18, United States Code, to grant exemptions or approvals for individuals appointed pursuant to 3 U.S.C. 105 and 3 U.S.C. 107(a), is delegated to the Counsel to the President.

Sec. 403. Delegation Regarding Civil Service

The Office of Personnel Management and the Office of Government Ethics, as appropriate, are delegated the authority vested in the President by 5 U.S.C. 7301 to establish general regulations for the implementation of this Executive order.

Part V: General Provisions
Sec. 501. Revocations

The following Executive orders are hereby revoked:

(a) Executive Order No. 11222 of May 8, 1965.
(b) Executive Order No. 12565 of September 25, 1986.

Sec. 502. Savings Provision

All actions already taken by the President or by his delegates concerning matters affected by this order and in force when this order is issued, including any regulations issued under Executive Order 11222, Executive Order 12565, or statutory authority, shall, except as they are irreconcilable with the provisions of this order or terminate by operation of law or by Presidential action, remain in effect until properly amended, modified, or revoked pursuant to the authority conferred by this order or any regulations promulgated under this order. Notwithstanding anything in section 102 of this order, employees may carry out preexisting contractual obligations entered into before April 12, 1989.

Financial reports filed in confidence (pursuant to the authority of Executive Order No. 11222, 5 C.F.R. part 735, and individual agency regulations) shall continue to be held in confidence.

Sec 503. Definitions

For purposes of this order, the term:

(a) "Contracting officers and procurement officials" means all such officers and officials as defined in the Office of Federal Procurement Policy Act Amendments of 1988.

(b) "Employee" means any officer or employee of an agency, including a special Government employee.

(c) "Agency" means any executive agency as defined in 5 U.S.C. 105, including any executive department as defined in 5 U.S.C. 101, Government corporation as defined in 5 U.S.C. 103, or an independent establishment in the executive branch as defined in 5 U.S.C. 104 (other then the General Accounting Office), and the United States Postal Service end Postal Rate Commission.

(d) "Head of an agency" means, in the case of an agency headed by more then one person, the chair or comparable member of such agency.

(e) "Special Government employee" means a special Government employee as defined in 18 U.S.C. 202(a).

Sec. 504. Judicial Review

This order is intended only to improve the internal management of the executive branch and is not intended to create any right or benefit, substantive or procedural, enforceable at law by a party against the United States, its agencies, its officers, or any person.

George Bush
The White House, October 17, 1990

CENTRAL INTELLIGENCE AGENCY

Code of Conduct

Employee Bulletin No. 911
February 3, 1982

The DDCI has requested that this bulletin be circulated to all employees concerning the standards of conduct they are expected to meet both during and after their Agency service.

1. Current and former CIA personnel are expected to maintain high standards of conduct consistent with the Agency's mission. There has long been a tradition of discipline and loyalty to the Agency that has guided the conduct of Agency personnel in the performance of their official duties and in their private lives. The Agency continues to rely heavily on this discipline and loyalty, not only during the period of employment but, of equal importance, after employment.

2. Certain types of activities are specifically prohibited by law or regulation. These various prohibitions and other standards of conduct which

employees are required to observe are set forth in Agency regulations. This bulletin summarizes information contained in regulations and with which employees must be familiar and are required to review annually. Additional standards of ethical conduct are imposed on Agency employees by Executive Order 11222. This order, among other things, restricts the receipt of gifts, limits the use of insider information, bars the use of public office for private gain, and directs employees to avoid situations which might result in or create an "appearance of impropriety." Given the special position of trust in which employees are placed by virtue of their Agency service, employees are expected to honor this trust through their own integrity and conduct in all official actions. Because of this special position of trust, certain obligations also are contained in each employee's contract agreement to protect from unauthorized disclosure information that is classified, information concerning intelligence sources or methods, and other sensitive information the disclosure of which may adversely affect CIA or national security equities. The obligation to protect such information from unauthorized disclosure applies during an individual's employment or other service with the CIA and at all times thereafter. On occasion former employees and others may try to exploit their prior and current relationships with Agency personnel. The conferring of any preference or privilege upon former employees as a result of past or present relationships should be avoided, and Agency personnel constantly must be on guard to ensure that such relationships are not being misused. Once an employee has terminated his or her service, that person is not entitled to be treated any differently than other individuals conducting business with the Agency.

3. Besides the continuing obligations contained in a former employee's contract agreement, the Agency expects, and indeed depends on, continued adherence by former employees to the same high standards of conduct which governed them during their employment. This continuing duty is implicit in their seeking and accepting Agency employment. Certain postemployment activities are restricted by explicit provisions of law (18 U.S.C., Section 207). Beyond these requirements provided by law and contract, former CIA personnel also are expected to avoid any personal or professional activity which could harm or embarrass the Agency or the United States. In this regard, former Agency personnel may draw upon their prior training and experience in pursuing second careers or opportunities outside the Agency. An employee's former Agency status should not be traded upon to obtain preferential treatment for the employee or his or her private employer, or to otherwise create any appearance of sponsorship, endorsement, or approval by the Agency of such activities or transactions. This does a disservice

not only to the individual involved but also to the Agency and its present employees.

4. Former Agency personnel also should avoid entering into financial transactions in reliance upon information, contracts, or relationships developed through and available only as a result of Agency employment. The use of such "insider information" for personal profit is an abuse of the position of trust which employees occupy, which abuse adversely affects the confidence of the public in the integrity of the Agency and its mission, brings discredit to the individual involved, and may involve a possible violation of law. Former employees also should carefully consider any proposed involvement with or provision of services to a foreign government, particularly any military, intelligence, or security service of such government. In this regard, various provisions of law apply to such business transactions and should be reviewed by the individual before engaging in the proposed activity. When former personnel have questions as to whether a proposed activity may fall within the Agency's concern, the Agency is prepared to provide guidance upon request. Former employees who are rehired by the Agency are subject to the above standards of conduct and are expected to fully comply with and familiarize themselves with this Code of Conduct.

THE DEFENSE INTELLIGENCE AGENCY PROFESSIONAL'S CREED "AT DIA, WE ARE COMMITTED TO EXCELLENCE"

In providing the finest, on-time **intelligence** to American warfighters and peacekeepers, to Defense planners, and to the leaders whose daily decisions affect the fate of our nation.

In executing our **mission**, approaching every task with dedication and strength of purpose, knowing that American lives and the well-being of the nation depend on it being done right.

In answering the call to **public service**, mindful that DIA belongs to the American people and that we must earn their trust by serving their interests, conserving their resources, and responding appropriately to their elected representatives.

In our approach to **customer service**, by actively engaging our Defense Intelligence consumers, anticipating their requirements, meeting their changing needs, and unfailingly delivering quality products anywhere, anytime . . . guaranteed.

In ensuring the absolute **integrity** of our intelligence products and services, and in abiding by the highest **ethical standards** of personal conduct.

In guaranteeing sound **management**, based on principles of empowerment and inclusion; open, honest, user-friendly communications; teambuilding; coordination; corporate decisonmaking; and the full professional development of each and every member of our organization.

In maximizing our **individual and collective potential**, by encouraging creativity, initiative, and the free exchange of ideas; by taking personal responsibility for exploiting all available professional growth and development opportunities; and by promoting collegiality and cooperation—with the aim always of improving the quality of everything we do a individuals, as team members, and as an Agency.

In fostering harmony in our **interpersonal relations**, creating an atmosphere that promotes fairness and openness in all personnel practices, nurtures self-esteem and individual worth, and respects human cultural diversity and the rights of others.

In remembering to balance the demands of service to DIA with **personal, family, and community responsibilities**.

In providing good **leadership** for the betterment of the Agency as a whole and Defense Intelligence in general, and in directing our contributions to the security of the United States of America.

Mission

Provide timely, objective, and cogent military intelligence to warfighters, defense planners, and defense and national security policymakers.

Vision

Integration of highly skilled intelligence professionals with leading edge technology to discover information and create knowledge that provides warning, identifies opportunities, and delivers overwhelming advantage to our warfighters, defense planners, and defense and national security policymakers.

Values

We are committed to . . .

- **Service** to our country, our community, and our fellow citizens.
- **Dedication, Strength,** and **Urgency of Purpose** to provide for our nation's defense.
- **Customer-Focus** on the products and services we provide.
- **Integrity** and **Accountability** in all of our actions and activities.
- **Commitment** to inquiry, truth, and continuous learning.

- **Creativity** and **Innovation** in solving problems, discovering facts, and creating knowledge.
- **Teamwork** through internal and external partnerships.
- **Leadership** at all levels within Defense Intelligence and the Intelligence Community.

FEDERAL BUREAU OF INVESTIGATION CORE VALUES

Listing on Website

The FBI will strive for excellence in all aspects of its missions. In pursuing these missions and vision, the FBI and its employees will be true to, and exemplify, the following core values:

1. Adherence to the rule of law and the rights conferred to all under the United States Constitution
2. Integrity through everyday ethical behavior
3. Accountability by accepting responsibility for our actions and decisions and the consequences of our actions and decisions
4. Fairness in dealing with people
5. Leadership through example, both at work and in our communities

Listing in Agency Offices

1. Rigorous obedience to the Constitution of the United States
2. Respect for the dignity of all those we protect
3. Compassion
4. Fairness
5. Uncompromising personal and institutional integrity
6. Accountability
7. Leadership

NATIONAL SECURITY AGENCY AND CENTRAL SECURITY SERVICE PLAN 2004–2009

Vision: Information Superiority for America and Its Allies

Intelligence and Information Assurance complement each other. Intelligence gives the Nation an information advantage over its adversaries. Information Assurance prevents others from gaining advantage over the Nation.

Together the two missions promote a single goal: information superiority for America and its Allies.

Mission: To Provide and Protect Vital Information for the Nation

The National Security Agency/Central Security Service is the Nation's key cryptologic organization. It is the world's best. It affords the decisive edge by providing and protecting vital information from the battlefield to the White House. It assures the security of U.S. signals and information systems and provides intelligence derived from those of the Nation's adversaries. NSA/CSS works with its customers to understand their requirements and then collaborates with its partners to deliver premier cryptologic products and services that exceed our customer's expectations.

GOAL 1: Deliver Responsive Signals Intelligence and Information Assurance for National Security Under Any Circumstance

GOAL 2: Radically Improve the Production and Protection of Information

GOAL 3: Enhance an Expert Workforce to Meet Global Cryptologic Challenges

GOAL 4: Create and Integrate Business Management Capabilities Within the Enterprise and With Stakeholders

Personal Obligations: Each of us bears personal responsibility for the transformation of NSA/CSS.

Our actions will be guided by the following principles:

- Integrity and Stewardship
- Lawfulness
- Loyalty and Commitment
- Openness and Respect
- Teaming and Collaboration
- Continuous Learning
- Service

THE NATIONAL CRYPTOLOGIC SCHOOL GUIDING PRINCIPLES

Service to the customer: We are dedicated to giving all of our customers the best possible service. Good Service depends on partnership with our customers and teamwork within the National Cryptologic School.

Effective leadership: Leadership is everyone's responsibility. Our success depends on making an enthusiastic partner and leader of every individual in the National Cryptologic School.

Excellence is a way of life: We want the National Cryptologic School to be known for its excellence. We believe that every task, in every part of our work, should be performed in a superior manner and to the best of our ability.

NATIONAL IMAGERY AND MAPPING AGENCY PRINCIPLES OF ETHICAL CONDUCT

Public service is a public trust, requiring employees to place loyalty to the Constitution, the laws, and ethical principles above private gain.

Employees shall not hold financial interests that conflict with the conscientious performance of duty.

Employees shall not engage in financial transaction using nonpublic Government information or allow the improper use of such information to further any private interest.

An employee shall not, except as permitted by applicable law or regulation, solicit or accept any gift or other item of monetary value from any person or entity seeking official action from, employees agency, or those interests may be substantially affected by the performance or nonperformance of employee duties.

Employees shall put forth honest effort in the performance of their duties.

Employees shall not knowingly make unauthorized commitments or promises of any kind purporting to bind the Government.

Employees shall not use public office for private gain.

Employees shall act impartially and not give preferential treatment to any private organization or individual.

Employees shall protect and conserve Federal property and shall not use it for other than authorized activities.

Employees shall not engage in outside employment or activities, including seeking or negotiating for employment, that conflict with official Government duties and responsibilities.

Employees shall disclose waste, fraud, abuse, and corruption to appropriate authorities.

Employees shall satisfy in good faith their obligations as citizens, including all just financial obligations, especially those—such as federal, state, or local taxes—that are imposed by law.

Employees shall adhere to all laws and regulations that provide equal opportunity for all American regardless of race, color, religion, sex, national origin, age, or handicap.

Employees shall endeavor to avoid any actions creating the appearance that they are violating applicable law or the ethical standards in applicable regulations.

SOCIETY OF COMPETITIVE INTELLIGENCE PROFESSIONALS CODE OF ETHICS FOR COMPETITIVE PROFESSIONALS

- To continually strive to increase the recognition and respect of the profession.
- To comply with all applicable laws, domestic and international.
- To accurately disclose all relevant information, including one's identity and organization, prior to all interviews.
- To fully respect all requests for confidentiality of information.
- To avoid conflicts of interest in fulfilling one's duties.
- To provide honest and realistic recommendations and conclusions in the execution of one's duties.
- To promote this code of ethics within one's company, with third-party contractors, and within the entire profession.
- To faithfully adhere to and abide by one's company policies, objectives, and guidelines.

Editor's note: "The Society of Competitive Intelligence Professionals (SCIP) is a global nonprofit membership organization for everyone involved in creating and managing business knowledge. Our mission is to enhance the skills of knowledge professionals in order to help their companies achieve and maintain a competitive advantage. Specifically, SCIP provides education and networking opportunities for business professionals working in the rapidly growing field of competitive intelligence (the legal and ethical collection and analysis of information regarding the capabilities, vulnerabilities, and intentions of business competitors). Many SCIP members have backgrounds in market research, strategic analysis, or science and technology" as stated at the web site (www.scip.org).

INTERNATIONAL ASSOCIATION OF LAW ENFORCEMENT INTELLIGENCE ANALYSTS (IALEIA) CODE OF ETHICS

Synopsis

Description: IALEIA Code of Ethics adopted April 30, 1988. The integrity of the International Association of Law Enforcement Intelligence Analysts (IALEIA) is dependent upon the conduct of its individual members in all membership categories. A code of ethical behavior is set forth herewith for the purpose of providing guidance in achieving a desirable individual and group standard members of IALEIA will not:

1. As an officer, director, or agent of the Association, engage in substantive discussions concerning:
    a. ongoing or prospective case specific investigations,
    b. intelligence activities, or
    c. official agency information.
2. Unnecessarily delay, refuse, or fail to carry out a proper directive or assigned duty.
3. Act or make promises or commitments on behalf of IALEIA without appropriate authorization.
4. Solicit funds in the name of IALEIA or any IALEIA function or project without proper authorization.
5. Acquire, use, or dispose of IALEIA property without appropriate authorization.
6. Discriminate or harass others on the basis of sex, race, creed, or religion.
7. Accept or solicit gifts, favors, or bribes in connection with official agency or IALEIA duties.
8. Knowingly make false or misleading statements, or conceal material facts, in connection with IALEIA functions or proceedings; or
9. Release any information pertaining to an IALEIA member, including the identification of his or her employer, position, address, telephone number, or level of professional expertise, to any non-member except:
    a. with the expressed permission of the member concerned, or:
    b. in the course of official investigative proceedings.

In exercising IALEIA duties and responsibilities, members will:

1. Maintain the highest standards of professional propriety;
2. Refrain from any activity which would adversely affect the reputation of IALEIA or IALEIA members;
3. Carry out all Association activities in accordance with prescribed IALEIA procedures and practices;
4. Report violation of IALEIA rules, bylaws, and ethical standards to the Board of Directors;
5. Avoid engaging in criminal, dishonest, disreputable, or disgraceful personal conduct;
6. Avoid personal and business associations with felons or persons known to be connected with or engaged in criminal activities;

7. Ensure that all personal financial activities, as they relate to IALEIA, do not reflect adversely on the Association;
8. Maintain a businesslike demeanor, be courteous, and demonstrate a respectful and helpful attitude whenever representing IALEIA.

Resource person or organization to contact for further information: Leo M. Jacques, CCA, Chair, Bylaws, Ethics & Resolutions.

Selected source: van de Werken, Tiffany. (Australian Institute of Criminology) *"Domestic Violence—Policing the 'new crime' in the Northern Territory"* (www.aic.gov.au/cgibin/).

B

Case Studies

1. SEX FOR SECRETS

Erica Lynne was 28 years old and a very attractive woman. Erica attended Catholic schools her entire life, and she was a graduate of a major Catholic university as well as an avid church attendee. Erica also was an agent for one of the intelligence agencies. Yesterday, her agency wanted her to intensify her collection of information from a suspected terrorist. Over the past several months, Erica had played her part perfectly. She and the suspected terrorist had "accidentally" met at the local supermarket, when her shopping cart ran into his shopping cart. Erica and the man again met several days later at a local coffee shop where she was invited to enjoy his companionship.

After chatting over coffee, Erica and this man began dating. She has known this man for several months, and there was also a strong reason to believe he was planning and financing several terrorist operations on the West Coast. The man had taken Erica into his confidence, and she was able to get some information that was both substantiated and substantial. Nevertheless, she and her supervisors knew, this was only the "tip of the iceberg." Erica had done her job perfectly. Maybe, too perfectly. Yesterday, the man had asked her to move in with him. Erica also knew that this meant consenting to have sex if this relationship was going to continue and more information would be forthcoming.

Now, Erica wanted to rethink her job and her values. Although she did not want to have sex with this man, much less have any kind of premarital relationship with this person whom she considered repulsive, or anyone else, this relationship could be extremely productive for her agency and her country. Meanwhile, at the agency there was a split among her supervisors as to what Erica should do. Some at the agency thought that Erica should not put her integrity up for sale by prostituting for the government and that her supervisors should not look poorly on her job performance. On the other

394

hand some co-workers felt that while citizens and soldiers were making the ultimate sacrifice of dying in the war on terrorism, it was inconceivable she would refuse this extremely important assignment by opting out of this operation.

If you were Erica, what would you do? Why? And does Erica's background have any bearing on your decision, and should it?

2. FABRICATING REPORTS TO SAVE LIVES

During the Vietnam War, Staff Sergeant Frank Thomas was under orders to establish a long-term reconnaissance unit in sector #24. This sector had a long history of extremely heavy coverage of North Vietnam soldiers. From technical collection sources, Staff Sergeant Thomas knew from experience and reports that if any reconnaissance unit went into this sector for an extended period of collection, it would be a suicide mission. Nevertheless, his commander did not trust the intelligence he received because he did not like using "technical means" and he wanted someone reporting via walkie-talkie from the sector.

Staff Sergeant Thomas also knew from troops and commanders from other units where this commander was assigned that he was considered a "daredevil" with other people's lives; some soldiers felt he bordered on being psychotic, while others saw a leader who would do anything for the mission. Staff Sergeant Thomas decided he would fabricate reports gleaned from other sources, and tell his commander that it was human intelligence (HUMINT) since he knew that nothing significant would be gained by having these soldiers almost certainly lose their lives in this heavily infested enemy territory.

Was he correct in his actions? Why?

3. HAVING A NEED TO KNOW

A military operation, code named "Dusty Dog," has been in the works for several days. The intelligence community has been conducting reconnaissance using all available electronic intelligence (ELINT) and human intelligence (HUMINT) resources to include some special forces on the ground. The operation requires deep attacks using rotary wing assets to conduct an air insertion of troops or air assault behind enemy lines. Meanwhile, as the aircraft is about to take off, extremely sensitive and highly classified intelligence is received. This intelligence could be vital to the success of the operation and it may save many lives. However, there is no time to conduct a brief to the pilots or commanders of the ground forces preparing to leave the base. Further communication with the pilots and troops will be impossible.

Do you pass this very sensitive and highly classified information directly to the pilots and commanders, which would compromise the collection source by allowing personnel without proper clearances to see the message?

4. THE INTERCEPT

You are working with native civilian linguists listening to intercepts between enemy military commanders and their troops reporting from the field. These civilians, all contractors whom you are supervising, were literally hired "off the street" for their language skills. None of the civilian linguists in the group have a background working in intelligence. On this night, one of the linguists intercepts radio traffic about a relative being killed; however, because he heard about this through an intercept, he was told not to contact his family concerning the information, nor could he tell anyone until they first told him. He is extremely upset and asks you to justify your action in preventing him from passing along this information.

How would you handle it if the intercept was received before the killing occurred and there was enough time for the civilian linguist to warn his relative to flee for safety? Would you do it, even if it may compromise and possibly expose your collection efforts?

5. A RELIABLE POLYGRAPH

You are working with a remote village militia group in a counterinsurgency operation. In response to your request, your agency has sent a polygraph examiner out to your location to test the veracity of a newly acquired source whose loyalty and veracity is in doubt. (His time-sensitive information is quite valuable if true, however.)

Unfortunately, the examiner proves to be incompetent, and his examination will clearly be useless in deciding the issue. Rather than wait indefinitely for another chance to test your source, you tape a block of C4 (explosives) to his chest, run the detonating wires into the polygraph machine, and tell him that a false answer will generate an electrical impulse that will detonate the C4. (The wires are, in fact, not connected to anything, and there is no danger to your source from the C4).

Should you receive a reprimand from Headquarters or an award for your quick response in validating your source for intelligence?

6. INTERNATIONAL INTELLIGENCE

During a multinational military operation, where intelligence is freely exchanged between countries during the mission, a senior military officer from your country does not want to pass intelligence to the allied commander in the peacekeeping operation because he "does not trust foreigners." The allied commander is authorized to receive the intelligence.

Should you take it upon yourself to bypass your senior officer because you feel the allied troops are as entitled to this information as your troops? Would it matter if you discriminated in what you thought was important, and thus only some of the information would get passed but not all information? Would you be willing to accept the responsibility if you are brought up on charges for passing "unauthorized" information to foreign nationals?

7. WARNING FROM THE INSIDE

Frank is the analyst for the country of Tsgnua. Over the last several months, he has been seeing increasing reliable and valid intelligence that the country's majority tribal faction is about to go to war against the minority tribe that now holds power in the government. While every indication concludes that thousands of deaths will occur on both sides, ultimately the minority tribe would face genocide. There are no reports of this in any of the media. Your supervisor has told you that administration officials have unofficially let it be known that administration officials are not interested in getting involved in this part of the world, either diplomatically or militarily. Soon your intelligence briefs are no longer requested, and you are moved to another department to focus on another country. One night, you go to a party and meet an old friend, who works at a major newspaper. Nothing has appeared in the media of this impending war that will likely lead to genocide.

If you were able to "leak" classified information to the press, in an attempt to seek international attention and action to this emerging problem, would you? What if the information can easily be traced to you and it would lead to prosecution and losing your job, would you still disclose the information?

Consider the opposite situation. The administration is seeking an excuse to enter Tsgnua, and you know the intelligence in the reports is false. The administration then decides to enter Tsgnua militarily. Would you be willing to quit, rather than use false intelligence? Would it matter if the intelligence reports you wrote were being used falsely in other people's assessments?

8. DEFINING A "HIT"

Background

The Republic of Pixxie has surface-to-surface missiles that barely qualify as a military threat. The missiles are very old and outdated, and are usually at the mercy of the winds. However, these missiles are one of the few ways

Pixxie can directly attack coalition forces and other countries in the region. However, Pixxie does have highly reliable and advanced surface-to-air missiles, and there is pressure to show results from the bombing campaign to the coalition of nations involved in the war.

Situation

You are a young imagery interpreter, specializing in missile imagery analysis, and you are supporting the hunt for the missing surface-to-surface missiles. A frame comes across the imagery interpretation table. The target was a "suspected missile airframe" thought to be hiding in a culvert. The culvert was attacked with several warheads, but it is obvious to you this is not a "hit." The sortie received several surface-to-air missile attacks, barely escaping.

There is no evidence on the imagery that any enemy missile airframe has been destroyed. There is a small blast area on one side of the culvert, but the scar is too small to be the result of a direct attack on a missile, and your assessment is that it is more likely the result of a blast from your own military warhead. The Targeting shop is literally looking over your shoulder challenging every call and you know they *need* to find some successful missile explosions that would indicate they have been blown up. Meanwhile, your boss asks, "Are you sure it's not a hit? What about this 'secondary explosion'? Look at these impact points. Anything in that culvert is dead. Are you sure it's not a hit? (Do you want to keep your job?)."

Do you report the culvert as a "hit," giving your commander the results he is looking for so he can reassign aircraft to other "more important sectors" and maintain cohesion in the coalition; or do you call it a miss, and risk sending another sortie into harm's way to strike an empty culvert?

9. SCREENER FOR INTERROGATIONS

You are assigned to a detention facility as a screener for interrogations. You have screened several thousand detainees over the course of your time at the facility. You have developed a good sense of who is able to provide intelligence and who has been captured solely for being at the wrong place at the wrong time. Recently, a new commander has taken charge of the facility. Previously, you would recommend discharge of those detainees who cannot provide intelligence.

However, this new commander insists that all detainees be interrogated before they are released, even though his screening staff has deemed them of no intelligence value. Holding these detainees, who likely have done nothing wrong, until they are finally interrogated could take months. In the meantime, they are unable to provide for their families by working and are missing out on all these months of their free lives. You are extremely uncomfortable with this and you have aired your concerns to the new commander. The new commander feels that screening is not an effective way to find out if a detainee has intelligence and maintains his policy.

Do you choose to follow this policy quietly, so as not to rock the boat? Or, do you take it higher, risking your reputation and possibly your career, in order to stand up for the rights of the detainees being held for no good reason?

10. WHAT'S IN A NAME?

You are the commander of an interrogation unit. Your unit has been involved in the interrogation of suspected members of an international terrorist organization which has the stated goals of attacking your country. Some recently released former prisoners have claimed that they had been abused by their interrogators while in custody. When asked to give the names of the interrogators, the former prisoners state that the interrogators did not wear name tags. Officials at higher headquarters had directed that all interrogators will wear complete uniforms with name and unit patches conspicuously displayed whenever they conduct interrogations so that future cases of suspected abuse can be more easily investigated. As the commander of a squad of interrogators, you understand that if interrogators show their names and units of assignments, there is a good chance that this terrorist organization could order retributive action against the interrogators or their families back home.

Do you follow the directives of higher headquarters?

11. TO ATTACK OR NOT TO ATTACK: THAT IS THE QUESTION

For the past several months your unit has conducted low-level HUMINT collection operations in a hostile environment. One of your subordinates has developed a very well placed source that has provided highly reliable information over the past few months. The information which this source has provided has enabled your forces to avoid or thwart attacks which would have led to large-scale casualties. Fifteen minutes ago, the source contacted your unit and informed you that he will attend a high-level planning meeting in two hours. He provided the exact location of this meeting. He further informed you that most of the principal leadership of the resistance movement will attend this planning meeting. The meeting will be at a location that would be impossible to use ground forces to attack or disrupt it. The only possible option is to attack this target with precision-guided munitions, which are available and can be launched on your order.

If you use precision munitions on this meeting site, you will in all probability eliminate the leadership of the resistance force. But you will also, in all probability, kill your faithful and trustful source. What do you do?

12. CATCHING A STOWAWAY

Background

Tom Jenkins is a civilian intelligence analyst on a ship tasked with conducting at-sea boardings of suspect merchant vessels in the Mediterranean Sea. This particular task has been undertaken on a rotating basis by Allied ships for two years now in response to intelligence that terrorists are using merchant ships to transport weapons, money, and themselves from North Africa to southern Europe. Nine months ago, intelligence analysts were given permission to ride on these ships as a means of collecting, conducting initial analysis, and submitting their findings back to intelligence agencies more quickly. Allied nations agreed on the condition that they see the fruits of this faster intelligence "turnaround" and are kept informed of any leads. Ultimately, the intelligence analysts are tasked with finding trends in passages, cargo, and companies that may be involved in terrorist activities. Tom is the first intelligence analyst to participate in this mission.

Situation

The HMS *Godfrey Jones* has received permission to board the M/V *Torella* at first sighting. Her last known position was twenty nautical miles off the coast of Libya, and the HMS *Godfrey* has been instructed to wait until she has left Libyan territorial waters. Intelligence is keeping the HMS *Godfrey* informed of her position every hour. After waiting several hours, the HMS *Godfrey* sees the M/V *Torella*, queries her, and receives permission to board. Tom boards with the rest of the inspection team but then gets separated. He is inspecting one of the below-deck containers when he sees a pair of eyes. At closer inspection, he finds they belong to a small boy, no more than thirteen. At first Tom merely assumes that the child is attempting to stow away, trying to get to Europe. He decides to say nothing, but then remembers something from his terrorism class before he began his ship duty—terrorists know no age limit.

Tom takes the child into a nearby stateroom and demands to know what he is doing there. At this point, the rest of the ship is still unaware of the boy's presence. The boy pleads with Tom, saying he escaped from a terrorist training camp in northern Sudan. Tom realizes that this boy could provide a wealth of information about terrorist training tactics with a few simple lies about promises of a better life in the United States. He also knows, however, that if he alerts the ship's crew about the boy's presence, he will be arrested, interrogated, and later deported back to Sudan.

Should Tom have compassion for the boy and say nothing? Or should he lie and then interrogate him for whatever intelligence he can provide and then send him back to Sudan, where he could be sent to another training camp and decide to lead the life of a terrorist based solely on his treatment by Tom?

13. THE DIRTY INFORMANT

While conducting counter-drug operations in a politically volatile Latin American country, you have an informant who is well-connected with the local drug lord you are working to bring down. Though this informant has provided extremely valuable intelligence that has led to a significant advance in U.S. operations against this drug lord, he is also employed by the drug lord as an assassin who is responsible for the deaths of many local civilians. He is also wealthy from the profits of the drug operations as part of this drug lord's inner circle in the very impoverished country. These facts are understood by your superiors who approved of the recruitment of this source several years ago. You receive reliable intelligence that the drug lord is positioning himself for a coup against the popular ruler in the next few weeks.

Your source comes to you in a panic the following day. He overheard one of the drug lord's confidants expressing the possibility of a mole in their operations that has cost them dearly in the past few months. Your informant tells you that it is a matter of time until the drug lord identifies him as the informant and begs you to relocate him and his family in the United States. He and his family, to include three children, will be executed when the drug lord discovers his connection as a U.S. informant. The standard policy is to relocate useful informants in situations such as this.

Should you relocate this informant knowing of his connections and murders with the understanding that you would be sentencing him to death if you don't?

14. JOINT COLLECTION CHALLENGE

You are a Coast Guard member of a joint service collection unit. As a Coast Guard member, you are on the team because you have the authority to col-

lect and use information for law enforcement purposes and on domestic entities. Your specific duties are to transcribe and record all collection
information that may involve law enforcement or domestic entities, regardless of which watch station gets the collect. Your Department of Defense
counterparts strictly work with the information concerning foreign entities.
Signatures on the reports record who performed the collection and provide
the legal proof that the collections were kept separate.

Due to the compartment size onboard the ship, all personnel are aware of
what is being collected at each station. DOD personnel are aware of and have
witnessed your domestic collects, but you have always done the actual processing. Personnel regularly cover each other's watch station for head calls,
chow runs, etc., and complete the reports for each other, but the issue of a
law enforcement or domestic collect has never come up.

That morning you come in to watch, and breakfast is not sitting well with
you at all. The corpsman has given you some medicine, but you still have an
upset stomach. You take leave of your watch station to run to the head. When
you return, your Navy counterpart tells you that he covered your station for
you while you were in the head and has a report. He has it written and
printed it out for you, and all you need to do is sign it at the bottom. As you
read the report, you realize it is a key piece of information for a big ongoing
case. However you also realize the reason he gave it to you to sign is that it
has law enforcement information on a domestic vessel. Your counterpart is
very competent and you have no reason to doubt the accuracy of the report,
but you question whether you should actually put this report through since
it contains domestic information and you weren't even in the space when it
was collected.

*If you fail to put it through, the case may be lost. This information will be
used only to tip off law enforcement assets and will not come up in court. Your
signature is, in many ways, for administrative and audit purposes only. What
do you do?*

15. DETENTION FOR NO REASON

Abu Ali has been captured during a firefight in Fallujah, Iraq. Upon capture,
Abu was found to have no weapons or any other incriminating items that
would indicate he was actually involved in the fight. On his capture documents, the Infantrymen wrote that he had been "hiding" beneath a fruit cart
when they found him. Because it is general policy for the Infantrymen to
arrest anyone who could possibly be involved with an insurgency, Abu was
taken with all the other young men who were still alive in the vicinity.

Upon arrival at the detention center, Staff Sergeant Brookings is assigned
as the screener for Abu. Staff Sergeant Brookings discusses with Abu the

circumstances of his capture and finds Abu to be very cooperative. Abu details how he had been selling his fruit on the street corner, as he does everyday, in order to feed his eight children, all under the age of 12. He goes on to say that he has been working extra hours lately because his wife is pregnant again. Abu says that when he heard gunshots, he was afraid to run because he did not want to desert his fruit cart, so he got as low as he could to avoid getting hit by a stray bullet. Throughout the screening conversation, Abu continually questions Staff Sergeant Brookings about the disposition of his fruit cart. Abu is expressing genuine concern because without his cart, his livelihood is ruined.

Staff Sergeant Brookings decides that Abu should be released. It is general policy that a screener recommends to the commander whether a potential source is deemed to have intelligence information or not. If not, he is generally released. The commander, however, decides that Abu, and anyone else who is initially detained, will be held with low priority until a full interrogation can be conducted. This could mean three to six weeks. Staff Sergeant Brookings goes personally to the commander to explain Abu's circumstances. The commander says that report numbers are down and that they need all the interrogation reports they can possibly produce. The only option Staff Sergeant Brookings has is to contact the next higher commander and inform him or her that the detention center commander is taking people away from their livelihoods and children solely for the purpose of beefing up the numbers of reports. However, if Staff Sergeant Brookings does this, he faces persecution from the detention center commander and a negative evaluation that could seriously impact his career.

Are this man's life and children's lives worth that chance? Should Staff Sergeant Brookings chalk it up to war and move on? Is it ethical to detain people for no good reason? Is it even Staff Sergeant Brookings' issue to worry about?

16. PUBLIC OPINION DETERMINES TECHNIQUE?

Following the media coverage of the detainee abuse that took place at the Abu Ghraib detention center in Iraq, interrogation and detention policies were rigorously scrutinized. Public revulsion and outcries and the incessant display of the photographs of hooded prisoners with barking dogs caused the U.S. to develop a whole new policy for interrogators. Previously acceptable interrogation techniques like sleep deprivation and placing detainees in an uncomfortable position for a period of time were outlawed by this new policy. The public and the media now deemed these "torture."

Major Super had been interrogating detainees in Iraq for approximately eight months when these new policies were sent down the line. Major Super is in charge of a small facility right outside of Baghdad that houses 100 detainees and employs six interrogators. Major Super recognizes the benefits of these previously acceptable interrogation techniques and notices a sharp decline in useful intelligence information once the use of sleep deprivation is halted.

All of the interrogators in Major Super's facility have expressed their frustration with the new policies and have confirmed Major Super's suspicions that without the sleep deprivation, it is ten times more difficult to acquire useful information. The now bright-eyed, alert detainees are more stubborn than ever. Major Super and the interrogators are worried that some of the information that their detainees may have could save hundreds of soldiers' lives. Major Super is struggling with whether or not to quietly, unofficially re-implement the sleep deprivation technique, even though the new policy states that it is not allowed.

Should Major Super follow the rules, even though he is aware that information that could save U.S. soldiers' and innocent Iraqi civilians' lives is not being gained? If Major Super implements his own policies, in direct violation of the new U.S. policy, is he sending an unethical message to his subordinates? If Major Super does not allow the use of sleep deprivation, in accordance with the new policy, is he allowing soldiers to die because useful intelligence is now unattainable?

17. NOT CLEARED FOR THAT

Ms. Foxy is the security officer at the battalion headquarters. She has been evaluated for promotion and is waiting for notification from her superiors. She recently purchased a new house and is eager for a raise, so this potential promotion will be a joyous event for her. Some of Ms. Foxy's duties include passing security clearance information for unit personnel who will be on temporary duty (TDY) at other locations. Ms. Foxy takes pride in her job and has never had a security violation on her watch. This week, she is passing several clearances to the National Ground Intelligence Center (NGIC) for a conference that some members of her unit will be attending in two weeks.

Ms. Foxy's supervisor has asked her to send clearances for two officers who have only SECRET security clearance. The conference requires only a SECRET level clearance, and information presented there will not go beyond the SECRET level. However, in order to get into the building, a person must have a TOP SECRET clearance. When Ms. Foxy points this out to her supervisor, he asks her to just write down that the two officers have TOP SECRET so that they can attend the event. Her supervisor tells her that it's really no big deal because there will not be information presented above SECRET anyway. Further, the officers would have TOP SECRET clearances if their current duties required it, but since they don't they were not able to request the investigations. The supervisor assures Ms. Foxy that both officers are quite responsible and there is nothing to worry about.

With Ms. Foxy's promotion being deliberated, she is concerned that if she does not do as the supervisor asks, she will be passed over. She rationalizes that doing this will hurt no one since the information at the conference is at the level of the officers' actual clearance anyway. It's just a technicality to get into the building to have a TOP SECRET clearance.

Should Ms. Foxy obey her supervisor? If she doesn't, should she report her supervisor? If she doesn't report him, is it possible that his attitude toward security could result in a devastating compromise of classified information in the future?

18. LIFESAVING INFORMATION THAT IS LIFE THREATENING

Kadira is a high-level source being held in a Central Intelligence Agency (CIA) facility in Iraq. Kadira is the wife of one of the most-wanted insurgents who is known to be a leader in the local insurgency. Kadira has been present for several high-level meetings between her husband and several other insurgency leaders and planners. Kadira has even participated in the bookkeeping and other administrative tasks for the local insurgents. Kadira's cousin, who also lived with Kadira and her husband, told all of this information to the CIA. Kadira's cousin, however, was never present for the meetings and has very little information about plans, intentions, or suppliers of the local insurgents.

Several agents have tried to get information from Kadira. She has been in custody for about a month. Kadira has refused to speak to anyone. For the last few days, Agent Buford has been assigned to Kadira's case. He has been pushing his activities to the edge of the law by allowing Kadira to sleep, but ensuring there is incessant, loud noise in Kadira's cell. He has also been feeding her extremely sparse meals. Kadira is obviously in a distressed physical state, and it is affecting her ability to think clearly. Agent Buford knows Kadira is on the verge of breaking and telling him everything.

Agent Buford takes Kadira into a questioning room. She is hardly able to walk and is mumbling in Arabic. Agent Buford speaks fluent Arabic and recognizes that she is talking to her abdomen, repeating, "It will be okay, little one." Agent Buford proceeds with questioning her. Unlike during other sessions, Kadira begins to give up small bits of information. Agent Buford is encouraged. He now knows the names of some of the leaders of the insurgencies. Halfway through the questioning, Kadira falls from her chair and passes out temporarily. Agent Buford helps her off the ground and back into her chair. Kadira begs to see a doctor.

Agent Buford knows that he is legally required to allow medical personnel to evaluate any detainee who is ill, but he is concerned that if this session is interrupted, it may be the last information he gains from Kadira. After all, he has spent the last five days setting this session up by "softening" Kadira up. It is apparent that Kadira is extremely uncomfortable and that she is having difficulty breathing. She is continually holding her stomach and moaning. It is obviously possible that she is pregnant and that the baby could now be in danger. Kadira could miscarry if not treated soon. However, Kadira's knowledge could save hundreds of lives. The capture of the leaders of the insurgencies or the halt of their supplies could be the most important event in ending the deaths of civilians and soldiers in this area.

If Agent Buford continues his questioning of Kadira, both she and her unborn child's life are at risk. However, if he calls in medical personnel, they will surely discontinue the questioning and demand that she be placed in the medical area of the facility for several days. By that time, Kadira will have regained her strength and reoriented herself and she will surely clam up again. Agent Buford must decide between potentially saving the lives of hundreds of soldiers and Iraqi civilians, and ensuring the safety of an unborn baby, who has done nothing wrong.

19. AM I MY BROTHER'S KEEPER?

Fareed and Mohamed are brothers. Fareed is a local shopkeeper with a large family. He is a devout Muslim who scorns terrorism and openly speaks out against the local insurgents. Mohamed, however, never married and took a different path in life. With nothing to lose, Mohamed has been active in planning several car bombings and proudly boasts that he has been responsible for the deaths of dozens of "dirty Americans." Recently, American soldiers took Mohamed into custody when he was discovered with a trunk full of explosives that failed to detonate at a highway checkpoint.

Mohamed has not cooperated at all. He will not even reveal the minutest details about himself, let alone anything about his insurgent comrades. During one cell inspection, the military police discovered a letter that Mohamed wrote to his brother, Fareed. The military police turned the letter over to the interrogators for exploitation. While there was no intelligence value in the letter, it was apparent from the content that Mohamed loves and respects his brother very much. Mohamed wrote in the letter to his brother where to find his money in his house because he wanted to ensure that Mohamed had extra money to feed his family. Mohamed further expressed in the letter how much he loved his nieces and nephews and that he hoped Fareed's business would pick up so Fareed would be able to feed his family every day instead of sporadically as he has been doing as of late due to slow business.

The interrogation team leader comes up with an idea. If they arrest and detain Fareed, he will obviously be unable to make any money whatsoever and his family will surely suffer. If they place Fareed in the cell next to Mohamed and tell Mohamed that Fareed cannot be released until he talks, Mohamed's guilt will surely make him talk. The interrogation team leader realizes that this is punishing an innocent man and his family for no reason. However, this is a last resort. After all, they will not be doing any sort of illegal activities like sleep deprivation or physical pressures that have recently been outlawed. Fareed will be returned to his work and family soon enough.

In the meantime, a few hungry kids and an inconvenienced shopkeeper are surely less important than the lives of soldiers, aren't they? Wouldn't it benefit the greater good to get the information from Mohamed that could save so many lives by inconveniencing a few innocent people for a few days or weeks?

20. TURNING A BLIND EYE

Situation

Foreign military and police forces derive their authorities and missions from constitutions and laws that differ significantly from those of the United States. Commonly, Latin American militaries have authority for police actions, including arrest, detention, and interrogation of people suspected of committing crimes. While working with the Serrian Republic Army, a U.S. liason intelligence officer witnesses the detentions and interrogations of numerous campesinos suspected of aiding or abetting guerrilla fighters. These Serrian Republic Army interrogators detain and question these farmers to obtain information or raw human intelligence (HUMINT) on locations of guerrilla camps and personnel and to determine the degree of the farmers' complicity. The Serrian Republic Army uses this raw HUMINT to legally and successfully ambush and capture many guerrillas.

Dilemma

Although the farmers are not tortured, the U.S. liaison intelligence officer is responsible for reporting what he witnessed. However, if he does report this information or raw intelligence, approval and funding for future bilateral operations with the Serrian Republic Army might be eliminated or reduced, because the UN and U.S. do not approve of such tactics, especially such military to civilian interaction. Additionally, he knows that his Serrian Republic Army counterparts will no longer trust him, resulting in decreasing effectiveness of the bilateral operations and increasing success of the guerrillas.

Knowing this, should the U.S. liaison intelligence officer attempt to prevent such tactics and report everything he witnessed?

Contributors

Fritz Allhoff is a senior research fellow at the Institute for Ethics of the American Medical Association. After completing his B.S. in physics at the College of William & Mary, he attended graduate school in philosophy at the University of California, Santa Barbara, earning his M.A. and Ph.D. His research interests include metaethics, biomedical ethics, and philosophy of law.

Jean Maria Arrigo, Ph.D., is a social psychologist (formerly a mathematician) and daughter of an undercover intelligence officer. Her 1999 dissertation developed an epistemology of intelligence, summarized in "The Ethics of Weapons Research: A Framework for Moral Discourse between Insiders and Outsiders," 1999, *Journal of Power and Ethics* 1(4), http://www.spaef.com/JPE_PUB/1_4/v1n4_arrigo.html]. The University of California at Berkeley, Bancroft Library archives her Oral History Series on Ethics of Intelligence and Weapons Development. She has created educational theater performances, including *Redemption from Black Operations* (2001, Carnegie Mellon University) and *You, the Interrogator and The People Who Disappeared Twice* (2003, University of Texas Medical Branch, Galveston).

James A. Barry is a senior research fellow at the Center for International Development and Conflict Management, University of Maryland. He is also a visiting faculty member at Salve Regina University in Newport, Rhode Island, as well as an independent training consultant. Prior to joining the Center he was a visiting associate professor at George Mason University, where he taught courses in International Politics, Ethics, and Management. Mr. Barry served with the federal government for more than 30 years, specializing in national security policy and arms control. He is the author of

The Sword of Justice: Ethics and Coercion in International Politics (Praeger, 1998) as well as numerous studies and articles on foreign policy issues.

Charles R. Beitz is professor of political science and dean of faculty at Bowdoin College. He writes frequently on ethics and international affairs. His book *Political Theory and International Relations* is a major contribution to understanding normative approaches to international relations.

Lincoln P. Bloomfield Jr. was principal deputy assistant secretary of defense for International Security Affairs.

Martin Bulmer is a lecturer in social administration at London School of Economics.

Darren Charters is a lecturer in business law at the School of Accountancy, University of Waterloo. He is a member of the Law Society of Upper Canada and holds degrees in arts (Queen's University) and law (University of Toronto), as well as a graduate degree in business administration (Wilfrid Laurier University). He has also practiced as a corporate/commercial lawyer. He may be contacted at the University of Waterloo, School of Accountancy, Waterloo, Ontario, Canada.

J. E. Drexel Godfrey is director of the Masters of Public Administration Program, Rutgers University in Newark, New Jersey. He served in the Intelligence Directorate of the Central Intelligence Agency from 1957 to 1970 and was for some years director of current intelligence. Prior to 1957 he was professor of political science at Williams College and is the author of *The Politics of the Non-Communist Left in Post-War France and of The Government of France.*

Robert M. Gates served as director of the Central Intelligence Agency from November 1991 to January 1993. He is the only career officer in the CIA's history to rise from entry-level employee to director. He holds a doctorate in Russian and Soviet history from Georgetown University. He is currently the president of Texas A&M University.

Jan Goldman is on the faculty at the Joint Military Intelligence College, where he teaches ethics and intelligence. His experience includes intelligence support to special operations, and he is the author or editor of several publications, including the recently declassified *Anticipating Surprise: Analysis for Strategic Warning* (University Press of America, 2004), a field manual on counterinsurgency operations, and a glossary on forecasting, intelligence, and homeland security to be published by Scarecrow Press.

Roger Homan teaches in the Department of Sociology and Education at Brighton Polytechnic in the United Kingdom.

Arthur S. Hulnick wrote his article while coordinator for academic affairs at the Central Intelligence Agency. After his retirement from the CIA in 1992, he was appointed associate professor of international relations at Boston University. Professor Hulnick is a veteran of more than 35 years in the profession of intelligence, including 7 years as an intelligence officer in the U.S. Air Force and 28 years in the Central Intelligence Agency. He received his B.A. from the Woodrow Wilson School, Princeton University, in 1957.

Loch K. Johnson is regents professor of political science at the University of Georgia and author of several books on intelligence. He has been special assistant to the chairman of the Senate Select Committee on Intelligence, staff director of the Subcommittee on Oversight on the House Permanent Select Committee on Intelligence, and special assistant to Les Aspin and professional staff member on the Aspin-Brown Commission on Intelligence.

R. V. Jones, often called "the father of scientific intelligence," was a British physicist for the British Air Staff in World War II. He is perhaps best known for the development of methods to defeat the Germans' radar and their use of radio-beam targeting. He was the author of several popular books and he is the namesake and first recipient of the Central Intelligence Agency's R. V. Jones Intelligence Award for Scientific and Technical Research. He died on 17 December 1997.

John P. Langan, S.J., is the Joseph Cardinal Bernardin Professor of Catholic Social Thought at Georgetown University. He is a senior research scholar in the Kennedy Institute, where from 1987 to 1999 he served as Rose Kennedy Professor of Christian Ethics, a professor of philosophy, and a member of the core faculty of the School of Foreign Service at Georgetown. He teaches courses on ethical theory, ethics and international affairs, human rights, just war theory, and capitalism and morality. He holds a Ph.D. in philosophy from the University of Michigan, entered the Society of Jesus, in 1957, and he was ordained to the priesthood in 1972. He has edited or coedited six books, and he serves on the board of directors of several associations. In January 2004 he was elected president of the Society of Christian Ethics, the main academic organization for scholars of religious ethics.

Daniel W. Mattausch cowrote his article while a Ph.D. candidate at Georgetown University. He received his M.P.P., Georgetown University, in 1988, and his B.A., Seattle Pacific University, in 1986.

Kent Pekel wrote his article while serving as a White House Fellow. He was a special adviser to the Deputy Secretary of State.

David L. Perry is professor of ethics at the U.S. Army War College in Carlisle, Pennsylvania. He teaches courses on ethics and warfare, strategic leadership, and U.S. defense policies, planning, organizations, and processes. He also edits and writes materials for a web-based educational module on Just-War Theory, and is an author of core-course lessons on ethical reasoning, the military profession, military ethics, and critical thinking. He earned a Ph.D. in ethics at the University of Chicago Divinity School and taught ethics at Seattle University and Santa Clara University. His numerous publications have addressed recent conflicts in Afghanistan and Iraq from a just-war framework, ethics and war in comparative religious perspective, and diverse ethical issues in medicine and business.

Tony Pfaff is a lieutenant colonel in the U.S. Army and a Middle East/North Africa foreign area officer who has most recently served on the Joint Intelligence Directorate (J2), the United Nations Iraq-Kuwait Observer Mission, and the faculty at the United States Military Academy, where he taught philosophy. LTC Pfaff holds a B.A. in economics and philosophy from Washington and Lee University and an M.A. in philosophy from Stanford University, where he was a graduate fellow at the Stanford Center for Conflict and Negotiation. He has also deployed to Operation Desert Shield/Storm with the 82nd Airborne Division and to Operation ABLE SENTRY with the 1st Armored Division.

Joel H. Rosenthal has been president of the Carnegie Council on Ethics and International Affairs (since 1995) and editor-in-chief of the journal *Ethics & International Affairs*. He lectures and writes frequently on ethics, U.S. foreign policy, and international relations. He received his Ph.D. from Yale University (1988) and B.A. from Harvard University (1982).

Michael Skerker, Ph.D., is an adjunct professor in the religious studies department at DePaul University. He has written on numerous topics relating to ethics and national security.

Linda K. Trevino is associate professor of organizational behavior at the Smeal College of Business Administration of the Pennsylvania State University. She received her Ph.D. in management from Texas A&M University in 1987. Professor Trevino teaches, consults, and conducts research on the management of ethical conduct in organizations.

Veteran Intelligence Professionals for Sanity (VIPS) was created in January 2003 when its founders saw that intelligence analysis was being corrupted by political pressure to "justify" an attack on Iraq. The organization includes over 50 former professionals from CIA, the Defense Intelligence Agency, the Department of State's Bureau of Intelligence and Research, Army Intelligence, the FBI, the National Security Agency, and other U.S. intelligence agencies. VIPS's first paper, a *Memorandum for the President* on February 5, 2003, was a same-day critique of Secretary of State Colin Powell's address to the UN, in which VIPS strongly urged the president to "widen the discussion beyond the circle of those advisers clearly bent on a war for which we see no compelling reason and from which we believe the unintended consequences are likely to be catastrophic." The thrust of VIPS's next two prewar memoranda can be gleaned from their titles: "Cooking Intelligence for War" and "Forgery, Hyperbole, Half-Truth: A Problem." To date, eleven such papers have been published corporately; individual VIPS members frequently publish under their own bylines as well.

Gary R. Weaver is assistant professor of management in the department of business administration for the College of Business and Economics at the University of Delaware. He received a Ph.D. in philosophy from the University of Iowa in 1980 and a Ph.D. in management from the Pennsylvania State University in 1995. Professor Weaver teaches, consults, and conducts research on business ethics.

Andrew Wilkie, a senior analyst in Australia's Office of National Assessments (ONA), resigned nine days before the U.S.-U.K. attack on Iraq, for which he saw no justification. Later, he gave evidence to the Australian and British parliaments about how his government had "skewed the truth" and he indicated that ONA had told Australia's leaders that "the U.S. was intent on invading Iraq for more important reasons than weapons of mass destruction and terrorism." Wilkie exposed the fact that, as one journalist put it, Australia's leaders were "conned by master manipulators masquerading as purveyors of objective intelligence." The prime minister's office retaliated by trying to discredit him, claiming he was mentally unstable. In retrospect, it is now clear that Wilkie was correct. On October 7, 2003, the Australian Senate censured Prime Minister John Howard for misleading the public in "justifying" sending Australian troops off to war.